ALSO BY STEPHEN HUNTER

Now Playing at the Valencia

Havana

Pale Horse Coming

Hot Springs

Time to Hunt

Black Light

Dirty White Boys

Point of Impact

Violent Screen: A Critic's 13 Years on the Front Lines of Movie Mayhem

Target

The Day Before Midnight

The Spanish Gambit (Tapestry of Spies)

The Second Saladin

The Master Sniper

AMERICAN GUNFIGHT

**The Plot to Kill Harry Truman—and the
Shoot-out That Stopped It**

Stephen Hunter

and

John Bainbridge, Jr.

Simon & Schuster

NEW YORK   LONDON   TORONTO   SYDNEY

SIMON & SCHUSTER
Rockefeller Center
1230 Avenue of the Americas
New York, NY 10020

SIMON & SCHUSTER and colophon are registered trademarks
of Simon & Schuster, Inc.
For information about special discounts for bulk purchases,
please contact Simon & Schuster Special Sales at
1-800-456-6798 or business@simonandschuster.com

Designed by Paul Dippolito

Manufactured in the United States of America

10 9 8 7 6 5 4 3 2 1

Library of Congress Cataloging-in-Publication Data
Hunter, Stephen, date.
    American gunfight : the plot to kill Harry Truman, and the shoot-out
that stopped it / Stephen Hunter and John Bainbridge, Jr.
        p.   cm.
    Includes bibliographical references (p.) and index.
    1. Truman, Harry S., 1884–1972—Assassination attempt, 1950.
2. Collazo Oscar, 1914–   3. Torresola, Griselio. 4. Nationalists—
Puerto Rico—Biography. 5. Assassins—Biography. 6. Blair House
(Washington, D.C.) 7. United States. Secret Service—Officials and
employees—Biography. I. Bainbridge, John, date. II. Title.
    E814.H36 2005
    364.152'4'09227295—dc22   2005051587
ISBN-13: 978-0-7432-6068-8
ISBN-10: 0-7432-6068-6

Photo Credits
Grateful acknowledgment is made to the following for permission
to reproduce illustrations:
AP/Wide World Photos: 11; © Bettmann/Corbis: 3, 7, 8, 10, 16;
Carmen Zoraida Collazo: 5; © Phil Licata Photography LLC: 14, 15;
United States Secret Service: 6; University of Puerto Rico Library
System: 1, 2, 4; © John G. Zimmerman: 12, 13.

To the - -R-I- -

CONTENTS

Authors' Note   *1*

Introduction   *3*

1   A Drive Around Washington   *5*

2   *Griselio Agonistes*   *12*

3   Revolution   *18*

4   The Odd Couple   *36*

5   Mr. Gonzales and Mr. De Silva Go to Washington   *40*

6   Early Morning   *50*

7   Baby Starches the Shirts   *54*

8   Toad   *62*

9   The New Guy   *74*

10   The Buick Guy   *83*

11   The Guns   *86*

12   The Ceremony   *100*

13   Indian Summer   *104*

14   The Big Walk   *109*

15   Oscar   *113*

16   "It Did Not Go Off"   *128*

17   Pappy   *133*

18   The Next Ten Seconds   *138*

19   Resurrection Man   *141*

20   So Loud, So Fast   *152*

21   Upstairs at Blair   *156*

22   Downstairs at Blair   *161*

23   Borinquen   *167*

24   Oscar Alone   *181*

25   The End's Run   *184*

26   Good Hands   *186*

27   The Colossus Rhoads   *194*

28   Oscar Goes Down   *200*

29   The Second Assault   *203*

30   Pimienta   *206*

31   Point-Blank   *223*

32   The Man Who Loved Guns   *228*

33   The Dark Visitors   *236*

34   Mortal Danger   *240*

35   The Neighbor   *243*

36   American Gunfight   *244*

37   The Good Samaritan   *252*

38   The Policemen's Wives   *258*

39   The Scene   *260*

40   Inside the Soccer Shoe   *267*

41   Who Shot Oscar?   *273*

42   The Roundup   *278*

43   Taps   *286*

44   Oscar on Trial   *289*

45   Deep Conspiracy   *298*

46   Cressie Does Her Duty   *308*

47   Oscar Speaks   *310*

48   - - R - I - -   *317*

Epilogue: Destinies   *323*

Source Notes   *327*

Bibliography   *339*

Acknowledgments   *349*

Index   *355*

". . . I found the greatest difficulty . . . was to put down what really happened in action; . . . the real thing, the sequence of motion and fact which made the emotion and which would be as valid in a year or in ten years or, with luck and if you stated it purely enough, always."

—*Ernest Hemingway, Death in the Afternoon*

AUTHORS' NOTE

Everything in this book is true according to transcript, interview, secondary source, or official document. Interpretations, deductions, and opinions, which should be clear from context, are our own.

INTRODUCTION

On November 1, 1950, two Puerto Rican Nationalists named Oscar Collazo and Griselio Torresola pulled German automatic pistols and attempted to storm Blair House, at 1651 Pennsylvania Avenue, Washington, D.C., where the president of the United States, Harry S. Truman, was at that moment—2:20 P.M. on an abnormally hot Wednesday—taking a nap in his underwear. They were opposed by a Secret Service security detail led by Special Agent Floyd M. Boring, consisting of Special Agents Vincent P. Mroz and Stewart G. Stout, Jr., and White House police officers Leslie W. Coffelt, Joseph O. Davidson, Joseph H. Downs, and Donald T. Birdzell. In the brief exchange—under forty seconds—between twenty-nine and thirty-one shots were fired in an area about ninety feet by twenty feet, though the exchange broke into two actions at either end of the property, where the ranges were much shorter. When it was over one man was dead, another was dying, and two more were seriously injured.

The story was of course gigantic news—for about a week. What's remarkable about it is not how big a story it was but how quickly it went away. Today, few Americans even remember it, or if they do, they have it mixed up with a later event. In 1954, four Puerto Rican Nationalists pulled guns and shot up Congress. Soon enough the two stories melded in the U.S. folk imagination under the rubric of stereotype: hot-tempered Latin revolutionaries, undisciplined, crazy even, pursuing a dream that made no sense at all, Puerto Rican independence.

Even those few North Americans who could distinguish between the two events couldn't prevent the actual thing itself from eroding, losing its detail and meaning and settling sooner rather than later into a kind of comforting folk narrative. For Americans, it always encompassed the following points:

The grievances Oscar and Griselio were expressing were fundamentally absurd: Puerto Rico had been given the gift of United States culture and political traditions and was rapidly becoming Americanized, as it should be. What was wrong with these two that they didn't understand how benevolently they had been treated?

Americans believed they were a little crazy. The evidence is clear: the assault was thrown together on the run by these two men of no consequence and no meaningful cause. One of them didn't even have a gun, so the other had to go out the day before and buy him one. They were upset by newspaper reports of what was going on in Puerto Rico, where an equally silly group of men were attempting a coup, like they do down there all the time, something equally stupid and futile.

In Washington, the two gunmen further expressed their deep state of mental disorganization by acting in strange ways.

On the morning of the attempt, for example, they went sightseeing. It turned out they thought Truman lived in the White House, and a cab-driver told them the president had moved across the street while the White House was being remodeled. Then, back in the hotel room, one had to teach the other how to work the gun.

One of them even went up to the hotel clerk on the day of the attempt as he was leaving and inquired about an extended checkout time.

And that was the smart one!

The dumb one was an unemployed salesman, a ladies' man, an abject failure in life. Nothing at all is known about this fellow, but why should it be, since he is so predictable: like so many disgruntled would-be assassins, this was his chance to count in a world that had denied his existence. They had no plan and no understanding of tactics.

In the actual fight itself, the Secret Service and the White House policemen essentially brushed them aside.

The two never came close to getting into Blair House. And even if they had, it would have made no difference, as an agent with a tommy gun was waiting just inside the door.

Harry Truman was never in any mortal danger.

In the end, many Americans concluded, it was more a joke, a farce, an opera buffa, than anything else.

There is only one trouble with assigning these meanings to the 38.5 desperate, violent seconds of November 1, 1950.

Every single one of them is wrong.

1. A DRIVE AROUND WASHINGTON

This story could start in a great number of places. It could start with Columbus's arrival on a Caribbean island called Borinquen in 1493, or General Nelson A. Miles's arrival on the same island, now called Puerto Rico, in 1898. It could start at a Harvard graduation, a football game in DuBois, Pennsylvania, the collapse of a staircase railing in the capitol in San Juan, even a Virginia farm boy's decision to go to the city and become a police officer.

But no matter where it starts, it ends in the same place: a fury of gunfire that broke apart a quiet afternoon on Pennsylvania Avenue in Washington, D.C., just across from the White House, November 1, 1950. It ends as most gunfights do: with men dead, men wounded, wives in mourning, causes lost, lives shattered, duty followed hard, and regrets that never pass.

But let's begin—arbitrarily, to be sure—at 3:18 P.M., September 23, 1950, in Washington. On that day at that time, a father and a daughter slipped out the back door of their Federal-style townhouse, climbed into a well-waxed specially built black Lincoln driven by a tough-looking customer who carried a gun, and went for a little drive. The old man may have looked like a rich snoot out on the town but "rich snoot" doesn't describe him: he was famously plainspoken, hardworking, sensible, tough and had the common touch. He was sixty-six, well dressed, a giver-of-hell from the Show-Me State, a man who stood in the kitchen no matter the heat. He was the thirty-third president of the United States, Harry S. Truman.

His daughter, half a head shorter, was an elegant, poised young woman who took more after her mother than the pepperpot ex-haberdasher, ex–artillery officer who was her father. Margaret Truman, twenty-six, was pursuing a career as a concert singer, touring the East Coast; she always had the dignity of a diva. She had taken this weekend off and had returned

Friday afternoon by train from New York—Compartment A, Car 250, Train 125, accompanied by Special Agent Theodore Peters—to visit her father while her mother, Bess, was off in the Truman hometown of Independence, Missouri.

The mansion the president departed that afternoon bore the name Blair-Lee House, sited diagonally across Pennsylvania Avenue from the White House. A regal, elegant dwelling from the outside, it served as substitute home for the chief executive family while the 130-odd-year-old living quarters of the White House across the street were being modernized.

The father and daughter were close: he was a devoted and doting dad who a few months later would fire off an angry letter to *Washington Post* music critic Paul Hume, who had said unkind things about his daughter's singing. "Some day I hope to meet you. When that happens you'll need a new nose, a lot of beefsteak for black eyes, and perhaps a supporter below!" the president wrote, giving hell as was his style.

The drive, to nowhere important, lasted a little less than an hour, until 4:12 P.M. The day had clouded over but it was warm—74 degrees at 3:15—and it is not recorded what the two discussed as they traveled. But it can't have been a happy time.

For even as they moved through the quiet streets of the capital and enjoyed the pleasure of an early fall day, a political drama played out under the big white dome that stood upon the hill that dominated the federal triangle. Possibly the president didn't look at the Capitol; he suspected he was going to lose this one, and his mood must have been disgust and contempt.

The drama, at that very second dominating the U.S. Senate, swirled about the McCarran Act, an eighty-one-page accumulation of internal security—some would call it "red-scare"—legislation proposed by an old enemy of Truman's from the Senate, the seventy-four-year-old Democrat from Nevada. Pat McCarran, a man with "a profile that belonged on a Roman coin: a large hawkish nose that seemed to incline lower with age and thick, wavy white hair cresting high on his head," was a shrewd politician and, unlike the more famous but less effective Joseph McCarthy, he was an insider, "a master of parliamentary procedure."

His bill was a patchwork of the many different security bills that had been circulating around the Congress in the years after World War II when, in the wake of several security scandals such as those involving Alger Hiss, Klaus Fuchs, and the Rosenbergs, the fear of communist espionage and subversion was at its highest; the act mandated, among other things, that communists and front groups register with the government and declare their literature as propaganda, that communists not hold passports or governmental jobs, and that it was now a crime to commit "any act that might contribute to the establishment of a totalitarian dictatorship in the United States," whatever that might be.

When he introduced it on September 5, McCarran had all but declared war on his opponents: "I serve notice here and now that I will not be a party to any crippling or weakening amendments and that I shall oppose with all the power at my command any move to palm off on the American people any window-dressing substitute measure in the place of sound internal security legislation."

Truman wasn't an anti-anti-communist—in 1946, he crafted a temporary loyalty security program for the federal government and made it permanent in 1947—and he was aware that his administration had a reputation for being "soft on communism." But this was too much. Like many, he believed the bill was a modern-day version of the Alien and Sedition Acts of 1798 and he had "a bedrock belief that the Bill of Rights was the most important part of the Constitution."

It was a classic Washington mano a mano: two strong-willed men at opposite ends of the Mall locked in bitter opposition over a principle of governance, each willing to fight to the end to win the day, no matter the cost.

Thus, when the bill was passed by both House and Senate after much shrewd maneuvering by McCarran and despite dire warnings from many on Truman's own staff and even his vice president, Alben Barkley, who knew which way the wind blew, Harry Truman chose to stand against the wind: he vetoed it.

The veto was immediately overturned in the House, and now this very day, this very hour, the Senate argued the issue. The president had made his position clear to that body the day before in a message read by the clerk: "I am taking this action only after the most serious study and reflection and after consultation with the security and intelligence agencies of the government. . . . We would betray our finest traditions if we attempted, as this bill would attempt, to curb the simple expression of opinion. This we should never do, no matter how distasteful the opinion may be to the vast majority of our people."

Now only a few argued for the veto, but they held the floor, primarily on the efforts of Senator Bill Langer, a Republican from North Dakota, who had well-known libertarian tendencies; Langer had embarked on a kind of one-man filibuster. In the Senate it was Langer against the world, and everybody knew who would win.

As he drove about the town with his beloved daughter next to him, Harry Truman knew that there was nothing left to do but wait.

The president had another, more dangerous, adversary that day than the senator from Nevada. Where a Pat McCarran came at him with brilliant parliamentary moves, with subtleties of agenda, with fakes and jukes and feints, the angry Puerto Rican Nationalist Pedro Albizu Campos would come more directly—he would send men with guns.

Albizu Campos, sometimes called "El Maestro" or "The Maximum Leader" or by his intimates "The Old Man," was smallish, olive-skinned, and electric with an almost religious fervor to his beliefs. Harvard-educated and by most standards brilliant, and committed to the ideal of an independent Puerto Rico, the fifty-seven-year-old was a riveting speaker, a shrewd plotter, and commanded the allegiance of a small army of armed, black-shirted soldiers. On this same day, September 23, 1950, he gave a fiery speech that revealed his intentions, not that they had ever been secret and even if they flouted an infamous act called Law 53, which outlawed the expression of such sentiments in Puerto Rico. His words make an interesting counterpoint to Truman's veto message to the Senate and reveal the essence of this other 1950 mano a mano between two strong men, with not the Mall but an ocean and a culture and a history between them.

At 3:00 P.M.—Harry Truman, lunch and his last official appointment behind him, was getting ready to leave Blair House with Margaret— Albizu appeared at the Gonzáles Theater of Lares, a mountain town a few hours to the south of San Juan, before an audience of three hundred. The speech he delivered was recorded, and broadcast that same evening over radio station WCMN of Arecibo.

It was the climax of a busy day for the Old Man, as his watchers from the Insular Police Internal Security section carefully noted.

They had observed him all day, as they did every day, and they recorded everything.

For example, they recorded that at 7:00 A.M. Albizu left the home of

Oscar Colón Delgado in Barrio Pueblo of Hatillo for Lares, "to participate in the NPPR [Nationalist Party of Puerto Rico] celebration 'Grito de Lares' which refers to a day in 1868 when a group of Puerto Rican Nationalists succeeded in temporarily overpowering the Spanish garrison at Lares."

Discreetly, they followed him, to note that he arrived by eight and joined a group of Nationalists in the town plaza. At the head of the group were four officers and thirty-seven members of the NPPR Cadet Corps, in black shirts and white trousers, who quickly gathered into formation. The paramilitary unit led the way to the church. Then at 9:30 the marchers moved on a narrow road, up a hill, to the Lares Cemetery, where they placed flowers on the graves of the martyrs who fell in the revolution of Lares. Then they moved to the plaza and placed another floral offering at the base of an obelisk raised in memory of "the heroes of 1868."

At three he appeared at the theater. One must imagine the scene: the ornate venue in the center of the picturesque mountain town, the three hundred sweating Nationalists packed into it, the temperature high and humid—it was 89 degrees in Lares that day, building toward a rain that would fall at four—and at the center of this, the small, messianic figure on the stage. He had piercing eyes that seemed to see into people and disarm them immediately. He nearly always dressed the same, almost priest-like in his severity: a black jacket shrouding his narrow shoulders, over a white shirt, and set off by a black bow tie. But when he spoke he became more: he was a fiery, spellbinding orator who knew how to draw a crowd to him and then bring them along, either to lay siege or to share a romantic and imaginary journey to an independent Puerto Rico where the modernity of the Anglo world would be irrelevant to the ideal life of the worker on the land.

It was a long and dense speech—he allowed himself many of the rhetorical indulgences of the great orator, fully aware that his personal magnetism would carry the crowd over the duration of his performance— that cited history and religion, culture and tradition. And it did not shy from the boldly direct.

"It is not easy to give a speech," he began, "when we have our mother lying in bed and an assassin waiting to take her life. Such is the present situation of our country, of our Puerto Rico: the assassin is the power of the United States of North America. One cannot give a speech while the newborn of our country are dying of hunger, while the adolescents of our homeland are being poisoned with the worst virus, slavery."

He argued that a state of conflict existed between his country and its oppressors and he cited the philosophic underpinnings of it, the illegality of the United States's rule over Puerto Rico, its very presence an act of war: "And here the yanquis have been at war fifty-two years against the Puerto Rican nation, and have never acquired the right of anything in Puerto Rico, nor is there any legal government in Puerto Rico, and this is incontestable."

He railed against the presence of American troops on his island: "Well, are the armed forces here to defend Puerto Ricans? [No,] TO KILL PUERTO RICANS!! That's the only government here, the rest are scoundrels, and all that crowd of bootlickers [who] say that this is a democracy, the yanquis laugh at them."

He evoked the standard themes of anti-imperialism: the waste of Puerto Rican manhood in the Korean War, the possibility that germ warfare had been tested on Puerto Ricans, the unfairness of a system that made it necessary for Puerto Ricans to go to the United States to earn a living wage after American capital had wrecked the agricultural economy.

It went on and on, for over two hours, through the rainstorm that came at four, through its cessation, through the coming of cooler weather, the fall of night, on and on.

He finally got to the immediate political issue, which was the upcoming voter registration days—women on November 4, men on November 5—for a later referendum on whether to draw up a new territorial constitution. He opposed the registration, not because he detested constitutions but because he detested the U.S. influence that such an enterprise would necessarily entail. Then—spent, one guesses, exhausted by the passion—he concluded with a promise of things to come and that golden dream of ripping freedom from the bosom of the oppressor.

"All this has to be defied, only as the men of Lares defied despotism—WITH THE REVOLUTION."

Senator Bill Langer fought on. Asked to surrender the floor, he said furiously, "I said I would not yield." Like Mr. Smith in Frank Capra's fabled movie, he alone would stem the tide.

But if his spirit was unbowed, the same cannot be said of his body. At that point, he "stopped speaking, swayed slightly and crashed to the floor."

He had passed out, and would be removed by ambulance crew to Bethesda Naval Hospital.

The inevitable end came swiftly enough. A few parliamentary maneuvers mounted by the liberals were quickly defeated, and another speaker, Paul Douglas, the progressive Democrat from Illinois, took the floor but eventually relinquished it. Finally, almost twenty-four hours after Truman's veto message had been read, it was time to vote.

At 4:30 a roll call was taken.

The veto was overturned, 57 to 10.

The McCarran Act became law.

"One of the most distressing political defeats my father ever suffered," Margaret Truman later wrote.

But Truman got on with his life and the next day saw his daughter off on the train to New York. He wrote his cousin, Ethel Noland, that evening discussing the trying weekend, but only in personal terms, chatting about "Margie" and how she moaned when she found out that her maid had forgotten to pack two fur coats she meant to take with her to New York and how he chided her about not doing things for herself and "I didn't sympathize with her at all and that made her mader [sic] than ever."

But then he had an odd moment, almost like a premonition.

"You know," he wrote cousin Ethel, "I have a valet, four ushers, five butlers, seven or eight secretaries, a dozen or so executive assistants, an assistant president—three of 'em in fact, and I can't open a door, get my hat, pull out my chair at the table, hang up my coat or do anything else for myself even take a bath! I won't be worth a damn when I come out of here—if I ever do."

If I ever do.

2. GRISELIO AGONISTES

An unseasonable heat hung over New York, Sunday evening, October 29, 1950. It was freakishly warm all over the Northeastern and Middle Atlantic states. But it was certain that a young man standing twenty-five feet over the river on the bridge that separated the Bronx from Harlem didn't notice or care. He appeared anguished.

He was a handsome young man, with a wisp of mustache, and he was intelligent, ambitious, and committed. Everyone who remembers him comments on his vitality, his pep. He was known for his loyalty and his strength of character. A superb athlete, he played shortstop on the ball fields of his youth, a position that demanded a particular grace of hand-eye coordination, so he was used to being the star. This evening he seemed distraught.

Standing on the Willis Avenue Bridge, amid a mesh of steel girders with their gigantic rivets and thick coating of gray all-weather paint, as four lanes of dense traffic roared thunderously between the two boroughs, he could look off to the immediate southwest and locate a symbol of his pain, in the form of the lights of a spire clawing to the sky. That would be the Empire State Building, from this distance at this time of night just a streamlined, aggressive silhouette. For a man of Griselio Torresola's sensibilities, it must have mocked him. That would be the United States of America: proud, beautiful, gigantic, indifferent, distant. He was but nothing to it. He was intense and concentrated, his mind so abuzz with ideas it was all he could do to speak without shouting. That is because, more than a handsome fellow, more than an athlete or a worker or a father or a son, he was a man of politics and a man of action.

Griselio was something of an anointed one, a special child. He was raised in a mountain town, Jayuya, a long way from San Juan. His memories of the past were golden: he recalled high mountain valleys, three green peaks, forests, and sparkling streams. That, to him, was Puerto

Rico: a valley of lush beauty where his friends and his family all lived together and everybody was happy and had enough. It was in his mind an image of his nation.

It was in that valley, under those three mountain peaks, that through the actions of his charismatic cousin, the redoubtable social worker and landowner Blanca Canales, sister of one of Puerto Rico's intellectuals, he met and grew up with an even more imposing charismatic: the great Don Pedro Albizu Campos, leader of the Nationalist Party of Puerto Rico, fighter against imperialism, plotter of revolutions, a man of almost saintly composure and assuredness. How could Griselio possibly grow up any other way than devoted to this man who dazzled them all with his courage, his strength, his absolutism, his wit, his powerful oratory, and his way of seeing through things, to the absolute core.

He would die for Don Pedro and the cause of freedom for Puerto Rico, of that he was sure.

But that might not be enough. He had other responsibilities. He has been Albizu's secret revolutionary representative in New York since his arrival in the United States two years ago; he has been working in politics, raising money, communicating with the New York junta of the party, carrying messages, buying ammunition. It was all for the revolutionary future they were so certain approached. On November 4 and 5, women first, then men, were scheduled to register to vote on a constitution put before them by the oppressors. Instead, the island would be struck by heroic revolutionary action in key cities as the men of the barrios become the soldiers of the barricades and make a statement the world will never forget. And Griselio has steeled himself: he is to be part of that statement. He has an immense responsibility but he knows he is up to it.

In his pocket he carried an extraordinary document, all but giving him total power over the action units of the Nationalist Party of Puerto Rico here in the United States, a high position for one so young—he is but twenty-five—but one reflecting his judgment, his poise, his commitment, his loyalty.

My dear Griselio, the letter reads, *If by some circumstance it may become necessary that you assume leadership of the Movement in the United States, you will do so without any kind of qualms. We leave everything concerning this affair to your high patriotism and sound discretion. I embrace you, Albizu Campos.*

Additionally, he had a document, also signed by Albizu Campos, giving him access to various monies raised by the party to finance actions he deemed necessary. That is an awful lot of power for one so young, but again, he knew he was up to it. That is the depth of his commitment.

But word has come that two days ago, Don Pedro's bodyguards, following him home from a rally, were intercepted and arrested by the police. Alas, in the car were weapons intended for the revolutionary action, including pistols and several bombs, plus ammunition. That would tip off the police that something was planned. These men, so close to Albizu Campos, knew of the plans. What did the arrest portend for the stroke so carefully planned for November 3? Possibly that is what had Griselio so upset, and upon getting the news, he rushed to the apartment of one of the wisest of all the men of the party he knew, an older fellow, much experienced, much traveled, one of Don Pedro's closest friends and allies in the United States. He went to see Oscar Collazo.

Oscar and Griselio had left Oscar's apartment for the bridge. And thus they walked, two men, hell-bent on a mission, not seeing the Bronx on either side of them, the bodegas, the tenements, the others in the busy dramas of their lives. In each head a revolutionary anthem was playing behind a revolutionary newsreel: buildings burning, executions, soldiers with bazookas and machine guns, the hopeless heroism of the outnumbered and the passionate, the dream of self-realization, of that green thing called liberty, by which each man was his own master and no masters ruled from behind fancy desks or in fancy Lincolns.

Soon they reached the bridge and Griselio's anguish must have come pouring out.

The older man offered calmness. He was a student of history and philosophy. In his armchair at night, he merged minds with the greatest thinkers in history. And for two years, the great Albizu Campos himself had lived downstairs from this man in the same building, and on a daily, intimate basis they had shared thoughts. This man was highly placed here in the Nationalist junta of New York.

Griselio was back from Puerto Rico less than two months. He had seen Don Pedro. It was all set. The revolution was like a giant train on the tracks and it couldn't be stopped, as people all over the island had their assignments and their timetable. What if the police arrest Don Pedro and he is incommunicado? Who makes decisions?

The older man listened patiently. He wore a suit—always, even on the way to work as a metal polisher—and had a scholarly mien. He had an impeccable work record, a wife he loved desperately, a daughter, two step-daughters, and a dog named Smoky.

Both were short but only by U.S. standards. Griselio Torresola was the smaller, at five foot five inches tall, weight a mere 112 pounds. That's close to jockey weight, yet it's unlikely he was over-freighted with a small man's need to make an imprint beyond the scale of his body. That's because he was a superb athlete, he'd been well loved as a child, and his height was quite normal among smaller-statured Puerto Ricans.

Oscar Collazo was an inch taller and twenty-eight pounds heavier and older, by eleven years. He had built a life, a reputation; he was a part of society, and, outwardly at least, appeared to believe in its structures and organizations. He worked as one of the best metal polishers at a buffing wheel at the Gainer Corporation in New Rochelle, where he shined women's purse frames. He was very good at it. Griselio, meanwhile, had worked briefly at a bookstore called El Siglo on Fifth Avenue, but really was a full-time political operative. His whole life, his whole mission, was politics. He lived off the government dole.

Both had fiery internal lives. They were true believers in their Puerto Rican-ness, in Eric Hoffer's sense, men who had given themselves over to a leader and a movement and for whom no rational argument against had any meaning. Both were committed members of Don Pedro Albizu Campos's party, and both knew and loved Albizu Campos himself. Though neither had criminal records in the United States or Puerto Rico, both had been exposed to revolutionary violence. Revolution wasn't romantic to them, or abstract: it was street action, violent, harsh, irre-versible.

They talked. They talked. They talked.

Yet to this day, it is not entirely clear what they talked about. One of them later testified that it was their intention, at this moment, to return to Puerto Rico. This is revealing, for the revolution to which they meant to give lives and fortunes had not yet broken out at this moment. So clearly, they knew it was planned. The beliefs of their leader and his policy goals are also known, as are what others said of his methods of leadership and how he selected some men—Griselio was a particular favorite of his—for special assignments.

But for this night, the sole survivor would later say the next idea was his own, to return to Puerto Rico and take part in the fighting (which had not yet broken out). However, to return to Puerto Rico, a gun was necessary. He claimed at this time Oscar asked about a gun, because Griselio would know of such things, being far more practically versed in the intricacies of revolution.

A price was discussed. Oscar had access to $1,250 in a postal savings account, money he and his wife, Rosa, were saving to buy a house. They had chosen a postal account because they didn't think banks were secure enough. A gun was clearly affordable. The sole survivor would later testify that on Sunday evening, October 29, after two hours of intense conversation, Oscar turned over $50 to Griselio for a gun.

But questions remain. Whatever the mission planned, why would Oscar be part of it? He was sedentary, a thinker, older, inexperienced, not by any means a young fighter. He hadn't the skills, the training, the temperament for such work. He was the patient one, the organized one, but in these matters of action and speed, a hopeless, hapless amateur. In a practical sense, to take him along, any fool would have known, would be to doom any action. In the middle of an action is not a place to learn about actions. Why was Oscar involved?

For years afterward, the Secret Service believed and tried to prove the deeper conspiracy, the larger conspiracy—that as an act of political policy the Nationalist Party of Puerto Rico ordered Griselio to commit the deed and he recruited Oscar. And of course what is meant by the party is the man. The government believed that Pedro Albizu Campos, as part of his revolutionary strategy for 1950, ordered two assassinations, one targeting the governor of Puerto Rico, Luis Muñoz Marín, and the other the president of the United States, Harry S. Truman. These two events, in concert with the proclamation of a Free Republic of Puerto Rico in Jayuya, and cities in flames across the island, would have been the first step toward the long and brutal war of revolutionary liberation.

The evidence never rose to a threshold of legal action. It may have been convincing, but still it was a series of inferences of intent, of patterns, of possibilities, of probabilities. These inferences must be considered.

What is known is that the one survivor testified later that Griselio agreed to buy Oscar a gun.

And so at around 11:00 P.M., the two parted on the bridge between Harlem and the Bronx, each to return to his life and their plan.

What they don't know, and can't know, is that they were already behind events. Somebody was about to start the revolution without them.

3. REVOLUTION

It was the day of death. *El día de la muerte.*

A man named Gregorio Hernández Rivera sat in the back seat of a dark green 1949 Plymouth. It was mid-morning, October 30, 1950, in San Juan, Puerto Rico, the morning after Oscar and Griselio had met on the bridge in the Bronx. Gregorio was wearing his Sunday best, his best suit, his best shirt, his best tie. He was preparing to die.

Fighting had already broken out all across the island. At 4:00 A.M. in the Barrio Macaná in the town of Peñuelas, Nationalists ambushed Insular police officers. In Ponce, at 9:00 A.M., an Insular policeman was assassinated. At 10:30 A.M. in Arecibo, the police station was under fire. At 11:30 A.M. in Utuado, shooting broke out between Nationalists and Insular police and national guardsmen. At noon in Jayuya, the police station was attacked; parts of the town were burning. Yet this was not the master stroke that had been in the works for two years, but some diminution of it.

For reasons yet unknown, the revolution happened out of coordination, over a space of eight hours, one unit lurching into action too soon, the others hesitating, men not showing up, arms not appearing, the attacks too small and uncoordinated to be effective, El Maestro, Don Pedro, himself trapped in his house by police units, and now, it was said, soldiers and detectives, alerted by the actions in other cities, waited on the roof of the target of Gregorio and his friends. It was said that certain death awaited them.

Gregorio had an automatic pistol. And the other men had automatics as well—in all, a Belgian .38, a Colt .45, two Lugers, and a P.38, the last three in 9mm. Only their leader, Raimundo Díaz Pacheco, had a submachine gun, the American M-3, a .45 commonly called a grease gun for its similarity to the common garage tool. That would be their best chance;

you point such a gun and press the trigger and *ziiiiiip* the bullets buzz out. Also in the car were three rifles, one a Winchester (in the trunk), ammunition and forty-four pipe bombs; twelve Molotov cocktails, the insurgent guerrilla's best friend; eighteen sticks of dynamite; and twelve commando knives. It was time. Raimundo Díaz Pacheco, who had served as commander in chief of the Cadet Corps (sometimes called the Liberating Army) of the Nationalist Party of Puerto Rico and was a man of notorious, even brazen, aggressive tendencies, gave the signal. It was time to go.

Did they want to go? Who would want to? To go was to die, it is that certain. It was an ambush; surprise had been lost. Everyone knew this. But they had an obligation; they had concluded their lives meant nothing compared to their deaths. Even if the police and the soldiers knew they were coming and were on the roof of La Fortaleza, the ancient structure that served as the governor's mansion in the old quarter of San Juan, it didn't matter. Sacrifices must be made.

But Díaz Pacheco was no fool. As much as he understood the necessity of sacrifice, so too he understood the necessity of preservation.

And thus, just a few minutes ago to the sixty men that had gathered there in the cobbled Plaza Dársenas in Old San Juan in front of the Customs House and the U.S. Post Office, in the shade of a great tree, he gave an order.

There had been no sense in wasting lives. He sent most of the men away to fight another day.

And so off they went, and now only these five remained: besides Gregorio and Raimundo Díaz Pacheco, there are Domingo Hiraldo Resto, Roberto Acevedo, and Manuel Torres Medina. They were the designated martyrs. They knew it. They will do it.

That is one variant of the story, possibly the most romantic. In another variant, of the sixty to seventy revolutionaries scheduled to show up, only these five did. The others may simply have concluded it was a bad day to be a revolutionary, with the secrets blown by the actions in the other cities now on the radio. Particularly damaging to the assault on La Fortaleza was the absence of a second car. A Nationalist insider later testified that they had originally planned that "[o]ne [car] was going to shoot from a certain spot to get the police's attention and the other was going to go on to Fortaleza." Without a diversion, with police awaiting them, the attack was certain to fail.

What is almost certain is that Díaz Pacheco's squad took a last look around before leaving the square. What they saw summed up the reasons why they were about to do what they were about to do. They could look in one direction and see the immense U.S. Post Office. Next to it was the Customs House, where U.S. tax collectors took their share of all that came into San Juan. Beyond that, the bay, sparkly and beautiful, and beyond that the green of the island as it humped up into a spine of some of the loveliest mountains on the face of the earth. For these men, those mountains *were* Puerto Rico. The two American government buildings, meanwhile, were symbols of the oppressors' heavy presence, and on this day, they would die to protest it.

Nevertheless, no one was eager for what was ahead. As the Nationalist insider relates, "[T]hey just drove around in circles. Raimundo was more nervous—I think he had a firecracker in there—but Raimundo is a kid of a man—always like a little kid—a man that would say that when he was trembling that he would fire a shot into the air to calm himself . . . to get in the groove. . . . So, they had driven a lot of circles around [the neighborhood of] Santurce, around San Juan."

Eventually, they pulled up the street from the square, going uphill, for much of Old San Juan is on a hill set on the tip of the peninsula that forms the Rich Port that provided the island with its name, then turned left down the narrow street called Calle Fortaleza. The street, being four hundred years old, was bumpy with cobblestones, and the colonial buildings built in ox cart days looming a couple of stories above seemed to bend in, permitting the illumination of only a ribbon of sky. Normally crowded, it was this day sparsely occupied, for everyone knew trouble brooded in the air and most civilians preferred not to risk an errant bullet. The arcades and doorways, the little shops, all flew by.

Ahead of them loomed the structure that gave this street in Old San Juan its name. La Fortaleza, the governor's mansion, is where the first democratically elected governor of Puerto Rico, Luis Muñoz Marín, resided, behind the crenelated white walls of a fortress, though the walls were carpeted in flowers. Neoclassical in style, it stood on a cliff, overlooking the beautiful bay, on the lee side of the triangular peninsula that forms Old San Juan. It expressed the grandeur of Spain's aspirations for the New World. But it was a fortress so incompetently placed for its strategic mission that the Spaniards in the very year of its completion, 1540, began building another, more soundly located fortress at the tip of the landform, where bay meets Atlantic, which was called El Morro. It was a good move, as from El Morro, in 1595, the Spaniards defeated Sir Francis Drake's invasion, sending hundreds of Britons to the bottom.

The British came back, and ultimately their flag flew over La Fortaleza. But not for long. The heat, the disease, the intensity of the tropical experience was not for fair-skinned northern peoples; they abandoned the city back to the Spanish in 1598. The Dutch tried their hand in 1625 but were unsuccessful, and the island continued under Spanish rule until 1898, when the Americans arrived. La Fortaleza was rebuilt in 1640, then again in 1800, and finally, taking this configuration, in 1846.

But the men in the car were not concerned with such historical tidbits. They were on an assassination mission that had become a sacrificial offering.

Thus were certain themes immediately established. They were armed, determined, willing to die. More importantly they were willing to die to kill; assassination was a part of their worldview, as was suicide. What they lacked in finesse they made up for in what their victims would call zealotry and what their followers would call heroism. Possibly it's a Latino thing, inherited from a culture where politics and honor seem to involve the spilling of blood. Or possibly it's a colonial legacy, as imported to the hemisphere by hard-eyed, gold-hungry Spanish conquistadors who took what they wanted, and paid in violence when their will was denied. Or perhaps the Americans, landing in 1898 and advancing behind piety and bayonets, changing their language and customs and even the spelling of the name of the island itself, taught them the lesson. Or perhaps it's the invention of their leader, the fiery Pedro Albizu Campos, Harvard law school grad with a knot of fury in his brain for all things *norteamericanas*. Whatever, it was certain absolutely that they were willing to kill and to die.

Thus they had a feeling they had to do their part. They must strike a blow for Puerto Rican independence. They must do as their Maximum Leader, Albizu Campos, directed.

Steadily, unflinchingly, they approached the fortress.

The hero of their dreams was not far away. He was, in fact, less than six blocks distant, in his apartment at 156 Calle Sol, on the second floor. Below his apartment was a sign advertising a bar, La Borinquen. The bar may or may not have been open but in any event it's more important as a symbol than a tavern. It happens that the name *Borinquen* is Puerto Rico's original Taíno name, and it represents, in certain imaginations, the rural purity that was destroyed by yanqui invaders from 1898 onward, the rural purity that should be restored by all means, violence included. The building was square, stucco, and altogether unremarkable, except for a party headquarters sign below a window and a flagpole jutting heroically outward from it, displaying the symbol of the Republic of Puerto Rico. A balcony looked out on the other side, and now and then Don Pedro, in striped pajama tops, could be glimpsed through the windows or even standing on the balcony. He was not alone: he shared the dwelling with his compatriots in the revolutionary elite of Puerto Rico, such as his ardent secretary, Doris Torresola, and Carmen María Pérez, as well as university student José Muñoz Matos. But at this particular moment, he can't have been happy, for the grand stroke he had engineered was rapidly collapsing about him. By a stroke of bad luck or perhaps even internal treachery, police forces last Friday, October 27, pulled over the car containing his bodyguards, which was trailing him after a speech in Fajardo as part of his campaign against the upcoming vote on a new constitution engineered by his bête noire, the governor, Muñoz Marín. In the car, the police found three pistols, several bombs, and ammunition.

Everywhere the fear of what the captured men might spill in interrogation passed through the air like electricity, and one by one, uncoordinated, the revolutionary attacks began today, on Monday. As a Nationalist insider later testified, "They went for it on October 30th because there were already several errors committed amongst them . . . they knew that the police would now carry out raids after . . . [the arrest] in San Juan—so they said the time has come . . . the signal would be a shot—the first shot that was fired."

In Jayuya, Albizu Campos's friend and admirer Blanca Canales had led a squad of men with Doris's brother Elio Torresola among them to occupy the post office and declare the Free Republic of Puerto Rico. But National Guard airplanes were called to bomb them out. Now only two planned events were left, one here, at La Fortaleza, and one in the United States. The war had to be brought to the United States. Otherwise, Albizu knew, what happened in Puerto Rico would be just a little news item about crazy Latinos shooting one another. He understood America very well. He was, after all, a Harvard graduate.

Then there was the problem that he was surrounded.

Ever since the arrest of the bodyguards, elements of the police and the National Guard had taken up positions outside his house far more aggressively than their usual not-so-subtle surveillance. But at 12:20 P.M., more police arrived, and Albizu Campos greeted them with a few incendiary bombs that didn't detonate, though one broke a police windshield. He or someone on his side fired a few shots as well. So the police blockaded the streets of Calles Sol and Cruz, isolating the apartment–party headquarters. He was effectively stalemated from fighting in his own war, and for a man of such energetic personality, such dynamism and passion, the forced inaction couldn't have been easy.

Action was always his preference. Photos convey a little of his intensity. Slight at five foot four, dapper, he looked like a stick of dynamite in a pair of suspenders and a bow tie, even at fifty-seven, after a lifetime of turmoil and travail as well as a stretch in the hoosegow. The pajama top he now wore was atypical, perhaps indicating the drama of the situation. Otherwise, he always dressed like the Harvard law student that he had been. His cheekbones were prominent, his eyes brilliant, his mustache perfectly trimmed. One can never imagine him at repose, or out of politics, or as having a life separate from his belief system. By policy and persuasion, he was a man of a single, absolute personality, expressed in spellbinding oration and direct, vigorous action. One man said of him, "He is rather tall than short; thin; his olive-skinned color characterizes him as a Creole; his eyes, the same as his glance, have the expression of the look of a saint." But mainly he can be summed up in a single word: smart. He was very smart.

He claimed two birth dates, one in 1891, the more likely one in 1893. He was born of a Basque father and a peasant mother. One can see easily enough the play of those origins. From his Basque side, he inherited a willingness to go to far places and do hard things. This is a Basque specialty, and it is no surprise that many of Columbus's crew were Basque, that the Basques roamed the world, that they succeeded as shepherds in Montana and merchants in Puerto Rico and the Caribbean. Also, notoriously, they have difficulty with authority, and have been fighting in their motherland for freedom for centuries. And they tend to zealotry: Ignatius Loyola was a Basque, and he founded the most intense form of Catholic clergy, the Jesuits. They are, then, a formidable people. But from his mother, the daughter of a slave, he inherited a deep love of land, of place.

He learned the skill of abiding, of getting through hard times, of never letting a conqueror conquer your interior landscapes even if he had overwhelmed your exterior landscapes, and rode on horseback and wore a splendid uniform and commanded respect and attention and the worship of an alien flag and culture.

The birthplace of the future Nationalist firebrand was Ponce, "La Perla del Sur," the pearl of the south; it's a coastal city eighty miles down and across the island from San Juan, the second largest on the island. It was, like Cuba's Santiago, a city of rebellion always, a font of discontent. In 1937, a famous massacre took place in Ponce, and those embittered by it provided the foot soldiers of the revolution who would march to Albizu Campos's commands. But not yet: he had much to overcome before he commanded men and plotted violence. His birth was problematic: the father was well-known merchant Don Alejandro Albizu Romero, known as "El Vizcaíno," from the Spanish province of Vizcaya. His mother, Juliana Campos, was—well, there's some debate. Albizu Campos's most admiring and romanticizing biographer, Federico Ribes Tovar, says that in her veins "flowed the blood of Spaniards, Indians and Africans," which would make her mestiza. The anonymous spook "District Intelligence Officer 10ND" of Naval Intelligence HQ in San Juan is less circumspect, calling Juliana, in 1948, "a colored mother."

There is also some suggestion of mental instability in the mother. In her biography of Albizu Campos, Marisa Rosado wrote, "Juliana, Albizu's mother . . . was affected by her mental faculties and on various occasions she tried to bring her children to a pool in the Bucaná River . . . she brought them there to 'drown herself with them.' . . . In her delirium, Juliana burned the garbage inside the house. She would walk on the streets of Ponce speaking to herself."

She was drowned when Albizu was almost four years old, trying to cross a river on planks that she had brought for that purpose. The planks gave way and her body was carried to the beach.

Because his skin was dark, most Americans, particularly the authorities, have inevitably considered Albizu a Negro. Americans have always ascribed his fury at the United States as being racially rooted, the pathology of a man who had suffered the ugliness of racial prejudice and therefore marshaled his intelligence, his anger, and his courage to destroy it. But this is not quite the case; nothing is ever that simple. He himself denied it, saying, "For us, race has nothing to do with biology. Nor dusky skin, nor frizzy hair, nor dark eyes. Race is a continuity of characteristic virtues and institutions. We are distinguished by our culture, our courage, our chivalry, our Catholic sense of civilization."

The low caste of Albizu's mother and his bastard origins aside, his talents were recognized early in Puerto Rico in the years between the turn of the century and the First World War. Indeed, the kid had "star" written all over him, and wherever he went, he impressed people, won awards, was guided onward to better, higher goals. Graduating from high school in Ponce, he attracted the attention of Ponce's school superintendent, Charles Terry, who recommended him to a Masonic group, the Aurora No. 7 Lodge of Ponce (Albizu's father was a Mason, possibly explaining the first contact), which in turn obtained for him a scholarship at the University of Vermont.

One can only imagine the isolation the dark-skinned, wren-boned, electrically charged Latin intellectual felt in the cold climate of Burlington, but, as Albizu did everywhere, the young man worked hard, applied his considerable intelligence, and excelled. In a year he had attracted the attention of a Harvard professor, who arranged for him to transfer to that institution in 1913. His Harvard records suggest a young man of strong work habits who impressed most people not with his brilliance but with his diligence and his excellent manners. He first took courses in 1913 as an "unclassified student" with the understanding that he had to pass fourteen courses with at least a C grade to get a bachelor of arts degree. In 1916, halfway through his third year, he wrote to the Committee on Admissions, stating that he had taken fifteen courses and pointing out that eye difficulties had bothered him during his second year. It's in this letter, an ultimately successful application to waive the C requirement (he had received a D in chemistry) so that he could receive an appointment to Harvard Law School, that he writes, "My ambition has been to learn as much as possible while in College and while in this country in order to become a faithful interpreter of both to my people."

He took courses in English, German, French, government, economics, education, chemistry, and mineralogy. He taught high school Spanish in the winter of 1913–14 at the Walpole High School in Walpole, Massachusetts, then at the Country Day School in Newton, Massachusetts, and tutored Harvard students in Spanish, French, and chemistry (he charged $2.50 an hour). Although he had excelled during his year at the University of Vermont, earning mostly As, his undergraduate grades at Harvard appeared to be predominantly in the B and C range. Some of his professors were guarded in their praise: "A gentlemanly Porto Rican; not brilliant intellectually but of good habits and appearance," one wrote. Another observed that he was "an unusually courteous and 'gentlemanly' young man, and also unusually serious. His work, if not brilliant, has always been thorough and absolutely satisfactory. . . . He will prove to be a devoted and painstaking teacher, I am sure."

It is said by his defenders that all during this time he was noting the impact of racism upon his experiences, but in truth it seems that there was nothing preventing him from anything; he was, after all, in the cradle of American liberal culture, presumably the most tolerant and welcoming city in the world, even in the benighted early 1910s. He earned his A.B. degree from Harvard in 1916.

Many date Albizu Campos's anger from his army experience. In World War I, empathetic to the French who were being slaughtered in the trenches, he enlisted in the Harvard ROTC. In May of 1918, he interrupted his studies at Harvard Law (he had registered September 25, 1916) and returned to Puerto Rico. There he founded a Home Guard Force on the beach of Ponce with 180 men. He was a soldier for ten days in the F Force of the 375th Regiment. Then for three months he served as a first lieutenant, again with the 375th. But sometime in there, something happened: the sensitive young intellectual was confronted by the harsh realities of the racist institution that was the army.

One could then track the consequences of racism as they rippled outward through society, through the long war between Albizu Campos and his oppressors, the bombs, the murders, the shootings, the whole sense of anguished anarchy that stalked both Puerto Rico and the United States as this issue was played out over the years.

Yet at the same time, and once again conforming to pattern, his extraordinary intelligence declared him special, different, a star. Somehow he ends up a general's aide. There's even a formal portrait of him in full uniform, and it certainly looks as if the young man is enjoying every inch of being an officer and a gentleman in the United States Army, as he sits there proudly, his legs crossed, his elegant riding boots polished brightly, his cap with its gleaming American eagle set trimly above his bold, fierce eyes, which gleam with dark purpose at the camera lens. Never sent to Europe, he never saw combat; but still, he was well enough known, according again to one of his biographers, to be asked by some factotum of President Woodrow Wilson's to attend a congress in Paris and even to travel by American warship, with full honors. At a Southern port, when he saw how Negroes were treated he refused to travel farther; later, rejecting a reserve commission, he declared that Puerto Ricans should not be the Sepoys of the American army.

It's a revealing metaphor; the Sepoys, native Indians in the employ of the British East India Company's army, revolted in 1857, in an epic bloodletting known as the Sepoy Rebellion to the Indians and the Great Indian Mutiny to the British. Thousands died, atrocities were the rule of the day, and a scar was cut into the British and Indian imaginations that would never heal. Albizu Campos was clearly moved by the image of a gigantic conflagration, as the oppressors are put to the sword and then retaliate with all the fury of their might, turning a subcontinent into a graveyard of ruins.

But when he left the army, under an honorable discharge, he did nothing particularly radical, nor did he entertain despair. He was not like Hemingway's Krebs in "Soldier's Story," or Nick in "Big Two-Hearted River." That whole dynamic of postwar disgust and the concomitant crisis of faith seems to have evaded him entirely. Instead, ever ambitious, his course set, he returned to Harvard to resume his law studies. His second stay at Harvard was equally successful; he quickly became a famous radical, a leader of independence movements. He met and was influenced by two international visitors to the campus in the late 1910s, the Irish leader Eamon de Valera and the Indian patriot philosopher Rabindranath Tagore. It is reported that on a certain evening at Harvard, a high church of Anglophilia in those years, he was the only speaker to come out in favor of independence for Ireland, and despite the apostasy was pronounced the giver of "the speech of the evening."

At Harvard also he made another decision. He joined the Catholic Church. One may fairly ask, was he not a Catholic to begin with, as were so many Puerto Ricans? Until then he had evidently tended toward agnosticism, to a sense of the world as rational, to possibility as achieved by labor, not prayer. But at Harvard he met two priests, the Irish Father Ryan, with his stories of valiant sons of Eire standing against the English, and the priest-scientist Father Luis Rodes, from the University of Ebro, who showed him that faith and rationalism could coexist.

Later, in 1966, Puerto Rican Nationalist poet and ex-communist Juan Antonio Corretjer said of Albizu Campos's conversion that it represented a choice of the Catholicism of old Puerto Rico as opposed to the Protestantism of new America.

Even at Harvard and upon his return to Puerto Rico after law school (now married to Peruvian intellectual Laura Meneses, whom he had met while a student at Harvard), according to at least one of his biographers, he was subject to many offers. These included lecture tours at $200 a month, a $15,000-a-year job as an executive in the Spanish-American division of a Protestant organization, a clerkship to the U.S. Supreme Court, and a diplomatic career in the State Department, beginning with an assignment to the Border Commission to work with Mexico. He turned them all down.

Instead he settled down as a lawyer in La Cantera, a poor section of Ponce, where he represented the impoverished, again turning down many munificent offers, including a judgeship, a government job, and an appointment at the University of Puerto Rico. He practiced poverty law, taking on hopeless cases in which he believed. But he did not join the Nationalist Party immediately; rather, he flirted for some years with trade unionism, ultimately discovering he had little in common with workers and could not communicate with them effectively. Thus, in 1924, he joined the struggling Nationalist Party, and almost immediately it ceased to be struggling.

This is not a political history of the Nationalist Party of Puerto Rico; in general, though, it can be said that in this party, eventually, Don Pedro Albizu Campos found the perfect vessel for his rage, his brilliance, his talent, his labor, his full, intense, messianic personality. Using the full measure of his intellect and will, he quickly became a force. Partially, this was a stroke of luck: in Ponce, he began writing for the weekly *El Nacionalista de Ponce*, which gave him a voice. His articles quickly attracted attention, and he had a talent for self-dramatization. In 1925, he gave a speech in San Juan, but before talking, ostentatiously removed the American flags that adorned the handrails of the podium, a theatrical gesture that won him immediate notoriety.

In 1927 he began, at party behest, a two-and-a-half-year tour of Latin America, acquainting himself with "conditions" in the Dominican Republic, Panama, Cuba, Mexico, Nicaragua, and Peru, the home of his wife. He gave speeches, he met friends, he made allies, he essentially networked the radical anticolonial culture of Latin America on that trip. When he returned in 1929, however, he found a party in chaos. By 1930, he was its president and guiding it toward victory at the polls.

This was his democratic period. At that point he was a reformer, driv-
en by his rejection of all forms of what he considered colonial oppression,
but not a revolutionary. He believed in working through the system, that
by explaining his cause, by inspiring his followers, by building a political
base, he would eventually liberate his people.

But all that changed in 1932, when he has what some might call his
purest epiphany and what others might call his final snapping point. He
stood for election as a senator-at-large and attracted a substantial following; other party members stood for positions in the legislature. But as one
of his ever propagandistic biographers has it, "Overwhelming forces and
powerful influences had resolved to strangle the liberation movement."
This is another way of saying he lost the election. He himself won only
about 10,000 votes out of 384,000 cast; his party members received even
fewer, about 5,000.

This is a key moment. Every revolutionary suffers it. It's the moment
of decision. When the people speak and they speak against the party, then
it is the people, not the party, who must change their ways. For Albizu
Campos it must have been a relief: no more of this nonsense of election-
eering, of giving moderate campaign speeches, of lobbying and reading
laws. No, from this moment on, it was far simpler: us against them. It
was from that moment on he decreed a policy of abstention from election
and direct violent action against the United States's interests.

He instructed his followers to take part in no more "colonial elections," which served only to appoint "high employees of the colony."
"Where tyranny is the law," he said, "revolution is order."

Thus begins his outlaw period. Now the Nationalist Party of Puerto
Rico would wage war; it would seek direct violent confrontation; it would
repudiate the "Yankee military invasion" set forth by the Treaty of Paris in
1899. From his new headquarters in the town of Aguas Buenas, surrounded by a cabinet and a small armed guard, he declared himself the
president of the Free Republic of Puerto Rico.

The violence thus began: in 1932 a march on the capitol resulted in a
panic in which a man was killed and several others injured. In 1932, he
established the Cadet Corps, which he called the Liberating Army of the
Republic.

According to the FBI's confidential report "Nationalist Party of Puerto
Rico," dated November 8, 1950: "During the period 1935–1938 the
NPPR became especially noted for its violence. In October, 1935, four

NPPR members were killed in Río Piedras . . . in a gun fight with the Insular Police. Many bombings occurred in public buildings in 1935 and these were attributed to the NPPR. In February 1936, the Chief of the Insular Police, E. Francis Riggs, was shot and killed by two nationalists."

True enough; the FBI fails to report, however, that the two assassins were assassinated themselves almost immediately in police custody.

The report continued, "On July 31, 1936, Pedro Albizu Campos and seven other leaders of the NPPR were convicted in the Federal Court in San Juan for inciting rebellion and for conspiracy to overthrow the government of the United States."

He spent six years in the Atlanta Penitentiary, during which time most violence in Puerto Rico halted. He was released, finally, in 1943. After two years in a New York hospital, he spent more time recuperating in an apartment building in the Bronx where a man called Oscar Collazo lived; when his parole was up in 1947 he was finally allowed to return to Puerto Rico and, for the next few years, as the FBI states it, "NPPR speakers throughout the Island gave numerous addresses of a bold and defiant character in which they called for an end to the tyranny allegedly exercised by the United States over Puerto Rico."

He returned December 15, 1947, to be greeted by his followers in a blast of enthusiasm and hope. Raimundo Díaz Pacheco, in the full uniform—white trousers and black shirt—of the Cadet Corps of the Nationalist Party of Puerto Rico, led the honor guard. Among the young men in the formation of cadets was Gregorio Hernández, standing straight, at attention, enjoying the jubilation. Placards waved gaily in the crowds attracted by sound cars all day: "Don Pedro, your sacrifice has not been in vain," one proclaimed. "Puerto Rico awaits you anxiously," said another. And "Death to Yankee Imperialism." El Maestro had returned, and nearly four thousand people had arrived at Pier No. 8 to greet him. He declared to Customs that the only thing he had to declare was "one seed, and I have brought it back."

Another young man in the crowd that day: Griselio Torresola.

Unbowed, the fiery leader left the steamship, and there was Raimundo Díaz Pacheco, commander in chief of the Cadet Corps, ready to do as ordered. He would spend the next three years, under the guidance of his leader, recruiting and training men for the Great Day. Drill, target practice, all to prepare. Meanwhile, in the United States men were sent to raise money for arms, men like Doris's brother, the impassioned Griselio in 1948, a shortstop on Jayuya's ball fields, and others, there already, joined in, like that methodical metal polisher and amateur intellectual, Oscar Collazo. Theirs was to prepare; it was the mission of the Liberating Army to strike.

Noon, October 30, 1950. The car approached La Fortaleza and halted in a courtyard just before its facade. On either side of the entrance stood an armed policeman. For a second or so, nothing happened.

Then it was Díaz Pacheco himself who leaped from the car and opened fire. According to one account, "When he arrived, he fired a shot, like saying, here I am, a minute before jumping out of the car."

Exact details of the gun battle are contradictory. Díaz Pacheco opened up with his grease gun, a slow-firing automatic weapon that pounds out heavy-caliber bullets known for their ability to incapacitate, wounding one guard severely, driving another away. The wounded officer crawled to cover; later that day, he would bleed out and die. One can wonder at many curiosities of this event: for one thing, with fights raging all over Puerto Rico, and snipers and detectives on the roofs, why were these two men left out front to do little but die? But that seems to be the way it was.

The other occupants jumped from the car.

Did they have any intelligence as to the location of Muñoz Marín? Evidently not. Did they have any fire-and-movement skills by which to maneuver close enough to apply the killing bursts to their target or take him captive? Clearly, no.

So the five men commenced to shoot out windows. Again, the grease gun ruled the action, spitting its heavy slugs across the facades, chewing stone dust from the ancient building, fracturing windows. The other men opened fire with their automatic pistols and revolvers.

In Muñoz Marín's office a bullet went through the blinds and buried itself in the opposite wall at about three meters height. The governor, who had been in conversation with Attorney General Vicente Géigel Polanco, went to the floor and crawled out of his office. The governor's daughters—nine and ten years old—leaned out the window as if the spectacle were a western, but when they saw what was happening they hid behind a chest of drawers in tears.

But while this was going on, the men on the roofs were calmly zeroing in on their targets, cocking their weapons, getting comfy behind the trigger, maybe smoking a last cigarette. Detective Carmelo Dávila had arrived at La Fortaleza at 11:45, carrying orders about the suspected strike. He'd even had time to situate himself on the roof.

The guard force opened fire.

Superior firepower is difficult to argue with. It declares its intentions so forcefully that the area of its concentrated attention has a name: it's called the beaten zone. And now, in the beaten zone, the Nationalists did what men in beaten zones the world over have done since Sir Hiram Maxim perfected the first machine gun—the Devil's paintbrush, it would later be called—in the 1880s. They died.

It's not pretty. The first to be hit was Domingo Hiraldo Resto, who was driving. He got it in the temple. He fell against the left door of the car with his head almost underneath it. But there's also a story that, hit, he crawled to a wall, and waited until the shooting was over. The police approached him with drawn guns.

"I am already dead. Please don't shoot me anymore," he proclaimed.

They shot him again.

Whatever, Raimundo turned and ordered his men back under cover, that is, the Plymouth. Then he ran toward the right, firing his grease gun, bouncing bullets all over the place.

Roberto Acevedo, tall, heavy, jumped out of the right side of the car, shooting, and made it maybe twelve or fifteen steps. Someone hit him squarely and he went facedown with a dust-raising thud to the earth.

Manuel Torres Medina circled the car, shooting all the time. Then he headed toward the main entrance of the building and he met the slug with his name on it and went down hard.

Just a few seconds had passed and three men were dead already. Then, on the roof, the detective Carmelo Dávila took careful aim with his carbine, fired once, and Raimundo Díaz Pacheco dropped dead. He made it closest to the building itself. He died in the sun, near the door.

Only Gregorio Hernández was left alive. He did not go easy. No thought of surrender occurred to him. He was still in the car because he had been in the middle with Torres and Acevedo to his right and left. He fired from the car at an agent he saw, and brought him down with a bullet to the neck. Then he got out and ran to the entrance, but police fire lit up the universe. He tried to get in and he was hit first in the arm and second in the knee. So Gregorio turned, raced through the hail of fire to the Plymouth, ran around back to open the trunk where heavier weapons were stored. He was shot in the face and the abdomen.

He ducked behind the car. Lying there, he saw a man in a window and winged a shot at him, missing, but striking a flag flying from the window that happened to be a United Nations flag. Later, the hole in the flag is offered as proof of the rebels' fury at the organization.

Gregorio huddled next to the car, bleeding a lot. The bullets pummeled the 1949 Plymouth mercilessly. Occasionally he fired a shot, and even reloaded. He hit a police officer in the leg. Then he was hit again and again, once in the left side. He felt his heart hammering terribly. Then he was shot in the throat. He passed out.

The Plymouth was ventilated. Gregorio had been hit many times but mostly by shrapnel—shreds of bullets shattering on impact, pieces of car spun supersonically, stones and clods of earth set to dancing. He had five actual bullets in him. He pretended to be dead. Nobody else had to.

It wasn't much of a battle. One account, by a writer who calls the killers a "commando," as if to confer upon them the élan of a Special Forces unit, says the shooting lasts an hour. But the New York Times, quoting an eyewitness, puts the fight's duration at more likely ten minutes.

The United Press International arrived shortly thereafter, and some enterprising photog got a shot that depicts the classic squalor of a hopeless battle lost. The press photographer was sited in a balcony, overlooking the car, and meanwhile many official-looking vehicles have arrived. Soldiers and police officers stand around, in the listless poses of the already bored, facing a few more hours of duty, the taking of notes, the collecting of cartridge casings, the official photography, the identification of the dead, the application of first aid to the wounded. The Nationalists' car, right-hand door open, is parked in the sunlight. The bloody Gregorio has been hauled off to the hospital. A palm frond droops from overhead. Two dead men can be seen, and like most battle dead, they are without dignity, simple sacks of now inanimate flesh tumbled clumsily upon the earth. They lie like broken dolls in the sunlight, arms outthrown, shoes off, oblivious to style.

Back at Albizu Campos's apartment, the police finally decided it was time to take the Maximum Leader himself prisoner. He was ordered to surrender, and refused. Thus the order to fire was given.

Three machine gun volleys ripped into the apartment that afternoon. The besieged Nationalists responded with a few desultory shots from a desultory arsenal. A UPI photographer got a nice shot of the window to the apartment in the immediate aftermath of this probing by fire. It happens, by irony, to be the window over the sign announcing the site of party headquarters: PARTIDO NACIONALISTA DE PUERTO RICO, say the letters in an arc over the crossed flags of the revolution, and underneath that, JUNTA NACIONAL, national headquarters. The helpful UPI photo editor has directed that an artist indicate with arrows the bullet holes—that is so 1950s newspaper—and they spread across the sign, running from the center to the right-hand upper corner, signifying the jump of the gun in the inexperienced gunner's hand. Then he found the range and brought the shuttered window above into sight and really beat up on it. The louvers are shattered, the frame is askew, and above the top of the frame, heavy gouging damage has been done to the stucco, though it is possible these ruptures were caused later, by missed tear gas shells.

Inside, it can't have been pleasant, for gunfire, particularly of an automatic nature, vaporizes, atomizes, or liquefies all that comes before it. You do not argue dialectics with it, you simply pray it doesn't notice you. The young people in the rooms and the old man they loved must have involuntarily gone to ground and lain there as around them the room shuddered under its pulverizing.

Doris Torresola lay on the floor, shot in the throat. Blood must have spurted everywhere, for throat wounds are particularly bloody. Again, it is not known what conversation ensued, but it must have been pointed out that absent rapid attention, the girl would bleed to death. One presumes that the senior among them, Albizu Campos himself, ordered them out. He had known Doris for years. She was of the beautiful Torresola family, in the beautiful valley of the Three Peaks, just outside Jayuya. She was a student of his ardent follower, the great Blanca Canales; her brother Elio was leading the fighting at Jayuya even now, along with Blanca; and her younger brother, the bright boy called Griselio, the shortstop, the dandy, the one everybody loved so passionately, so intense was his charisma, he was in New York. He was the chosen one. So Albizu Campos knew that Doris must be spared. He would stay, alone, and face whatever must be faced.

Her two young colleagues, Carmen María Pérez and José Muñoz Matos, carried her out to the street, not on a stretcher as in the movies where such transfers are smooth and dramatic, but as best they could, clumsily, her slack body and dead weight rendering all of them awkward and vulnerable. Outside, they were quickly engulfed by police and arrested.

The Old Man was alone in the house. The shooting continued.

And in Manhattan, Doris's brother Griselio would soon get the word that his sister had been shot and captured, that the rebellion had collapsed, that his boyhood hero, his mentor, the man who would give meaning to his life, Pedro Albizu Campos, was alone and under siege by police.

4. THE ODD COUPLE

The news was very bad and both Oscar and Griselio faced it by the afternoon of Monday, October 30.

Death, catastrophe, men imprisoned, the great Don Pedro besieged in his home, the heroes at La Fortaleza shot to ribbons. Nothing, in fact, had been accomplished, at least from an American point of view. Oscar spent the day at his buffing wheel, watching the felt of the wheel take the burnished, imperfect coloration of the brass purse frames and transform it magically, by applications of touch and judgment, into something with a golden glow. He was one of the best men on the floor at this tricky task.

As for Griselio, he had nothing to occupy himself. He could not escape. There was no escape. He had political duties.

What now? There was nobody to turn to, no leader available, all contacts with the island were cut off. By Don Pedro's edict, he was the leader. He had to decide. But on what basis? There was no news. And on that day, as the FBI later learned, many in the Puerto Rican Nationalist community came by his room for news of loved ones back in the fighting at home. What could he tell them? He only knew what was in the papers or on the radio. He would have to utter assurances, counsel them to accept the wisdom of the Old Man and to believe in the brilliance of the plan. That was what an officer in the struggle did under these circumstances.

But it was no one-man job. It simply couldn't have been. Thus, rushed and improvising madly, he tried to adhere to the plan. Griselio walked down to the apartment of a friend, Manuel López, again according to the FBI. He urged Manuel to accompany him "back to Puerto Rico" to join in the fight; but clearly this was some kind of subterfuge or coded language, because the island was closed down during the insurrection. Under those circumstances, no invitation to return to Puerto Rico can be taken at face value; it was an invitation for other actions. Manuel declined because his wife was pregnant, but he did walk Griselio back to the hotel, presumably trying to get the depressed young man to buck up. During the next few hours, Griselio worked the phones and tried to find an accomplice. But no one would go "back to Puerto Rico" with him.

At 9:00 P.M., he went back to the Willis Avenue Bridge to meet with Oscar Collazo. He had a gun with him.

It is another part of the legend of this event that Oscar gave Griselio $50 to pay for the gun on October 29 and that Griselio, a professional revolutionary after all, was so worldly in the ways of obtaining weapons he was able to buy one and give it to Oscar the next evening—with $15 change.

But the revolution had not broken out yet on October 29, so it would not have prompted a need for guns. Instead, Griselio almost certainly brought the gun to the bridge the second night for a specific reason: he knew what he had to do, what he had to accomplish. As for the gun itself, he may already have had it—he hardly had time to buy it on the busy Monday of the 30th, as the FBI later re-created his many duties. It was later testified that Griselio went to someone who had been active in running guns to Puerto Rico for the movement. But why was that necessary?

They were again standing on the Willis Avenue Bridge, between the Bronx and Manhattan, the Harlem River sluggishly rolling by twenty-five feet beneath them, the traffic honking and screeching and stopping and starting on the span over it. One assumes they were turned, facing away from the traffic; otherwise the gun would be visible, police might be called, the whole thing might go awry at its very point of inception. In the dark, though, amid the strut work, slanted and crisscrossed, almost web-like in its density, they may have been all but invisible.

A gun is a special object, especially, as in Oscar's case, if you've never handled one so sleek and rakish before. (He told Nelson Canals, a Puerto Rican activist who visited him in prison, that he had fired pistols before, but not this kind of pistol.) It was a roughly treated German automatic called a P.38, a brilliantly designed weapon meant to replace the more arcane and intricate Luger, which is what Griselio had, as the sidearm of the armed forces of the Third Reich. The P.38 is dense and compact, it's heavy beyond its scale, there's something final about it, something that triggers the imagination.

Oscar held the dull, scraped thing in his hand, watching the play of

light even on the finishless surface, feeling the heft of it, his fingers locking on the grip, his index finger running the taut curve of the trigger, feeling a slight give at the pressure. Almost certainly it frightened him, for
the first time a man takes up a gun, the gun is uniquely charismatic. It's
like meeting a movie star. Then, shaken, he must have rapidly wrapped it
up in the towel it had arrived in, and stuffed it into his waistband, out of
sight under his jacket, and turned to face Griselio.

Here is the key moment in this affair. In the sole survivor's version it is
Oscar who broaches the idea.

The survivor later testified that Oscar said to Griselio that he had concluded that in Puerto Rico they couldn't do so much. They could only
shoot at soldiers, and die. What is that? What can that mean? What does
that accomplish?

It was later testified that Oscar said: We should go to Washington. We
should make a demonstration in Washington. In the United States no one
knows or cares about Puerto Rico or the conditions. If we could do something to make them know, to draw Puerto Rico and the situation down
there to their attention. That would be the way to change history. That
would be the stroke the situation demanded.

The survivor never recanted, adjusted, or equivocated. The whole
thing was Oscar's idea, hatched on the bridge. It would be some sort of
vaguely conceived "demonstration" in Washington to attract attention to
events in Puerto Rico, and once the Americans understood what was
really going on down there, the greatness of Albizu Campos, the tragedy
of the yanqui invasion, then the situation would be rectified or at least
noticed, the first step to rectification.

There are some difficulties with this version, however. For one thing, it
was Griselio, not Oscar, who by virtue of the letter from Albizu Campos,
had command authority. It was Griselio, not Oscar, who was just back
from Puerto Rico and knew of the plans for November 3. It was Griselio,
not Oscar, who was one of Don Pedro's favored sons. It was Griselio, not
Oscar, who had come back from Puerto Rico a changed man. It was Griselio who had the action personality, who was always the bold one, not
Oscar, who was sedentary, intellectual, a homebody. It was Griselio and
not Oscar who was already an accomplished shooter. He could break
down the weapons, he could shoot them well. He was confident enough
with them to teach them to the unlettered Oscar. He had practiced shooting in Puerto Rico, where he was a member of Albizu Campos's body-

guard in Jayuya, and he carried a German Luger and with brother Elio and revolutionary leader Carlos Irizarry practiced in the mountains.

Thus it makes far more sense to assume that it was his idea.

Did Griselio show Oscar the letter that essentially gave him command and made Oscar his lieutenant? Possibly not. But likely so, for at the time Oscar was secretary general of the New York junta. In any event, whatever his regrets over leaving the life he had built up, Oscar would have had no hesitation.

And thus both men, standing on the bridge between the Bronx and Spanish Harlem on the night of October 30, 1950, in the unseasonably warm weather of an Indian summer, committed to what they believed was right and proper and heroic and self-sacrificial, the action of a soldier of the struggle: the idea of assassinating Harry S. Truman, president of the United States. And the idea of dying in the battle, exactly as Raimundo Díaz Pacheco had.

5. MR. GONZALES AND MR. DE SILVA
GO TO WASHINGTON

Smoky needed an airing. So Oscar took the dog—part German shepherd, part Eskimo spitz—up to the roof of 173 Brook Avenue, and let the dog—and possibly himself—enjoy a last surge of freedom, of clear blue skies (it was warm and cloudless), and of the solitude for contemplation. His tenement is gone now, and a housing project takes its place; but when it was there it surely resembled any of the thousands of tenements left in that part of the South Bronx: a four-story building with architectural flourishes like bricked arches over each window, a stoop, three windows per floor, part of a row of such units, with flat roofs. Once the essence of upscale, out-of-town living, before the turn of the century when the Bronx exploded as an alternative to the city itself, it had degraded significantly with the passing of time, the outward movement of prosperous people to farther zones, and the arrival of wave after wave of impoverished immigrants. So now the proud old building was besmirched with grime, turning the original red of the bricks a smear of indeterminate color. Inside, it had been chopped with cheap plasterboard walls into smaller units, and Oscar, his dog, his wife, his three daughters, all crowded into five rooms on the third floor. The halls were dark; the building dreary, the neighborhood appalling.

Yet in this unpleasantness, within the apartment itself, he and the family had constructed an oasis: he had a little corner that he used as a study, and there, when he wasn't off on countless political or good-works errands, he read industriously. He was a reader.

On this day, October 31, 1950, he went up the ancient stairwell, presumably creaking as it zigs and zags up a brick channel, opened an ancient door, and stepped into light. He found himself on an asphalt promenade broken by vents and chimneys, a classic New York scene. The sun was hot, perhaps the asphalt was sticky-soft, yielding ever so slightly to his tread.

Up there with Smoky, Oscar could see the weirdly asymmetrical crests of the two spans of the Willis Avenue Bridge, where the scheme had been broached. He could see the river, the skyline, the spire of the Empire State Building. If he looked immediately over the precipice of the roof, down to Brook Avenue, he saw a cobblestoned way jammed with other tenement units, swarming with people who have been driven up from the island to the South Bronx and its squalor in hopes of, somehow, making a better life for themselves.

He was up there for a few minutes with the dog, the frisky animal pulling this way and that on a leash, the dog itself emblematic of a certain kind of imagined middle-class life he had to be aware that he was abandoning eternally. Maybe he noted the beauty of the day, maybe he didn't. What is clear is that he did his last little job as head of household: he walked the dog. Not exactly what one would presume of an assassin.

Then there was the issue of the sick call to the Gainer Corporation, formerly called the Randolph Rand Company, in New Rochelle. His wife, Rosa, an equally committed Nationalist who by now understood and supported her husband in his task, which she later claimed was to return to Puerto Rico and fight with Albizu Campos, handled this responsibility. He met her in 1940 and she got him a job at the Majestic Metal Specialties Company, in Moosup, Connecticut, where she worked; she was on the buffing wheel next to his in that plant, and someone has called it a "buffing wheel romance." They married on August 3, 1940.

Next, he must buy clothes. Assassins frequently buy new suits before their self-appointed missions begin; the dowdy Lee Harvey Oswald was the exception, not the rule; it tends to be a dandy's profession. For Oscar, with a stash of $1,250 hard earned and hard saved in a postal savings account, the choice was a blue chalk stripe. Oscar also bought three new shirts. Again, this might seem a ridiculous gesture: one to travel in, one to die in, and the third to be buried in? But maybe not so much so. You can read into it—in fact, into everything he is known to have done over this two-day period—the drama of his rational self in combat with his fanatical self for control over his personality. The new wardrobe is part of this struggle. He is getting into costume. As Eric Hoffer notes in his book *The True Believer*, "Dying and killing seem easy when they are part of a ritual, ceremonial, dramatic performance or game. There is need for some kind of make-believe in order to face death unflinchingly. . . . It is only when we see ourselves as actors in a staged (and therefore unreal) perfor-

---

mance that death loses its frightfulness and finality and becomes an act of make-believe and a theatrical gesture."

Next Oscar packed, with his usual meticulous care. He bought a small suitcase, and even remembered to include his hay fever pills. He added a whisk broom, some hair oil, and a somber dark tie for the next day's labor, choosing to travel in a brighter, gayer one.

Finally he was ready. He and his wife walked along Brook Avenue to the busier 138th Street, turned west, and headed up it, looking for a taxi. They passed a Spanish-language theater where a lurid film entitled *La Virgen Desnuda* was showing, and the theater was festooned with appropriately revealing posters. The metal polisher did not notice; instead, at last, he found and hailed a cab.

He turned to Rosa. "Goodbye," he said. "Pray for me."

The cab is another intriguing detail. In those days, the fare from the South Bronx to Penn Station must have been considerable for a poor working man with three children, a dog, and a sense of foreknowledge that very soon his income would be terminated forever. And he was such a good man at responsibility too: he paid his bills on time, and all through the ordeal of the next day continued to live by the rules of frugality so that in the end he still had $75.47 of the $100 he had taken out in expense money on his person. So the cab was a luxury. Perhaps it represented a secret longing: just once in his life, he'd be the king of the hill, traveling first-class as the big yellow Checker moved across the Willis Avenue Bridge, then 125th Street in Harlem, then turned downtown for Penn Station at Broadway and 34th. Midtown held no surprises for him; but his view had always been that of a dishwasher in the early years, before he learned his trade, when he had come to the city off and on to try and eke out a living while staying in a cheap boardinghouse, trying to put together a little estate on bitterly hard labor at bitterly tiny wages, haunted by memories of a farm, in his memory and imagination destroyed by a pair of hurricanes, American capital, and imperialism. And now here he was, in a taxicab, in a new suit, on an important mission from the great man Albizu Campos, headed bravely forth to meet his destiny, in the uniform of the struggle, dignified and serene.

As for Griselio he too had a busy next day. He had a wife and a baby daughter at home and he almost certainly returned there and explained his intentions to Carmen Dolores, who was pregnant with their son.

He lived, according to FBI documents, at the Hotel Clendenning, at 202

West 103rd Street. This was on the Upper West Side, a part of the spread of Spanish Harlem into new territories, with subsequent difficulties. Now the neighborhood has become chic, but in those days it was so far from chic that, just a few years later, the state flattened it—and the Clendenning—and built one of the first big American housing projects there, the Frederick Douglass Homes. Like the Bronx, this West Side was not a cheerful place to live, and if you were raised in the visual splendors of a Jayuya, with its lush green valleys and resonant, mythic peaks, that dreariness must have impressed itself upon you every single day.

The 1939 *WPA Guide to New York City* describes the dreariness of the general area well enough: "Built up solidly with tenements, old apartment houses, brownstones converted into flats, and occasional small frame residences, [it] is a poor man's land. Half a million persons are crowded into its three square miles—the largest single slum area in New York. . . . The Spanish Harlemites reflect in their recreation, their public markets, and their changing social life, the traditions in which they were reared. Unfortunately, this native picturesqueness has in large part been preserved by extreme poverty, with its overcrowding, illiteracy, malnutrition, disease and social dislocation."

The Clendenning was a grim building in the heart of this malaise; it was, if the extant buildings in the area are any indication, ornate in stonework from an age when labor-intensive construction was cheap and necessary. It was located on the block between Broadway and Amsterdam, and the Broadway subway station on the line that ran up to the Bronx was at the corner of Broadway and 103rd Street, a fortuitous location for a conspirator because the underground transportation gave him speedy access to all parts of New York.

Those few blocks of the Upper West Side happened to support a cluster of other Nationalist sympathizers, and indeed sometimes the party rented a room on 108th Street for meetings or used the upstairs of the San Juan Bar in the neighborhood. In that very small area some of the neighbors included party members Manuel Ovidio López, at 239 West 103rd Street; Irma López, 147 West 100th Street; Juan Pietri Pérez, 244 West 99th Street (the party treasurer); and the party president, Julio Pinto Gandía, who was living on West 34th Street—in a YMCA, to which he had repaired after being kicked out of his apartment by his wife. So Griselio was essentially living in a tiny pocket of Manhattan that was the Free Republic of Puerto Rico already; he saw, he socialized with, he neighbored to, he performed, he cadged money, he got dumped by one wife and picked up a new one, he fathered a daughter from the second and missed a daughter from the first, all in two rooms in that grim hotel.

People came and went at all hours of the night; the phone rang constantly; letters in what appears to be in code arrived from Puerto Rico, gun parts were bought and shipped on. Everything he does is consistent with the image of him functioning as a kind of clearinghouse for Don Pedro's clandestine aspirations, as apart from the formal party headquarters and consistent with no other pattern of behavior. He's a figure out of Conrad, handsome, yet furtive; clever and brave, yet limited; depressed and doomed, yet ebullient.

Still, it was hard to know Griselio. You looked at Oscar and in some way, you knew him: he had an open friendly face, his eyes were kind, he had jug ears. There was nothing at all about Oscar that seemed disconnected from life as it is lived by most people. The riddle of Oscar is how a man so like everyone ended up so unlike everyone.

Griselio was different. Griselio was a man apart. A formal portrait reveals a kind of Spanish Tom Cruise, a perfect little man. He had a noble brow, a squarish head, beautifully formed features, an elegant and restrained nose, a firm chin. His hairline was square to the line of his forehead, and his hair was thick, the black-and-white film turning his lustrous brown-blond far darker than it was in life, but still pointing out its unusual beauty. He was in his Sunday suit, a chalk-striped, wide-lapeled banker's suit. His shirt blinded with its whiteness, his tie somber, tightly tied, and perfectly placed. He could have been the young doctor at med school graduation instead of the man with romantic troubles (it turned out his legal wife, Dilia, had *not* divorced him, as he had thought; so he was still married to her while he was living in common-law marriage with Carmen Dolores) and Secret Agent of the Revolution, tasked with the impossible, touched by destiny, the special chosen apostle of Don Pedro. And where Oscar's eyes, in his wedding portrait, warmly contacted the camera lens, his head nestled gently against Rosa's, a kind of half smile playing across his face, Griselio was without smile. His mouth was a tiny dash, uncurved by emotion or perhaps kept rigid by pride. He did not make eye contact with the lens in front of him and, instead, he looks off to the left, his beauty radiant and eloquent in and of itself.

But there is a different picture of him. That picture, not widely seen, was reprinted in his friend Heriberto Marín Torres's book, *Eran Ellos*. It's a

Griselio the world had never seen, the Griselio of Jayuya: this time his beauty was more spontaneous, less posed, less rigid. He's what you might call a lad, handsome and buoyant. His curly brown-blond hair tumbles impishly off onto the corners of his forehead. His head is cocked slightly, and the angle lends him a jauntiness, a cockiness, a youthful sense of comic swagger. Nothing could have been further from his mind when this shot was snapped than political killing; he looks as if the Jayuya Tigercats had just beaten the Ponce Seabirds 9–8 and he, the shortstop, had made a diving grab on a liner through the box in the last of the ninth with the bases loaded to save the game. He also looks like he knows all the girls love him. A smile plays across his face, and his bright eyes are crinkled in merriment. He looks utterly at home in the world.

A few years later, all that glee had vanished. On the morning of October 31, 1950, he too had things to do. He rose early, went to the relief office on 42nd Street to sign for an unemployment check slated to arrive November 6. But when he returned home, Carmen later told the FBI, he had a new suit in a box. But he was not done shopping; the two of them, with baby Rebecca, walked to a store on Broadway where he bought a dark blue suitcase for $6. Then they went to another store—near 99th Street and Amsterdam—and he bought two white shirts at $2 apiece and a light gray tie. He didn't say where the money came from; Carmen had been under the impression there was only $5 left in the family apartment, which certainly suggests access to a secret revolutionary fund, as one of Don Pedro's letters had authorized.

They returned home at noon, and Carmen ironed the suit, some underwear, and some handkerchiefs, and packed them in the suitcase, along with toilet articles. She didn't see a gun, she later said, and she packed the entire thing by herself. Then she made lunch.

Griselio stood alone at the bureau in the bedroom. He had on his new suit, carefully pressed, his white shirt, his gray tie. Like the warrior, he was ceremonially dressed for the ordeal ahead. One presumes he had the Luger tucked neatly in his waistband under the drape of the banker's gray chalk stripe. But Griselio was not only a soldier, he was a father. And now, as the enormity of what was about to transpire settled across his small frame and handsome features, he wrote two notes, one to each daughter.

The letters, identical, were to his daughter Rebecca by Carmen Dolores, and back in Puerto Rico, his daughter Áurea by his first (and still legal) wife, Dilia.

He wrote: "Remembrances of your Daddy," then signed them with his first name, as if reaching out for them one last time.

He and Carmen Dolores ate lunch.

Then he kissed his wife goodbye and left.

Carmen later maintained to the FBI that he was going off to Puerto Rico.

Griselio and Oscar met at Penn Station at 3:00 P.M. Both wore suits. Both were small, polite, undemonstrative. It was Tuesday afternoon. The Penn Station of 1950 was a far more glorious venue than the cramped, low, many times refurbished space under Madison Square Garden that it is now. It spoke of empire, of America's destiny, of grand cities and wide visions, though it's unlikely that the two assassins paid too much attention to it, and in any event the glories of civic architecture were not on their agenda.

Here's the telling fact. Oscar bought two one-way tickets to Washington. You can make what you want of this or that, but the one-way ticket certainly suggests they knew they were on a one-way ride to fame or infamy, to hell or glory, that there was no coming back from this one. Nobody noticed them. Who would: two men in suits, somber, professional, calm.

They bought that day's *New York Times* for its reports on events on the island; then boarded the train. The trip took four hours, the Pennsylvania Railroad's electric GG1 engine drawing three or possibly six cars down through the Middle Atlantic, with the same stops then as now. Newark, Trenton, Philly, Wilmington, Baltimore, and Washington. The train too had an imposing name, *The Congressional,* running hourly down to the capital city. They sat in straight-backed leather seats, felt the sway of the car as it glided over the roadbed, and New Jersey and Pennsylvania and Delaware and Maryland passed by outside, mostly rural flatlands broken with monochrome forests (though it was hot, the leaves had fallen, according to pictures taken then), then cities that thought quite highly of themselves.

The one recorded detail of the trip is the stop at Philly. They got off the train on its ten-minute stopover, and bought a copy of the afternoon paper the *Bulletin,* which had later news in those days when papers published updated editions six or eight times daily.

COUP ATTEMPT IN SAN JUAN screamed the headlines. It featured the photo of the dead at La Fortaleza next to their shot-out car in the courtyard, the cops standing around prosaically, the sun bright, the squalor inescapable. In the reporting, the details were hazy but not inaccurate: the story described the shooting as an attempt on the life of Muñoz Marín.

It made no mention of the wounding and arrest of Doris Torresola.

Did Griselio know of his sister's or his brother Elio's fate as he approached Washington? Surely if Griselio knew that Albizu Campos was under siege he realized his sister was in grave danger. He knew that Puerto Rican Air National Guard planes were strafing and bombing in Jayuya, where Elio had led a squad of men and one woman—Blanca Canales, whom he had known and loved since childhood—to occupy the police station and the post office. He knew both the Insular Police of Puerto Rico and the National Guard had tendencies to shoot a lot first, then shoot some more, then shoot a whole lot, then ask questions. Yet so set on mission was he, so locked into Hoffer's notion of performance, that he allowed no play of concern to afflict his features or blur his behavior.

The other curiosity is how obtuse to the lessons of La Fortaleza the two appeared to be, at least from a rationalist perspective. It taught exact knowledge of what not to do in an attempt on the life of a head of state. For in its peculiar way, the attack on Fortaleza represented a model of their own action to come. Yet it never seems to have occurred to them to analyze it tactically, to consider its lessons. They were not critics or tacticians but soldiers. They simply put on their grim game faces and did what they believed must be done.

At 7:30 that evening, after dark, they arrived in Washington. Neither had ever been there before. But the city's ceremonial beauty was cloaked in darkness and though they would not prove immune to its seductions, that night they must have been too tired from the hasty arrangements, from the travel, from the self-imposed pressure.

Thus they walked from Union Station—the Capitol dome, lit for drama, loomed above them to the left as they angled through a park toward Massachusetts Avenue—and within a block had encountered another grim hotel, this one called the Harris and as much without charm or allure as the Clendenning; it was in fact a kind of farewell house, as suicides tended to use it as a transfer station to the next world. They walked in.

Here was the first small act of the drama. Here you can sense them getting into their roles, Oscar in particular becoming a man he wasn't, trying on the new life he was in the process of inventing. At this point, since they had no reason to believe anyone was tracking them and their enterprise—not even the FBI's fleet of snitches in the party, Confidential Informants T-1 through T-5, was aware of their existence—and it was all but impossible that they would survive the next day, there simply was no premium on deceit. Yet they could not help themselves from partaking in the theater of espionage for the first time, one assumes, at least in Oscar's case, Griselio being a somewhat trickier character (there is some evidence, to be detailed later, that he had bought ammunition and magazines under a nom de guerre earlier).

At the entrance to the professional-class traveler's hotel, they paused. Both are Hispanic, both are slight, both are dressed in suits, they arrive together. They are conjoined in look, culture, space, and time. Yet, preposterously and to no point, at the entrance, they part and approach the desk separately.

Oscar goes first, requesting a single room with semiprivate bath. The cost was $3.50.

So Oscar peeled off the bills, plucked out the four bits, and registered as Anthony De Silva, of 150 Aldridge Drive, Aldridge Village, Connecticut—the Connecticut fabrication recalled the happiness of meeting and marrying Rosa, of making her two daughters his own—and in return took the key to Room 434.

The clerk's regard for Oscar later became a signal irony in the case, much reported, a part of the small mythology of the event.

He looked, the clerk would say, like a divinity student.

After Oscar cleared the desk, it was Griselio's turn. He duplicated the process, sustaining the deceit that he was unconnected to his near-twin who had just completed the same transaction. He registered under the nom de guerre Charles Gonzales, of 167 Ponce de Leon Avenue, Miami, Florida. He was imagining a life he surely understood now he would never have. He was assigned to Room 436, which shared a bath with Oscar's.

Both men went to the elevator for the trip to the fourth floor, still pretending not to notice each other.

But once they were securely in their rooms, Griselio came through the common bathroom and they gave up the charade. In fact, in a few minutes, hungry, they left the hotel together, went to a restaurant, and ate dinner. Then they walked over to Union Station Plaza, bought some newspapers for the latest from the island, and returned to their rooms.

What happened next is the only record of any tactical planning for the event they intended to perpetrate. They sat in Oscar's room and pulled out the telephone directory with a map, on which they located the White House. A map. That's all, a map in a phone book in a cheap hotel. Perhaps they talked, but what they said is not known and it would be pointless to conjecture.

And thus, at around ten in the evening, October 31, 1950, they went to bed, Mr. Gonzales and Mr. De Silva, strangers in a strange city not their own.

6. EARLY MORNING

Shortly the men who would protect him would awaken, followed by the men who had come to kill him. But on November 1, 1950, nobody got up earlier than Harry Truman.

The president customarily arose at 5:30 A.M. He went through a stack of work and three or four newspapers. At 6:40 he left for his famous early morning walk. He would dress—in a suit, always, in case there happened to be photographers or voters about—and take off for a vigorous one- or two-mile walk in the neighborhood, down or up Pennsylvania Avenue, left or right on 15th or 14th or 18th or 19th, sometimes out to the Washington Monument, or down the Mall toward the Capitol, then back around in what someone called a "fast, easy-moving stride." He traveled at the army's 120-steps-per-minute pace, two miles in half an hour. "I've always walked at this speed—ever since I was in the army," he told the novelist and journalist John Hersey. As of 1950, he had been walking for thirty years. He carried a cane, though not to assist himself: he was in excellent shape, at five feet nine and 167 pounds, nearly the same height and weight that he'd been as an artillery officer in France twenty-six years before.

The walks came hell or high water for him. In fact, on his first day in the White House after the death of Franklin Delano Roosevelt, with a whole world of anxiety on his shoulders, he left the mansion at 6:00 A.M. with only a single baffled Secret Service agent trailing him, utterly confounding his unprepared protection detail in the main office, which was used to his predecessor's more leisurely morning style. Two other agents took off at a dead run to catch up with him. He'd already made it way up Pennsylvania Avenue with only the single agent—four agents, by iron protocol, were the minimum assigned to a chief executive anytime he left the White House—and they raced after him as he turned down 15th Street, out of their sight.

They finally caught up with him a half a mile later.

He grinned and said, "Mornin', gentlemen. Nice day, isn't it? Nice of you to join me!" and kept on walking.

"I walk early to get a chance to think over things and get ready for work of the day," the president confided to his diary in 1953.

The walks were also the source of much humor. One history of the Secret Service recalls an episode where the president saw a chance to play a prank on an old acquaintance.

"During Truman's walks, agents would remain a few steps behind him unless he invited them to stay by his side, which he frequently did. One morning as an agent walked beside him up 16th Street in Washington the president said, 'Here comes old Johnny Smith. I haven't seen him for months. Let's see if he recognizes me.'

"The agent noticed an elderly man approaching. When they were practically abreast of him, the man glanced casually at the president and at the Secret Service man, then looked away and continued on past them. The president chuckled as he turned and called out, 'Hey Johnny! Aren't you speaking to your friends these days?'

"Johnny stopped and looked around. His face brightened with recognition as he smiled, walked back to the president with his right arm outstretched, and said cordially, 'Well, *Senator!* How are you? Where have you been keeping yourself?' "

It was typical of the president's modesty, which may have had its roots in what Hersey noted as a tendency to think of himself sometimes in the first person and sometimes in the third. "Toward himself, first-personally, he was at times mischievous and disrespectful, but he revered this other man, his tenant, as a noble, history-defined figure. Here was a separation of powers within a single psyche, and a most attractive phenomenon it was, because Harry Truman moved about in constant wonder and delight at this awesome stranger beneath his skin."

John W. Snyder, the secretary of the treasury in the Truman administration, recalled in 1969 the difficulties of the Secret Service agents of the midnight–to–8:00 A.M. shift in keeping up with him.

"With Mr. Truman, who was very active and quite a walker, they had a change in pace that took them some months to get accustomed to. And he did love those walks. He sometimes nearly walked them out of breath on those sprints he would take every morning. At first, they weren't accustomed to that but they soon got used to it."

He liked his Secret Service companions, most of whom came from small towns or backgrounds much like his own, and none of whom ever asked anything of him. "I like them more than all the top-notchers," he once told his daughter. He enjoyed chatting with the two or three who regularly accompanied him on the morning walks. He knew where they came from, whether they were married or had children, which church they attended. When one of them, Floyd M. Boring, had a child, Truman visited Floyd's wife, Ruth, in the hospital.

"He would treat us almost like sons," remembered another agent, Rex Scouten. "He talked nearly the whole time as we walked—about the army, about his growing up in Missouri, and the Civil War. He'd go by a building and he'd tell you all about the building and why it was designed the way it was."

Still, he gave the Secret Service fits. U. E. Baughman, the service chief at the time, recalled, "The walks took place in exposed sections of a great city; they were usually over the same route; and they occurred at almost the same time every day. They represented the kind of 'habit' that was hand-picked for the assassin.

"Walking along a street," Baughman continued, "usually deserted at such an hour in the morning, made Mr. Truman a slow-moving target, the delight of a sharpshooter. A rifle with a telescopic sight slipped unobtrusively out of any of a thousand windows along the route, with plenty of time to aim carefully, and we would have been helpless to protect our charge." Baughman goes on to lament the fact that in public, his men couldn't carry tommy guns, though, as he puts it, "Believe me, I thought of it often enough."

It is not known exactly where he walked November 1, but it is certain that Truman used the time to mull over the day's schedule and set himself for another grueling sixteen-hour day, with its share of appointments, ceremonial events—a Medal of Honor presentation was scheduled, as well as a speech at Arlington National Cemetery—military deliberations, political considerations, domestic initiatives of his own, and of the Republicans to be blunted, good news and bad, so forth and so on. He almost certainly noted the weather, which at the time of his walk was around 59 degrees and hazy, but he knew it would be getting hotter and hotter today, all the way up to 85. He had a passion for the weather, always reading the U.S. Weather Service maps in the morning. He loved to bet his Secret Service guys on the weather; he always won.

When the president returned from his walk, according to a November 6, 1950, memo from Assistant Press Secretary to the President Eben Ayers, he returned not to Blair but to the White House, and there went for a swim in the pool. He returned to Blair House for a shower and then dressed again. As an ex–clothing store owner, he was a meticulous dresser. Today—possibly because of the Medal of Honor ceremony and the speech—he dressed almost formally, in a dark double-breasted suit, a white shirt and a dark tie with white polka dots and a pair of well-shined black oxfords. His appearance was one key to his character. "You only had to glance at the president's well-scrubbed, bandbox appearance, the starched handkerchief peeping out of the breast pocket of the sharply pressed double-breasted suit and showing the regulation four points," someone wrote, "to realize that here was a person who valued orderliness and predictability." And he had one more ritual before sitting himself at the breakfast table. He had a nice tot of bourbon, just to get the day off to a healthy start.

Then he and Bess had breakfast together in the Blair House dining room. He told John Hersey, "I'll eat half the breakfast I want and then go hungry all day long." He had "a strip of bacon, a scrambled egg, a piece of toast, and a glass of milk. No coffee." Truman explained, "I don't crave coffee. It hurts the peculiar talent I have for lying down and dropping right off to sleep in two minutes."

With that, flanked by the 8:00 A.M.–to–4:00 P.M. Secret Service detail just come on duty—he knew all their names and faces, their hometowns, their wives' names, how many kids they had, who they were, and today it would be Floyd and Vince and Stu, with Floyd in charge because Jerry had taken a day off—he walked across Pennsylvania Avenue to the Oval Office, to do that day's duty.

7. BABY STARCHES THE SHIRTS

On the morning, every morning, Baby ironed Les's shirt. A dutiful woman with a strong sense of where she belonged and what she expected, she saw the ironing as one of her primary duties. She had washed the shirt the night before, then sprinkled on the starch, then rolled it up overnight to take a set. Now, she unrolled it, ironed it hard, using all her muscles, really leaning into it. It was a knack, and Baby had it. She got all the lines straight and parallel, the collar stiff and never bent, a kind of heaviness to the front of the shirt so that no creases ever showed, the material never lost shape and bagged. Les had to look that smart. It was for the president, after all.

So on a typical morning, as Baby ironed, Les would get up and make breakfast with Jane, who was called Janie. Janie was the teenage niece, down from Pennsylvania, where she'd grown up. Janie and Les would cook, and Baby—her given name was Cressie and she was Les's wife and Janie's aunt—would unreel a shirt, and run that steam iron over it, and the limp, thick, shapeless thing would emerge crisp and perfect. Then Baby would dress to go to Hecht's. She also had to look nice.

That was how the mornings were at 1915 North Wayne Street, in Arlington, in the apartment in the old yellow clapboard house they'd rented from a sergeant in the Arlington County Police Department named Dudley Rector. The three of them, the two women, the aunt and the niece, and Les, forty, just the sweetest old bear in the world, who loved them both and would until the day he died.

Leslie Coffelt was five foot eight, and weighed 172 pounds. He had light brown hair and one of those faces that would be called open. It was slightly rounded and the eyes were set deep and radiated warmth. He wasn't a big man but neither was he small; he couldn't dominate with bulk, like many a cop, nor was he pint-sized, with a small man's bitter anger and urge to make the world dance a jig to his call. He had the middle-sizer's sense of fitting in already, a calm demeanor, no known temper, a feeling that he knew and accepted who he was and, with grace and dignity, that which the good Lord provided.

As a consequence, people liked Les. Les presented a much softer image to the world than most cops do. Many years later Janie would remember, "He was the type of person that the minute you met him, he was not a stranger. He was very thoughtful, very kind and considerate." Les just drew people in. He was so nice that even when tourists would ask him to pose next to the building he guarded, he'd happily oblige, and sometimes, later, these pictures would be sent to the president, with a nice note on what a decent, friendly man the officer was.

On November 1, 1950, he was mandated by regulations to dress in winter uniform even though it would be in the 80s that day, and he knew it, and he'd be outdoors, in the sun all day, but of course he'd never complain. Les was not a complainer. If there was a burden to be borne, he would bear it, without making a fuss or demanding much in the way of attention.

So Les would pull on the trousers he'd hung so neatly the night before. He'd button on the freshly ironed white shirt. He'd tie his black tie tight. He'd put on his spit-shined black oxfords. He'd pull on his officer's coat, tailored by S. Livingston & Son, dark blue, worsted, designed for chilly fall weather of the sort that Washington should be, but was not this particular day, having. Finally, he'd remove his belt and holster from the bureau where he placed it every single day. He'd pick up the six .38 Special 158-grain lead round-nose cartridges he'd so carefully removed, open the action of the weapon—it was a Colt, the model called "Official Police," a sturdy, heavy, utilitarian revolver with four inches of barrel, checkered wood grip—and slide the six cartridges into the six chambers of the cylinder. Then he'd snap it closed, feeling the vaultlike lockup that was characteristic of American revolvers in those days. For Les, it was as familiar as taking out the garbage or brushing his teeth. He'd grown up around guns and had hunted his whole life. The gun was not remarkable to him; he knew it the way you'd know an old friend. Then he placed it in the duty holster, and strapped it down. Finally he cinched and buckled the belt, with its complement of twenty more cartridges held in loops; the loaded holster with a slight density to it, off his right side, surprisingly low like a cowboy's because it had to be reachable under the hem of the jacket. The weight would be familiar to him as well, as he'd worn a gun on a hip most of his professional life, after a total of eight years with the Washington Metropolitan Police and seven years—broken up by a stint as a hotel employee and meat cutter and by army service in the war—on the White House Police. And he could shoot too; he was a member of the White House pistol team.

The funny thing was, he wasn't even supposed to be working that day! It was his day off! But one of his best friends, Officer Bradley H. Allen, Jr., needed to take some time off to paint his house. He asked his old pal Les, and it was part of Les's radiant personality to want to help folks. So of course Les said yes and agreed to work the extra day.

So maybe that's what Les was thinking about. But maybe not. Just as likely, he was thinking of the little details of a life lived earnestly. Possibly he was thinking of the Masons. He was a member of the 564-member Potomac Lodge No. 5, FAAM, in Georgetown. Early members of the lodge had laid the cornerstone of the White House in 1792, and the Capitol in 1793. Les had been raised a Master Mason on September 28, 1945, and now he was preparing to assume the position of a lodge officer, a junior steward. He would have a lot of ritual to learn if he decided to progress through the chairs (that is, advance to progressively higher positions in the Lodge) and possibly become a Master of the Lodge one day. But many men found meaning in simply belonging to the Masons. Les was one such man.

Both Cressie and Les were members of the Order of the Eastern Star, the affiliated organization for women. Much of their social life revolved around the Eastern Star, and they were a constant couple at Star parties and gatherings, and looked forward every year to the social highlight of the season, the Night of Thrills, a large social gathering held at Griffith Stadium to raise funds for the Masonic and Eastern Star Home in Washington, D.C., an assisted-living facility for Masons and their wives. Clark Griffith, owner of the Washington Senators baseball team and an active Mason, donated the stadium every year for the event.

Or possibly Les was thinking of music. That was another theme in his and his wife's life, because every night Baby would play the piano, both before and after dinner, and he and Janie would make the dinner, and after dinner, they'd wash the dishes—"Oh, he knew how to wash dishes, that's for sure," Janie would recall many years later—while Baby returned to the piano and beat out popular ballads and classical melodies. She had to have her piano, that was for certain. Or maybe the music in Les's thoughts revolved around the church choir in which both Les—he was a powerful baritone—and Baby were enthusiastic members except that . . .

Well, *which* church choir? It seemed that Cressie had an extremely rigid sense of her own centrality to every situation, and so one reality of the couple's life was that they were forever leaving this church for another one. Already they'd run through the Calgary Methodist, the Full Gospel Tabernacle, and the National City Christian, while Janie stayed loyally at the Community Methodist Church, about two blocks from home. But Les didn't mind. He worshipped the strong, formidable woman he had married back in 1937, and in his eyes, according to Janie, she could do no wrong. "He absolutely adored her . . . anything she wanted or did was fine with him."

But the chances are Les wasn't thinking about any of these things. The chances are he was thinking about that certain tension in the air which had to be the central fact in his domestic life, and that was the turbulence between Janie and Cressie. It filled the small apartment and it must have torn him up, because he ran into it time and time again, every single day.

What was it with Cressie? She always had grudges going, she was always annoyed. "She didn't get along with anybody," says Janie, grimly, remembering. "She just would rather sit and let somebody else wait on her, and he'd rather help somebody out," another friend who knew them then remembers.

In the Coffelts' case, this took yet another turn toward tension by virtue of the presence of Janie in the house. Janie was nineteen, and blond, and wore her hair in a short perm. She was of medium build, five foot four, with hazel eyes and a quiet disposition. She had visited in the summers all through her girlhood and now had moved down to Washington where Les had gotten her a job working at the Veterans Administration at Vermont and K, taking dictation. She liked it much better than Pennsylvania. She made friends both at the VA and at youth groups at her church. And she had one thing in Arlington that she didn't have in Pennsylvania: she had Les, whom she adored.

Janie and Cressie were alike in many ways: both were tough as nails, both had strong independent streaks, and in Janie, Cressie would have to see something that reminded her of herself so she'd have an overbearing instinct to prevent the young woman from making the mistakes she had made.

So that must have been weighing on Les's mind that morning, all mornings, for it was the single dominant fact of the domestic atmosphere at 1915 North Wayne Street. Sometimes it took bizarre turns as it worked itself out.

One day, Janie was tap-tap-tapping away at her job in the Veterans Administration when she got a call from Cressie. You will be, her aunt told her, at a certain lawyer's office at 4:00 P.M. Then the aunt hung up.

Dutifully, but resentfully, Janie showed up (she got off work at three). In the office she found her aunt and some attorney poring over a document that turned out to be nothing less than a contract which required that Janie could have but one date per weeknight and must on that date be home by ten, and one date on the weekend, during which she could stay out as late as eleven. Clearly, Cressie did not like the young man that Janie was seeing (and was secretly engaged to and, for the record, would marry in January and stay married to until his death, forty-nine years and six months and four daughters later). Janie refused to sign; a scene ensued.

It turned out on that day that Les drove them home, and the screaming continued. Les kept saying to Cressie, Now, Baby, be reasonable. Janie, to this day, remembers Cressie's response, and expresses it in the vernacular of another age: "She ripped him a new one. But he stayed calm. He was always calm."

So finally at about 6:30 A.M., all the getting-ready gotten ready, Les and Janie left the big yellow clapboard house just off Lee Highway and found Les's beloved green Nash parked on the little strip cresting a hill that is North Wayne. It was his joy and pride: he paid $1,154.40 for it just last year when the family moved from Q Street and out here, and he kept it shiny as a new penny, with long hours of washing and waxing on his off days.

And again, the dynamic of the family is neatly summed up by the driving arrangements. Les and Janie will drive downtown, because Blair House is so close to where she works at the VA; it's so close that sometimes she comes over to visit him during his duty day, which mostly consists of rotating between guard positions at the temporary executive mansion where the president of the United States now lives, as the White House, just across Pennsylvania, is being extensively remodeled. And their hours are the same, the 7:00 A.M.–to–3:00 P.M. shift. Meanwhile Baby, who works much farther downtown at Hecht's, takes the bus because she's not due in till just before the store opens. The driving accommodations have merely made official what was long before evident. That is an unofficial, but evident, kinship between Janie and Les. You'd think it odd: the niece and the aunt's husband. Yet the two bonded almost from the start and during her many summer visits to Washington when she was in high school, it was Les, not related by blood, who took the girl and then the young woman all around Washington and who developed a warm relationship with her, the classic old-young thing of teasing and gentle flirting and mock admonitions.

"When I was younger [and they lived on Q Street] I used to walk his lunch down to him at the White House. It wasn't the showcase or museum that it is now, it was a home. There were many parts of the White House that we had access to. When he would be on duty, he would take me with him through the whole place. Once I almost fell into the swimming pool!"

He took her everywhere, including that tourists' standard, the Washington Monument. "He took me up and I'm afraid of heights and I wouldn't look out. He thought that was so bad but he had me walk downstairs with him because I was so afraid. He tried to convince me to look out and I wouldn't do it."

There were a lot of things between them, private things, and it was clear that they enjoyed each other's company in a profound way. And possibly modern thinkers who've seen too many movies are thinking they know what's going on here. But they don't, not really. Because yes, something is going on, but it's not what you would expect.

What is going on is that Janie wasn't Baby's niece at all, as Les and the whole family have known from the beginning, even if they never talk about it directly. Janie was Baby's daughter.

The story was melancholy and not without its shame. Sometime in her late teens, Cressie met a man who said he would marry her. But he didn't. The child was raised as her niece and always felt something like an outsider, or as if she bore a stigma though she herself had done nothing wrong. That was one reason she liked D.C. so much more than Pennsylvania, because no one knew anything about her in the bigger city. And she had Les, who always treated her as if she were his own.

They pulled off Wayne onto Lee Highway, and Les headed the small green vehicle down the hill, through Arlington toward D.C. As the two of them drove out of the hills and approached Key Bridge, they saw a low city on the other side of that water, its roofs dominated by a few movie-Rome monuments. They could see the Capitol, of course, that gleaming white dome, and probably the Parthenon-like precision of the Lincoln Memorial, as there was no Kennedy Center yet to obscure it from the southwest. But the Washington Monument would have predominated, rising white and straight and graceful, lit by a low morning eastern sun. All the rest would have been the flatness of office roofs. Les once said to a hometown friend, "Irene, we don't have anything but cement and asphalt."

Les and Janie crossed the Key Bridge, which is an imposing structure a hundred feet over the broad Potomac; it could have been built by Romans eager to leave their mark on the world. From it, they were deposited in the congested little byway known as M Street, which runs through a crumbling village called Georgetown, not yet glamorized by the young Kennedy set and in 1950 just a jumble of Georgian mansions and town homes running around still cobbled streets, all of them in that pre-refurbishment era looking a little worn down.

But soon enough Pennsylvania Avenue veered off M; it was the main drag of the United States government. As you follow it—just a few miles, really, nothing like the mighty metropolitan boulevards of a New York or a Paris or a London—you'd run by Foggy Bottom on the right, where the empire that was the State Department nestled in the trees, where the decisions of America's way in the world were overseen by a stern gentleman named Dean Acheson, with a guardsman's mustache as bristly as his dignity. And soon enough, you'd hit the 1600 block of Pennsylvania Avenue, which is the cerebral cortex of the executive branch of government. To the right was the wedding cake structure of the Executive Office Building, just beyond it the gutted hull of the most famous house in America, the white one. Directly across Pennsylvania is the ornate creation called the Court of Claims, an arabesque fantasy of red brick and arches. And next to that was the understated two-building residential unit called Blair House, where the most important resident was named Harry S. Truman.

But Les wouldn't have stopped there, not yet. He would have proceeded to Lafayette Park, turned left, and dropped Janie at the VA.

Then he would have circled around, recrossed Pennsylvania, and looked for and probably found parking on Executive Avenue behind the White House, which was wide open in those days.

Then on foot he would have headed over to 16th, up that avenue, crossed Pennsylvania, and arrived at last at his place of employment, and his job, which was posing for pictures, giving directions, presenting a brilliant ceremonial face to the world, and not least of all, guarding the life of the president of the United States.

8. TOAD

Toad awakened.

He was a big man with some scars—left side, a knifing; shins and ankles, football cleats; knuckles, punches—and rolled from bed. He felt, as he usually did, pretty darned good. He wasn't one of those grouchy ones, not even on a day like this, on day shift when he must arise at 6:30 A.M. He was to duty a slave, but his attitude—he's a teaser, a josher, a poker, as befits a man of sublime physical confidence hard-earned in athletic fame—was to look for a moment of fun wherever.

Fully mobile quickly, Toad walked through the small apartment in his pajamas to the kitchen where his wife, Ruth, fixed breakfast. He ran a quick check on his watch, saw he had plenty of time (hell, he'd never been late for anything in his life), and sat still for a cup of coffee and a piece of toast. Put a dab of jam on it too, just as he always has, just as he always will. He wanted to get an early start today, because he'd be running the daytime 8:00 A.M.–to–4:00 P.M. tour, since Jerry McCann was on vacation, and Toad did not and would not allow anything untoward to occur while it was his watch. That's the kind of mind he had.

The apartment was in Anacostia, in Washington's southeast, across the Anacostia River from the main chunk of city that most think of as the "official Washington." But Anacostia might have been a more real city than the one with the monuments across the bridge: it was full of vets starting careers and families in the big town, and they've crowded into its rows of low apartment buildings and small houses. They could see the other Washington across the river, as represented primarily by the Capitol dome, which, standing on a hill, lords it over the western landscape. But they'd grown used to, even blind to it, and in Anacostia, where rents are cheaper, hopes are higher, life goes on without much pretense or affectation. It wasn't the Washington of fancy dress balls, ambassadorial teas, and press interviews, and you didn't need a guardsman's mustache and a pedigree down here; it was blue-collar, hardworking Washington. It was Washington as city, not as capital.

And here Toad lived with his beautiful wife, Ruth—the football hero always got the prettiest girl, then as now—and his two daughters, Judy and Katie, in three rooms furnished with pieces brought down from DuBois, Pennsylvania, Ruth's and Toad's mutual hometown, where furniture prices are much lower.

You'd think it a busy scene at breakfast, but it wasn't. Judy, eight, was still asleep; after Daddy leaves, Ruth will awaken her and get her ready for school at St. Theresa's. Katie, the baby, is only eight months old. She'll snooze until Judy is dressed.

Done eating, Toad rises, and heads back to the bedroom for the male morning ritual conveyed by three letters S, S, and S. Only the third S was remarkable: Toad was the proud owner of one of the new Schick electric razors, which he switched to some months back when he tired of walking around with little bits of toilet paper stuck to his face by a drop of dried blood.

And now: which suit?

Well, let's see. It's going to be hot today, dammit, even though it's November. Yet it wouldn't be somehow right to wear a summer linen. Toad—so called because as a kid he had an unusual number of warts on his hand—picked a light suit, unusually light for this time of year, but still of substantial weight and drape. It wasn't a summer suit but gabardine. Maybe it's a little more relaxed than most of his others but it felt right for that day's expected heat.

Toad—Floyd M. Boring, Special Agent, United States Secret Service— was a suit guy. He worked in a suit and he was proud of his suit. He wore a uniform for the Pennsylvania State Police for many years, so to be in a suit, with a tie on, that was special. He was proud to make a living in a suit, something his father never managed, so proud that once, when he was asked by someone if he was wearing a sport coat, he responded, with typical Toad brusqueness, "Hell no, I never wore a sport coat one day in my damn life."

He bought them at Louie's, near 7th and D streets. Louie had reasonable prices—no Hecht Company for Toad, who was always a shrewd man with a dollar—and, even better, upstairs Louie had a selection of factory rejects. They had flaws in the material or were mis-sized or mismatched; for a few bucks, a fellow could look pretty sharp if he didn't mind knowing that the second button was two inches lower than it should be. He just had to remember never to button it up.

But why would he button it up? The whole point of his job, after all, was the small Colt .38 Special he wore in a holster at his right hip, an unobtrusive six-shot revolver with a snubby barrel called, with melodramatic flourish, a "Detective Special," or, more commonly, a "Dick Special," which seemed to show up in every movie Humphrey Bogart ever made. It had never happened, but in theory sometime or other Toad might have to get to it and get it into action fast, and for that reason his suit would never be buttoned. This is a theme in the duty that was his life and it continued to all aspects of the job: always ready. You never knew when the world would go screwball on you. Hell, even if he was at something formal, he'd slip the Dick Special into his dinner jacket, it was that small, and always feel its weight; he could easily grip it too, in the shield of the pocket, and nobody would know.

As was common with men for whom guns are tools of a trade, the gun was to him simply another piece of equipment. Once he'd dressed, he took it out of the dresser drawer, nimbly opened the cylinder to see six gleaming cartridge heads with their central circular primers and their little inscription ".38 Spec.-Winchester" curled around the primers, snapped it shut, holstered it. Then he checked his "flapper," as the vernacular had it, a leather pouch worn on the belt that contained a rubber strip, which held five .38 cartridges. You could get those slugs off the strip and into the gun fast, if you had to. Then, the gun ritual finished, he pretty much forgot all about it.

His white shirt was immaculately ironed, particularly the collar, which was a flawless administration of flats and angles well disciplined by a day's worth of starch that will not melt in the hottest or the wettest of weather. That's one of the many things Ruth does well and effortlessly, like many of the agents' wives. Next, tie—hmm, why not a bow tie, for the Boss frequently wears them and they're popular again, and Toad thought of himself as a dapper dresser. With practiced fingers he figure-eighted the band of silk ribbon and drew it tight, so that on either side of the square central knot the bows were perfectly symmetrical and the knot itself was tight enough, but not too tight, so that any unusual rigor would not loosen it and pitch the whole construction toward anarchy and dissonance. On comes the coat, then he checks himself in the mirror because he's always got to look right.

He sees what the world sees: a biggish man with an athlete's grace and confidence—he was in the DuBois, Pennsylvania, high school football hall of fame and was a four-year varsity letterman. He saw a wide face, a broad forehead, tanned from the sun, a few careworn creases from a life lived out-of-doors mostly. He had a nice crop of hair, dark brown and full, in the style of the times. Toad, as he was called by nearly everybody, had an open, uncomplicated face. He was a man of direct action, of precise procedures, of utter self-confidence. He was the man who always knows what to do next, almost instinctively. He was never at a loss, and there was no crack in the facade of his confidence and presence. Nothing affected him much. He wasn't terribly contemplative, and would rather work with his hands than read a book, unless that book were a bankbook, which was his favorite kind of book, as he once remarked.

It was time to go. He kissed Ruth goodbye and told her he loved her and left the building. Already the sun was bright, and it would get brighter. Toad's used to brightness; he saw it on the highway many times. So Toad had the state policeman's most recognizable affectation, aviator's sunglasses. He hooked his around his ears; they were high-quality optics, prescription lenses for a slight diminution in his vision (he's 20/30), gold-framed, big-lensed, teardrop-shaped, tight to his ears for a rigid hold against his nose in case of severe action. Thus armored, the thirty-eight-year-old Secret Service agent heads to his car.

It's the best little buggy he's ever had, or ever will have. It was a dark blue 1939 Ford coupe, which he bought new in that year for $700. It packed eight cylinders under the hood and displaced 189 cubic inches. Baby, it could hum. He tuned it himself, changed the oil, changed the filters.

The car took him through the light early morning traffic. He crossed the 11th Street Bridge, turned onto Potomac, slid down a ramp to Independence and took that one on in to the White House. Seven miles, start to finish, and maybe he listened to the radio, a little news, a little traffic info, but on this day, as on most days, there was nothing memorable. Washington, D.C., hadn't awoken yet at 6:30 A.M., even with a war raging, an anti-commie crusade gathering steam in the Senate, China gone red, Joe Stalin still kicking up trouble in Russia.

Toad pulled into one of the four Secret Service reserved parking spots at the White House, and headed into the Secret Service office, which was in the basement of the East Wing, which was still functioning as the administrative headquarters of the executive branch, even if, because of the living quarters repairs, Harry Truman lived across the street at Blair.

There was no security system. Nobody wore IDs on lanyards. Nobody was searched and poked. It was just a place of work, banal and matter-of-fact, like all other places of work. Moreover, there wasn't a huge intelligence gestalt, with instant communications sent by code, no analysts poring through things, no steady flood of bulletins and warnings and briefings, no dit-dit-dit-dah-dah-dah of Teletype machines rattling importantly.

The Secret Service office in the West Wing of the White House consisted of two brown desks in a tiny office. There were a couple of guys there from the late shift and a coffee urn. There were phones, a portrait of Harry Truman and one of U. E. Baughman, the chief of the service. There were some logbooks, probably a locked gun cabinet with tommys and Winchester pumps, but as for drama, the room was sorely lacking. He looked in, maybe chatted briefly with the boys on duty, saw if there was any new information or anything big on the schedule—there wasn't.

Toad then headed across the street where, with the same lack of security ceremony, lack of inspection or briefing, he takes up his daily duty. No doors are locked. No IDs were demanded. He knew everybody. Everybody knew him. That's just how it was.

Everybody on his shift was either in or would be shortly, and no checking was done. There was no sense of urgency. Toad didn't bother to look at the duty roster for his own agents, much less the one compiled by the White House Police, which was a division of the Secret Service but jealously guarded its own administrative prerogatives, as do most official entities in Washington. Toad already knew that Jerry McCann was on vacation, the new guy Vince Mroz and Stu Stout, an old buddy from the Pennsylvania State Police, would arrive shortly. He knew Les would be in and so would Joe Downs. Joe Davidson and Don Birdzell, the uniform guys, will show up when due. The whole thing was relaxed, confident, and everybody knows everybody.

Toad knew all the players at Blair too. He knew the ushers, who basically administer the place. He knew the wait staff, which was primarily African-American, though the term he used, without prejudice and simply as a reflection of the common usage of the time, was "colored." He knew the administration people who will accompany the Boss everywhere and always be at his beck and call. He knew the Truman family, including of course the Man himself, the formidable First Lady Bess, the daughter, Margaret, who was now off on a trip and not in residence, and Bess's brother Fred Wallace, a sometime problem in official Washington, and for the Secret Service in particular, because he was—to use the 1950s term—an alkie, at times putting the Secret Service agents in dubious situations.

During this time on this day it was like any other day. Everyone showed up, everyone looked spiffy as they should, and then the push begins. The four White House policemen push outside, moving from duty point to duty point, the Secret Service agents push inside, and it's set up so that once a day, you get an hour off for lunch or relief. And there are other breaks in the day. When Harry Truman leaves Blair promptly at 8:30 A.M., two agents slide in next to him, and take him on the short walk across the street to the West Wing. Or, during the day, to avoid crowds, that transfer, to and from, will be handled by car, the president leaving from the back entrance to Blair in a Lincoln limo, again escorted by two of the men.

And there'll be other interruptions in the duty day, and Toad had one he couldn't avoid. It's called Qualification, something he and every other agent must do once every six months. This was his day. So at about ten, when his hour off is slated, he heads across Pennsylvania Avenue, enters the West Wing, goes downstairs, and heads to the Tunnel.

The Tunnel was built in the 1940s for the secretly paralyzed Franklin Delano Roosevelt; it runs from the basement of the White House to the basement of the Treasury next door, out of public view. Roosevelt used it about once, as it turned out, but it became a handy shortcut to the Treasury Department Range, in the basement of the large, cathedral-like building just east of the White House. An agent would cut through the White House Police dressing area, where the White House cops had their lockers, and come to a big door that looked almost medieval and had to be opened by a big flat key, "like a prison," someone said. It wasn't much to experience: it was dark and poorly ventilated and led to the Treasury Cash Room. In another sector of the basement, the Treasury branch known as the United States Coast Guard ran a shooting range for armed Treasury officers, primarily Secret Service and Tobacco and Alcohol agents. Toad shoots officially once a month, as required by his service; the score was recorded; he practiced on his days off and sometimes shot in informal matches out at the Arboretum or up in Baltimore against other police units. He had to maintain a high average, and if you shoot in the upper percentile six straight months, you are awarded the Distinguished Marksmanship Award. He got his in 1948.

Firing ranges are characteristically dark, dirty places, even if run by a federal agency. They are tidy, after the military fashion, but all those lead particles and powder fumes roiling perpetually in the air leave a stench and a sheen on everything so you always feel like you're in a boiler room. Cold or hot, the places always feel greasy for some reason. The Coast Guard petty officer who runs the place, named Frenchy, supervises the eight lanes, and the pride and joy of his domain is a large, bulky reloading machine, whereby used shells—deposited by shooters who must gather their spent shells—are mechanically resized, reprimed, repowdered, and rebulleted with drumlike lead wadcutters, the most accurate load possible, used almost exclusively for target shooting.

This reveals the theme of law enforcement shooting at the time, and it was a theme that was to persist into the 1970s. It was a kind of willful disregard for reality, an insistence on ceremony at the expense of practicality. It refused to acknowledge the true nature of the gunfight, which was chaos and movement as propelled by fear and excitement and complex physiochemical reactions to intense stress.

But Toad was a man of orthodoxy, not a visionary radical, and played exactly by the mandates of his organization; thus he will practice exactly as he has been trained and ordered to practice.

There's a locker room to one side, and Toad went to it, took off his jacket, hung it up. Then he went into the reloading room, where glittery boxes of fifty flat-nosed reloaded wadcutters are out; he picked up five boxes, stacked them, picked them up awkwardly and headed to the shooting range, after stuffing two empty shells backward into his ear channels, for the noise of a discharging firearm was intense, especially when contained in a small, closed room.

Toad sets up in a booth. He takes his Dick Special from the holster, and with practiced fingers unsnaps the cylinder latch, then carefully babies the cylinder out of the frame. In movies all the time actors perform this revolver act with some brio for maximum dramatic appeal, but like most real-life shooters, Toad wouldn't think of such a thing. A revolver is a little perfect matrix of pins and struts and springs and screws and beautifully machined so that everything lines up superbly. To bang it around is to risk throwing some little thingamajig or other out of alignment and that's a sure bet to happen when you need it the most. You pull, the gun binds, and you're out of the fight and maybe out of your life.

So, gently, he pushed the cartridge plunger so that his six heavy-nose 158-grain lead Winchester cartridges slipped out, set them aside, then loaded in six drumlike, lower-powered wadcutters. The practice of law enforcement shooting was built around the conceit of bull's-eye shooting.

Even Colt itself had an investment in this faith. The procedures are very well pronounced in the instructions given with every gun. "Proper Grip or Hold," runs the title of a block of type full of advice for shooters as issued by the Hartford gun makers for seventy or so of the last century's one hundred years. "It must be comfortable and natural, not strained. Rest the thumb above the latch (but clear of the hammer), and allow no unequal pressure at any point. A uniform 'squeeze' is the basis for hits, unequal pressure with a 'jerk' on the trigger, the chief reason for misses."

The instructions display in photographic close-up the perfect grip for further guidance, with the revolver cupped gently like a Fabergé egg, a delicate treasure, the relaxed thumb splayed against the latch, the loose entwinement of fingers supporting the weight of the gun, the whole thing a study in relaxation therapy, and no sign of a second hand in sight. It's a one-handed pose, involving particularly the muscles of the upper shoulder, to keep the gun not so much pure steady as trembling under control, according to certain rhythms and vulnerable to certain anticipations, so as the gun's front sight settles momentarily on the six o'clock of the target while well framed by the notch of the rear sight, then that soft finger can press ever so gently and the whole thing comes together in sweet syncopation. It helps if you're a first-class athlete with big old hands and have unusually refined hand-eye coordination. Then it works. How beautiful, how delusional, how absurd. Surely in a gunfight, the fingers will clench the gun desperately and there'd be no time for a perfect arrangement of the hand to the grip, for the perfect placement of digital pad to trigger curve, and the whole operation will take place in super-time, desperately improvised by fingers fat as sausages and clumsy as potatoes from adrenal release, as guided by a man so far into oxygen debt that his IQ has just dropped seventy-five points.

But Toad, ever obedient to those above him as he expects those below him to be ever obedient to him, practiced the ideal, not the real. His target was the "Official 50 Ft. Timed and Rapid Fire Pistol Target," a two-and-a-half-inch black bull's-eye, a dot at the fifty feet to which he runs it out via a pulley system. It hangs, resembling nothing at all in the real world, except a black dot. That black dots are largely absent in the real world, and even if present rarely attack, concerns nobody. He finds the right grip, orders his body and hand into a state of relaxation, and with his strong, big thumb pulls the Colt's little hammer back. It slides as it compresses the subtle mesh of springs within its stout frame, then locks. The gun settles into his hand. Toad takes over his own breathing, holds it down to a minimal in-out rhythm, one per second, turns his body to find his ideal aiming position—this is the near-mythical body-set by which the gun axiomatically is pointed dead-on to target—and, finding it, brings the gun, lightly gripped, to the target. With his great athlete's vision he locks on the front sight, which is contained in the little groove machined into the top of the frame that serves as a rear sight. He nests his left hand in his left pocket. He never cheats by secretly locking his foot on the edge of the booth for additional steadiness, as some of the less gifted shots are known to do. He lets his body relax, he finds a certain amount of air in his lungs, he watches the sight settle until it's nestled with perfection under the circle of the black dot so far away, and without willing it, without thinking of it, somehow his subconscious takes over and manages to compress the trigger with a slow p-r-e-s-s until BAP! the revolver fires. He is correctly watching the front sight; the target was a blur.

Five more times Toad carefully reenacted this ritual, gathering himself, marshaling his concentration, for each placement. Finally, the gun was empty, the gun smoke hung in the air, and he reeled in the target to see a satisfying cluster of holes dead-on in the black. The Colt revolvers, after all, are sublimely accurate machines and Toad had physical gifts far beyond most men's. And he's worked hard, not only down here and in the matches, but at home or in the office, practicing an exercise then called dry-snapping (and now dry-firing), by which the gun was emptied, then the shooter shoots, clicking on an empty cylinder, working on trigger pull, steadiness, stamina, rhythm, repetition, without the distraction of the actual shot. It's an agency-wide practice, and, alas, many field offices are peppered with bullet holes in the wall where a young agent has forgotten to check, then check again, then check a third time that the gun was empty. Toad has seen his scores rise steadily; when he joined the service, he was a 160 shooter and now he's a 280 shooter.

So the target looked like a six-leaf clover has been die-cut in it, for a signature of a wadcutter on paper is the perfect penetration of the bullet through the medium, and the holes looked as if drilled by a machinist's fixture in the center of the bull's-eye. At fifty feet, one-handed, that's shooting. No doubt about that. The Secret Service pistol teams were regular winners on the informal circuit of pistol shooting matches that were part of police culture, and Toad was a regular on the team, venturing up to Sparrows Point in Baltimore or out at the Washington Arboretum to shoot against other law enforcement units.

But was it the right kind of shooting? Toad probably knew it wasn't; he'd been in two lethal confrontations before, and this kind of shooting had nothing whatsoever to do with the outcome of those two events.

Sometime in the 1930s, he was serving warrants, then a common state police officer's job. He was a tough guy, or so he thought. Usually it's a two-man job, but Toad, after all, was a man who'd dominated every physical and social transaction he'd ever taken part in, so it never occurred to him, when his partner called in sick, to forswear that day's scheduled arrests. He drove out to the house near Ebensburg where this particular Joe was known to be located—it wasn't big, possibly robbery, no Dillinger deal, nothing that would ever make the papers—and knocked on the door.

Big cop, the sunglasses, the uniform straight and neat and perfect, representing all the state's rectitude and authority. He knocked again, and heard the pitty-pat of big feet making tracks. Guy's come out the back and was running like hell down the dirt road to the highway. Toad took up the pursuit and in a few bounding receiver's strides reached the fugitive and brought him down. That's cop work: the chase, the coming together of the bodies, the strength against the strength.

The two men grapple in the dirt, going this way and that; first it's the guy with the advantage, then Toad, who's probably not too scared and more than a little angry that his uniform's now a dusty mess, that his hat fell off somewhere, that his paperwork burden has just increased. Then the knife came into play.

It went into Toad's side, cutting open a nasty slice. The pain wasn't there, then it was, harsh and strong. Then the blade's withdrawn for another stroke, and for just a second Toad lunges and tried to control the stabbing arm, but then concludes, hey, it's him or me and I don't want this baby to do any more cutting.

He broke free, went to his sidearm, a six-inch Colt. There was no time for a prissy hold, for the proper adjustment and equalization of finger to weapon, for the drawing back ever so gently of the hammer, for the search for natural aiming position, for the careful downward arc of revolver to target, for the search for the front sight, for the mastery of the tremble impulse, for the application of all those subtly mastered but talent-based hand-eye calculations, for the smooth, even press of the digit against the soft curve of the—

BANG! No *bap!* here, for the cartridge was a high-powered one, loaded to maximum velocities for penetrating automobile bodies, typical state police arrangement for the time. The range was two feet if that, and the shooting was desperate, improvised, done in super-time without reflection. It was from the id. And from Toad's id, it flew straight. At one later point in his life, he said of this incident, "He didn't testify because I hit him in the head."

The results were swift: the anatomical result of the bullet's collision with the skull, the sudden surrender to gravity of the stricken man, his almost immediate cessation of signs of life, his open but blank eyes, the slack dull look upon his face, the clumsiness, the squalor, the incoherent nature of his fall to earth. In any case Toad, who'd seen a lot of highway death and knows what metal does to flesh, isn't particularly moved or stimulated. He's damn glad to be alive, even if he's bleeding through his shirt and he's got a lot of uniform maintenance to do and he knows that when he tells Ruth he almost got killed today, she'll be stoic about it, but underneath profoundly disturbed. But all that's in the future.

For now, he straightened up, made sure (as would any cop) to recover the knife—it was a butcher's thing, as domestic as they come—to preclude any suggestion of wrongdoing, as improbable as that may be. The rest was just regulation crap. Toad telephoned it in—the radio car wasn't in vogue yet—waited for the boys to show, then headed off to the hospital. It's typical of law enforcement in those rougher, looser days that the entire episode was no big deal. Hey, guy had a knife, Toad had to clip him, end of story. No inquiry board, no psychological grief counseling, no shooting-related suspension while the investigators do their thing, none of that. It happened, he got through it, he shot well to save a life, his own, it was part of the job, now let's go on.

But it had one lasting residue. At the hospital, after he was sewn up, he was given a tetanus shot. And the next day, all his warts fell off!

"I had a whole bunch of warts on my hand, and one right here for a long time. As soon as I took that tetanus shot, the damn warts fell off. The next day they were gone. I told Dr. Graham, who was Truman's doctor, he wrote that baby down. That's a mystery."

Did memories of that horror in a very small place come back to haunt Toad? The answer was, no more than the warts ever did. His mind doesn't work that way. He's not one for being haunted or for pondering the nature of paradox either. His nature was just to get the damned job done, dammit. So no memories of violence past dog him, and he continues with his shooting for about an hour, one man in the basement of Treasury, watching the little holes cluster at the black dot fifty blurry feet out, knowing at some level the foolishness of it but not letting himself be bothered.

The session over, Toad shook the last six target shells free of the Colt and dumped them into the cardboard box, for return and refill. Then he reinserted the six heavy-nosed Winchester rounds, slid the cylinder into the gun till it locked tight, then put the gun in his hip holster, snapping the safety strap over it, and promptly forgot all about it.

He turned his targets in, signed them, bantered with Frenchy and some of the other guys who are coming in and out, checked his watch, and moved on. He'd wash his hands because lead is greasy and the stuff congeals to flesh, leaving you feeling as if you've been eating ribs. That done, he took his coat off the hook, threw it on, checked himself out in the mirror to make sure the gigline was still straight, the bow tie trim, ran a hand through his thick shock of hair, and headed back through the tunnel. In a few seconds he's back on street level, then out, crossing Pennsylvania for Blair. He links his sunglasses around his ears.

The sun was bright and by now it was really hot out, mid-morning, getting near 80. The trolleys ran down Pennsylvania and everywhere people thronged, enjoying the last fling of temperate clime before the arrival of winter weather. Floyd M. "Toad" Boring, thirty-eight, of DuBois, Pennsylvania, headed across the street for another day on the job. He passes by Lafayette Park and, up ahead, that canopied structure, as elegant as any in the better parts of London, that would be Blair House, where, for now anyway, the president of the United States lives.

9. THE NEW GUY

Maybe Vince wasn't quite as cocksure that morning as Toad was. After all, Toad was the star, the boss man, a favorite of U.E.'s. Vince was a little further down the pecking order. He was the new guy. That meant a lot here, as it would anywhere in an environment where lives may be at stake.

On the face of it, the two should have loved each other from the start, they were so alike. Like Toad, Vincent P. Mroz was a big guy. Like Toad, Vince was a great athlete. On top of that, both were ends. Can't you see them as a one-two punch, Boring and Morose (the newspapers would have a field day), so the other team couldn't concentrate on one, because then the other'd kill them. You can imagine them having a nice long toss before a game, warming up, the ball floating gracefully through the blue air like a zeppelin, each fellow snaring it in strong, big hands.

Then there's background. Both were strapping sons of tough American Rust Belt industries, one from a Pennsylvania rail town, the other from a Midwestern steelmaking city. Both were immigrant stock, both lost their fathers early, both fought their way from nowhere, from nothing, to stand at the left and right of the president of the United States. Both made their parents, spouses, and children proud beyond measure.

But the gulf between them is larger than you might think, and it has to do with the culture of the United States Secret Service, the institution that spawned and defined and nurtured and rewarded both of them. It's a peculiar institution too, a government entity whose members, far from being paper-pushers or bureaucratic turf-guards or committee-room warriors, are sworn to give up their lives at the drop of a hat or the pull of a trigger for another, more powerful man. The conceit of that sanctified sacrifice has never even been examined; it simply *is*, an article of faith. A man jumps in front of a bullet meant for another man, and meant also to pierce the heart of a nation. You know that they would just intercede and put their flesh in front of the flesh they were meant to protect, without giving it a second thought. And that's what's so special about the Secret Service, that willingness to take the shot aimed at the Man. It's a powerful core to build a faith around. And possibly it explains some of the service's cultural peculiarities.

The Secret Service, history insists, was founded on July 5, 1865; it was a division of the Treasury Department and its stated mission was to suppress counterfeit currency, which at that moment in history threatened to overwhelm the United States's financial system. The agency's mandate was swiftly expanded to include investigations of "persons perpetrating frauds against the government," including Ku Klux Klanners, distillers, smugglers, mail robbers, and land-fraud practitioners. In 1894, among other duties, it began an informal part-time protection of the president.

But the Secret Service to which Toad and Vince and Les belonged was really born Friday, September 6, 1901, at the Temple of Music at the Pan-American Exposition, one of the world's many jamborees of showing-off that seemed to be so in fashion around the turn of the century. The locality was Buffalo, New York, and the time was 4:07 P.M. William McKinley, the amiable, large-bodied, and enthusiastic Republican president of the United States, put out his hand for a shake with a slight young man. He received instead two bullets in the stomach from an Iver Johnson .32 revolver, which had been concealed in a handkerchief in the hands of the fellow, a man of low intelligence named Leon Czolgosz, who was obsessed with the glories of anarchy. One of the bullets bounced off McKinley's button it was so low-powered; the other plowed through his intestines and came to rest near his spine, trailing massive trauma, unleashing massive infection. He died eight days later, on September 14.

It's not that McKinley was unguarded. Surrounding him were a couple of Secret Service officers (one of the operatives had been repositioned away from McKinley to accommodate Pan-American Exposition president John Milburn while he introduced the guests in the rope line to the president), a squad of Buffalo police detectives, and, nearby, a platoon of American infantrymen. But he was unguarded *professionally:* no effort had been made to screen the crowd, no files were kept on possible assassins in the area, no sharp-eyed guards scanned the clothes of the people in line for telltale lumps or, in Czolgosz's case, a hand-obscuring handkerchief ideal for concealing a small revolver.

Any of those commonsense preparations might have averted the

McKinley assassination; and one even suspects that had it come to it, any one of those Secret Service operatives would gladly have put his own body between the gun muzzle and the president. But there wasn't time; in those days, and even in days that followed, the president expected and planned to meet and mingle with the common man. On New Year's Day 1907, for example, Teddy Roosevelt, McKinley's successor, shook hands with about eight thousand of his countrymen in Washington. Any one of them could have had an Iver Johnson .32 concealed in a handkerchief, and, again, the agents wouldn't have had time to be heroic.

After the death of McKinley, Secretary of the Treasury Lyman Gage and presidential secretary George B. Cortelyou instructed the Secret Service to continue to protect the president. Aware of this understanding, Congress requested permanent protection, and made that official in 1902, when two full-time agents were assigned to the White House detail. There seems to be some controversy as to the legality of the Secret Service's new obligation, but legally or not, the Secret Service was and is on duty to prevent recurrences. In 1906, Congress actually got around to paying the bill for presidential protection through the Sundry Civil Expenses Act. The agency's protective responsibilities grew, and in 1908 it assumed responsibility for also protecting the president-elect. In 1930, the White House Police Force, which had been started in 1922, was placed under the supervision of the Secret Service.

Those are the historical details, the who-what-when-where of how Congress engineered in good faith the expansion of the service. But it doesn't communicate inner details, the culture of the agency that really has more to do with the way a career there would be experienced by a Floyd or a Vince. For one thing, it was a small agency then (it still is, relatively speaking); it had fewer than four hundred special agents, for another it was notoriously underbudgeted, and for a third thing, it considers itself an elite organization by virtue of its sacred mission and sacred responsibility. Thus its cultural attributes are different from any other federal agency; what it most resembles is the United States Marine Corps, another institution high on spirit, small in size, and low on budget. It works, moreover, on certain inevitable patterns of human fellowship of the small-organization variety: a man gets in, does well, acquires influence, and he brings in a buddy who, in turn, helped by the first, brings in another buddy, and sooner or later you have a collection of fellows from one particular locality or institution—the Pennsylvania State Police is a perfect example, as would later be the Michigan State School of Criminal Justice. Thus, friends are always looking out for friends.

And here's a funny thing about the Secret Service up through the 1960s at least: though it's called the Secret Service and though to outsiders it maintains a wall of secrecy, within it, there were no secrets. Everybody knew everybody and everybody knew about everybody. Word got around; there was no anonymity within it, and a mistake or a bad impression stayed with you forever, while a spectacular performance could make a career for life. There was also—agents deny this routinely, but the signs are abundant and obvious—an informal pyramid within its three divisions: the special agents of the Protection Detail were the highest of the high; they were drawn from and will return to the Investigative Branch, which targets bunco artists, check forgers, and funny-money engravers, and was seen as slightly lower down the pyramid. Then, finally, there were the White House policemen, who wear uniforms and stand inspections as well as guard and were largely drawn from Metropolitan patrolmen. They were more or less the enlisted men. Culturally and bureaucratically, they stood apart.

Given that the executive protection detail considers itself an elite within an elite, its members guard their position with some energy. It's not a thing easily earned, and they are not terribly willing to share its prestige with those who haven't earned it, in their eyes. One of the agency's main administrative antagonists throughout the years, for example, had been J. Edgar Hoover of the more powerful Federal Bureau of Investigation, who, with his political brilliance, his public relations genius, and his imperial zeal, had always schemed to take over the role of protecting the president. Thus it was known within the agency that complacency might equal co-option. That is why in 1948, U. E. Baughman made a decision that challenged the culture of the institution and explains the difference between Toad and Vince.

Whereas for many years the Secret Service had drawn its men, fully formed and well trained, from the ranks of America's state police, particularly Pennsylvania's, Baughman determined that from 1948 onward, Secret Service agents should come from universities. Previous police experience was no longer required; a bachelor's degree was. The nominal reason for this was to get his men higher pay grades faster, since by federal law a college degree gets them in as GS 7. In a year you jump to 9, and in another year you jump to 10. So you're making more money faster, whereas the ex–state cops, lacking the premium of the college degree, start at 5 and take forever to get up to 9.

Like so many nominal reasons, there's truth to it, but there's also some subterfuge. Baughman was quietly upgrading the savoir faire quotient of the Secret Service. He was ever so subtly easing out a culture of men who said "It don't matter" and "They was going south," who spat indoors as well as out, who blew their noses loudly into handkerchiefs and maybe didn't trim their fingernails often enough or used too much Brylcreem, that sort of thing, common in prewar America, a drawback in the new, modern, postwar America. If these men protected a president who also occasionally mangled verb and noun agreement and who had himself never seen the inside of a college dormitory and whose memories and tendencies included spitting, handkerchiefs, and Brylcreem, that didn't matter; new presidents, Baughman understood, would be slicker, college-educated, more presentable, and so would the new generation of their protectors. The world was changing and he would change his agency with it. Why, already the FBI was demanding not only college degrees but also advanced work in either law school or accountancy.

And of course the old protectors understood this as well. They understood—people understand the secret messages of their workplaces faster than anything—that they were in some sense a last generation, that their kind would no longer walk the earth, that the young men they were training would replace them, would in fact usurp them. There might have been just the slightest bit of resentment. The new men, the inheritors, would not be loved and embraced by the men they were replacing. It doesn't work that way, not on the planet Earth at any rate.

So when Vince, after just eight months in the Chicago office, joined the White House Protection Detail in 1949, he was the junior guy, he'd never been a street cop or made an arrest, much less gotten a knife in the gut and handled the situation with a .38 slug to the head. And his promotion to the big time came not because he'd made a spectacular bust, but because when the president visited Chicago and Vince stood next to him, people noticed Vince, his size, his bearing, his good looks. He was "discovered," you might say, like a movie star.

"Boring and [agent Stu] Stout, they were senior to me because I came to the detail in 1949. We sort of more or less took orders from them; the junior men on the shift always got the, I wouldn't say the *worst* duty or anything," he remembers, meaning of course that he is saying yes, the junior men got the *worst* duty, always, inevitably. That's the workplace; that's the way it goes.

It didn't matter that Vince is one of the few men who has a varsity letter from and is a member of both the S Club at Michigan State and the M Club at the University of Michigan, or that he spent the war as a marine officer aboard an aircraft carrier and a battleship in the Pacific. It doesn't matter that he's a graduate of Michigan State School of Criminal Justice, or that he bulled his way out of East Chicago, Indiana, because of his great athletic gifts, winning a football scholarship to Michigan State, fighting a stepfather who wanted him to stay home and go to the mills instead. It didn't matter that he caught a touchdown pass against Ohio State. None of that mattered. He was the new guy. He was the college kid.

So that morning Vince woke up in his apartment in Southeast Washington in a residential complex called Fairfax Village, at Pennsylvania and Alabama Avenues. It's a very nice place for a nice young couple with a fourteen-month-old daughter, and a whole bunch of other agents call it home, like Rex Scouten and Jerry McCann and Bill Shields and Roy Kellerman, who was in the front seat of the Kennedy limo thirteen years later in Dallas. Vince picked a light blue double-breasted suit. He slid his gun into its place, another Colt Detective Special, like Toad's, as a perk of rank, for the uniformed White House officers hadn't any choice, had to carry a four-incher. The gun will all but disappear in his paws.

Vince was a big man, with giant hands, and an athlete's grace and confidence. He was the sort that's been through too much already—getting out of East Chicago wasn't easy—to let anything stop him. His gifts were mathematical, and he had an advanced mind for engineering. Whatever he tried that involved organization and precision, he succeeded at. He was a sandy-haired guy, and in profile handsome in a way that the movies would classify as Solid Leadership Type (he looked a little like William Holden), and as a marine officer grew easy in the ways of command. That's probably why taking directions and orders from a Floyd Boring probably secretly grated against him, and it's probably why he and Toad never became the closest of friends.

And there was probably another reason. Vince may have been just too smart for this kind of work. He had a questing mind, never still, always looking for problems to tear into. Thus, he was a natural investigator, a natural organizer who always sees a better way. Solving crimes was the perfect vessel for his IQ-driven restlessness. A crime was like an equation to be cracked, it took certain methodical steps, a jump powered by intuition, an assembly of parts into a whole, the ability to distinguish a pattern, to make connections, and then there's the physical outlet of the actual pursuit. It's a complete and satisfying narrative.

Protective details are something else again. There's a monotony to them, a sameness. You are passive 99.999999 percent of the time, and not since 1933, at the shooting of Chicago mayor Anton Cermak in Florida near FDR, had shots been fired in the vicinity of an American president. So mostly it was rote work, still work, patient work.

The service understood that. The system was called "the push," and it was shrewdly based on psychological realities. Everyone got bored sitting around. Therefore, during the eight-hour duty shift, no one sat in one place for eight hours. The five Secret Service agents push. That is, every half hour, they rotate through the security positions, which are coded on the D rubric so that the eastern guardhouse in front of Blair is D-1, the stairway up to the front door is D-2, and so forth around the perimeter: from doorway to doorway, bottom of the stairs to usher's office, inside the doorway to basement office. They're always on the move, the idea being to keep their eyes from growing still, their minds from turning dull, their senses from clogging, their reflexes from turning off. The White House policemen push too, moving around between their three designated positions, the easternmost and the westernmost guardhouses, two little shacks that are essentially doghouses high enough to stand in, sited at each end of the 130-odd feet of Pennsylvania Avenue frontage that Blair House commands; and, third, a standing tour at the foot of the Blair House steps. There's another man out back, commanding the rear approach to Blair.

Then there are excursions and preparations, which break things up a little bit. For example, today the president was scheduled to travel to Arlington National Cemetery at 3:00 P.M. to officiate at the dedication of a statue for a British field marshal, Sir John Dill, who had died in Washington in 1944, in honor of his wartime service. This means at 1:00, a small contingent of the security force will depart by car for that destination, coordinate with (which means supervise) park police, sweep it, set up posts, and secure it against any possibility of threat. It means trips too, as when the president visits Kansas City or heads south to Florida— there an agent saved the president's life as the banty little man proved to be less of a swimmer than he thought he was—or missions overseas. All good fun.

The walks in the early morning hours were also good fun, as Harry Truman bounded along with his cane, which was by rumor carried more to bop disgruntled voters than to assist the sixty-seven-year-old's sprightly step, and the agents flanked him, huffing to keep up, nudging the 6:00 A.M. curious aside, watching this way and that. Fun, if exhausting, but over so quickly.

But today was so normal; other than the Dill excursion, nothing was scheduled. So it was riding the push, keeping alert, following Toad's orders for this job or that, and getting through the day best as possible.

In the kitchen Vince hugged his baby. Her name was Barbara, and after she squiggled and twisted and babbled, as ten-month-old babies will do, he grabbed a quick breakfast and then he too is off for another dull day of duty. His morning was almost exactly like Toad's as a matter of fact. Except in one extremely important detail: he got *dressed* before breakfast and Toad got dressed *after* breakfast. No toast for Vince! He usually ate eggs and pancakes, which his wife rose heroically to fix, and then sat down with him and had a cup of coffee and maybe a piece of toast while he ate, although she isn't a breakfast person herself and had the baby to contend with as well. Shirley would usually make his lunch the night before, putting it in the fridge. He knew exactly where it was, and he'd just grab it and go. In other respects, the details were almost identical, and Vince's suits also came from Louie's, near 7th and D streets, were also seconds (Jim Rowley, head of the White House detail, seems to have made the first connection with Louie, and it grew to be a detail-wide thing). And Vince liked bow ties too; but today he chooses a regular tie.

Sometimes he'd tell Shirley where he was going to be, if he knew ahead of time. Today, she knew he was going to be at Blair House.

Like Toad, he too drove, a black, four-door 1937 Olds he'd owned since before the war. His folks bought it used, and while he was off on carriers in the Pacific, it sat on blocks in the garage in East Chicago. It was only about ten minutes to work as there's hardly any traffic at 6:30 A.M. in Washington in 1950. He was a good way out, practically in the suburbs, just barely inside the District line. It was different out here: leafy, hilly, more private, actually. Two big parks just down Pennsylvania from the Alabama Avenue intersection had the effect of cloistering Vince's development, of separating it from the city.

As he drove, he liked to turn on the radio and listen to the big bands, Glenn Miller and Tommy Dorsey, Jimmy Dorsey and Harry James. He and Shirley loved to dance—their first date at Quantico, during the war, had been devoted to dancing.

But no matter the music, there was no doubt of his destination. If you happened to look forward as you moved westward, you'd notice right away that Pennsylvania is oriented, by the iron rule of L'Enfant's grand plan, directly toward the Capitol. The road stands out like a silver ribbon as it runs downhill, and you can trace it directly to the large dome, gleaming in the sun, nearly five miles distant. It certainly impresses on you the permanence, the totality, the seriousness of the state. Maybe he'd grow used to it, but Vince was still new to D.C., and the giant scoop of vanilla ice cream that was his government still stirred him.

He watched it grow closer, listened to the radio, checked his watch. Here it came. It got closer and closer, then so close it lost all sense of scale as he drove by the ornate building, with its thousands of stairs, its gardens and landscaping and walkways and glades and its aura of benign grandeur. Who could look on such a sight and not see utter benevolence?

Then the Capitol was gone and in minutes he was pulling into one of the Secret Service parking spaces on West Executive Avenue and heading to Blair House and a day of pushes.

10. THE BUICK GUY

onald Birdzell, forty-one and dead-solid tough, liked complete. He liked tidy. He liked organized. He liked fixed. He liked beds made, light bulbs lit, sidewalks swept, pictures hung straight, everything dusted, and he'd dust it himself if Helen was busy. He could wire a socket, build a bookshelf, change the oil or the wiper blades, hang a curtain rod, repair a shingle, or rewire a toaster. He'd begun doing crossword puzzles—later in his life it would become an obsession—and it seemed the process of solving the puzzle and neatly watching the blank spaces running this way and that in the little grid fill up with letters that became words summed up the way his mind worked: a strictness for order, an internal logic, a pleasure in completion. Life was 4 across, "in order," N-E-A-T, and 5 down, "scrubbed," C-L-E-A-N.

Donald took a puff on his morning Lucky Strike and exhaled a cloud of nicotine-flavored gas into the atmosphere. Then he took a gulp of Black Magic, as he called coffee, which he loved.

Donald and Helen—he was a Birdzell from the Midwest, Champaign, Illinois; she was a Murphy—were a part of the wider Catholic Murphy clan of Washington, D.C., and to them, family was the main thing. The clan gathered every weekend, and many nights during the week, and it was always a merry time. They played games: lots of cards, penny-ante poker, pinochle, and cribbage, lots of eating, lots of yelling and needling among the boys, talk of fishing trips to the bay come again in the spring, while the women chattered about family and recipes and victory gardens, and the kids ran this way and that.

It was a happy mob, the Murphys, so happy nobody ever held it against Donald that he was a Methodist, and sat in the car Sunday morning when everybody else was at mass.

It was early by most people's standards, but not by Donald's, because the way his job was set up, every week he's on a different shift and there are three shifts, so it's not like he's set on one getting-up time. This was the best shift, the day shift, even if it was so darned hot and he'd be out in the sun all day.

He went into the bedroom and like all the men of the security detail, he put on his belt and then he loaded his Colt Official Police, one round at a time in the cylinder (he shot Expert, 273, on the last qualification), then snapped it shut and put it in the holster. Then came the tunic, too heavy for the heat that's been squatting on the Northeast all week long.

Donald was a handsome man in that 1930s and 1940s fashion. He had heavy brows, a blade of a nose, a forehead furrowed from much responsibility or concern, beautifully slicked-back movie-star hair. He had a stern, lean jaw over a prominent chin, all of it permanently sheathed in a shadow of whisker. His voice was taut, sometimes gruff, and he spoke with the deep confidence of authority. He cut a stolid figure in uniform— Don liked uniforms and kept his in top condition—with that weight of command going for him, his easy way with giving orders. He was never Officer Friendly like his pal Les; people approached him less readily, because of the steel in the eyes under his heavy black brows, the muscularity of his frame, the professional set of mouth and face and demeanor.

What people saw was what they got: they just saw a big guy, a cop guy, a guy's guy, and they saw him in the cop personality that was his armor whenever he left the perfect little row house, second from the end, with the porch and the garden and the neat hedged and trimmed lawn at 4937 New Hampshire Avenue NW.

Now he was ready. Gun on, belt on and tight, tie up and tight, new Lucky Strike fired up, last cup of Black Magic terminated, a hot, long duty day ahead of him, memories of the war in the Pacific probably not haunting him, because he wasn't a guy for ghosts and demons, he kissed the fabulous Helen goodbye.

He headed to the Buick, a policeman, a veteran twice, a Lucky smoker, a fisherman, a penny-ante poker champ, a handy man about the house, a rock to the Murphys, a lover to Helen, a father sub to Joan— and a Buick guy.

Don was the type of guy, he sets his mind on something, it stays set. He always bought Buicks. He believed in the Buick. The Buick is the car for him, and his brand loyalty is a symbol of his bundle of other loyalties.

He got in, shut the door, felt the shudder of a well-made unit fitting solidly into another well-made unit, listened to the baby purr to life, and headed down the street, straight down New Hampshire Avenue where it's green and lovely and shady and all the homes are well kept into the unruly city where duty and fate await. There was a block's worth of rise as New Hampshire climbed a hill, then crested out right next to Rock Creek Cemetery, with its wrought iron fences sealing off the legions of the dead from the living. Then downhill, to a big traffic circle; beyond that, New Hampshire widened, four lanes straight to the heart of the federal city.

11. THE GUNS

On the day that they planned to kill the president of the United States, Griselio Torresola and Oscar Collazo dressed carefully. Oscar chose a blue shirt, a white handkerchief, a brown leather belt. His suit was blue and chalk-striped. He wore a pair of brown shoes of a brand called Crusader and, under this sober business or church attire, added one touch of color: green and orange socks.

Griselio was a little more subdued; his socks were gray. His suit was a lawyer's gray chalk-stripe, his shoes were black, his shirt was white, his tie was gray. He had a brown hat, from a company called Adams. His belt was cordovan, an in-between color meant to unify black, brown, and gray. He wore Arrow underdrawers and undershirt.

Then they went sightseeing.

The grounds of the U.S. Capitol were just a short walk from their hotel. No, the trees weren't full of leafy grandeur, and by this time, late in fall, the grass had lost its lush greenness, but still the grounds of the old place were majestic. So the two of them walked it.

What was the mind-set of the two gunmen at this particular moment in their lives? Certainly the trek to the Capitol represents their duality. They were radical operatives, assassins on the hunt, and, in their own view, sacred warriors facing sure death; yet they were also out-of-towners who had a chance to experience a thrilling visit to a thrilling, world-famous locality, and with an hour or so to waste, they couldn't resist the temptation.

Maybe it was a form of therapy. Maybe it was a way of backing off from the reality of the day. For the Capitol grounds, blasé reality to longtime Washingtonians, are a charismatic bit of the theater of government, in and of themselves compelling. Few can walk them without profound emotional engagement; they make you feel humble in the cleverly crafted architecture of political grandeur. They were the emblem of the city on the hill, that dream of democracy, and the structure of the building is itself a powerful communication. The dome encloses, it doesn't divide; it gathers in, it absorbs, it aspires to unite. It lacks the rococo vanity of European capitals, or the stylistic connection to a tradition of aristocratic castlery. It's not dark, gray, or imposing in the authoritarian sense; it doesn't carry the message of absolute power and the will triumphant that is buried in so much civic architecture the world over. It's nice and friendly, somehow. For many Americans it cannot be looked upon without significant emotion.

Weren't they touched by the sense of tradition and history, weren't they impressed by the monumental greatness, didn't the expanse of patriotic message reach them? How could it not? They too were citizens.

But there's another possibility as well. Perhaps Griselio and Oscar looked upon it as an exercise in hypocrisy and used its beauty as a way to rev themselves up emotionally for the action they were about to initiate. Perhaps everything they saw offended them, seemed cheap and tawdry, enraged them. In the dome they saw not inclusion but immense weight, the weight of empire. In the trees and gardens, they saw camouflage of the empire's true meaning. In the vast stairways that lead up, up, and up to the grand mall entrance, they saw the vast distance between their humble, tiny selves at bottom, representative of their humble, tiny island civilization, and the elite rulers so far above them, encased in marble.

It is not known. What is known is that after an hour examining and interpreting the centerpiece of the American legislative system, they hailed a taxi and headed to the White House, where the president lived.

It was the cabdriver who says to them, No, no, he don't live there. See, they're rebuilding the White House.

He took them exactly for what they appeared to be. Two slightly foreign tourists, well dressed, serene in manner and curious in disposition, in for a visit to the capital of the greatest country in the world. No blame can be affixed to this man; he was simply doing his job as professionally as possible and telling his passengers what most of the nation already knew.

Both Griselio and Oscar were slapped in the face by the truth of his statement. That's evident from Pennsylvania Avenue, where from the cab the official mansion of the president of the United States, behind its wrought iron fence and its elaborate ceremonial landscaping, stood. There was even a steam shovel outside. It was all shell. The insides had been torn out, and essentially a new house was being constructed within the facade of the old. This engineering necessity was a long time coming, as the old mansion degenerated further each month, but Harry Truman, with his customary brio and decisiveness, put it into operation. He and his wife, Bess, and their daughter, Margaret, had moved out on November 21, 1948, almost two years earlier.

The driver then helpfully pointed across the street. Griselio and Oscar confronted for the first time in their lives the site of their destiny—just three hours or so before it became their destiny.

They paid the cabbie, got out on the far side of the street, in front of the ornate Executive Office Building, and, amid the hundreds of hurrying midday Washingtonians, looked at what lay before them, across the busy street.

The house they saw was really two houses, one, Lee House, built in 1858, the second, Blair House, in 1824. That is, it's two houses from the outside, a view that gives no sense of its interior complexity, as the two units have long since merged into one, of the intertwined mesh of rooms and stairs and passageways inside, which is why the formerly accurate appellation Blair-Lee House has vanished from usage and the whole structure is known as Blair House. But from the outside, one sees two separate buildings, one late Federal in style, the other mixed Federal and Victorian, symmetrical, elegant, graceful. Both are brick edifices, flat to the avenue, just a few yards off the sidewalk, checkerboarded with windows guarded by shutters. Every line is straight, every angle acute, the only ornamentation a kind of castellated effect of stonework set in the brickwork right at the vertical boundary of the two houses, running the full three stories from roofline to shrubbery. The landscaping is subdued: a couple of leafless trees, a box shrub running at the base of each house, a six-foot shelf of lawn separating the house from the very public sidewalk, a wrought iron fence set in concrete at the boundary of lawn and sidewalk. Each house has a grand, centrally located doorway, reached by marble stairway. A slight imbalance is created by the fact that Lee House is three window rows wide, with the doorway in the dead center of the lower level of three, but Blair House is four window rows wide, so its doorway is set asymmetrically in the second row of windows from the west.

The houses reflect the people who owned them: the first house was built by a prominent physician, Dr. Joseph Lovell, first surgeon general of the United States, an illustrious man who also had time to found the

Army Corps of Engineers, and clearly he had an elegant imagination for balance. But in 1836, he and his wife died within weeks of each other, leaving their eleven children orphaned and the house on the market. Francis Preston Blair, Sr., a Kentucky newspaper publisher and Jacksonian democrat who came to Washington to advance the political fortunes of Andrew Jackson, bought the house. Francis built the second house abutting the first in 1858 for his only daughter, Elizabeth "Betty" Blair, and her naval officer husband, Samuel Phillips Lee. The second house, though larger, seems almost like an afterthought and lacks the warmth and beauty of the first structure. Meanwhile, the Blairs—père et fils—throughout the Civil War were what Washington would recognize as "players": people of power and influence, who moved behind the scenes in the higher circles of government, who gave and attended dinner parties, who knew admirals and generals, senators and secretaries, and, most importantly, who had the ear of the president. Portraits of the Blairs still hang in the house, and the most revealing depicts the man himself, Francis Preston Blair. It was painted by society portraitist Thomas Sully, and no matter what Blair paid for it, it shows the world a homely fellow, Dickensian in his singularity, balding and ascetic with a half-open mouth.

It's still a whale of a house, where parties and conferences were held, where careers were advanced or ended, where gossip was one of the currencies of the day, where politics was played hard amid soft, lovely damask, Asian porcelains and oriental rugs, gleaming wood and severe portraits of great men in goatees and beards. The government acquired it in 1942, when an in-town residence was needed for the parade of visiting dignitaries a world war conjures.

But what Griselio and Oscar see has nothing to do with any of this. They were looking at security precautions, at the obstacles that stand between them and what they want. What they saw does not on the face of it appear particularly imposing. At each end of the 130-odd feet of Blair House frontage at the sidewalk stands a one-man guardhouse, carpentered to imitate the graceful stylings of Lee House with shingles and a peaked roof. In each sat a White House police officer in uniform. At the entrance of Blair House, at the foot of the elegant stairways that are themselves encased in green canvas canopy to give the structure a yet more imposing stylization, stood another uniformed White House policeman. The plainclothes Secret Service officers more or less circulated between these positions, entering and exiting Blair House itself by two basement doors directly behind the guardhouses at the margins of the property. Their headquarters was the Secret Service office on the first floor, directly behind the easternmost guardhouse, with immediate access to both a stairwell down to the basement door and the first-floor hallway that leads to the house's formal entrance on Pennsylvania. Griselio and Oscar could also see that the door to Blair was open and that only a screen door, easily punched through, stands between themselves and what lies within.

It's doubtful whether Griselio and Oscar looked at the men on duty themselves. They wouldn't have noticed Les, content and friendly in his guardhouse, answering the monotonously similar queries of tourists in that pleasant way of his; they wouldn't have noted Toad, the big guy with the take-charge demeanor, the John Wayne type in the bow tie and the light suit and the cool shades, rotating between spots; they wouldn't have paused on the blade-thin, movie-star-handsome younger fellow in the double-breasted coat, Vince, in the same rotation.

Instead, they noted physical details observable from across the street and marked targets. Clearly a guard by the stairway to Blair is a target. Clearly a guard in a guardhouse is a target. Clearly the point of the action is to get into the house. Clearly in the house, sooner or later, they'll find what they're looking for, and they can strike, as long as they have the surprise, before their opponents get over the shock of the assault, and before reinforcements can arrive.

For weeks afterward, the attack plan the two men invented there on the spot will be condemned by the press and other commentators as utterly insane. It will fit neatly into stereotypes of screwball Latino revolutionaries with more guts than sense, who go in with guns blazing like cartoon characters, the whole thing skewing, as time passes, into an opera buffa of stupidity and waste. Yet in retrospect, it seems a pretty sound plan: they understand the necessity of shock and surprise, they understand the importance of suppressive firepower, of the doctrine of fire and movement that is the fundamental small-unit war-fighting theory of most of the world's armies. Given their limited resources—sheer bravado being the most important, Griselio's marksmanship skills being number two—it was a plan that could very well have worked.

The plan was quite elegant. They would approach from different directions down Pennsylvania Avenue, Oscar from the east, Griselio from the west, timed to reach the outer limits of the Blair House frontage simultaneously. Oscar would pass within the first guardhouse and, when he reached the Blair House steps, wheel and shoot the guard at the foot of the steps. Simultaneously, Griselio would fire on the guard in the western guardhouse, then offer covering fire, engaging the men in the eastern guardhouse. This made sense; he was the better shot. Under cover of his fusillade, Oscar would vault the steps to Blair, break through the screen door, and shoot whoever was inside. Total time of operation: three seconds. Griselio would follow him in, but Oscar would lead the way upstairs. The whole point of the plan was to overcome the defenses with a stunning blast of firepower, disorient and dis-coordinate the response, then hunt the president down in Blair. It was Oscar's job to clear the way. Almost certainly the two assassins would have been in the house before any waiting agent would have time to unlimber weapons, which included a Thompson submachine gun. Possibly Oscar would have died there, going down shooting, taking that man with him. That was his job. But the way would have been opened for Griselio, who was determined to bring Don Pedro's war to Washington, D.C. Griselio didn't know that Harry Truman was sleeping in his underwear on the second floor just a few feet from the head of the Blair House stairs he would have climbed, but he would have encountered him in seconds, and done his job.

From that point on, with armed reinforcements arriving from all over the city, it's a rat hunt in the dangerous corridors of Blair House, and many rounds would have been fired. And they had many rounds; each carried three magazines of 9mm ammunition, plus assorted loose rounds. And one senses a certain thing about Griselio: he would have gone down hard, guns blazing, Don Pedro's words screaming from his lips.

But all that was in the future by a few hours. They study, but don't linger long enough to attract attention. Then, the details frozen in their minds, they decided to walk back to the Harris Hotel. It was time for the guns.

For the purpose these guns ultimately served, they were an excellent choice. Griselio knew what he was doing, he had thought it through, applied his considerable raw intelligence and his fury against the problem. They were service automatics of the Third Reich, brilliantly designed, and though one was new and one old in design, both were highly efficient lethal weapons. They were better guns than American policemen had, firing a high-power cartridge (the 9mm) that had extremely convincing terminal ballistics as well as steel-jacket bullets. The 9mm of 1950 struck with an impact of around 365 foot-pounds at close range, while the common police round, the .38 Special, hit with only

250. Moreover, the two automatics could be loaded quickly, with magazines that held seven rounds, while the police revolvers had to be loaded one round at a time and held only six rounds. The triggers on the automatics let off a shot with a single crisp, short pull; the police firearms demanded either a long, slow pull for double-action firing, or the mechanical act of cocking the hammer for each shot with the thumb before the shorter, crisper single-action pull could be managed.

But there was more too. There was an issue of fashion, of taste, of the subjective attributes of firearms that a Griselio Torresola, a very good shot and practiced gun fancier, would know. Clearly, the guns provoked his imagination, but in different ways.

His own Luger, which was a late production run, built in 1939 at the Mauser Oberndorf am Neckar plant in Württemberg, one of 38,500 manufactured with that date code, was a prize. Of all the Lugers snatched up by GIs in blown-out tanks or pillbox rubble or ruined farmhouses, this was one of the best. It's sleek blue with almost no cosmetic imperfections, other than identifying scratches and numbers in the finish performed by law enforcement personnel for establishing chain of custody for evidentiary purposes and also by Truman Library and Museum curators for inventory. It shows almost no wear; it could have left the factory yesterday. The checkered walnut grips are deep, sharp, and grainy; the magazine grip, two little finger-sized dish-outs in the magazine base by which the empty magazine is pulled from the gun, have been polished to a high, silver sheen, giving the gun a glittery highlight that plays off the slide stop, itself also polished a bright silver. It's a beautiful gun, for people who recognize beauty in guns.

Yet there's more to it still. The Luger is one of those rare firearms that have transcended their banality of task as a sidearm and become icons. It is almost universally recognizable, then and now. With its sleek, forward-leaning design, the streamlined rake of its grip, the checked knurl of its toggle action, it's almost art nouveau (it was designed in 1903, the heart of the art nouveau movement). It lingers in the imagination. It's the Nazi officer's gun, the spy's pistol, the detective's weapon; the movies loved it. It's not just a gun; it carries with it all sorts of connotations from popular culture.

Possibly it had a great emotional meaning for Griselio: it was either donated to the party by a Puerto Rican GI or sold to a party member. Possibly the location of this transaction was Puerto Rico, and it was given to Griselio when he was one of Don Pedro's bodyguards in the mountains of Jayuya in 1947 and 1948, probably the happiest time in his life. Or possibly it was acquired in New York or Chicago by gun-buying Nationalists.

The other weapon isn't a trophy or a totem at all. It's a tool. It's a P.38, originally designed by Walther in the mid-1930s as a replacement for the more complex, more precisely engineered Luger, manufactured in 1941 at the Walther factory in Zella-Mehlis, one of 111,000 manufactured that year, during wartime when needs were greater and standards lower. It is by far the more modern of the two, though it doesn't look it, or this one doesn't. It employs two radical features. Unlike the Luger, it is made largely of stamped parts; thus it can be mass-assembled far more inexpensively and practically than the Luger, which demands intensive machining, which is more of a jigsaw puzzle, a matrix of tiny, perfect pieces that must lock together precisely and that is difficult to take down and difficult to reassemble.

The P.38 breaks down into key components and reassembles quickly. It has a revolutionary operating system, much cleverer than the Luger's. Though both are semiautomatic, the Walther is the first service automatic in the world that is of a variant called double-action. This means that once loaded and primed by withdrawing and releasing the slide, the safety functions as a hammer drop mechanism. By snapping it, the hammer is safely lowered to rest against the receiver. At that point, the gun may be fired by pulling the trigger like a revolver, though, like a revolver, the pull is typically hard, long, and gritty—the strength of one's finger is providing the mechanical force by which the hammer is drawn back. After that first hard shot, the gun cocks itself on the power of the detonating cartridge, and the subsequent trigger pulls are short and brisk. One has to learn, therefore, not merely two trigger pulls, but the transition from the long one to the short one. However, if and once mastered, this system is highly efficient, and in fact most of the modern service firearms of today—the Beretta, the SIG, the H&K, the Smith & Wesson—use it. But it is more complex than the Luger, and its learning curve is higher. Its protocols must be made subconscious by many hours of practice. This is the gun that Griselio gave to Oscar, who had never fired a semiautomatic pistol before. That is a decision that will have ramifications.

The aesthetics are something else indeed. This gun, in comparison to

Griselio's own, was a gun without vanity, pretension, or beauty. It was just a gun. It looked like it had been towed behind a tank or dropped from a Stuka.

It was also a gun without much grace or style. Compared to the rakish grip angle of the Luger, the P.38's is almost 90 degrees; the Bakelite, industrialized grip simply distends without angle from the prosaic details of the overbusy receiver. Its genius is internal, unevident to the naked eye. It has all kinds of little devices projecting off it, a safety and hammer-decocker, a slide-stop, a magazine release, so it looks uncommonly busy and intimidating. It has almost no place in popular culture, except that it featured in one 1950s movie, a Sam Fuller shoot-'em-up, *House of Bamboo*, and one of the guys on *I Spy* carried a snub-nose version. Clearly, it had no penumbra of imagination.

Given the year of its manufacture, it had to be a World War II bring-back, which may not disprove later testimony that Griselio bought it for $35 the day before they left for Washington, but certainly brings it into doubt. Clearly Griselio was already experienced enough with it to teach it to Oscar, and most of the guns used by the revolutionaries of 1950 were World War II bring-backs; both Lugers and P.38s were carried in the attack on La Fortaleza.

Now Oscar had to learn to fire the gun. In the hotel room, he contemplated it: its angles without nuance or grace, all squares and planes and no roundness anywhere upon it. It lacked the sleekness and the beauty of Griselio's Luger. More importantly, it lacked a cylinder, which meant it lacked familiarity.

One of the great myths of the attack on Blair House is that Oscar was a complete novice with guns. The American press played with the theme of the crazy Puerto Rican who had never fired a gun before. In fact, Oscar had fired guns before—handguns. He had helped organize Don Pedro's Cadet Corps and had stood alongside Raimundo Díaz Pacheco on the firing range, watching the young men practice their marksmanship and himself taking part now and again. But those guns were revolvers, not semiautomatics. They were the sorts of guns Floyd Boring, Vince Mroz, and Les Coffelt carried, with a cylinder that rotated outward for careful, one-at-a-time cartridge insertion; they were fired by first locking back the hammer, then aiming carefully, then touching off the trigger. That is how Oscar was trained; that is what he knew. And that, a few hours later, is what betrayed him.

But in the hotel room, he faced a semiautomatic pistol of advanced design. Few weapons in the world of 1950 were as well designed as it was for combat purposes. It was probably one of the, if not the very, best combat pistols in the world. However, like any advanced technology, it had to be mastered. It has a complex set of protocols to be accomplished before it can be fired, and if any are done out of order, the gun is dead to the shooter until he goes back and undoes what he has mistakenly done.

Moreover, it was almost impossible to master theoretically. To learn the semiautomatic pistol, one needed two things, primarily: a firing range and lots of ammunition. That is because the power that makes the gun operate is the chemical energy stored in the form of powder in the cartridge; when that is ignited, the dynamic process is initiated and the gun goes through changes as it fires, then cocks itself again. All sorts of things happen: the slide flies back with a thunk, a spent cartridge spins off to the right, the slide slams forward, leaving the hammer cocked and just a little bit of tension in the trigger. One must have some experience with these small dramas before the gun can be effectively used.

For Oscar, even with Griselio's tutelage, that was impossible. Oscar's mind was a methodical instrument, precise, patient. He would try. That is his very *Oscarness,* somehow. The two men sat in Oscar's room in the Harris Hotel. They had walked back, they had eaten lunch.

Oscar held it. It didn't feel like a revolver, which nestles comfortably into the hand. It felt clumsy, because the angle of the grip to the frame is possibly too acute and thus it doesn't point agilely, as would a revolver.

Griselio instructed: the bullets fit into these boxes, called magazines. Griselio took the gun, and handled it with his shortstop's dexterity; he loaded a magazine. Oscar watched as the trimly engineered box, which cants slightly forward at approximately a 60 degree angle, slid into the grip of the pistol until it locked with an authoritative snap.

Does this mean the gun is loaded?

Anyone would say yes. But the answer is no. A cartridge must be chambered, allowed to pass through the magazine into the belly of the gun. Griselio's strong young fingers clamp to the slide of the pistol, yank it back, and let it fly forward with a resounding CLACK! and shudder.

With the mechanical precision of his mind, Oscar studied what had been demonstrated. He understood the principle: the cartridge, contained in the magazine, was allowed to move upward when the slide was pulled backward; then the slide sprang forward, carrying the bullet from the magazine, carrying it like a delicate cargo an inch or so forward, and inserted it precisely in the chamber.

Now it would be ready to fire?

Yes, but here's where this gun is special. Griselio held the pistol, which looks primed for action, its hammer locked backward, ready to spring forward and fire the weapon.

With a blur his thumb stroked against a lever on the left side of the pistol; the hammer falls with a snap, yet the trigger was not touched. The gun does not go bang.

That was the safety. That made the hammer fall but it did not fire the pistol. Now the loaded gun is safe to carry. It will not go bang in your pocket on the streetcar.

He handed the thing over. Oscar tried it. It was dead. The trigger yielded nothing; it just came back a little, then hung up. It was weight in his hand.

With the thumb, push up the lever on the left. That is the safety.

Oscar, with little hands, tried and eventually got the safety lever up.

Now pull.

Oscar pulled, feeling the long grind of the trigger as it fought him, as its leverage drew back the hammer through a double-action pull, and then with a snap, flew forward.

Here Griselio faced the immensity of his task. How to explain to him that after that first long pull, the gun reset itself in the single-action mode, so that subsequent pulls were short, simple releases of a sear set against a ledge. And did it matter? It probably did not.

Griselio determined that the best way for Oscar to carry the gun was with a round in the chamber, the hammer down, the safety off. That way, the only thing Oscar had to do was pull the trigger and he was shooting. The gun would fire as many times as he pulled the trigger, until it was empty, and then the old magazine could be discarded, a new one inserted, and by the simple drop of a lever, it would shoot again. It would be better if Oscar just left the safety out of the process altogether.

But this information was almost impossible to convey in the abstract. It must be seen, felt, experienced. And to learn it in an hour in a hotel room without live fire? Impossible.

But in war, one does what one must. And so for another half an hour, Griselio drilled Oscar. He showed him how to carry the gun in the waistband of the slacks—they didn't have holsters—then pull it out, thrust it toward the target, and pull that trigger the first time, until the gun goes off.

More time was spent on loading. The loading was crucial for the plan: Oscar must keep up a steady stream of fire so that Griselio can advance to the target. Draw, fire, reload. That is the drill. Draw, fire, reload. Remember. Point the gun, pull the trigger. When the gun is empty, drop the magazine by hitting the button on the heel of the butt. Insert another magazine.

In time but two obligations remain. The first is the oiling of the guns. Guns, especially the semiautomatic pistol, run on the principle of metal sliding against metal. It must all be smooth. Lubrication is needed.

Pinching a can of gun oil, Griselio squirted out droplets of lubricating fluid on the slide or toggle rails of each gun, turned each over and deposited a droplet inside the trigger. Then he ran each gun hard, to distribute the oil, the slide or toggle flicking this way. When he was done, the two machines ran slickly; no little dry spots or burrs of metal, no powder deposits, no motes of dust or hair will interrupt the smoothness of their functioning. He wipes them off.

And now the last thing.

He takes out of his valise a bagful of loose 9mm Parabellum cartridges, their war surplus origins denoted by the fact that the FBI will later identify them as German "steel-jacketed bullets." They were purchased for 8 cents apiece in Morton's, a Manhattan gun and sporting goods store. In fact, by their bullet weights (two of 98 grains and one of 124 grains) as determined in later FBI forensic investigation, they may be identified as German SE cartridges (the 98-grain bullets) and a German steel-jacket lead-core bullet (the 124-grain bullet). The SE designation connotes a late World War II modification of bullets made entirely of compressed steel powder. The bullets then were unusually hard and would not deform; they were meant to penetrate, and were originally designed for use in German submachine guns.

They were well prepared, with a total of sixty-nine cartridges. That is a lot of firepower. Griselio began to thread the cartridges into the magazines. It was a matter of finding the right angle of entry, compressing the spring beneath the magazine's follower, as the piece that guides the cartridge into the chamber is called, and sliding the cartridge in to be locked under the lips of the magazine.

That task complete, Griselio took the P.38 and inserted a loaded maga-zine. He yanked the slide back, let it fly forward, and as the slide picked up the bullet and shoved it forward, it did so with a different noise and less velocity. He dropped the hammer via the safety lever with the charac-teristic loud click, then handed the gun to Oscar, along with the two spare magazines.

He loaded his own Luger with the same confidence, pulling back on the toggle, then letting the whole assembly uncoil. He didn't bother with the safety, which in a Luger is poorly placed and difficult to maneuver. He'd just carry the primed pistol in his belt. Then he loaded seven more rounds into his two extra magazines, and put the loose, leftover ammo in his pockets.

The guns were tucked in the waistbands of the trousers, the ties tight-ened, the hands washed clean of oil, a last little run-through of brush to hair, then the coats came on, the mirrors were checked so that each was satisfied with the formal perfection of suit and tie and hat, and the two were off.

What happened next was apparently so odd that it becomes an icon in all accounts of the event, much remarked upon by all its chroniclers. No one gets it and it's another one of those little twists that tilt the event off toward farce.

But not so at all. In fact, the little micro-event perfectly reflects the mind of Oscar Collazo, that orderly, disciplined place, where everything is thought through. It is what made him such a great metal polisher, father, political operative, student, and intellectual.

When the two reached the lobby, Oscar walked alone over to the desk. He asked the clerk if he would be charged extra if he missed the checkout time at 3:00 P.M.

What was he thinking? so many have wondered. He was going to die, or be imprisoned for the rest of his life. Yet he stops to ask about check-out policies at the Harris Hotel. Is that not an indicator of craziness?

He was thinking about the gun.

He had two and a half pounds of loaded automatic pistol under his coat. As a man who had never carried a gun before, he was exquisitely aware of it. He was as self-conscious as it is possible to be. The first time you carry a concealed weapon in public you feel as if it weighs forty pounds, is bright orange, and sticks out of your coat like a feather boa. He assumed all eyes were on it, that it was visible to the world like the mark of Cain. Thus, he needed desperately to reassure himself that it was invisible to outsiders and that he could interact with the public without suspicion. So he engineered a small, stage-managed interaction, just to prove to himself that the gun was not evident, that its presence was not suspected, that his nerves were steady, his voice calm, his manner serene.

Having assured himself, he rejoined his friend, and they went outside to find a cab to Blair House.

12. THE CEREMONY

That Wednesday began with his usual 10:00 A.M. staff meeting, where, among other things, the president expressed his desire to take a short vacation trip after the election. He would go home to vote, then take some time off before returning to Washington. The other topics of discussion were the campaign itself, a speech he had planned for St. Louis on Saturday, and appointments to the National Science Board.

Then, the appointments started. Harry Truman sat in the Oval Office, his suit immaculate, his polka-dot tie tight, his hair combed, and received the first of many guests that day.

It was the Broadway and Hollywood composer Rudolf Friml, who had scored big hits in the 1930s with *Rose-Marie* and *The Vagabond King,* along with eighteen other shows; inevitably he'd moved on to Hollywood and scored over twenty movies. He was a specialist in lush, romantic operettas, and the president, an admirer of his work, had asked him to call whenever he was in town. Friml took him up on it and had come by to pay his respects. Friml wondered why the president was not out playing golf on such a fine day. The president, in his polite, Midwestern way, joshed with the creator of "Indian Love Call" and "Donkey Serenade." The conversation turned to music, one of Truman's deep enthusiasms, and the president probably reiterated an opinion he was well known for.

He liked the old masters, Mozart, Mendelssohn, Beethoven's Fifth, Chopin, Bach too. But he didn't like "noisy" music, he told Friml.

Next it was more serious business. He spoke at length with Delos W. Rentzel, chairman of the Civil Aeronautics Board, followed by Nelson A. Rockefeller, the Standard Oil family scion who was at that moment the head of the International Development Advisory Board. Truman also got the disturbing word from the new CIA chief that thousands of Chinese communist soldiers had joined the North Koreans to fight U.N. troops.

By then, it was almost noon, and the president probably had his best moment of the day.

He left the Oval Office for the Rose Garden, on that day splashed with sun. The warmth—it had risen to 75 degrees on the way to the 80s—permitted an outdoor ceremony. Hedges defined the Rose Garden just as surely as the white trellises, and they were still green from the warm fall, immaculately shaped from careful trimming; the garden had a friendly, less formal feel to it than any of the portrait-laden ceremonial rooms inside the White House.

The event must have meant a lot to a man who knew a great deal about war, having fought one close up and dirty in France in 1918, and who once said under similar circumstances, "I would much rather have that medal around my neck than to be president of the United States."

The medal went to a marine colonel, Justice Marion Chambers, who had performed heroically on Iwo Jima as commanding officer of the 3rd Assault Battalion Landing Team, 25th Marines, 4th Marine Division in his fifth amphibious assault of the Pacific Theater.

His citation read, in part, "Exposed to relentless fire, he coolly reorganized his battle-weary men, inspiring them to heroic efforts by his own valor and leading them in an attack on the critical, impregnable high ground. . . . He was directing the fire of the rocket platoon when he fell, critically wounded."

Chambers, who had retired from the Marine Corps because of his war wounds and now worked as assistant chairman of the Federal Personnel Council and a staff advisor to the U.S. Senate Armed Services Committee, was the sort of man Harry Truman knew and understood. He came from modest beginnings in Huntington, West Virginia, worked his way through Marshall University and the George Washington University Law School, and without connection or favor rose through the Marine Reserve, beginning as a private in 1929. Called to active duty in 1940, he ended up the only reserve officer to command a line battalion.

And the Medal of Honor was only the climax of a storied battle career in the Pacific. He served initially in the fabled Edson's Raiders, the marine commando unit, where he'd won the Silver Star for evacuating wounded and directing a night defense of an aid station on Tulagi. Already seriously wounded, he was a patient at the time!

Later, on Saipan, he suffered blast concussion, but returned to lead his unit there and on Tinian, all as prelude to Iwo Jima. Besides the Medal of

Honor and the Silver Star, he had been awarded a Legion of Merit with Combat V, Purple Heart with two gold stars, the Presidential Unit Citation with three Bronze Stars, the Marine Corps Reserve Unit Medal with two stars, the American Defense Service Medal, the American Campaign Medal, the Asiatic-Pacific Campaign Medal with one silver star (denoting five campaigns), and the World War II Victory Medal.

But the photographs of the event don't show a great warrior; they show a father.

The place is full of bigwigs brought in for the occasion. In fact, the guest list reads like a Who's Who of the Naval Service in Washington in 1950: George C. Marshall, secretary of defense; Francis Matthews, secretary of the navy; Admiral F. P. Sherman, chief of naval operations; General C. B. Cates, commandant of the Marine Corps; and Lieutenant Colonel R. M. Thomas, aide to General Cates.

The Important Men stand around, looking important in their uniforms or suits, most with hands clasped before them, the stern look of higher ranks on their earnest, jowly faces, their hair combed back. Up front of this solemn crowd is another crowd, a crowd of Chamberses, most of them under the age of twelve. Jumping Joe, as he was called because of the funny way he ran—one leg had been shortened as a result of a childhood polio episode—had five children with him as well as his wife, his two sisters and their husbands, his father- and mother-in-law, and some friends. But the kids pushed their way up front: they were Patricia, John, J.M. Jr. ("Mike"), and finally Peter and Paul, who were twins and seven months old.

The White House staff photographer captures an extraordinary moment. There's Jumping Joe, the great hero, all six foot three of him, with a broad smile on his handsome, ruddy face, the Congressional Medal of Honor on a blue ribbon around his neck, kids to the left, kids to the right, and in each arm an unruly boy baby. The twins, Peter and Paul, of course have no idea where they are, what all this is about, and although they're trying to behave, they're just seven months old. One of them, Paul, in Jumping Joe's left arm, has suddenly taken a liking to a certain fascinating thing he sees before him, white, perfect, trim, and most wonderful of all for a curious child, within grasping distance. It happens to be the handkerchief in the suit pocket of the president of the United States. So the child reaches out and grabs the handkerchief, and the president's face lights up with joy at the spontaneity of it all, Colonel Chambers laughs merrily, the older kids show embarrassment.

At that moment the president, in a relaxed and jovial manner, smiled, and gently inserted his fingers into the baby's grasp, delicately removing the hand from the handkerchief. It was just a moment of sweet human contact in the otherwise rigorous ceremony.

After the citation and the presentation, Colonel Chambers spoke briefly. His daughter, Pat, many years later, remembers her father saying something like "This is for my men." It was not a phony, let-me-thank-the-little-people comment, but represented something Chambers truly believed. "Dad always felt that the award was given to his unit, that he was representing them." It was a typical moment of modesty—Truman would have liked it so much, because his own style was modest to a fault—from a man who later told his grandson, "You are never to talk about my accomplishments or bring them to the attention of others."

After that ceremony, the president hurried back to the Oval Office and there met Sir Anthony Eden, later prime minister of Great Britain but then a well-known diplomatic figure, and the British ambassador, Sir Oliver Franks. Certainly the conversation veered toward Field Marshal Sir John Dill, a British general and member of the Combined Chiefs of Staff, who had died in Washington during the war and was the twenty-second foreigner to be buried in Arlington National Cemetery. That afternoon at three, Truman was scheduled to appear at Arlington to unveil a statue of Sir John.

The final appointment before lunch was with W. Stuart Symington, the fellow Missourian, if a transplanted one (born in Massachusetts, he was raised in Baltimore and moved to St. Louis as a young man, where he had a brilliant business career). Symington was chairman of the National Security Resources Board and would later become a distinguished senator from Missouri, serving for over twenty years. He was an old political ally of Truman's.

At one o'clock, surrounded by a protection detail from the White House office of the Secret Service, the president returned to Blair House for lunch with Bess, where, in the casual intimacy of a long, happy, and secure marriage, he probably waxed sentimental about the heroism of Justice Chambers.

After lunch, it was time for a nap.

13. INDIAN SUMMER

At 2:20 Les was frying. He'd been on duty since 8:20, as he called in from Post D-5 to the Army Signal Corps phone room right off the White House Police squad room in the East Wing of the White House, and very professionally someone had logged him in on the duty roster of the White House Police. That meticulous document would trace his progress, hour by hour, from station to station around Blair House. At 9:23 he moved to Post 2, at 10:19 to Post 3, at 11:21 to Post 4, at 12:24 to Post 1, and at 1:20 back to Post 5. Joe Downs was just this second back with the groceries. So there Les was in the dog-house, D-5, his world the little slice of the 1600 block of Pennsylvania Avenue; he could see across to the wedding cake of the Executive Office Building. And he wasn't even supposed to be here today! He could have been waxing his Nash, cleaning his guns for deer season, helping Baby with important errands.

That was Les. He was a trouper. He sat there, hour after hour, while presenting his best face to the public, locked in the thing called duty. It's a humble calling, a far cry from any sort of heroism, but that's Les too. He abided. He was strong. He carried, he suffered, he endured. He put up with all manner of absurdity.

Excuse me, Officer, is that the Smithsonian? he must hear ten times a day.

No, ma'am.

But it looks like the Smithsonian.

They were inevitably asking about the Court of Claims at the corner of 17th and Pennsylvania, right next to Blair. It was red brick and big and looked like a castle and people get confused a lot. But he'd patiently explain to them that the Smithsonian was on Constitution, a mile or so away, and give directions.

His shirt was sodden under the heavy coat, and here, in the little guardhouse, the air was still and dense. His heavy wool pants assailed him. Another White House policeman later said, "You were hot with sweat running down the crack of your rear end, and it was hot. You had to wear a tie. Everything was neat. You had to wear your cap at all times." Les sat on a straight-backed wooden chair, next to the Signal Corps phone on the wall to the right. The chair, on a box, elevated him; he could see out the windows cut in the box as well, so it wasn't completely dark.

His gun must have felt as if it weighed a ton that late in the duty day. But even if it was over 80 degrees, there weren't any mosquitoes and that was a blessing. In the August summertime in Washington, it can be terrible with the heat as well as the constant hum of the bugs. Something about the town being built on a swamp all those years ago.

And suddenly, in his limited vision, a man slid before him as if out of a dream. He was a handsome little devil, and he was wearing a hat and a suit of somber aspect, a churchgoer's suit.

As Les sat, the sun was at about two o'clock in the sky, and since it was November, it was low, just above the skyline of the buildings along Pennsylvania. And it was a bright sun. That meant it cast shadows. When the little man stood before Les, he cast a shadow across him, like a biblical premonition.

It was cooler where Vince was. At 2:20 his rotation has deposited him in the little Secret Service office on the first floor of Blair, the southeast corner. It was a ratty place: the government spends its money only where the money can be seen and is part of the luster of the image of a great and magnificent organization for all the public to see. Behind closed doors, where the real work takes place, you can expect grim plain walls, beat-up old furniture, the smell of storage and usage, the general dullness of a place where people go and work and watch the years pass. It looked like the junior officers' wardroom on a ship, and Vince had been in plenty of those, a combination workspace and relaxation space. This is where the phones were; this, modest as it is, this little dumpy room, this would be headquarters of the Secret Service detail at Blair House.

Vince has been through the rotation once already, been on the door, been at the two guardhouses, been at the usher's office just inside Blair's door, and now he's here, on what passes for a break in the duty day. He's sitting there with taciturn Stu Stout, and Stout, an older guy, hasn't said a word. That's Stout. Vince looked at his watch. The Boss, according to schedule, was taking a nap. A break in the day is coming, because at 2:30, the Boss will be awakened and at 2:50 the Secret Service agents will slide into the seats of a presidential Lincoln next to the Man himself via a back door to Blair used in all transfers of the chief executive to another location, and the vehicle, plus a follow-up, will head out to Arlington.

It was 2:20, his watch says, and—say, what's that?

Big, gruff Don Birdzell had the worst duty station. He was standing, at a sort of parade rest, next to the ten marble steps that lead up to Blair. He had no place to sit, and in the withering heat, he can't have been comfortable. At least, he could move side to side on the stairway to position himself in the shade of the canopy as the sun rotates across the sky—White House police officers were not military rankers, like the guards at Buckingham Palace who must stand at full, steely-eyed parade rest over their full duty tour—but still he's got to maintain a solid professional deportment, unpleasant in extreme weather. At this moment, the only thing Donald could know was the heat, the discomfort, the length of the duty day yet before him, possibly the ache in his legs, the harshness of thirst, and sweat collected inside the heavy coat he is wearing. To his immediate east, about twenty feet though shielded from his vision by the Blair stairways, a wrought iron fence, and some vegetation, he knew his Secret Service supervisor, Floyd Boring, had stopped to chat with Joe Davidson. He couldn't see them because he happened to have moved a little to the left of the stairway, and had pivoted, so that he was facing the building. So neither did he see the little man with the jug ears come up behind him. He didn't know that the little man had a loaded pistol and was about to draw it. He didn't know that, by all that's fair in the world, he was already a dead man.

Besides Toad and Vince and Les and Donald, there were three other agents and police officers at Blair House at 2:20 P.M., November 1, 1950. They were Joseph Davidson, White House policeman, and the already mentioned Secret Service agent Stewart Stout and White House policeman Joseph Downs. There was also one man in the basement and one man in the back of the house, well out of the course of the action about to unfold.

At this precise moment, each was attending to duty in his stolid, unspectacular way. For example, Joe Downs always has the grocery detail. Every day he went to a grocery store in plainclothes and bought food for that night's dinner. Each time he went, unpredictably, to a different store; the idea was to preclude any attempt at poisoning of the chief executive, and it's possibly an indication of how sluggish the bureaucratic mind is that in its wisdom, the service retained control of the shopping, as if poisoning were a particularly menacing threat, whereas the president now lived and worked in a house that was but seven feet from a heavily traveled public thoroughfare, and the glass was not bulletproofed or anything. Anyone with a grenade could have killed Harry Truman in a flash, and there were plenty of grenades floating around, as bring-backs from the war. But that possibility never occurred to anybody, any more than the possibility that armed men would try and shoot their way in did. They had the poisoning menace defeated, however.

So Downs was just returning from the grocery run, he'd chatted briefly with Les Coffelt, and turned off Pennsylvania at the far end—the western end—of the Blair House complex and was headed in the basement door at that end of the house.

Then there was Stewart Stout. You would never forget Stu Stout if you saw him; in fact you'd be so impressed you'd say, "Mr. Hoover, sir, it's a pleasure to meet you." For Secret Service Agent Stewart Stout bore a remarkable resemblance to J. Edgar Hoover, the famous chief of the FBI. He had that bull neck, that squat bulldog's face, those dark eyes, and he didn't talk much.

Chance, as played out by the push, had deposited Stu Stout in the Secret Service office next to Vince Mroz, down the hallway in Blair. There he'd be able to go to the front door or down the steps. He sat, in his suit, aware that at least theoretically he was a last line of defense. In this duty, however, he was not alone. A monolithic piece of furniture that looked banal from the outside actually contained, behind its locked door, a gun rack, and in the gun rack was, beside a number of short-barreled riot guns, one Thompson submachine gun. This is a formidable piece of ordnance. That's why gangsters loved it—it starred in the St. Valentine's Day Massacre—but in military modification, it was the weapon of choice of all the army and Marine Corps point-of-contact units: paratroopers and rangers carried them all through Europe, and the marines used them particularly well in the savage late war in the Pacific. Thompsons were also deployed most terrifyingly at the Ponce Massacre, in Ponce, Puerto Rico, in 1937. But the gun doesn't know to what use it's being put: it's simply a brilliantly designed if somewhat heavy fast-firing, powerful, reliable, and extremely lethal tool, unleashing a heavy 230-grain .45 bullet that will punch through nearly anything made of flesh and blood. As were all the agents, Stout had been well trained in its usage and its deployment; he could get to it fast, get it loaded and cocked and into play fast.

At the easternmost guard post, White House policeman Joseph Davidson was chatting with his boss for the shift, Floyd Boring. Toad roamed the outside of Blair House, moving from post to post, keeping up with the boys, keeping their spirits up, teasing, joshing in that special Toad way. Davidson was a favorite of his, because Davidson was the only bachelor on the Security Detail, and a macho wit like Floyd can have a great deal of fun with an unmarried guy.

In fact, exactly at 2:20 P.M., as Oscar Collazo has ambled by Davidson's eastern guardhouse and turned to face Officer Birdzell, Toad was tweaking Davidson about the pretty girls on the streets.

Davidson laughed.

But at that moment they heard a click, sharp and metallic. Only one thing on earth makes a click like that. Their eyes flew to the source of the noise to discover a drama twenty feet away. A small man in a suit seemed to be addressing Don Birdzell, whose back was turned. Then Floyd noticed what was in the little man's hand. It was a pistol. At first Floyd thought the man must be an old friend, one of Donald's war buddies, and he's got a battle trophy he wants to show off. That would be the only explanation for a pistol in a man's hand in front of Blair House in the middle of the afternoon. It seemed to make sense, even if it didn't, for just the smallest sliver of time, and then the gun went off.

14. THE BIG WALK

scar and Griselio, on what they believed to be the last day—the last hour, the last minutes—of their lives, got out of the cab at the corner of 15th Street and Pennsylvania Avenue at around 2:12 P.M. That was directly across from the Treasury, and by another of those coincidences that illustrate the intertwining of Puerto Rico and the United States, they found themselves in front of the Riggs National Bank, an imposing, cathedral-like structure whose Greek Revival architecture was designed to suggest it too was part of the government as it sat there across from the Treasury. The Riggs Bank was known for its trust department and its service to the very richest of Americans over the years; it was also credited with financing the Mexican War. This small fact is worth noting only in the historical oddity department because a scion of the illustrious Riggs family of Maryland, Colonel E. Francis Riggs, had been the appointed chief of the Insular Police in Puerto Rico in 1933. An ex–military man and Yale graduate, he was on his way home from church in San Juan and stopped to investigate some errant gunshots. Two young Puerto Rican men, Elias Beauchamp and Hiram Rosado, both members of the Nationalist Cadet Corps and presumably (though not verifiably) acting under orders from Albizu Campos, approached the unarmed man, and shot him three times. Death was instantaneous and so was arrest. The two Puerto Ricans were hauled off to the police station and—here's a treasured trope from less enlightened days of law enforcement—were "shot while trying to escape" in a back room, less than an hour after their action. It was a bloody day in San Juan. The episode was yet another in the bitter stew of acrimony between Americans and Puerto Ricans, as many in the big country thought justice had been done to assassins and many on the small island thought it but another example of totalitarian oppression, resulting in the martyrdom of two heroes.

There's no evidence that Oscar and Griselio connected these dots; they had other matters on their minds. Still, Oscar was a reader; he knew history, and the connection may have struck him as he got out of the cab, if he hadn't noticed it on the previous trip. Maybe something fluttered through his mind, some connection with a political-historical past that was of help to him to get through that which he had determined had to be gotten through.

Now their assignation with political violence was but minutes away. One was twenty-five; one was thirty-six. One was handsome and beloved; the other was a family man with a reputation for self-control. One had physical gifts and was quick and daring; the other was a sedentary fellow who loved best of all to settle in with a good encyclopedia after a long day at the buffing wheel. But neither was mentally disturbed. They were simply profound believers. They were animated by a cause so passionate it drove them toward their deaths and neither of them flinched.

Griselio was probably the more aggressive psychologically. He would have had physical confidence. He was well trained. As far as the actual mechanics and physics of the act they'd planned, he was the most adept. He was younger, probably hotter-headed, and lacking an older man's wisdom, more committed by passion. He knew his brother and sister were shedding blood or had shed blood already and he had to live up to their example. Moreover, he could not let down Don Pedro, the man who had guided his life.

Oscar—well, who can see into Oscar? Not even Oscar could see into Oscar, and his later accounts of the event were distressingly bland. He always played his cards close to his vest. At this moment he gave his life up to God and to what he viewed as his country. He cannot have been confident; the gun was still largely mysterious to him and he must have had great anxiety about operating it with the necessary efficiency. But did he think of his wife, of his two stepdaughters, of his own daughter and what the effect of his actions would be upon them? Did he think of how they would get along without a breadwinner, how they would be stigmatized here in America, where they'd chosen to live? No evidence exists, except his rather passive-aggressive expression in action. He was a man, like Griselio, who was sold.

They seem also not to have the subtly competitive relationship by which each goads the other, each is afraid of letting the other down or not living up to the other, and so they do things as a tandem they could not do individually. That's a fairly common criminal pattern, but Oscar and

Griselio were not psychologically intimate enough for it to come into play. It's a long-term, carefully evolved relationship; the two never socialized and knew each other only through politics. Their families didn't know each other, at least not beyond the acquaintanceship stage. Essentially, other than through their political selves, they were strangers to each other. If Oscar knew Griselio, it was only in memory, of a young kid running around in the fabled purity of Jayuya. As for Griselio, Oscar can only have been a dimly seen older fellow, not a part of his set of young hotheads, anxious to fight, anxious for change.

Perhaps to calm nerves or perhaps for sound tactical reasons, they decided to take another casual stroll by Blair House. This was for last-minute checks, to see if anything was radically different from before. The inspection produced immediate results: nothing is different. There'd been no alert, nobody was on special guard, it was the same: four men outside, three in uniforms, one in a suit, paying attention yet also in the numbness that stationary duty necessarily produces. Griselio and Oscar knew they had surprise and shock on their side as well as history.

Then they returned to the corner of 15th and Pennsylvania. It was time. No other thing was left to do.

According to their plan, they separated. Griselio crossed Pennsylvania, turned west, passed in front of the Treasury, the White House, and the Executive Office Building on that side of the street. He very carefully walked at a normal pace, so as not to attract attention.

In a way, it must have been harder on Oscar. His approach to Blair was much shorter. It had to be timed so that his arrival from the east coincided exactly with Griselio's from the west. Thus he had to dawdle while Griselio manfully strode onward. He moseyed along the north side of Pennsylvania, clearing the bank and the buildings on the eastern side of Lafayette Square; then he came to Lafayette Square itself, a joyous splurge of imperial splendor in the heart of downtown Washington, a splendid, be-statued park directly across from the White House, its trees and benches and equestrian statuary giving scale and harmony to the elegant building across the way, alas marred this day by the presence of a steam shovel out front. In Lafayette, the trees still had their leaves even if the grass was brown, but the sun was bright, the breeze warm, the park full of citizens enjoying the weather. Meanwhile, he would have seen the center occupied, amid a circle of cannon, on a marble pedestal, by General Lafayette, in the saddle of his rearing steed, waving a jaunty tricorn at the president of the United States, or, that is, at his white, splendid house one-hundred-odd yards away across Pennsylvania. Oscar had a fondness for American revolutionary history—Washington was a favorite of his—so he would have known who the French general was, and how he came to the aid of the struggling revolutionary state in 1778 with his brio and his dash and his courage. Oscar didn't have dash or brio, only courage.

He also didn't realize that the general on the beautiful copper mount in Lafayette Park wasn't Lafayette, but Jackson. The statue of General Lafayette, obsidian black and not mounted on horseback, nestled obscurely in a glade of trees at the park's southeast corner. In any event, Oscar too soldiered on, slowly, adjusting his speed so that it was well under Griselio's more forceful stride as it covered the longer distance.

The street that separates Lafayette Square from the block on which Blair House is situated is Jackson Place. Oscar at last crossed it, possibly noting a bank of swank mansions along its way that matched, more or less, the elegance of Blair House. Or maybe he didn't. It was so close now.

As he approached Blair House, he could see his compatriot ahead. Griselio had reached 17th Street, crossed it, passed by the rococo Court of Claims, and was fast approaching the western guardhouse just 135 feet away.

Adjusting again, Oscar sped up and his little feet ate up the distance. In seconds he was by the guardhouse where two men, one in uniform, one in suit, bow tie, and sunglasses, chatted amiably. Then he was at the canopied base of the stairway.

Did a signal pass between him and Griselio, now just thirty-five feet away and edging up to the western guardhouse? Eyes lifted, a wink, a nod, just a glimpse of human eye contact? Nobody will ever know.

Oscar, just inside the canopied stairway to Blair House, turned to face the back of a large man in police uniform. There was an awful moment of awkwardness. One can imagine the hammering of Oscar's heart, the heaviness of the fact that he was leaving, at that instant, the known world far behind. He reached into his jacket, his fingers closed on the butt of the P.38 and he pulled it out, fumbling to do the right thing—let's see, cock, not cock, what about the safety, ah, let's see, have I got it right?—and thrust it awkwardly at the cop's broad blue back, heard but did not understand a sharp click that made the gun shudder ever so slightly.

Then Oscar Collazo pulled the trigger.

15. OSCAR

O scar was born into paradise, as he remembered it. For Oscar paradise was a small town called Florida, in central Puerto Rico. He was the baby of a very large family, fourteen children by Eduardo Collazo Gago and Trinidad López Dávila. Oscar was born there January 20, 1914, and named after a character in a French novel, as his mother was a voracious reader who told stories to her children every night.

Paradise was a forty-acre farm, and the lord of paradise was Eduardo Collazo, who commanded fifty workers on this place, the major crop being coffee. In Oscar's mind it was a model of what Puerto Rico could be: lush, self-sustaining, a haven of equality and labor and happiness, producing coffee for the world. It ended when Oscar was five and his father sold the farm and then died.

Many years later his daughter, Zoraida, would relate Oscar's version almost verbatim. "The farm was lost," Zoraida said, "because the Americans came in, and after the Americans came two big hurricanes. After those two big hurricanes came the American loan companies lending money to these farmers, and of course the next year it was one hurricane one year and the next year another hurricane; next year they couldn't pay the loan company, and they were going to repossess it. So my grandfather sold it. He didn't lose it. He sold it, and what he had left after he paid the loan he bought a house in Manatí where he died." But one of Oscar's sisters told the redoubtable *New Yorker* reporter Robert Donovan that Eduardo Collazo had health problems, that managing the farm became impossible, implying therefore that the collapse of the farm was subsequent to and a function of natural causes, that is, Eduardo's health. It could not have been avoided, and no outside forces were involved.

Thus was Oscar cast out. Actually, he wasn't cast that far out. His oldest brother, now the man of the fractured family, took him in. Various other siblings went to various other relatives, but Oscar went to live with

Salvador in Jayuya. It was Salvador who first taught Oscar to love his land and his people with the intensity he would feel for the rest of his life.

Ah, Jayuya! Font of revolution! Linchpin of nationalism! Breeder of Torresolas and Canaleses and Irizarrys and Marín Torreses and other revolutionaries!

Yet when Oscar moved to Jayuya, Griselio was not born. Moreover, not much was happening; Jayuya was a sleepy mountain town nestled in a valley along a stream; it was approachable only by more than three hours of hard negotiation with roads that crisscrossed through the forested slopes as they climbed. But maybe it wasn't so far from revolution as it might have seemed. There's a theory that coffee growers make the best revolutionaries, in the way that sheepherders make the best soldiers. Sheepherders, as the great military historian John Keegan puts it in *The Face of Battle*, are used to staying up all night in the worst weather, to moving suddenly and unpredictably, to working long hours at the point of exhaustion, and to killing swiftly and surely, all prerequisites for battle. Coffee growers, for their part, tend to be small-time entrepreneurs, men used to living by their wits and labor. They are not employees, they are not anonymous masses; they have a strong sense of self-identity, of making a living off a free market and their own hard work. Moreover, the near vertical nature of the landscape on which they live and work tends to reward hardy self-reliance and discipline; if you rise at four every morning and go off by yourself, climb a mountain in rain or fog or killing heat, and make a living off such an enterprise, then you don't need an empire to tell you what to do, what language to speak, what flag to salute, and what heroes to worship. Thus coffee culture is a natural breeding ground for rebels.

So that was in the air then, even if Griselio would not be born until 1925. Moreover, Griselio was a country boy, from the valley of the Three Peaks, a barrio—in Spanish, the term has the neutral meaning of "community"—called Coabey, six miles outside city limits. Oscar, meanwhile, eleven years older, was a city boy, or rather a town boy. Salvador ran a little grocery store next to his house in Jayuya, and he rapidly put Oscar to work—in Puerto Rico, nobody didn't work; times were too tough not to work. He began working for his brothers and sisters in their businesses. At first, he did little errands and cleaned up their shops. As he grew, they gave him more important tasks such as clerk and salesman. Business had an appeal for Oscar. Once he even started his own, but a lack of money made him give it up.

He roamed the countryside, it is said, and so it is quite possible that he wandered east to Coabey, whose soil he would later call "sacred," and there encountered the valley of the Three Peaks, where green mountains rise like sentinels from the lush valley and one has a sense of being enclosed in the bosom of God. There he began to understand liberty as he watched mountain birds fly free. His world was quiet and lovely and magical, blessed with the simplicity of rural living.

And he would have seen the big gray house where Blanca Canales lived, where she taught, where she ran her salon and gathered all the Coabey children to her to speak of freedom. She would not meet Don Pedro until 1928, but she would have feelings so profound and so important she could not help but express them, and she could not help but create a culture in which Don Pedro's more formal constructs would grow like wildflowers. Her cousins the Torresolas would have been there too, running all over the place, blond and beautiful kids with strong European heritage (Griselio's sister Angelina Torresola, now eighty-nine years old, looks like a Roman aristocrat). Others too swarmed to the place, including Carlos Irizarry and Griselio's older brother, called Elio. Certainly Oscar would have heard of Blanca Canales and her set because she was that well known. The social worker, the woman of position, who came back home after a college education—unusual among Puerto Rican women then—and gave back to her people. But he was so busy and his own feelings were so unarticulated and he was, after all, an outsider, it's extremely doubtful that he came under her aegis. That would happen much further down the road, in 1932, when Don Pedro Albizu Campos became the magic force by which all these disparate folks were brought together and unified; it would also be the event that left Griselio and Oscar shooting it out with Floyd Boring and Les Coffelt in 1950.

But by seventeen, Oscar had run out of options. It was 1931: high Depression. No work. Markets depressed the world over. In Jayuya, no prospects. Possibly that's the real exile that haunted him, for he loved Jayuya, enough so that when he died, he directed that half his ashes be spread across its valleys and peaks and creeks by the mountain winds. Possibly he intended that some of them would come to lie in the cemetery up the mountain slope to the north, where Griselio, Elio, and Doris now rest.

In any event, as would Griselio in 1948 and as did hundreds of thousands of his countrymen in the next years, he emigrated to the United

States. He was a little ahead of the curve; the bulk of his countrymen would make the trip in the 1940s and 1950s, when increased plane travel made it easier than taking the slow boat to New York, in steerage, a five-day voyage. He would have arrived bedraggled, exhausted, impoverished, and, one suspects, seasick. Hardly the beginning of a great crusade.

Yet this is a moment to conjure with, for it's one thing that bound Griselio to Oscar and Oscar to Griselio and that whole generation of Puerto Rican immigrants to one another. It's a thing gringos wouldn't quite understand, because when they themselves, centuries ago, immigrated, they reversed the process: they went from the squalor of an old world to the splendor of a new world. For the Puerto Ricans especially, the journey was more depressing: they went from splendor to squalor. They went to the Big Apple.

The New York, New York that's a hell of a town, where the Bronx was up and the Battery down, eluded them, except via the bitter low rungs of the service economy. The town where Fred and Ginger tripped the light fantastic: they swept up the garbage after the shoot. The Algonquin Circle, where wits and wags threw pearls of polished venom at each other: no Puerto Ricans invited, except for the busboy who policed the martini glasses with Dorothy Parker's smeared-lipstick cigarette butts in them. The New York Athletic Club, where the old Irish Catholic politicos who ran the city took their steam baths: the Puerto Ricans gathered the sweat-soaked towels. Toots Shor's, Lindy's, the "21" club: busboys and dishwashers in all those places. Ernie H. smacking Max Eastman in the nose with a book before the horrified eyes of Max Perkins at Scribner's on Fifth: Manuel emptied Mr. Perkins's wastebasket at 3:00 A.M. that morning. "Oh, what a beautiful morning/Oh, what a beautiful day!" Picking up the garbage in the bleak Broadway dawn. All that, literary New York, ironic New York, theatrical New York, artistic New York, political New York, musical New York: not for them unless it was with a broom in hand.

What the new arrival—particularly one from Jayuya—must have experienced immediately was a sense that the fundamental nature of the universe had changed utterly: it had gone from green and balmy, blue-skied, sweet-scented, beflowered, and crusted with mountains tall enough to inspire but small enough to climb, to the city: dark, brackish, dangerous, full of angry noise and biting octane fumes, with many, many ways to make a mistake, and very few ways to make a buck. As with every immigrant population, the only way out is up, and the only way up is to start at a bottom so low it's invisible to everyone else. The available jobs stink: they're the jobs the Irish and the Italians have had and passed on to a next generation of newcomers, clean-up jobs, service jobs, jobs shoveling shit, hauling garbage, scraping food. Jobs that somehow seem always to involve the glutinous secretions of life that human beings of a certain economic stature would prefer not to look upon or to acknowledge anymore. When you reach a certain income level, you can shield yourself from the reality of your own biology; let the Puerto Ricans deal with the reality of your biology. That's their place in the universe.

And so Oscar enters the great American pecking order at the absolute bottom: he was a dishwasher and kitchen helper at the Army and Navy Club, 30 West 44th Street. He got the job via the intercession of his sister Ana Reveron, already living in New York; he roomed in her house and through her husband, who worked at the club, picked up the job.

Professional dishwashing is not pleasant. The water is very hot, as is the atmosphere, which is full of drifting steam. The cooks are gods: you are scum. Do you like being yelled at? Good, that helps, because you get yelled at a lot. Do you like working in a medium of other people's rejected food—half-eaten piles of mashed potatoes soaking in cold gravy, gobbets of inedible fat, squished green beans, gnawed bones, maybe a little knot of rejected gristle here or there, and say, what about that salad bowl that turns out to conceal a little spew of vomitus? Get used to it. Do you like grease? Grease is everywhere. It clings to the surface of all things and you never get away from it. You can scrub till your fingers fall off and it never goes away.

Who could take this for long? Only the most hopeless. Oscar leaves New York after seven months, with a bitter taste in his mouth and a memory of life as the lowest of the low. It is now 1932.

A hot night in San Juan. It is April 16, 1932. The bright stars spatter the sky, forming bands of radiance, pinwheels, pricks of distant white flame. A breeze from the nearby Atlantic stirs the heavy palm trees. A crowd has gathered, and a nondescript young man fits anonymously into a crowd of listeners at a political rally in Plaza Baldorioty, a short distance from the capitol building. The issue seems to be the adoption of a territorial flag for Puerto Rico, a single white star on a blue triangle, the same flag that has been used by advocates of independence to represent the nation of

Puerto Rico. A bill to implement this change is before the legislature. Speeches, some shouts and cheers, the invocation of patriotic names such as José de Diego, an earlier advocate of independence, gives some sense of purpose in the night, but nothing unusual seems to hang in the air, and the young man is quickly bored.

But then the crowd stirs. Oscar redirects his attention to the podium, where a new speaker has approached the microphone. The young man has never seen such a figure before. The speaker is small, but strangely charged, as with electricity. His eyes are dark and piercing, his cheekbones sharp, his arms long, his fingers elegant. A murmur runs through the crowd. "El Maestro," someone whispers, and the description fires through the crowd like an electric current, coming simultaneously to all lips. The term "maestro" captures exactly his particular penumbra, and he seems somehow like a great pianist, about to sit down at his instrument and unleash the titanic fury of God above as harnessed by a genius like Beethoven or Mozart—a teacher, a master. The Master. The Master is here.

Oscar leans forward, as the little fellow at the rostrum begins to speak. He is wearing a kind of dark coat that envelops his body, a white shirt and a dark blot of bow tie; suspenders hold up his pants and he looks like a lawyer, and so it's no surprise at all that he *is* a lawyer. When he speaks something magical happens. His words have the force of powerful music. He finds a cadence. His language is direct, yet lyrical. He aspires to touch the soul and he does. The young man feels himself being absorbed somehow, yet also enlightened. He has never heard such a message before, but only felt its rightness in his heart somehow even if he himself could never articulate it with the power, the glory, the grace, and the beauty of this speaker.

Astonishingly, the orator sees through this sham of a political initiative. He denounces it as foolish, the work of tiny minds that would not face the real problem of the island. He considers the bill an insult to Puerto Rico's national flag, the flag the Nationalists use as their party's standard.

And he, this little man, he would face that. It is *them*, he declares. Down there. Those men. They claim to represent us, but they represent the yanquis. They represent our oppressors. They buy us off with gestures and think that will satisfy us. But we know what must be done. We know that we must liberate ourselves. We were illegally invaded by a conqueror who changes the name and the language of our nation and who exploits our labor and steals our land and who defiles our women and drives us from our land. We must go into a bitter exile in a far, dirty city to survive at all.

Oscar's reaction is profound.

Yes, that was it. Our land was stolen. Conditions were engineered cleverly so that we could not meet interest payments on loans taken out under complicated procedures, and if a crop failed or did poorly, it was forfeit. And thus did our land, where we had been born and died, where we had sweated and bled, where we had brought forth sustenance for family and nation, that land was taken from us, and the people in that building, they are the ones that made it possible and profited from it.

The speaker continued, reading out the names of senators who supported the offending legislation. "What shall we do?" he asked.

The crowd had come alive. It was an animal itself, savage with pain and hunger, needing only a leader to direct it. "Let's hang them," shouted the crowd.

And the leader leaned forward and he directed.

He gestured dramatically with his long arm toward the building where the legislators worked.

"To the capitol!" he screamed. *"To the capitol!"*

The speaker had them. The fact that the legislators were presumably home, enjoying a nice after-dinner liqueur, seems not to have occurred to anybody. Crowds, or rather mobs, which is what this assembly had been alchemized into by the philosopher's stone of Albizu Campos's rage and rhetoric, are notably not rational.

This one surely wasn't. It rolled violently through the streets as it stormed the half mile to the capitol, tearing down a wooden fence to arm itself with pickets as clubs or swords, prying up bricks and stones from the street to fire off as missiles on any group foolish enough to try to dissuade them. Albizu Campos himself led them, from the back of a car. And somewhere in the massed, anonymous madness, the dispirited Oscar Collazo was swept up, his imagination taken, his mind liberated, his power felt for the first time.

As it happened, the Puerto Rican Senate was holding a night session.

At the domed, white-marble building that housed Puerto Rico's form of representative government they ran into a crew of policemen hastily assembled to stop them. It wasn't much of a contest. The mob surged by the cops and pushed its way into the edifice and began to charge up stairways and down hallways, looking for legislators to hang. Alas, they were stopped finally not by police or National Guard action or by the wisdom of elders or the arrival of sunlight, but by a stairway.

As the mob rushed up a marble stairway from the first floor to the second, the location of the legislative chamber, they faced a second phalanx of police, who halted them at the top of the stairs; meanwhile more protestors clambered up the stairs and with that, the railing gave way: with a thunderous detonation, the thing shattered, and down they went. One can easily imagine the disaster. Clouds of dust filling the air like a vapor. A moment of silence after the calamity. Then, slowly, moans and even more slowly motion. People begin to pick themselves up, stunned into disbelief. They wander about with befuddled faces, bumping this way and that in the fog, wretchedly holding broken arms, stanching the spurt of bright blood from head wounds. The cries become general.

Albizu Campos is immediately arrested as a leader of the riot.

As police, then municipal rescue workers begin to arrive, then ambulances and volunteers, the results are not pretty. Most seriously, there has been a death. A man—his name was Rafael Manuel Suárez Díaz—died in the collapse, and several others were hurt.

But three significant things had happened. The Nationalists had gained their first martyr, they had put themselves on the political landscape in a big way and established the ardency of their desire and the quality of their leadership, and, finally and not least significantly, Oscar Collazo had found his life's work.

The disappointment of the election was the next station of the cross for young Oscar Collazo. He quickly volunteered to help the party and the master, then in the democratic phase of their existence. The election was coming up, and Don Pedro had put himself up for the post of senator-at-large. But to be on the ballot, the Nationalist leader had to first collect 28,000 signatures, and so an army of enthusiastic young people was quickly assembled. Oscar was an infantryman in this crusade; he went from town to town, all across the island, to collect signatures. In one of his stops, he found himself back in Jayuya, exactly when Don Pedro was there. This is probably his most likely interaction with Griselio Torresola, who in 1932 would have been seven. Whatever it was in the mountains in that period—hopeful, dreamy, full of confidence (the signatures were mounting; the rallies were getting larger and larger)—it had to be, for the young Oscar Collazo, the closest thing to sheer happiness he would ever feel. Oh, to be young and in love with a cause, to be doing hard, meaningful political work in the day, to be attending rallies lit by torches in the night, there hearing the party speakers, particularly the great Don Pedro, enunciating precisely what was in his occluded heart! Why, that must have been extraordinary.

And surely the epitome of this bliss, the epicenter, was found at Jayuya, when Don Pedro came and stayed with his famous follower, Blanca Canales, in the big gray house with the balcony in the valley under the Three Peaks in the neighborhood of Coabey. Paradise had been lost; now it could be regained.

Imagine Oscar then. He's still an outsider, one of the anonymous army of youths in love with Don Pedro and the Holy Cause. He's never spoken to the great man, he's far from the inner circle, he's young, he's unformed, he's desperate for leadership and a sense of his place in the world. But he must see Albizu and Blanca, possibly in the way a generation of Americans saw the Kennedys. They would have been such attractive people from afar, framed by the beauty of the land, animated by the politics of hope. Don Pedro, his beautiful Peruvian wife, Laura, his two daughters and son. Blanca Canales, cherubic but radiating passion and love. And the Torresola kids, a tribe of beautiful children running around in the middle of the most excellent adventure of their lives. Who could not have been touched by this intimate spectacle, who could not have wanted it to last forever?

It lasted until election day, and then the bitterness returned, only this time much more angrily.

The Nationalists as a party received only about 5,000 votes; Don Pedro, in his stand for senator-at-large, only ten thousand. The people, once again, had been wrong, and Don Pedro issued strict orders thereafter not to take part in any "colonial elections." "The motherland's right to independence shall not be discussed," he proclaimed. "And if it is discussed, it will be with bullets."

For Oscar the spiritual consequences of this result cannot have been kind. It must have seemed that a goal he had always had but could only recently articulate had been snatched away. There were rumors, of course, of American meddling in the election, of powers that were seeing the threat the Nationalists posed, and working under the surface to defeat them decisively. How could the weak stand up against the strong, the individual against the combine, the patriot against the empire? Albizu

Campos in December formed the Cadet Corps of the party, the black-shirted paramilitary unit; soon there were assassinations, a gunfight with police. Oscar did his small part in organizing this unit.

But Oscar was not a warrior and moreover had to deal with the immediate practical consequence of the election loss: this was the beginning of an unpleasant period of wandering the two worlds of Puerto Rico and New York in search of work. Nothing was settled, nothing was open, nothing lasted. He had fallen into the hell of living hand to mouth. Yet he never yielded on his pride. He returned, periodically, to New York, but never went on the dole. He always earned his keep, in small, debasing jobs, anything to keep the food in his mouth. He ended up working in a hat factory in New York in 1933; then as an analyst in a sugar factory by day and at night as a drugstore clerk in Manatí. While he was there, he met a girl named Carmen, married her, and soon had a child, a daughter also named Carmen but called by her middle name, after one of Oscar's sisters, Zoraida. But by 1937, he headed again to New York, because he couldn't make it in Puerto Rico. Eventually he and his first wife separated. He took his baby girl with him; and he supported himself in the bars and restaurants around Times Square while his sister, with whom he was living again, looked after baby Zoraida. He was a dishwasher at a bar on Seventh Avenue near 59th Street, working from 10:00 A.M. to 9:00 P.M. for $15 a week.

And it's around here that what must be considered the heroism of Oscar Collazo begins to express itself. It's a ritual of adaptation and survival reenacted by millions of immigrants, taken as a whole and easy to overlook. When you examine it in its particularity, you must be impressed: Oscar found a wife, a family, a job, a skill, a career, a life. Somehow, from poverty and ignorance, on sheer guts and skill, he entered the mainstream, became what any and all would call a man. He provided. He built. He planned. He won.

At a Nationalist party in the Bronx sometime in 1940, newly divorced and working in Manhattan kitchens, he met Rosa Cortés, a divorcee, herself with two daughters. *New Yorker* reporter Donovan calls her "intelligent, active, buxom, with black hair, shining brown eyes and a dark velvety complexion." She had found a job—and her own life—in Moosup, Connecticut, near the Rhode Island line, working as a metal polisher for the Majestic Metal Specialties Company. Rosa got Oscar a job; he moved up to a suburb of Moosup and began to master the wheel.

It turned out that Oscar had the gift. It was his patience, his methodical mentality, his care, his involvement in details. Metal polishing is something of an art; gun manufacturers have artisans who have mastered it brilliantly, Colt being famous for the quality of its work. Majestic Metal manufactured much humbler artifacts, namely compacts for women's makeup, in a variety of materials such as chrome, nickel, and enamel.

It's not just work. It's art. It's skill. It's judgment. You stand at the buffing wheel, electrically powered, which whizzes and vibrates as it grinds remorselessly along, and to its spin and rush you apply the piece upon which you labor. But not crudely. You can't force it. It's a delicate matter, knowing just when to move and what angle to hold the piece at, and how long to apply it. You watch as a dull, clouded surface becomes something alive and perfect that catches and reflects the light, that can be rubbed against the cheek and feel smooth and creamy, that never catches on the fingers or in the pocket or the purse, so sleek is it. Oscar was good at this; he prospered.

In other ways, he prospered as well: he married Rosa, and the two, with Rosa's two daughters, Lydia and Iris, settled into a small apartment in the Aldridge Heights section of Moosup, the address being 150 Aldridge Drive, Aldridge Village, Connecticut. It's the address Oscar would use checking into the Harris Hotel October 31, 1950. Other changes followed; the next year, the family moved back to New York, where, after a time, Oscar continued to master his skill, working for a number of specialty shops in lower Manhattan. Ultimately he and the new family—his own daughter, Zoraida, would join them in 1947— settled into the Brook Avenue tenement house. And it was there that another major development occurred. One flight downstairs, for nearly two years, was nobody less than the Master himself, Don Pedro Albizu Campos.

The train of events that brought Don Pedro to 173 Brook Avenue in the Bronx is complex. The servo-mechanism of the arrival, however, is not: the Federal Penitentiary in Atlanta. In 1936, after the murder of the chief of the Insular Police E. Francis Riggs by two Nationalists, Hiram Rosado and Elias Beauchamp, a general roundup of subversives in Puerto Rico occurred, the biggest of these netted fish being Albizu Campos. Since, typically, no evidence could be produced that linked Albizu directly to the murder of Riggs, he was charged not as an accessory to murder but under the federal charge of sedition. Two federal prosecutors were sent to the island to assist the local prosecutor, and possibly it wasn't a coincidence that the most conservative of the judges in the federal circuit that included Puerto Rico heard the case. The result was not what the government anticipated and desired: a hung jury.

Historian Jaime Ramírez-Barbot, no Nationalist sympathizer, nevertheless characterized what happened next as "one of the most undignified and prejudicial actions of the American judicial system in Puerto Rico." A new trial with a new jury was ordered forthwith; the jury consisted of ten North Americans and only two Puerto Ricans, and the same judge, Robert A. Cooper, presided. On July 31, 1936, Albizu Campos and other Nationalists were found guilty of sedition, and though the sentences varied, Albizu received the three heaviest, one of six years and two more of two years apiece, to be served sequentially at Atlanta. Ten years' hard time. The sentences were appealed but upheld, and the Supreme Court, in 1937, refused to hear the case. Meanwhile, six policemen accused of murdering the two men who had assassinated Riggs were tried; four were acquitted, and the other two freed after a mistrial.

One consequence of this was the Ponce Massacre in 1937. For Albizu Campos, the practical reality was six dreary years in the slammer, while back home, at least for a while, anger rose, violence increased, and tension grew more explosive. Then the world war broke out, and the smaller struggle was subsumed in the larger one; without Albizu Campos's galvanizing presence, the war years in Puerto Rico were relatively calm.

In 1943, however, Albizu got a break, and no other word can describe it: he suffered a heart attack. He was removed from prison and transferred to Columbus Hospital in New York, where he was expected to die. Instead, he recovered, though his hospitalization lasted two years. During this time, he was actively involved with the Puerto Rican Nationalist Party in New York, and met the then presidente de la Junta Nacionalista de Nueva York, that is, Oscar Collazo. And so, in recuperation, it was logical that the old man in ill health would bunk with someone close to him, who loved and revered him. And that is how Albizu ended up in the same building with Oscar Collazo.

This is possibly another paradise that Oscar achieved and then lost. But it must have been thunderously thrilling for him to be so close to the man he had worshipped from so far for so long. Don Pedro himself: there, in the house. Zoraida recalls being introduced to the mysterious man on the second floor. He was with a visitor when Oscar and the child approached, and Don Pedro greeted both warmly, introduced them to the visitor, and proclaimed of Oscar: "This is nationalism personified."

Oscar, spending his spare time as an editor of a slick magazine the party called *Puerto Rico*, must have spent countless hours with the infirm old man struggling to regain his strength for the final act of the drama as it would play out when he returned to Puerto Rico. Again, this period is curiously undocumented. Oscar himself never remarked on it, and other chroniclers of these events don't pay it much heed, possibly because of the lack of information. What Zoraida remembers is primarily what so many say of Don Pedro: "I remember so vividly because I had never seen eyes like that. I never saw eyes like that. So full of love, and also when he looked at me I felt like he could see right through my brain, somehow. See my future, my past, everything."

So in a sense, Don Pedro became more than Oscar's hero, he became his mentor. That is why Oscar in turn became the elder, the advisor; he had absorbed all that intimate time with the great man.

But in 1947, his full ten years of prison time done (the two years in the hospital and the two years of bed rest were counted against the sentence), Don Pedro was free and clear and returned to Puerto Rico, there to be greeted by Raimundo Díaz Pacheco and his smartly uniformed Cadet Corps and hundreds of other well-wishers—including Griselio Torresola—and he began to mastermind the activities that would circle back and involve Oscar three years later.

As for Oscar, the next few years were marked by tranquillity and good works. He found employment as a metal polisher at the Randolph Rand Corporation on Wooster Street in New York; the firm changed its name to the Gainer Corporation and moved to New Rochelle, which meant that at 5:30 each morning Oscar arose, put on a suit and tie—everybody in the Bronx neighborhood must have thought he was a banker or a lawyer— and took the train to New Rochelle. There, in the plant, he changed to work clothes and put in his solid eight at the buffing wheel, bringing the luster out of the brass frames that Gainer then assembled into women's handbags. Sometimes he hit eight hundred in a day; he was considered one of the top ten metal polishers that had ever worked in the plant. He was hardworking, dependable, courteous, friendly, if typically reserved. His lunch hours he often spent teaching his fellow workers to read and write or pushing them to become involved in union activities.

Small reflections of the high esteem in which he was held abound. He was, for example, asked by the plant's union, the International Handbag, Luggage, Belt and Novelty Workers (of the AFL), to serve on the negotiating committee, where he was logical, reasonable, and willing to give and take. He was not a hothead, not given to tantrums or rants. He understood the system and abided by it.

At the same time, he would often spend his Sundays at La Guardia Field, helping newly arrived immigrants deal with their first confusing hours in the United States. He would serve as an interpreter and guide, walk them through the process of arrival and travel to their initial destination. On more than a few occasions he would act as an escort and take the newcomers via New York's complex subway system to their relatives or initial homes. He would try to find them employment. He was utterly committed to them; his imagination, one can infer, was compassionately engaged with "the people" and what had been done to them, and he was committed to doing what little he could to assuage that.

His private life over these last years of the 1940s was equally irreproachable. He and Rosa lived frugally and cleanly, paying $36 a month for the Bronx apartment; they were saving money for a house. Rosa spent $20 to $25 a week on credit at a nearby grocery store, and each payday Oscar would drop by and make the debt good. He gloried in taking his daughter and two stepdaughters—all of whom loved him—to art galleries and museums all around New York. "He used to take me to museums all the time," Zoraida later recalled. "I saw the Cloisters. I saw the Museum of the City of New York. I went to the Modern Art Museum. I went to all the museums in the city, the Brooklyn Museum, everything. That was fun for him and for me too. Sometimes in the summer when we couldn't go to the beach he would take me to the zoo, to the park, just for fun, just to walk around. He was a walker. He loved to walk."

"He did not drink, smoke, or dance, and none of his fellow workers ever heard him swear," the *New Yorker* reporter wrote.

And he read. Every night, for one hour, he settled in the corner of the little living room, sat in his maple-framed chair, and tore through books. He specialized in history, particularly the history of revolutions and liberations, including the American Revolution. He read Louis Fischer's *Week with Gandhi* as well as Benjamin Franklin's *Autobiography*. He read the Bible, even though he no longer practiced Catholicism ceremonially. He owned and frequently consulted encyclopedias. He read Shakespeare, Swift, Darwin, Sir Walter Raleigh. He experienced the world through books.

Yet underneath, always, the politics. He could not get over that which Don Pedro and Griselio and the other Nationalists could not get over: that the invasion of Puerto Rico in 1898, coming as it did after the Charter of Autonomy from Spain, was illegal, not an act of war. Therefore the American presence on the island was an occupation by force, exactly as the Germans had invaded France and Poland. The Americans weren't big brothers, helping their backward cousins into modern times, but military conquerors, there to loot, pillage, rape, and raze.

For a while in the early 1940s, the FBI took an interest in Oscar Collazo because of his Nationalist activities. A file was opened. But after a few years, based on informant information that Oscar had drifted away from the cause, the FBI decided that he was no longer worth keeping an eye on.

He had visitors, occasionally.

One of them was Griselio Torresola.

"I saw Griselio," Zoraida Collazo recalled. "He had come to the house with his first wife and the baby. He was working on 116th Street and Fifth Avenue where it's called El Barrio in New York. He was in a bookshop. . . . I saw him only once. My father knew him when he was a little boy because he was raised in the same town where Griselio was born [Jayuya]. That's what he said. When my father was fourteen, he said he must have been seven or eight [actually, he was two]. So he wasn't his friend, he was a friend of [Griselio's older brother] Elio and all the older kids. Blanca [Canales] was much older than they were. She would talk to them, but the way you talk to young kids."

He knew what he had to do, and when Griselio returned to his apartment and knocked at his door at 9:00 P.M., October 29, he was spiritually, emotionally, and practically ready. The man of words and good deeds, nourished by intimate contact with his Maximum Leader, would become a soldier.

16. "IT DID NOT GO OFF"

This is what happened when Oscar Collazo pointed his P.38 at Officer Donald Birdzell and pulled the trigger: nothing.

"It did not go off," Oscar later explained.

Why didn't it go off? Why didn't the cartridge fire, the bullet rocket forward and strike poor, unsuspecting Birdzell in the mid-back, driving him to the ground, putting him out of the fight, probably killing him? Instead—all accounts agree on this—somewhere in the drawing and shooting process there was a loud *CLICK*. This is one of the mysteries of November 1, 1950. It largely determined the choreography of the hectic events to follow over the next 38.5 seconds. And it may have had more to do with sparing the life of Harry S. Truman than anything the Secret Service, able and heroic though the Secret Service would prove to be that day, otherwise did.

Consider what should have happened.

Oscar shoots Birdzell; he drops instantly, disabled, possibly dying. Oscar rushes up the steps to Blair House. Two seconds have passed. Floyd Boring and Joseph Davidson rush from the eastern guardhouse to engage him. Coming down Pennsylvania, they run into Griselio closing fast from the west, who has already dealt with Les Coffelt. Griselio, a superb shot and a man they have not yet seen, drops them both with his powerful semiautomatic pistol. He rushes to join Oscar. Six seconds have passed. Griselio punches his fist through the screen door, unlatches the door. Fifteen seconds have passed. As they reach the central hallway, they encounter—nobody. Agent Stewart Stout has returned to the Secret Service office and is fighting to get the tommy gun out of the locked gun cabinet. Or, hearing them in the hallway, he lurches out, with his Colt Detective Special, leaving the still locked tommy gun. Griselio, hyperaggressive in battle, fires first. All agents and officers are down, Oscar has reloaded, and the two of them, heavily armed and unhurt, are loose in

Blair House. Vince Mroz has already gone down the stairs and out the basement door. The three other White House policemen—two in the basement, one in the backyard—race into the house and begin to hunt for the gunmen. Oscar and Griselio split up, Griselio upstairs and Oscar downstairs. There's a big, endless gunfight. Maybe Griselio makes it to Harry Truman in his bedroom, maybe he doesn't; but he's got a head start, the advantage of surprise, a powerful weapon, and a powerful will.

It didn't happen.

Instead what happened was a moment of disbelief. Birdzell heard the loud, metallic click—and turned to see a small man in a suit struggling with a pistol. He must have thought, as would any man in that situation, *hey, what the hell?* Meanwhile, twenty-five feet away but separated from these two by a wrought iron fence and some vegetation, still stunned into paralysis by the sudden strangeness that is unfolding, Floyd Boring and Joe Davidson didn't yet have a clear view of what was happening.

There are basically three explanations for the first shot failure. Some people believe what occurred was a genuine ammunition defect—a misfire. The trigger is pulled, the hammer falls and drives the firing pin forward, the firing pin strikes the cartridge primer, which is a little plate concealing a brew of chemicals in the head of the cartridge. The chemical glop on the primer—some form of silver styphnate—is supposed to detonate when the pin hits it, its detonation detonating in turn the powder that drives the bullet. But sometimes they don't go. They just don't go. The failure rate is microscopic, but it does have to do with the source, the components of the ammunition, the care with which it was assembled and has been stored, its age, all factors relating to its manufacture in 1944. And who knows what tortuous route it traveled, over the years, that finally deposited this one defective cartridge in the chamber of Oscar's pistol at this precise moment in history.

But the misfire interpretation is unconvincing. Yes, misfires occasionally happen. But to think that possibly events transpired as they did and not some other way because of no force except the random drift of the universe represents if nothing else a mind-boggling coincidence. The failure rate of handgun ammunition in that day and age was much higher than it is now, but it still had to be significantly tiny: 1 in 20,000? 1 in 50,000?

The second possibility relates to Oscar's own story. He told Secret Service agents after the event that when the gun did not fire, he pulled back on the slide to eject the bad cartridge and allow a new one to rise into the chamber. This is the appropriate clearance drill for a jammed semiautomatic pistol. However, the ejected bad cartridge—that is, unfired, with a dent in the primer from the firing pin—would have therefore been found; then there would be no mystery at all. But such a cartridge was not found. Of course there is always the possibility that someone—the site was unsecured in the immediate aftermath—stole it as a souvenir. Barring that possibility, the absence of such a dented round suggests that Oscar Collazo had actually forgotten to chamber a round in the first place, had dropped the hammer on an empty chamber, and thus when throwing the slide he would not have ejected anything. However, none of the witnesses reported that Oscar threw the slide; they all say that he "banged" on the gun, that is, hit it with his other hand.

Far more likely then, the phenomenon of "not going off" is related specifically to that gun and its operator. It was the interplay between Oscar and the P.38 that made the gun click and not go bang.

Oscar is drawing the gun. He has some familiarity with handguns, which almost certainly means he has a familiarity with revolvers. Revolvers in that era were shot by a mechanism called "single-action," meaning that the shooter thumbs back the hammer until it locks; then he acquires a sight picture, then trips the trigger, which, with the hammer cocked, has a resistance of but a few ounces. Thus did Oscar's memory confuse his intention. As he drew the gun, his subconscious remembered the shooting he had seen and done when helping set up Don Pedro's black-shirted Cadet Corps in the 1930s, and his thumb flew to the hammer of the P.38 and racked it back, even as another part of his mind screamed *no! no!* That was the conscious part of his mind that remembered Griselio's coaching him in the hotel room just an hour or so ago. Griselio would have said, *Forget the hammer. You don't need the hammer. Just point it and pull the trigger,* for that is the way Griselio would have set the gun up for Oscar, a round in the chamber, the hammer down, the only necessity being a long first pull to fire the first shot, at which point in the sequence the pistol recocks itself and will continue to do so, resetting the trigger in its short, single-action condition so that only a short pull is needed for each subsequent shot.

Oscar's unconscious, being faster and stronger, beat his conscious; but his conscious, being stubborn, caught up and overcame the subconscious. He knew that in cocking he had done something wrong and that he must instantly do something to fix it. In a fuddle of panic and confusion, he starts pushing things. The first thing he pushes is the first thing he feels, as it's right next to the hammer on the thumb side of the pistol. He pushes the safety. He pushes it down, which alas is on. But not only does he put the pistol on safety, also by the singularity of the double-action automatic, of which the P.38 is one of the first variants, the safety also encompasses a hammer drop. So when the safety is pushed down, the hammer falls, but harmlessly. Harmlessly and loudly. That was the heavy CLICK that everybody heard. It's that loud.

Oscar has drawn the gun, initiated the action. He thumb-cocks the gun, knows he's done something wrong (violating Griselio's instructions), and then pushes the safety and in that act, (a) alerts security, and (b) disables the gun. He is now standing in plain view of several armed guards outside the house of the president of the United States with a loaded gun which he himself has just disabled. He has, in one second, utterly destroyed the plan, and utterly destroyed the chance of any possible success. He has also almost certainly doomed himself, for the federal boys are about to draw and shoot.

But in the next second, it all changed. The unbelievable was about to happen again, and when it does, it resets the stage dramatically for the successful assassination of Harry S. Truman.

There is Oscar, having made the bad career move of his life. He must fix it. He has about one second to do so before the federals shoot him down.

He continues to push and twist things on the gun. Imagine the kaleidoscope of imagery in his dazzled mind. But very quickly and by utter chance, he finally does something right. He somehow recovers enough, or by sheer luck, pushes the safety up. Now he is back where he started; the gun is live. He just doesn't know it. He draws it to his chest and like a stern father begins to punish it by administering a beating. He is actually seen standing there, the gun clutched to his bosom in his right hand, and with his left he is striking it. And the gun cooperated. It fired.

Again, surmise. In striking his hand, he must have struck a nerve sharply and the nerve reacted by ordering his hand to clench. All the fingers tightened, including the one on the trigger. Therefore, it fired.

But the gun had not been oriented in any conscious direction; the simple geography of Oscar's body position had decreed that it should be more or less pointing north.

Think of all the places the bullet could go. It could smash itself into the stones of Blair House or the sidewalk, it could bury itself in the ground or a tree, it could pierce Donald Birdzell's aorta, it could ricochet crazily and kill some poor guy sitting in a barber chair some blocks away as he read the sports pages. Instead, it plowed into Donald Birdzell's knee.

17. PAPPY

Took a look at farming. No thank you.

Took a look at school teaching. No thank you either.

So a young man on the outskirts of Champaign, Illinois, in the mid-1920s turned to other thoughts of making a living. He didn't want to milk cows, or teach kids to spell and add, so he did what the posters advised him to do: he joined the United States Navy to see the world.

He'd seen enough of Illinois. Donald Birdzell had been born there, August 22, 1909, in Lerna, in Pleasant Grove Township, in Coles County. His dad was William Isaac Birdzell, the teacher and school principal; his mom was Iva May Scarcliff; both were from families long rooted in the soil of rural Illinois.

He was the second oldest of the family, and the staid, steady lives laid out before him didn't hold much fascination. If you don't have the farmer's gift for abiding and his talent for patience, what you see is a dullness never-ending, reflected in the even line of the prairie horizon, the straightness of the roads, the ceaseless, backbreaking toil that can shatter a man's spirit on the anvil of a bad winter.

It's no mystery why he joined the navy, why so many thousands of boys joined the navy. Because the sea, tedium itself, nevertheless delivers young men eventually into foreign ports, with all the pleasures of exotic cities, new mountains, strange forms of life either animal or human. Those giddy experiences are about as far from the flat, prim Illinois prairie as you can imagine.

Thus Donald, after knocking around in the lumber and cheese industries in Wisconsin, joined the navy to see the world, and see the world he did. He also saw a lot of teeth. The navy, in its wisdom, trained him and assigned him to be a dental technician, and his duties consisted of sterilizing the equipment and keeping the office spotless. Then it sent him to the Far East, where he helped the navy dentists fix or replace choppers knocked awry in back alley bar fights or boiler room punchouts. Or he helped fill the cavities for officers' wives, or their children. He took his liberties in Shanghai.

Was there a more storied place in the years between 1928 and 1935 in the world than Shanghai? Was there a town with more trouble available? But Donald was always too smart to do anything stupid. He didn't get a thousand tattoos or marry a gal named Mai-Ling. He just came back with a fine collection of silk shirts.

In 1934, Don was shipped homeward. By a fortuitous bureaucratic decision, he was seconded to the Naval Dental Office in Washington, D.C. In that same year, Donald met Helen Murphy, a clerk at the Veterans Administration who had been a yeoman 3rd class in the navy during World War I. He was at a party sometime that year and there he met the merry Helen. Neither was a kid. Donald was in his mid-twenties. He had been in the navy for about six years. Helen was a decade older, a sophisticated, big-city career gal, a "very stylish person, very well put together," in the words of Don's sister Wilma.

From the first moment it was clear to them that they had to be together and, after dating for a while, they were. It was, later commented Joe King, Helen's and Don's beloved nephew, a very strong marriage, one that lasted more than half a century.

They chose not to tie the knot in Washington, because in those days marriages within the District were listed in the paper and when the form was filled out, ages were required. They had just decided that age didn't matter and the difference between their ages didn't matter and they didn't want to bother with the whole thing and maybe there would be a little reluctance back in Illinois due to the fact that Don was marrying a woman not his own age. Why stir up trouble? Both were old enough to want to avoid trouble. So they traveled out of town and got married in Frederick, Maryland, a small city about forty-five miles outside Washington, where nobody asked and it was nobody's business. The Illinois kin never knew of the age difference until Helen's death, when the newspaper obituary gave it away. No, it wasn't a misprint, they were told.

Of course Don didn't want to kiss the new wife and find out the next day he'd been transferred to Manila or Panama City or some far naval port. So, after seven years, he left the navy. But he'd learned things in the navy that comforted him. He must have liked uniforms, ranks, the clarity of it all, the strictly observed hierarchy, the distinction between rankers and officers, the special place of noncommissioned officers, the sense of order, of steady progress, of rules, of authority, of loyalty, of reward. Maybe the navy was a big crossword puzzle. The only place that order could be obtained in civilian life was the police department, and so Donald applied to and was accepted as a Metropolitan policeman. But again, a problem. It was still the Depression, and one of the rules was that, jobs being scarce, husband and wife couldn't both be employees of the federal government. So Helen, though as a senior clerk she was making far more money, resigned from the Veterans Administration.

What followed for a few years must have been blissful. Don was absorbed into the bosom of her family, and it became their primary social hub. Like Helen, Don became a dapper dresser and the two often went dancing together. When he wasn't in uniform, Don often favored three-piece suits with a watch and chain, a small penknife as a fob.

There was enough money, somehow, to buy the pleasant row house on New Hampshire Avenue. He was the policeman, she was the policeman's wife, and both were long-term federal employees who knew the ropes and the networks, who got and accepted the system, who did their duties hard and honestly, who never missed a day. He wasn't the sort to go out with the boys after work, and the "boys," in any case, were his wife's brothers and brothers-in-law. The family Murphy must have been a great sheltering presence to both of them.

There's a picture from this period—it could be after the war, one supposes, as no date is recorded—that sums up Donald and Helen and their place in the Murphy clan. It's taken at some Chesapeake Bay beach, and Donald has just caught a fish. He loved to fish and he and the Murphy boys and in-laws made this activity a focus of their family culture. At this particular moment, Don, in khakis and work shirt, his hair as ever slicked back precisely, the part a straight-arrow line on the left-center of his head, is holding his catch aloft. It's fresh from the bay, and a chunk of solid, glistening protein, a five-pounder easily, hanging by its gills from the prongs of his fingers, probably a rockfish all rigid with indignation at its progress to the pan. The look on Donald's face is pure bliss, and the sense of family celebration—they're crowding in on him, taking pleasure in his pleasure, radiant in Don's small triumph over nature.

Of course all that changed with the coming of war—not the decency, but the family communion. The boys all went away to fight, and Don, even though he was thirty-four, was one of them.

Don tried the navy. He thought his earlier experience would qualify him to wear an officer's bars, but the navy turned him down. So Don, a veteran of seven years in the navy and not young by a long shot, went into the army in 1943, three years after he had switched from the Metropolitan Police to the White House Police. Joe King and Wilma think he volunteered, and Ruth, his other surviving sister, thinks he was drafted. First stop was Fort Dix, that sandy wasteland in the New Jersey Pine Barrens. His experience, his maturity, his solidity got him noticed and, soon enough, promoted. It wasn't long before he was a sergeant. But it was his age that got him his nickname. The kids called him "Pappy."

Don was made an MP, because of his police experience, and served in the South Pacific. Don never talked much about what he'd seen, of what he'd done. He was always insanely proud that he'd gone.

Then came the year 1944, and it was a disaster for the Birdzells. On one of the most remembered dates of that year, June 6, hundreds of American gliders loaded with infantrymen crash-landed behind the German lines as part of what is now remembered as the Normandy invasion. The Birdzells will always remember it for the death of Ivan.

Ivan, one of the glider pilots, was one of Don's two younger brothers, and he too had to fight. As a small boy, he caught the wild blue yonder bug and ran around with his arms outstretched pretending to be both plane and pilot. When war came to Europe, the bug was still with him, and before the Japanese attacked Pearl Harbor Ivan volunteered. In August 1943, Ivan went overseas to pilot those frail kites meant to surf the breezes behind a C-47, then disengage and ride the French winds to a landing behind a hedgerow. It sounds elegant but it wasn't. The gliders, nicknamed "flying coffins," were hard to handle and easy to stall, and you didn't so much fly or guide them as fight them all the way down, sweating bullets and cursing like a, well, like an army glider pilot. Then they didn't land, they crashed. Sometimes the crashes were soft enough so that intact men and functional equipment spilled out to fight, and sometimes the crashes were hard and sad. On that night in which history pivoted gigantically, there were thousands of tinier stories that never made it into the history books. Ivan's was one. His landing was soft enough—another Birdzell doing his duty—and when the boys were unloading, someone stepped on a landmine next to Ivan. He didn't have a mark on him, but the concussion killed him.

Then there was Kenneth. Unlike Ivan and Don, Kenneth had stayed in Illinois and given himself over to the farm. And for a while he flourished: he had six kids, he prospered, life was healthy and happy. But a farm is an awesome responsibility, and somehow, some way, it began to let him down. Then his wife died of cancer, his health broke, his spirit broke, and one day in 1944, profoundly depressed, he broke. He killed himself.

The family couldn't stay together. Thus it was that Kenneth's oldest daughter, the beautiful Joan, came to live in Washington with her uncle so recently returned from the war, and Helen, who was back at the Veterans Administration (rehired during the war when the no-couples rule was abandoned as the government geared up for maximum effort), got her a job there.

For about five years, Joan lived with Helen and Don. A rural, teenage farm girl from the Midwest, her family torn apart, Joan tried to cope with big-city ways, and her aunt and uncle tried to help. But as one family member said, "They didn't really set horses that well."

When Donald returned to Washington after the war—a case of ulcers that was to dog him the rest of his life was one trophy—he rejoined the White House Police Force. At 2:20 P.M., November 1, 1950, he turned at the sound of a click to see a man in a suit banging on a gun five feet from him.

The gun fired. Donald felt a searing pain in his knee and went down.

18. THE NEXT TEN SECONDS

The bullet hit the knee, veered to the left and exited, smashing against the Blair House facade. It pulled chunks of ligament and tissue and a spurt of blood with it as it bulled through. Donald, who got through two years in the Pacific without a scratch, was hit.

His leg collapsed; he caught himself as the pain soared and for a splinter of a fractured second was simply there, his leg aflame, his whole world spinning.

But here's the impressive thing, and it was not only true of Donald, but true of all the president's men that day: how fast they reacted.

No shock, no stupefaction, most of all no panic and no fear. They got to work.

Donald's leg ran hot aflame, then quickly went numb, but even as this was happening he was thinking. Not in sentences of course, not neat little things that can be laid out logically, a series of positions, but by the miracle of the subconscious in a rush of considerations that take but nanoseconds to compute.

Many will say afterward that Donald ran into the street to draw fire away from Blair House, where the president lived. That's certainly true. But he also obeyed the two iron laws of infantry combat, possibly reflecting his training and experience. The two laws are: take cover and return fire. Since there was no cover to be taken, he improvised his cover: he moved, knowing that movement was cover was survival and that firepower was survival.

That was Donald's war on November 1, 1950; he was hit bad, was bleeding, in a blast of pain and shock, and in a split second he somehow got his wounded, forty-one-year-old, three-pack-a-day body moving. He crabwalked out to the street, drawing as he went, sliding past Oscar, who must have been as surprised as anyone that the damn gun went off, that the officer twisted, then started to chug by him.

Donald got by Oscar, hooked to the west as he went, not straight across the street but curving toward 17th Street, until he was far enough. He drew, he fired. He was the first to return fire.

Almost certainly, he fired one-handed, single-action as he was trained to do. What he didn't have was a second to gather, to collect, to take control of his breath, to set. The gun was loose in his hand, he was moving, Oscar had turned and fired twice more at him, and Donald, one-handed, fired back. The bullets hit the facade of Blair, exploding against the stone, almost certainly twisting into 158-grain chunks as they veered away. No hits. But he was shooting, and in firefights missed shots are almost as important as hits, because they disorient your antagonist, they prevent him as well as you from setting up to aim, they slow him down, they put fear in him, and they hold him up so that others, better situated, can get the telling shot off. Donald prevented Oscar from turning his attention directly to Toad and Joe Davidson, twenty-five feet away on the other side of the sidewalk down by the guardhouse.

As for Oscar, his was a blurred experience. It must have been nothing but impressions for him. Did his mind scatter? Did he panic? Does a man with no experience at all in gun battle fall apart when the first incoming rounds whisper by his ear, and, when they miss and crash into something hard, begin to spray fragments in the air so a blistering wind of stone mist stings his eyes and wrists?

Not Oscar.

Oscar had work to do, and he set out to do it. He fired at the moving policeman he had injured. He must have fired quickly. This second shot must have surprised him also. That's because the action of the first shot, in the semiautomatic pistol, sets up the action of all subsequent shots. Where the first was long and grinding, a twenty-pound pull similar to dragging a rake across gravel, the second and subsequent shots are much lighter and shorter. So the P.38 must just seem to fire itself, and Oscar's shot at even a slow-moving target like Donald missed and sailed across Pennsylvania, where by the grace of God it did not strike anybody but instead just disappeared. It may even have grazed the tunic of a young Metropolitan policeman standing across the street.

But Oscar was now under fire himself, from another direction. Toad and Joe had joined the fight.

Toad went from standing there to gunfighter in about three seconds. The Detective Special was out, riding from the hip holster up in his big hand, and he found the hammer with that big thumb of his, and rocked it back to full cock. He hunkered down slightly behind the guardhouse and was aware of Joe Davidson maneuvering beside him, his gun also out. But Toad wasn't thinking that as the gun came up and through his dark glasses hunted for a target. Well trained, disciplined, and cool as ice, he had two objectives: to shoot to kill, and to kill the right guy, not any innocent bystander.

Where's the little guy? The vagaries of movement had suddenly removed him from visibility. He'd turned, dipped, and Toad can't see him through the blur of vegetation and the mesh of iron bars of the fence between them.

BAMBAMBAMBAM!

That was the sound of Davidson firing just to his right, fast, possibly so fast he's shooting double-action, and the noise, hammering against Toad's right eardrum from about a foot's distance, leaves a ring that will last for hours. It should have disoriented Toad. But it didn't. He's looking for a target, and suddenly the little fellow in the hat with the P.38 jukes toward the stairway of Blair and through the fence and around a tree and is suddenly, briefly, visible.

Toad put the front sight square on his head, goes rock-steady for just a second, and pulls the trigger.

I'm going to take care of this baby right here, he was thinking.

19. RESURRECTION MAN

They didn't play a different kind of football in Pennsylvania in the 1930s from the kind they do now, particularly in the hardscrabble western coal towns, but they played it without all the sensible safety refinements of the modern game. No face guards, the helmets were basically leather hats, and the shoulder pads mostly cotton padding. Noses got broken, teeth got knocked out, tongues and lips got cut, ankles got sprained, knees twisted, bells rung, scrotums kicked, and you just picked yourself up and kept playing. All the fury of young men locked in a dead-end economy in a dead-end town with nothing ahead but a lifetime of dismality came into play when the whistle blew.

So when the DuBois High Beavers faced the state championship–bound Windber Coal Barons on an afternoon in 1934, it was like a war. It wasn't graceful, smooth, sophisticated. It was just hitting, hitting, hitting. On that day, DuBois had some kind of magic going. Who'd have guessed? DuBois, a train town on the Buffalo, Rochester, and Pittsburgh rail line, maybe twelve thousand souls making a living not so much out of the mining itself—that's off in smaller towns—but by the loading of the product of the coal veins into the long iron cars for transport to Pittsburgh and elsewhere. Beating Windber? Beating a state champ? Unbelievable.

But true. Toad was seventeen, the right end, and he's big and strong and tough. And he's determined. He's not going to spend his life here, that he knows. His family is dirt-poor, his father is long gone, his mom's working as hard as she can, but Toad has ideas. Already, he had a dream, a dream of other places, other things. You got there on horseback. A man on horseback, on a black steed, a man in uniform, a man who must be respected and obeyed, who represents righteous force and an end to violence. A man who uses the animal muscle as a surrogate for his own and in that way affirms the will of the law and the sense of the tribe. That would be a mounted state policeman sent in to quell labor difficulties, and in an area where the cops must have been hated by most and seen as union-busting Cossacks, Floyd identified with them at a young age, wanted to be one. That was the way his personality was wired, the attraction toward order, discipline, respect, toward doing right.

But all that was in the future. Now there's nothing but this game here, this afternoon, this minute, this second, 2:00 P.M., November 4, 1934. As the anonymous poet-sportswriter of the *DuBois Morning Courier* notes, setting the stage with only the slightest of nods toward Grantland Rice, "A clear sky and perfect atmosphere for both player and spectator greeted this big game of the local season and the football interests of this entire region and much of the West Central Conference were focused upon the gridiron when the blue-clad miners from Windber and the militiamen of the house of Black and White crawled through the ropes. Bands representing each school lent a tuneful trend to the colorful situation."

The trend turned from tuneful to violent when Toad launched the ball with his educated toe. This was one of his specialties, and there's even a yearbook picture of him, in mid-phony-kick, arms side thrust for balance, right leg surging upward, face keen and concentrated, the big D of the House of Black and White emblazoned upon his chest. Toad's kick sends the ball booming through the thin air, and then the hitting starts in earnest. It's whack, smash, thud, grind, blast, grasp, shove, and maybe a secret punch in the pile here and there, for forty-eight long and grueling minutes. The guys on both teams play both ways, with but three substitutions all day for DuBois and two for Windber.

Toad may not be DuBois's best athlete on the field that day—possibly the right halfback, Shobert, was better, and certainly the little atom Garthwaite, who lines up at quarterback although Shobert is the actual passer, was flashier. But he was solid, dependable, always there when it counted. And if DuBois is to have any chance, it must pounce early and dictate; it cannot play catch-up. So let's pick a moment in the first quarter, when the game turns.

The ball came whistling its way toward Toad. He had big hands, he was big, he was strong, but he's not particularly fast, and when the pass seethes through the air, he snatches it. He lumbers left, lumbers right, and takes off downfield, even as the Coal Baron defenders swarm him. Hands claw at him, twisting, pulling, shoulders are driven into his midsection, he's pulled and yanked, but with those shoulders turned toward paydirt and those powerful legs churning, what force could bring him down? Finally, when they get him once again solidly moored upon the earth, he has gained twenty yards, which, according to the *Courier,* is the second longest pass reception of the day. But these are not just any twenty yards. They are twenty yards in what is called the Red Zone, close to the goal. A few plays later, the stolid Shobert plunges over, and DuBois is up six–zip.

You can never say that Toad took over, in that great athletic sense where one man so gifted dominates an entire field of play. He doesn't transfigure or transcend, he's not outlined mythically against a blue-gray November sky. He's just the big kid who keeps on thumping. He's just there, every damn time, doing whatever small, painful thing must be done. It's partly talent, and partly luck; but mainly it's commitment to duty, and commitment to duty is what Toad has up to his eyebrows. Everything he ever tried he succeeded at, and any anxieties he felt about his father's institutionalization had not made him fretful and unsure but made him a bulldozer.

Then came a moment late in the game when things got desperate. By a fluke—the alert Rossi stripped the ball from a Baron in the backfield and ran it in for a twenty-five-yard touchdown in the third quarter—DuBois is up 12–7, but had stalled deep in its own territory. The passing game has all but gone away as three straight passes have been knocked down, and it looks like curtains. A desperate situation demands a desperate play, and this is what the *Courier* scribe meant when he noted that "Thrill plays were frequent." Instead of punting as one would expect, DuBois's Shobert lofted a soft pass into the flat where speedy Garthwaite speared it, and turned upfield. Linebackers vectored in on him; he was only at the five and if he's nailed that deep, the Barons will surely grind in the winning score. When from out of the west who should come but Toad, and he gets those big shoulders rolling—"and with Boring cutting off tacklers," notes the *Courier* man—Garthwaite is sprung for a sixty-seven-yard dash to the twenty-eight-yard line, and the game played out over its last few minutes with DuBois eating clock in gulps while knocking on the door for a meaningless touchdown.

As the writer at the *Courier* limns it, "The sorely beleaguered Beaver of DuBois High School on Saturday lapped the blood from its wounds of body, mind and spirit, craunched [sic] back upon its haunches and lurched upon the Windber Coal Barons with such a savage attack that the

West Central Pennsylvania Conference champions were crashed to their first defeat of the season."

And that's how it ended. Not bad for Toad, who'd already died once in his life.

It happened on a summer morning sometime in the 1920s. He was just a wild kid, who lived in a not-so-nice apartment (intermittent electricity, crapper outside) with two older brothers named James and Colonel and a mom named Frances Mary Murray, Irish and tough. She had to be. She was raising the family herself. Dad, Earl Cleveland Boring, wasn't there. Everybody knows, nobody talks about it: Dad was in Warren State Hospital. He was a brakeman on the railroad and he started imagining he was talking to people. He started talking to them more and more and people started noticing. Then he stopped talking altogether. The diagnosis was schizophrenia. He was committed when Toad was three.

Toad ran free, played ballgames of all sorts (he was good at them), had buddies, got in a fight now and then, did well in school. If life was hard, he hadn't noticed. He didn't think much about his dad, his mother was working for the railroad that sustains the coal industry, his two brothers were working, it's the Depression. But no one told him it's hard, and so he's really having a pretty good old time of it, running around the low ridges crusted in pine, the gulches, the gaps, the rivulets, the forests that are the rolling coal country of DuBois.

DuBois, in Clearfield County about a hundred miles northeast of Pittsburgh, is a high town, about 1,400 feet above sea level. The air feels thin. The altitude means chills bite harder, winds blow harder, the sun burns hotter. The city itself spills across a gathering of hills and ridges lumpy and uneven on one side of a broad flat cut by the meandering Sandy Lick Creek. It's a town like most towns: the richer the owner, the higher the house. On the north side, for example, on DuBois Avenue, the mansions stand, looking like sentinels reconning the unruly flatlands beneath them.

The valley is dominated by trains. DuBois started as a timber town but now exists because of coal. Coal must be mined, then collected, then shipped out. DuBois's specialty, courtesy of B,R&P RR, is the shipping. It's a rail hub and the railyards dominate it, filling its air with the rancid odor of steam and kerosene, defiling its landscapes with alps of hauled-in coal, which, in transit, emits a constant vapor of dust. In the yards, endless miles of coal cars are linked together for the haul to points lower, where the coal will fire the engines that make America grow.

It's not a little town. Sinclair Lewis might have set a novel there, and John O'Hara, the great Pennsylvania writer, could have—though he didn't—based his on DuBois's aspiring gentry. The town's got a substantial run of urban downtown, four blocks of buildings that could have been surgically removed from Third Avenue in Manhattan and planted here in the mountains, and it has a row of restaurants and theaters and libraries and department stores, which Trautman's, an elegant emporium on Main Street, dominates. It has a middle class; it has beautiful, graceful homes on its mapley streets.

There's even a municipal tennis court, so that the well-born children of rail executives and department store owners can learn that genteel sport. And on the day that he dies, in high summer, Toad is racing by the tennis court on this or that adventure and one of the players on the court tees off on a ball and Toad sees the ball sailing in his direction and he leaps for it. He's played baseball and he knows the way a good player will track the trajectory, fade back, eyes up, intercept the flight, and pluck the thing out of the air, and that's certainly what he's thinking about, and his hands reach up and he leaves the ground and—

He had a whistle in his mouth. He swallows it.

The small wooden object catches in his throat. He cannot breathe. In seconds the oxygen debt occludes his brain. He's dying.

So Floyd, lost in the only panic he'll ever be in over his long and distinguished life, starts to run. He runs, he runs, he runs until the last cc of oxygen has been used for fuel. No fuel, no power, no run.

Down he goes in a dead faint, his life ebbing away. Until he hears a strange, faraway sound. TWEET.

It seems the laws of probability are suspended and the insanely unlikely becomes commonplace. What are the odds on the ball coming exactly as little Toad is not merely there, but that he has a whistle in his mouth? What are they then that when he leaps and lands, he involuntarily swallows, and the whistle, ingested, becomes a garotte? Then, when death is closing down on the boy, what are the odds that he would run in a panic, faint and collapse at just such an angle and speed that the surface of the earth itself performs the yet-to-be invented Heimlich maneuver on him, and the whistle, liberated from the gullet, goes down clean into the lung?

Yet this is exactly the chain of events that sent Toad to heaven, then brought him back again in a few seconds. Now, awake, he could breathe fine, it's just that on every exhale, he TWEETED like a canary in a cartoon that wouldn't be invented for twenty more years.

The trip to the hospital resulted in an X-ray, which in turn led to the prescription, "Cut the thing out." The problem with that was that you'd have to cut the lung out with it as well. Therefore the life that followed would be the life of the one-lunged man, low on stamina and strength, an indoors type forever. Think of the things Toad would have missed.

A Dr. Tucker, who had been in a class taught by the inventor of the bronchoscope, heard what had happened after the wheezing Toad was brought into the local hospital. He said, "Please don't take out his lung." He arranged for the boy to be taken by train to Philadelphia. That way, they could get the whistle out without dissecting Toad and more or less consigning him to a limp and timid life as a one-lunged man.

Two minutes, eight seconds of bronchoscope effort as used experimentally for one of the first times in medical history, and the TWEET was gone and Toad had his pristine lung back. His mother asked the doctor what she owed him. "Nothing. I'll just take this whistle we got out of your boy in payment."

Consider again the play of chance in this event. How lucky it was that the bronchoscope had just been invented, had just been invented nearby, and that a doctor in little DuBois had actually heard about it.

The whistle was later exhibited in Washington, so remarkable was the medical accomplishment held to be.

In fact, the whistle got to Washington before Toad did.

Toad survived whistles and football and the institutionalization of his father and the grinding poverty of his family, all without really noticing any of it. As he matured, he was, by reports, not averse to mischief. He was also Mr. Joker about the town. He didn't mind showing off a bit now and then. And he had a wonderful aptitude for vehicles, especially not his own.

The vehicles in question belonged to his older brother Colonel. One was an Indian motorcycle, the other a 1929 roadster, acquired by dint of Colonel's hard work at a bank and his cautious ways with a buck. They were Colonel's pride and joy, but every time he looked out his window, one or the other would be missing.

It is reported reliably that the mechanically gifted and highly coordinated Toad had one trick that was a specialty: he could rise upon the bike chassis until he crouched on the seat, then he could rise higher until he stood on one leg, the other outthrust behind him. He seemed to like to do this one when there were young ladies around and Colonel was nowhere to be seen. Then he and his pals would stop off at local watering holes and down a Budweiser or seven. And this wasn't Augie Busch's Bud. This was genuine DuBois Budweiser as brewed in that town (illegally for the seven years of Prohibition) by the local brewery.

After high school graduation, he worked a couple of jobs around town, one in a glass factory, one in a battery factory, while waiting on his State Police application. He had to hitchhike to Butler to take the test and to Harrisburg to take the physical and to Hershey to take the training. But he did it. Six months in Hershey—he got the six winter months—taught him how to ride both motorcycles and horses, how to shoot a revolver, what the motor vehicle laws of the state were. Pennsylvania's was one of the more progressive State Police agencies, and the training was rigorous and thorough, which is why that force became such a conduit to the Secret Service. But Toad couldn't know any of that yet; what he knew was that as a child he had admired the men on the horses who rode fearlessly into the crowds of angry miners and kept the peace, who halted violence by a benevolent application of nonlethal force, who protected property and lives, and now he had become one.

He was now the driver of the horse truck, a huge white vehicle with six horses and six officers, to whichever town the trouble has lit in. There, the horses are saddled, the six mount up, and ride to the strike.

The horse has been chosen for this task because no one argues with a horse. You just don't do it. No argument can be won against a horse. These horses were specially trained. They expected to be in and around crowds, they were calm by temperament, they responded well to their riders, and they didn't panic at noise or abuse or the presence of angry men, or even rocks thrown in their direction.

The cops weren't Cossacks; they didn't ride in and scatter the strikers, whipping them with swagger sticks or any such thing. Rather, the art was the art of keeping the warring sides separate, and nothing separates like a horse. Leg, leg, rein, that was the rhythm. The horses could walk sideways and just brush the crowd back. For troublemakers, a special technique was employed, and one suspects that the cops enjoyed this one. The troublemaker, pushed back, turns around, and when his back is to the wall of horses, one cop breaks free, leans over and snags the loudmouth by the belt and, lifting him like a sack of flour, canters away, the man dangling in the strong grip, probably screaming, certainly squirming and flailing. Five hundred feet away, he's dumped in a heap. The horse wheels and the big officer leans over and delivers a stern admonition.

There were other jobs, of course. Toad sometimes served warrants, and it has been noted what could come of that. Another day he was on a team that went to arrest a cop killer. The cops had shotguns, the bad guy had a handgun. They threw the body in the back of a meat wagon to haul it to the morgue.

Then there was Ruth.

"I think Ruth fell in love with him from the very beginning. There was never anybody else in her life except Toad, and I think he felt the same way about her," one of her sisters remembered.

You don't know when it's going to happen, but happen it does. It happened to Toad in 1937. He was doing a part-time job, helping a pal of his, a musician, set up for Jim Wilson's orchestra, at a place called K.C.—Knights of Columbus—in DuBois. It cost 25 cents to get in, and the kids walked through the snow to get there.

Since orchestras were the rock groups of the 1930s, then as now the girls flocked. Maybe Ruth saw a Johnny or a Frankie warbling a love song onstage and maybe she didn't but she did see a Toad and she liked what she saw. He was big and beaming with the vitality that radiated from him his whole life, that John Wayne thing but played for real, the sense that he didn't take crap but at the same time he didn't give crap either. They'd gone to different high schools—his public, hers Catholic—and soon they were talking and laughing.

Ruth is one of the willowy, beautiful Lehner sisters, tall, thin girls of regal bearing and grace, musical ability, and great senses of humor. Once they had enjoyed a comfortable station, but later their income diminished—the Depression—so the family had to move down the hill to the flats and ended up near the railroad. Ruth has memories of watching the engines trundle by and waving at the engineers, who waved back (as what man would not at a girl so pretty?). She and her sisters got to know all the engineers by name, and a helpful hobby was patrolling the yards for fallen pieces of coal, which would then fire the family stove.

The courtship was three years long and it boasts one movie moment. The flats had a problem, and Ruth was particularly disturbed by it: flooding. She was petrified by water. During heavy rains, Shaffer Ditch, which ran right by the Lehner house, would flood. One day in the late 1930s, she found herself upstairs, trapped by three feet of dirty black water.

But Toad had thrown on waders and plunged his way down the torrent, and the next thing you knew, he snatched her up, just like that football, and proceeded to high ground with her, past Pearson's Hat Store, where she sometimes worked, past the Swedish Club and Nelson's Restaurant at the corner of DuBois and Main, and he delivered her high and dry to safety.

And the next damn thing you know, it's 1940 and they are getting married.

Then the war started and he was exempt because of his eyesight, but a lot of the other men were drafted and the few that stayed behind started working longer and longer and longer hours. For a newlywed, spending all that time in the barracks where state policemen live during duty tours (like firemen in firehouses, not like policemen in police stations) was not a good situation. Floyd loved the State Police but at home he had the beautiful girl pining away for him. He left the police, spent his time with Ruth in an apartment in the back of a chiropractor's, and a baby named Judith Anne was soon on the way. Floyd started working at the National Tube Company, a subsidiary of U.S. Steel, and because of the police background, was appointed a lieutenant in the plant guard force and was running a security shift during the day.

But he doesn't like it. Not only doesn't he like it, he can't stand it. Perhaps this kind of work doesn't have the calling, the sense of mission, the position of community respect that the State Police had. He's a policeman. He was born a policeman.

So he called some old buddies at State Police headquarters and learned that the Secret Service was looking for trained, trustworthy, experienced men who could hit the ground running, as wartime urgency precluded extensive training. He applied, he was accepted, and in two weeks he was in the Secret Service.

There was really no training. It's not like it is now. Manpower was short, Floyd was vetted by virtue of the Pennsylvania State Police, and his first day on the job was November 9, 1943. His first assignment took him to Syosset, New York, with President Roosevelt's kids. From there he was assigned to the Protective Research Section in the White House, which was a kind of prelim for the White House assignment. It was an introduction in theory to what he would meet in the middle of a gunfight a few years later: that is, people with a grudge against the president of the United States.

The job was to go through the letters received and forwarded by the president's office, and classify them by threat level, then notify agents in a locality if a citizen appeared too angry to be trusted. If so, the agents would pick up the citizen and explain to him that he could disagree with the president all he wanted to, but he couldn't call him a son-of-a-bitch. He learned there were voluminous files kept on these angry folks and that sometimes they'd begin their letters nicely but get so heated up that by the time they were halfway done, they'd start spewing invective.

Maybe somebody liked Toad a lot, possibly because of his bearing, possibly because of his humor, possibly because he got along with the guys and fit in so perfectly and everybody knew they could rely on him. Or maybe Toad did so well because nothing ever impressed him as much as how hard his mother worked to put food on the table for three boys in the middle of the Depression. But very quickly, he became one of President Roosevelt's bodyguards, and suddenly, in a few months, less than a year, he'd gone from an employee at a tube factory in a small city in western Pennsylvania to a key member of the White House Protection Detail and very quickly found himself an eyewitness to history.

He goes places, he sees things. He's outside Roosevelt's window in Warm Springs when that great man dies, April 12, 1945. Then Toad was on the train all the way up to Hyde Park.

He meets Truman ten days or so into the new administration, when Truman's regular driver—he'd been Roosevelt's driver, possibly he was still shaken over the death—turned up drunk. Everyone knew Toad had driven that big horse truck in the Pennsylvania State Police, so he got the driving assignment, at least when they were outside the city. And one day the president said to him, "By the way, I see you are driving most of the time. How are you connected with me?"

Toad responded, "Well, Mr. President, I've been assigned to drive you."

"Well, could you tell me your name?"

"Sure I can. Floyd M. Boring, United States Secret Service."

"You don't mind if I call you Floyd, do you?"

"No, sir," said Toad, and he was ever after "Floyd" to Harry Truman, who never forgot his name or to send him and Ruth a Christmas card.

So he stayed. The job included doing advances for out-of-town trips, driving, running the shift, making sure things were always covered. It was a forty-eight-hour, six-day-a-week job, and he probably saw less of Ruth than if he had stayed a state policeman. But he saw enough of her to father a second daughter, Kathryn, in late 1949. And one day, he saved the president's life.

It was on the *Williamsburg,* the presidential yacht, in the Potomac. The president wanted to go swimming.

"The President gets in the water, and he was a bum swimmer. He was about like he was as a driver; he was going all this here [struggling to stay afloat] and losing ground. They were all getting excited and these fellows were going to drop a boat almost on top of him. I said, 'Hold on there, don't do that.' So I took one of these life preservers, and it almost went on top of him. He grabbed the thing and we pulled him in."

Toad was there in Potsdam when an army colonel said to the president, "Listen I know you're alone over here; your wife hasn't arrived yet. If you need anything like, you know, I'll be glad to arrange it for you."

The president said, "Hold it, don't say anything more. I love my wife and my wife is my sweetheart. I don't want to do that kind of stuff. I don't want you to ever say that again to me."

And Toad was the one who had to give the president some very bad news.

"Mr. President, your horse is going to run away with you if you don't close up that barn."

"Gee," said Harry Truman, buttoning his fly, "thanks very much."

That was the man Floyd was sworn by duty to protect, and the duty was not just to the man and to the country, but to his own sense of doing the right thing, of staying there, of not running away. And that is why he stood in plain sight on November 1, 1950, aiming at Oscar Collazo.

I'm going to finish this baby right now, he was thinking.

20. SO LOUD, SO FAST

The universe consisted of but one thing and that one thing was a target. The target happened to be a head, the head happened to be still, the range happened to be twenty-five feet, and it was a shot he had made thousands of times in his life. If you wanted one man to make one shot to save the life of the president, you'd pick this man.

Toad pressed the trigger. He had it just right. A moment when the little man's bobbing and ducking had ceased, when the little man was still. Toad saw the front sight calm and big in the center of the big hat, and he thought, *I'm going to finish this baby right here,* and he touched the trigger and the little Colt Detective Special, cupped so protectively in his big right hand, jumped in recoil. He expected to see the little man in the big hat go stiff, then lurch all deadweight to the pavement and begin to bleed copiously. That's the head shot. It ends everything fast.

Nothing happened.

How the hell could I miss, wondered Toad and the funny thing is, he didn't. He hit right where he was aiming and blew a .38 caliber hole in the man's hat. It's just that not enough of the man's head was in that part of the hat. It was a big hat but a small, flattish head. There wasn't much of it in the crown. The bullet, rather than punching through skull to the deep part of the brain, knocking out all the controls and toppling the brain-owner forward, simply cut a groove through Oscar's hair, flaying a laceration into his skull, and continued onward to hit whatever it did hit harmlessly.

But other factors may have made Floyd's shot all but impossible; he was hampered by the policies of two obdurate and narrow-minded agencies—his own bureaucracy, unbudgeable, and the laws of physics, unmalleable. As a cost-saving measure, the Treasury Department had installed a Star progressive reloading machine at the Treasury firing range, so that empty casings could be economically refilled with powder, refitted with primer, and replugged with bullets, and fired again—and again and again in practice. The cost savings per round rose as the number of rounds fired rose; it would have made any mid-level government accountant's heart warm and toasty. Floyd had, in fact, just finished firing three hundred of those rounds, reconfirming, even grooving for himself, the relationship between his sight picture and the strike of the bullet. Thus, when he aimed at Oscar's forehead, he had every expectation of striking Oscar's forehead.

Unfortunately, those target rounds—characteristically smaller amounts of powder pushing lighter drum-shaped bullets called wadcutters—will always strike lower than a full-power round of the sort Floyd then fired at Oscar. That is because the heavier, more powerful cartridge has a more significant recoil, and in the microworld of the firing handgun—measured in milliseconds—the amount of recoil causes the barrel to rise even before the bullet has left the muzzle. The more powerful load, recoiling more stoutly, causes the barrel to rise faster and higher; therefore, the bullet strikes higher, even at twenty-five feet. This tendency, furthermore, is exacerbated by the light, one-handed grip he'd been trained to employ, which liberates the small revolver to recoil even more aggressively. What this means is that if he aims at Oscar's forehead, he grooves Oscar's scalp; if he had aimed at Oscar's nose, he would have hit Oscar flush between the eyes. It's not a thing he could have known because it's not a thing his agency had thought out carefully.

But that is the world of the gunfight, the unpredictable magnified by the irrational. The fight becomes, as someone has said, what it wants to become, not what you want it to become. You adapt or you die. Meanwhile, there is no time, there is no sense. Everybody is catapulted into an adrenally charged mayhem. Bullets miss usually, but sometimes they hit. Results are governed by training and instinct as monitored by the universe's iron sense of whimsy. Notice what has already happened in the first ten seconds: Oscar has screwed up, then he's gotten the gun to fire and, by luck or grace, he's hit his target nonfatally. Donald has had the presence of instinct to move out of there, and the sense to cover himself with his own fire as he moved. Floyd has taken the good shot on a target that presented itself perfectly before him, without hesitation or indecision. He shoots to kill. He makes the perfect shot, and, by some unknowable dictate of the universe, the man before him happens to have a very small head in a very large hat, so the perfect shot accomplishes nothing.

Physiologically, the fighters have entered a zone that cannot be duplicated by man. It has to be real for you to get there: you feel nothing, you see only a little bit of what's ahead of you, you hear nothing. "Auditory exclusion" it's called: your hearing closes down. Meanwhile your fingers inflate like sausages and your IQ drops stunningly. Certain things that in real life might seem transparently absurd suddenly make perfect sense. Other things, bedrocks of the rational, simply disappear from your mind. Everybody is so deep into their primal being that all manner of weirdness ensues.

Yet it must be said that even in this confusion, in a world turned in a split second to lethal chaos, not a man flinched, not a man ran, not a man even ducked. Numbly the protectors did the necessary; earnestly, the killers tried to kill.

As for Oscar, he was too busy shooting to notice the bullet that scalped him. He just kept it up, best as he could. Not a trained shooter and not a man bred to or hungry for violence, he was simply yanking the now shortened trigger and experiencing for the first time the dynamics of the cycling semiautomatic pistol and the stout recoil of German steel-jacketed ammunition. The gun jumped each time he pulled—he couldn't have squeezed, he didn't know how, or if Griselio had told him, he'd certainly forgotten by this time—and he struggled to contain it. A skill in shooting is to set the gun up in the hand the same way at each shot, and that skill he lacked. The gun repositioned itself anew each time, which meant that any even cursory attempt at accuracy was utterly betrayed. He cranked out the rounds, oblivious to the men around him, oblivious to anything, really. You could say he was issuing suppressive fire, except that he didn't suppress either of the two men he was shooting at. You could more accurately say he had simply let his brain go into a hole somewhere and he was simply squeezing off rounds on pure instinct, on the half-formed suspicion that if he were shooting at them, they would be too busy ducking to be shooting at him.

Toad, heroically impervious to the bullets zinging through the air in his direction, quickly cocked, his big thumb flying to the hammer as he rocked it back till it locked, as his years of training had instructed him, and looked for another shot, but now the man seemed to have moved and was crouched. And then everybody was firing.

BAPBAPBAPBAP! a noise came hard against his ears and he winced at the multiple percussions that penetrated his ears, filled them with painful ringing. Next to him, Davidson had drawn and fired so fast he must not have bothered with the single-action drill and had simply thrust the gun at his target and squeezed the trigger double-action at full speed. Other sounds rose—Toad couldn't place them, but they had to be Don Birdzell on the street and, unknown to all of the men in the eastern sector, shots being fired in the west, where Griselio, Les, and Joe Downs were now mortally engaged.

All three guards at the eastern sector of Blair House were zeroed in on Oscar, who is himself in a mad dance of shooting and moving. Toad and Joe Davidson crouched behind the uncertain cover of the wooden guard-house, trying to get a better shooting angle toward Oscar. Donald Birdzell had reached the end of his crabwalk out on Pennsylvania Avenue, between the trolley tracks, and had turned and opened fire on his target.

But what is happening upstairs at Blair House to the man all are pledged to save or kill?

21. UPSTAIRS AT BLAIR

If ever a man deserved a nap that day, it was Harry S. Truman.

It wasn't that he had had a particularly busy morning. It certainly wasn't enough to tucker a peppy sixty-six-year-old farmer's son, used to hard work, long hours, and getting the job done on stamina rather than genius, which is itself a species of genius. But on November 1, 1950, Harry Truman had a soul-deep fatigue that the past few months had crushed into him. The strain radiated from his usually jaunty face at every public appearance. Even the papers that loved him had noted that the chipper whistlestop warrior who had stunned the nation with his upset victory over Thomas Dewey two years earlier now walked with a heavy tread. The crisp suits, the two-tone shoes, the snappy ties, the fabulous atilt straw Panamas, the cane he didn't need except for self-defense, all of those trademarks seemed unrelated to the dour oldster now in the autumn of his discontent. He had once said of Washington that if you couldn't stand the heat, you should get out of the kitchen. But he wasn't in the kitchen anymore; events had moved him to the epicenter of the blaze.

After his 1948 triumph, during the first part of 1949, things had gone reasonably well. "No calamitous domestic issues erupted. There were no sudden international crises to contend with. Greece and Turkey did not fall to Communist takeovers, nor would they. Nor would France or Italy. Best of all was a decided easing of tension over Berlin that began just days after the inauguration," notes David McCullough in his epic biography. Other developments were to follow: NATO was established, the Berlin Airlift succeeded, the "prospect of a prosperous, self-governing West Germany" emerged. The only bad news came from China, where Chiang Kai-shek's regime was crumbling. It was clear that China would go red, despite the $2 billion the United States had poured into Chiang's government.

A minor brouhaha sounded the change in fortune. This was called the "5 percent scandal," by which Harry Vaughan, Truman's military aide and a longtime friend, was dragged before a Senate committee and accused of selling influence, using his connection to Truman as part of the deal, and charging 5 percent on all contracts he managed to secure for his friends. The Republicans, especially a junior senator from Wisconsin looking for a way to make a name for himself, had a field day with that one!

But it got worse fast. On September 19, 1949, VERMONT arrived. VERMONT was the code name in high government circles for the Russian bomb, and on that day it was confirmed by scientists, working from data an air force weather plane had picked up on patrol over the North Pacific, that the Russians had detonated a nuclear device. This in turn, within weeks, led to intense pressure within the government to develop a trump card: an H-bomb. The arms race was on. Then, on October 1, in Peking, the People's Republic of China was officially inaugurated. China had been lost.

Meanwhile, the red hunts were ginning up, and Truman's secretary of state, Dean Acheson, picked an extremely inopportune time to voice his support for his friend Alger Hiss (whose brother was Acheson's former assistant), just found guilty of perjury for denying that he'd passed classified documents to a communist agent. The anger on the Hill was intense, particularly since Acheson was loathed already for being the man who "lost China." Richard Nixon, the congressman who'd led the Hiss crusade, accused the administration of a "deliberate effort to conceal the Hiss conspiracy." Then news reached Washington from London that a British scientist, Klaus Fuchs, who had served at Los Alamos on the World War II atomic bomb project, had confessed to being a Soviet agent.

More bad news arrived in the form of that junior senator from Wisconsin, Joseph McCarthy. At forty-one, a less-than-utter mediocrity, he had been recently voted the worst senator in Washington by the press corps. Looking for an issue—the 5 percent scandal was running out of gas—he settled on anticommunism. McCarthy first made news in February of 1950 on Lincoln's birthday, proclaiming that he held in his hand a list of 205 "known communists" in the State Department. He started his one-man bandwagon rolling and kept it rolling on the strength of his bullying demagoguery, his sullen brawler's fury, and his shameless willingness to say anything to anybody anytime and anyplace. He became so famous and so popular so fast—it was the beginning of the age of television—that the many members of his own party who detested him had to lend public support.

That circus dominated the political news and fortunes in the capital throughout the spring and early summer of 1950. At the same time the Democrats had their own star anticommunist, the same Pat McCarran of Nevada who was in the process of besting Truman in getting his McCarran Act passed over the president's veto. Though Truman tried to remain above the issue, many of his staff members and appointees came under suspicion, including the magisterial Acheson, of whom he thought so highly. In a rueful mood, Truman wrote to his wife, "You see everybody shoots at me, if not directly then at some of the staff closest to me." He didn't realize how soon the shots would cease to be metaphorical.

Then came June 25, 1950, a date that will not live in infamy forever. In fact, it has been all but forgotten, as has so much of what happened in the sixth decade of the twentieth century, which has receded into a collective folk memory of tail fins, TV antennas cluttering the roofscapes, rockabilly studs named Elvis, and little else in a national pageant called "The Fifties." But on that day—actually it was 9:20 P.M. on June 24, as Washington time was thirteen hours behind Korean time—Harry Truman, on vacation in his home town of Independence, received a phone call from Dean Acheson. "Mr. President," Acheson said, "I have very serious news. The North Koreans have invaded South Korea."

Thus began the Korean War. It was a monstrously dirty, violent fray, using up young lives in the thousands. But first of all, it was a massive international crisis for Harry Truman.

At meetings the next few days, the president stood firm on the principle of intervention and ordered U.S. land and naval forces to support the South Korean forces, which were in a state of near collapse as North Korean armored units penetrated deep beyond the 38th parallel and had already taken Seoul, the South Korean capital.

The war raged furiously all summer long. By August 25, American casualties were 6,886, by mid-September the number had doubled. Meanwhile, General MacArthur fought a campaign of retreat and advance, maneuvering brilliantly against the far stronger North Korean forces, holding the line here, retreating strategically there, attacking aggressively in still a third place.

And, just to make matters even more intense, at the same time Truman was having extensive dental work done. In three weeks in July he went to army dentists at Walter Reed twelve times, having two bridges, four single crowns, and a filling replaced—and he was only anesthetized once.

By August, MacArthur had fallen back to the Pusan Perimeter, an arc running 130 miles around the port city of Pusan. It was a bare toehold on the southeastern corner of the Korean peninsula. Desperate but brilliant, MacArthur conceived, and sold to Truman, a remarkable operation, a sunrise invasion deep in North Korea at Inchon.

The troops landed September 15, 1950; it worked brilliantly. By September 26, Seoul had been recaptured; meanwhile, other troops broke out of the Pusan Perimeter and began to work their way northward. MacArthur's men moved quickly, sweeping some of the North Koreans before them and isolating others, surging past the 38th parallel to the Yalu River.

On October 11, Truman left Washington on a 7,500-mile, four-day journey to Wake Island, a tiny spot on the Pacific Ocean that was little more than a landing strip. There he would meet with MacArthur, whom he had summoned to the island. The visit was primarily a public relations opportunity for Truman, a chance for a photo op with the popular general just weeks before the upcoming midterm elections. But the president was also worrying about the war and whether the Chinese would enter the fray. MacArthur assured him that that was unlikely and that even if they did, the United Nations forces could beat them.

Two weeks later, on the morning of November 1, the new CIA chief told Truman that the enemy in North Korea now included Chinese communist soldiers, perhaps as many as 20,000. This wasn't a guess; it had been "clearly established."

And that is why on November 1, 1950, Harry Truman, at 2:00 P.M., needed a nap.

And that is why the stakes of the battle lasting but 38.5 seconds between 2:20 P.M. and 2:20:38.5 P.M., November 1, 1950, were so high. The gunfight took place at an extremely anxious moment in the history of the republic. Americans of a certain age will always recall where they were when, years later, John F. Kennedy was slain in Dallas. Had Harry Truman been slain, that's the moment Americans of that time would remember and that would have been a moment of searing national trauma like none before and none after. It also could have marked the beginning of a tragic era.

But whatever might have happened did not.

Now, finally, it was nap time. Harry Truman went up the old stairs, turned right 180 degrees, walked about ten feet, then entered his bedroom. He entered a chamber that was about twenty feet by twenty feet by fifteen feet, with a window opening to the street below. And it was one other thing. It was not immediately above the Blair House entrance, as most of the newspapers identified it in the next morning's press. The bedroom itself is one window to the right, one window closer to the Lee House.

Since it was hot—and probably much hotter under the eaves of the old home without any air-conditioning—he had no desire to sleep in his clothes, so he stripped to his underwear, hanging up his suit. His bed, a high four-poster, abutted the eastern wall. He meant to sleep for only half an hour, for he had already instructed his doorman, James E. Wade, to wake him at 2:30.

But at 2:20—say, what the hell.

He came awake in a start.

What the hell was that?

Harry Truman's war had been an artillery war; it was big booms, beating at the eardrums. The slighter, distorted percussions of small-arms fire must have mystified him. And since Harry Truman was from Missouri, the Show-Me State, you had to show him. Or he had to show himself. So he rose, rolled to the left off the bed, and walked across the room to look out the window to see what the ruckus was all about.

22. DOWNSTAIRS AT BLAIR

s it happened, the 2:00 P.M. shift had left Stu Stout in the Secret Service office with Vince Mroz. The office was inside Blair, down the front hall to the east and in the eastern corner of the first floor. It was next to a stairway and next to the hallway to the front entrance. If you look out the window, you're about ten feet from the eastern guardhouse, separated only by that ribbon of yard, fence, bush, and tree.

Stewart Stout was a stocky man at five foot nine, whose nickname was "Slim" because he wasn't. He was known for his taciturnity. "He wouldn't tell you if your coat was on fire," his friend Floyd Boring said of him, laughingly. He was another ex–Pennsylvania state trooper, and a friend of Toad's. He was an older guy, a senior agent. He was born and educated in Easton, Pennsylvania, and was a state cop for four years before being appointed to the Secret Service in 1941. He had served time in the Philadelphia, Boston, and Washington offices, and on the Franklin D. Roosevelt, Jr., detail in East Norwich, Long Island, New York. He served in the United States Army from 1943 to 1946, initially in the infantry, where his math ability got him appointed to the Forward Artillery Observers, and later, his police background, as with so many of the other agents', having been noticed, with the Military Police, where he busted rackets in the Philippines. He came back with two war trophies: a bad case of malaria and a Bronze Star. He rejoined the Secret Service upon separation and went to the White House detail in 1947, where he and Toad had bonded.

He was decent, quiet, strong, and foursquare about his duties; some years later, he will be famous in agency culture for taking down a man— that is, to the ground—at a concert that President Kennedy was attending. The suspicious bulges in the man's jacket turned out to be drumsticks, and the man was legendary drummer Gene Krupa. At a

Republican convention, Stewart Stout almost arrested a man he saw carrying guns in the vicinity of President Dwight Eisenhower. Colleagues prevented him from pinching Wyatt Earp—actor Hugh O'Brian, in the costume of his TV series.

He was also an investigator of some note, and after retiring from the Secret Service in the 1960s went on to a career as an army investigator.

What made Stout unusual was that he looked just like J. Edgar Hoover. Even to this day, the people who knew him shake their heads with a little bit of wonderment.

His son, Mike, recalls that people would come up to him all the time and say, "Mr. Hoover," and Stewart Stout would just kind of chuckle and say, no, you've got the wrong guy, I'm just a Secret Service agent. He never got mad. But everyone knew he was the kind of man who'd take a bullet for the president—any president—without a second thought. That's how strong he was.

Stu was sitting there, probably smoking a Kent (his favorite brand), dapper in a fresh suit and tie, possibly thinking about the latest in hi-fi equipment (his passion) even with his senses alive, his mouth shut. Next to him, Vince Mroz was doing exactly what he was supposed to do, and one suspects that when Stu heard the sudden burst of gunfire outside the door, he did not react with stunned surprise or panic, he lost not one second in confusion, he had not a whisper of fear, doubt, or reluctance.

He rose without a word and raced down the hallway. He looked out the screen door. He could see nothing. But the nothing told him everything. People had scattered. The gunshots told him the rest. He did what he was supposed to do. He went back for the tommy gun, locked in a cabinet in the Secret Service office.

But there was a problem. The cabinet, a freestanding mahogany piece of furniture, was locked. Each agent and many of the White House policemen had a master key that would unlock it and several other gun cabinets throughout the White House. He set about unlocking the case. But whoever had planned the defense of Blair House hadn't thought out the realities thoroughly enough to realize that if one were to need a tommy gun, one would almost certainly need it fast. It represents in its way the eternal dilemma of the firearm, which is that to be effective it must be accessible quickly to trained personnel but at the same time it is so inherently dangerous to untrained personnel that it must be locked away.

Under great pressure, Stout was charged with inserting a tiny key in a slot. It may not have been doable by the physics of the universe in the time allotted. He got it open; he reached in, unlatched the door, pulled it open, and grabbed the tommy gun from a rack that also contained short-barreled pump-action shotguns.

Now he had to load and arm it. He inserted a thirty-round magazine in the housing just in front of the trigger frame, and slid it in, waiting for it to lock in place. Then he drew back the bolt—the nomenclature is actually "actuator"—on the right side of the gun until it locked, permitting a .45 cartridge to rise from the mag on the pressure of the spring and slip into the bolt. Then he checked the two levers on the left side of the frame to make certain the safety was turned to OFF and the fire-selector to FULL AUTO. It all took time.

Stout reemerged from the office. He ran down the hall toward the front door. He was at the decision point. He could turn left, kick open the screen door, and maybe he'd see bad guys running toward him. But he had no idea what was happening, who was out there, what the situation was. So maybe he stood there on the porch and saw a guy coming at him and sent a four-round burst from the Thompson into him. Or, maybe he stood there on the porch and someone across the street with a sniper rifle drilled him between the eyes, and a whole squad of North Korean commandos raced by his still form into Blair and a general massacre commences.

He didn't know. Nobody could know.

What he did know was his duty. His duty was to protect the president, no matter what, to the last cartridge, to the last drop of blood in his body.

Stu Stout turned right. He slid back a couple of feet to the foot of the stairway up to the second floor and the president's bedroom, pivoted, dropped to one knee, found a good kneeling position, leaned into the gun, and peered down its sight line at the front door. If anyone came through the screen door whom he didn't recognize, Stout would nail him.

"What are you doing?" a "high-ranking member of Truman's domestic staff" screamed at him. "Your mates are being shot down! What's wrong with you? Go help them!"

Stout was unperturbable, stoic, stolid, a sphinx with a tommy gun.

He kneeled, he waited, the gun alive in his hands, until relief came after the fight was over.

In Secret Service lore, he did the right thing. His job, it was said, was to protect the president, not aid his companions. U. E. Baughman, the then director, addressed himself to the issue in the book he wrote, *Secret Service Chief.*

"But Stout would not be bullied or tempted [by the shouts of the official]," Baughman (or his co-author Leonard Wallace Robinson) wrote. "He would not yield to the invitation either to achieve glory or save his reputation for courage. To him his duty was clear. That was all there was to it. Stout's refusal to move from his post was equaled that day only by . . ." and Baughman mentions the others. Baughman's assessment is that Stout "performed valiantly."

In fact, the image of Stout crouched behind his tommy gun has become a part of Secret Service legend, the image of the loyal retainer so disciplined that he locks himself in place, oblivious to everything except his duty.

There are only two problems with this. The first is that Baughman is also lobbying for himself and his plan, which he refers to several times as an elaborate "defense in depth" that he himself had engineered. It consisted of three "rings" of defense, the guards and agents outside (the outer ring), the guards and agents inside (the middle ring), and "the inside ring, [which] was stationed immediately outside the president's door. This ring had side arms and, concealed in a separate hiding place easily available to them, Tommy guns and other defensive weapons." Baughman's description of the attack is pretty much a demonstration of how his "in-depth" plan worked.

This is difficult to accept at face value. Basically, there were six men in the detail—Joseph Downs doesn't count because he was out getting groceries—and not one of them has ever acknowledged any "in-depth" plan. They had no plan at all. There wasn't time for a plan. They were where they were when the shooting started and they did what they did, brilliantly. But as for the whole notion of "rings," that sounds more like post-action creative thinking on Baughman's part. The "outer ring" was the whole show. The "middle ring" consisted only of Stout, who stayed, and Mroz, who left just as quickly for the outer ring. In the basement, near the housekeeper's office, were two more White House policemen who didn't figure in the fight at all and, given their position, probably couldn't have. There were also two men out back; they too, given their position, were unlikely to influence events. As for being yelled at by an unnamed staff member, that seems highly unlikely. The fight was over much too fast for that, and if something was yelled, it was yelled after the last shot was fired, in which case it was moot. And finally, that last "inside ring," with its sidearms and access to tommy guns and other defensive weapons, was problematical because it turned out to be only one man who had to struggle with a locked cabinet. There were no other agents in the upper floor of the house at the time. The only person besides Stout in the building between the president and intruders was the doorman, James Wade, and while Wade may well have given up his life for the president in a heartbeat, being unarmed, he would have presented no difficulty to the determined assassins.

But there's a more serious deficiency in Baughman's verdict. The afternoon of the incident, Stout filed a report. In it he states categorically that by the time he got back to the door with the armed Thompson, he saw "a man lying at the foot of the steps. At this moment the gunfire had stopped."

He was too late. There simply wasn't enough time to travel to the front stairs, travel back again, unlock the case, take out and load and prime the weapon, then return to the front, then return to a position near the steps. That took longer than 38.5 seconds. The gunfight was finished before he even got back into position with his submachine gun. Had either Oscar or Griselio made it into the house in the first 38.5 seconds, they would not have found a man with a submachine gun waiting for them. They would have found an empty hallway, while Stout was back in the office, unlocking, removing, and arming the Thompson.

This is meant in no way to dispute the notion that Stout performed "valiantly," only to point out the vagaries of timing in an extremely brief event, 38.5 seconds' worth of mayhem. If there is any blame to be assessed, it does not lie with Stout but with a plan that kept the guns stored in less than optimal circumstances.

But indisputably, and by his own words and in spite of the legend that obscures the truth, Agent Stewart Stout was in no position to prevent the attack on Harry Truman. That's why what happened outside, on the street, is of even more importance.

Meanwhile, across the street at the Secret Service office in the West Wing, Jim Rowley—the same man who will replace Baughman ten years down the line—was sitting in the office of Press Secretary Charlie Ross chatting, when the International News Service correspondent Robert G. Nixon burst in and announced that he's just heard that somebody's trying to kill Truman.

Rowley, a notoriously poor shot, nevertheless knew exactly what to do. He rose and yelled, "Where's my tommy gun?"

23. BORINQUEN

The island of Puerto Rico, in the name of whose freedom the gun battle raged at Blair House, lies a thousand miles from the United States on a south-southeast tangent. Most mainlanders are astonished to discover how distant it is. It sits at the end of the chain of islands called the Greater Antilles that runs along an east–west axis, and both Cuba and Hispaniola (Haiti and the Dominican Republic) are closer to the continental United States. Puerto Rico, by contrast, is much closer to Caracas than it is to Miami, much less New York. So it lacks the union of space that the nearer islands, Cuba in particular, share with the United States. It's an ocean voyage away.

It goes too far and is too melodramatic to point out that it's shaped like the point of a cupid's arrow, which has been fired away from the New World and toward Spain and to read from that its people's constant longing to return to a Spanish bosom. Nothing is that simple. But it *is* shaped like an arrowhead, flat at the western base, long and thin through the body, then tapering to a point or at least a suggestion of point at its easternmost extreme. It is not big. Compared again to Cuba, which is long and thin, or to Hispaniola, which is long and fat, it's tiny. It's less than 105 miles long and less than thirty-five wide.

Is it paradise? In the Puerto Rican imagination it certainly is, particularly as remembered from some grim barrio in the largest Puerto Rican city in the world, Nueva York, when the food is running low, jobs are scarce, the baby is crying, and a man can't seem to get a break. "Momma talked about Puerto Rico," recalls Piri Thomas in his classic memoir of Puerto Rican New York, *Down These Mean Streets,* "and how she'd like to go back one day, and how it was warm all the time there and no matter how poor you were over there, you could always live on green bananas, *bacalao,* and rice and beans." Oscar too thought it was wonderful; he spoke of "the sacred soil of Coabey" and described the place where he spent his adolescence as "beautiful. A wide plain surrounded by low hills."

But most Americans have no idea because if they go, they go only to a tiny strip of artificial paradise on a peninsula, an arm into the sea. What the norteamericanos will see is pretty much what they would see on a similar piece of geography—another long, skinny islet forming a bay—called Miami Beach: a series of dramatic and well-capitalized turista destinations suggesting a domino game played with giant hotels along the beach, amid swank homes, fabulous restaurants, and the swish-swish-swish of the undeniably sensual Puerto Rican señoritas. Flesh is always in fashion in San Juan. But beyond the hotel district in Condado, San Juan one-ups Miami Beach by virtue of tastefully re-renovated cobble-stoned streets and alleyways, the section called Old San Juan, a Hispanic Greenwich Village. There, balconied houses line the little alleys, along with restaurants, discount stores, old colonial mansions, and government buildings, such as La Fortaleza. The unpleasantness of 1950 at that site is nowhere acknowledged, and the bougainvillea and the vines and the flowers and the palms seethe in the humid, fragrant tropical atmosphere.

But there are other Puerto Ricos. For one, there's a mountain Puerto Rico. Most North Americans don't realize other than vaguely—the dim shapes glimpsed across the green plains and the bay as seen from the ramparts of the El Morro fortress at the tip of Old San Juan—that a line of mountains known as the backbone of Puerto Rico, intensely jungled, quite savage in their sudden verticality, runs the entire length of the island. That's where the coffee is grown, and revolution is fomented. Lower, where the mountains yield to plains on the way to yielding to the beach and sea, the green stalks coming out of the earth produce sugar, and the white grains are crushed from the sticky green stalks and shipped off, so that American addicts can sprinkle the stuff on their cereal every morning. That's the theory, at any rate, but the sugar economy is extremely complex and prone to manipulation by off-island sharpies, the weather, and other unpredictables, so it is not stable, and its frequent failures, both man- and hurricane-made, have yielded a tragic history.

In the center of the island, the devil weed tobacco is grown, to be fashioned into long, delicious tubes of death called cigars. The temperate climate and the brightness of sun produce an agricultural product some believe to be the equal, at its higher end, of the more famous torpedoes assembled in Cuba. These people would say: a Havana is only a Havana, but a Puerto Rican cigar is a smoke.

To the west, the landforms take up a sundered aspect, with short, sharp escarpments, like vine-sheathed ruins, jutting up everywhere. This is left over from sea bottom days, and it seems like a mythological landscape. Where are the dinosaurs? one wonders idly while navigating courses through these peaks on the way to Mayagüez. Then finally, offshore, there are tropical isles affiliated with Puerto Rico, like Vieques, reclaimed recently from half a century of naval bombardment. Its beaches and jungles are said to rival any in the South Pacific.

Still, mountain or plain, coffee or cigar, sugar or bikini-wax central, Puerto Rico may not be paradise but it certainly is uniformly glorious in that vivid, brightly colorful tropical way, rich in flower, zephyr, sea salt, undulating firm flesh, toenail polish, and dumplings (called empanadillas). Boys in the Bronx dreaming of it in winter have good reason to mourn its absence in their lives.

You cannot leave such a place unless under dire economic pressure, and that, alas, has been the dominant force in Puerto Rican politics and culture. For all its beauty, somehow the place was never self-sustaining; its masters, never really taking it seriously, patronizing it consistently, made decision after decision that kept it poor and barefoot. Aside from those in the tourist economy or those who identified totally with the colonial economic system, most lived tenuously. In 1950, after fifty-two years of U.S. rule, the island's economy put it at the very bottom of a state-by-state register of economic well-being. The per capita income in 1947 was $308; that on the mainland was $1,323. Perhaps one fifth of the population—84,000 families—lived in grinding poverty. High infant and maternal mortality rates haunted the jungles and mountains; there was a 10 percent unemployment rate in 1949. Meanwhile, between 1899 and 1940, the island's population nearly doubled.

In 1946, the University of Puerto Rico Department of Home Economics examined the living conditions on the island, with spectacularly squalid results. Only 8 percent of the population made more than $2,000 a year; 43.6 percent made less than $500. The per capita income of the 43.6 percent was less than $55. Eighty-four percent of rural families had no sink; 50 percent of urban families had no sink. Seventy-five point six percent of rural and 54 percent of urban persons slept three to four to a room. Only 4 percent owned a car. At the same time, the concentration of sugar production ownership in the hands of American companies at the cost of the old hacienda type of ownership by small landowners like Oscar Collazo's father was increasing. "By direct purchase, extending credit to small planters and then foreclosing on mortgages if it seemed desirable, by leasing lands for ten- or fifteen-year periods, by any and all means, four great American sugar corporations acquired fertile holdings on the island's level coastal plain that aggregated over 166,000 acres, of which 55,000 were held by one corporation alone." No wonder Nueva York, with its slums and cold and garbage and hostile environment, beckoned so fiercely to the island's young men.

This book is about 38.5 seconds' worth of gunfight, but to understand why the bullets flew that first day in November 1950, one must understand so much more. The context is tragic, except where it's merely sad. When Columbus sailed the ocean blue and showed up in 1493, he found a place called by its native inhabitants Borinquen, meaning land of the brave lords. Within a few years Ponce de León arrived and enslaved the relatively peaceful Taíno Indians. Half a century later, the Spaniards had run so low on slaves they began importing African slaves, which provided the island culture with its eternally spicy Afro flavorings.

Of the four hundred years of Spanish rule little may be said except that it was four hundred years of Spanish rule. That's the rest of the story right there. They didn't even get around to ending slavery until 1873, some ten years after it was ended in the United States, a fact the Spanish apologists tend to forget. And, to this day the Puerto Ricans adore their Spanish heritage, forgetting the blood, sweat, death, and rape that it must have entailed upon an almost daily basis across the four long centuries. They love the language, the culture, the rhythms, the colors, the traditions, the music of all things Puerto Rican in nature and cling to them with fervency. They even have a word for this difficult-to-define sense of heritage, *puertorriqueñidad,* which Nancy Morris, in her 1995 *Puerto Rico: Culture, Politics and Identity,* translates as "Puerto Rican-ness."

On the other hand, one can go too far in suggesting Puerto Ricans have a universal yearning to return to the bosom of Spain. The craziest thing about Puerto Rico is how such depth of feeling for a Puerto Rican identity can coexist with an adamant unwillingness to be torn from the bosom of the United States. What's amazing is how much Puerto Rican-ness is completely intertwined with a desire for U.S. citizenship and a connection to the United States.

In any event, the Americans were not greeted with open arms in 1898, when the U.S. Army arrived as an unintended consequence of the war with Spain. The United States then proceeded to advance a campaign that in later years might have been termed "winning hearts and minds." Its engineers understood that the campaign was cultural as much as political and set out to search and destroy vestiges of puertorriqueñidad. Language was among the first targets of opportunity. English became the official language of Puerto Rico, an insult to a people who loved their mother tongue.

Yet it is difficult to find evil in the hearts of the American colonizers who arrived in 1898 with a new language, a new educational system, a new way of doing and being. These men were not genocidalists. They meant their action to be a benevolence. The imperialists of the late nineteenth century really thought they were helping. They had no clear claim to the island except as war booty, and the war they fought didn't entail much in the way of struggle to justify their suzerainty, but nobody was giving anything back. When General Nelson A. Miles—"infamous Indian killer," left-wing historians sniff indignantly—landed in Ponce, the Spaniards retreated into the hills, after an initial invading fleet of 3,415 men had found only weak resistance in Guánica on the south coast. Miles's plan was to march across the island to take San Juan by land, not by sea. It might have worked too, but the Spanish surrendered before any serious battles could be fought. And once the Americans were there, they were there to stay.

Miles summed up his intentions: "This is not a war of devastation, but one to give all within the control of its military and naval forces the advantages and blessings of enlightened civilization."

So America shouldn't blame itself too furiously for imposing its colonial will upon the island. That's what empires, even new ones, as America was in 1898, do: they colonize, they exploit, they loot, they dominate, and they don't expect to be loved. And a vast majority of the Puerto Rican people have enjoyed and profited from their closeness to the United States, as countless polls have shown. But it's equally true and fair to say that in many cases the American stewardship of the island was not representative of the best traditions of democracy, goodwill, or fair play; therefore to see the Americans and their appointed officials as oppressors, as did many generations of Puerto Ricans up to and including Don Pedro Albizu Campos and his followers Oscar Collazo and Griselio Torresola, was at the very least an arguable proposition.

The root of the conflict goes back to the year 1897, before the start of the Spanish-American War. In that year, Puerto Rico obtained the Charter of Autonomy from Spain; over the years, this document has acquired enormous moral force among the Nationalists. And so at the conclusion of the Spanish-American War and the signing of the Treaty of Paris on December 10, 1898, Spain, in their view, had no legal right to give, and the United States had no legal right to receive, Puerto Rico as a possession. Thus, according to the Nationalist point of view, Puerto Rico's sovereignty was violated by "Yankee military invasion" begun under the guise of war when Miles landed and began his virtually unopposed march through the mountains.

But it's also fair to say that the possession of Puerto Rico was an afterthought to a war whose main objective was to liberate Cuba, only ninety miles from the United States, from Spanish oppression, and it offered a way of acquiring a naval coaling station for patrols in the Caribbean, as well as lots of bananas, sugar, and very fine cigars. This may have been jingoist and distasteful by the politically correct values of the twenty-first century, but it was a legitimate expression of the Monroe Doctrine.

But what was the United States to do with Puerto Rico (or, for that matter, its other unanticipated conquest, the Philippines)? Simply abandon these island nations? Give them up? Let them turn, as they possibly would have, into Haitis, Dominican Republics, Cubas? No, what the United States did, essentially, was what any colonial power at the turn of the century would have done: obey without self-examination its nature. It clung to what it had, it exploited what it had, it ruled what it had, realizing that Puerto Rico controlled seaway approaches to the Panama Canal; thus, under the doctrine of seapower as articulated by the influential Alfred T. Mahan, it militarized Puerto Rico; the island became another coaling station.

But its stewardship was hardly benign. In 1917, for example, all citizens of Puerto Rico, under the provisions of the Jones Act, were declared citizens of the United States. From an American point of view, this was an honor. But from a Puerto Rican point of view, it is an insult. It is saying to a people with a fierce national and ethnic identity, your country has no citizenship to offer, it does not exist. Therefore we make you ours, you little children, and now you must play by our rules. By decree of the Jones Act, the president appointed the governor, the commissioner of education, the attorney general, the auditor, and the Supreme Court judges. As well, decisions on economics, education, justice, and security were still made in Washington. And as an act of Congress, the Jones Act could be amended by Congress at will.

And many played by those rules, as statehood parties who yearned for closer ties to the newly self-appointed motherland grew in political power. But still there were enough men and women who believed in Puerto Rico as Puerto Rico, who had conceived an ethnic and a national identity of consuming passion, to render impossible the fusion of the smaller into the larger.

American policies did not help. Successive presidents appointed a number of mediocrities to the governorship of the island. Even the better appointees were typically men who ruled with America's interests first, Puerto Rico's second. At the same time, the FBI and Naval Intelligence began aggressive surveillance of radical groups; there were clearly different sets of rules for Puerto Rico than for the United States, despite the fact that both were governed by the same constitution.

Then, in 1948, Law 53 was passed. It was called the *ley de la mordaza*, the law of the muzzle, and it made it a crime to advocate or in any way agitate for the overthrow of the government of Puerto Rico. But it was purposely left ambiguous, and the definition of "advocating" was left to its enforcers. That ambiguity made it an important tool in controlling criticism and made it possible for the government to imprison people on the basis of their ideas, not their involvement in any revolutionary activities. Against all these developments there was a countervailing American liberal initiative, though almost always ineffective.

These grievances—the willful attempt at destroying culture and language, the construction of a political system that was controlled by off-island American interests in Washington, the institution of an economic system that uprooted people from the soil and turned them into migrants in a new, cold land, the subtly increasing tendencies toward totalitarian rule by a number of thick-headed colonial administrators—all had their effect. Many simply repressed any hostility; many simply went along and hoped for the best. Most worked hard, did their duty, accepted their lot, and prayed for better times. These people represented the third and largest group—beyond Nationalists and yanquis—at play on the island. Possibly any account makes it seem that the civilian population in the shadows is quietly supportive of the Nationalists, only afraid to come out and fight. But actually Puerto Rico doesn't fit that mold, which is what makes it so interesting. It should never be forgotten that although many Puerto Ricans at the time were very much in favor of independence, they rejected the Nationalists and their violence, and indeed thought that Albizu was crazy, not helping the cause in the least.

But while most Puerto Ricans accepted their lot, a small percentage— the Nationalists—felt a deep and abiding indignation. You cannot understand any of this if you do not visit Ponce, Puerto Rico's second largest city, on Palm Sunday of 1937.

You approach Ponce, which is on the southern coast of Puerto Rico, southwest of San Juan, out of the mountains. On the downslope, as the vegetation changes from plush mountains to tropic verdancy, you can see it stretched out on the plain before you, with the Caribbean blue-green in the background. The sun is bright, the sea sparkly, the city a mesh of earth tones and greenery on a grid. Some call it the most Mediterranean city in Puerto Rico and some the loveliest. The truth is, it's not particularly Mediterranean and it's not particularly lovely. It's just a working seaport, lacking the glamour and sizzle of the capital: it's flat and gritty, with its nicer sections and its uglier sections. It is notable to the Nationalist imagination as the birthplace of Don Pedro Albizu Campos, the site of his early education, his early law practice, and his launching pad into national politics as the incendiary columnist for *El Nacional.*

But by 1937, he was imprisoned in San Juan, awaiting transfer to the federal big house in Atlanta, rounded up and convicted (hastily) in the wake of the assassination of the chief of the Insular Police, E. Francis Riggs. The idea was to cut off the revolution's head and thereby kill its body. The problem was simply that the body refused to die.

In the first months of 1937, a situation of intense volatility had come to predominate. The Insular Police, being human, were still extremely upset at the murder of Riggs (and two other policemen thought to have been assassinated by the Nationalists, Orlando Colón and Antonio Gonzáles Cortea); the Nationalists were extremely angry at what they saw as the railroading of their leadership junta. And finally, the American governor, Blanton Winship, was concerned, and meant to stifle the Nationalist dissent by denying it an outlet.

Typically when the Nationalists applied for parade permits for demonstrations to express their anger at the sentence of Don Pedro and the others, they were usually denied all over the island (in San Juan, automatic weapons and gun crews were deployed along a proposed parade route as a further dissuader). This had not gone unnoticed in liberal mainland quarters; the American Civil Liberties Union will later argue that this policy intensifies, rather than diminishes, anger and dissatisfaction and makes inevitable that which indeed happened.

But that was the background. In the foreground was one of those absurd bureaucratic two-steps, a now-you-have-it/now-you-don't dance on the issue of a parade permit disallowed, then allowed, then at the last minute disallowed in Ponce, March 21, 1937. A week earlier, the Nationalists had petitioned municipal authorities for permission to mount a parade, which was denied because the mayor was out of town. When the mayor, José Tormos Diego, returned Saturday night, March 20, he finally granted permission. Meanwhile the new Insular Police chief, Colonel Enrique de Orbeta, had traveled to Ponce, examined the parade site, returned to San Juan, conferred with Governor Winship, and went once more to Ponce, determined to persuade the mayor to rescind the order, which he finally did, the very Sunday afternoon of the parade. Unfortunately, the parade had already assembled.

The intersection of Calles Aurora and Marina is to this day a pleasant setting. Flowery trees—poincianas, with their red-orange profusion of blossoms—overhang the area, the vegetation is plushly tropical, buildings are low and decidedly haciendaesque in charm and grace, whitewashed, with their overhanging balconies and terra-cotta fixtures. Then and now, it's not a slum. Then and now it's a mildly urbanized setting, what one might call a perfect example of twentieth-century civilization on the theme of the smallish, livable city, with homes and businesses in harmony, not too commercialized, not too residential. Churches are nearby, and it's a few blocks from the equally pleasant downtown area. Walk a few blocks in another direction and you find yourself at the doorstep of Local Aurora No. 7, the Masonic lodge that sponsored young Pedro Albizu Campos's education in America. It's just a nice place to be, except on the afternoon of Sunday, March 21, 1937.

On that corner, the Nationalists had their local headquarters (it's now a museum), a balconied two-story building in the Spanish colonial style, each window and doorway set inside a ceremonial framework of white wood, as if to give so humble a building a more regal bearing. The balcony, in a nice stylistic touch, curves sensuously around the corner of the

building—no acute angles here—where Aurora and Marina intersect, giving it the sweep of something more dramatic. Under the impression that
permission to march had finally been granted, the Nationalists had been
traveling to the club as a destination all day, many with their children
along, a sure suggestion that they weren't expecting a gun battle. By 3:00
P.M., the street was thick with them, maybe two hundred men, women,
and children, dressed in their Sunday best, the men in straw hats and
white linen suits, the ladies in their flowery print dresses, all full of purpose in expression of their faith and their anger. Children cavort in the
street. It looked like an afternoon in a park.

On the other hand, it must be said that while the parade, even when
legal, was mandated not to possess any military attributes, it did indeed
have a militarized theme. A group of eighty uniformed cadets of the
Nationalist Party—Don Pedro's junior paramilitary outfit—had arrived,
as well as a smaller contingent of twelve uniformed nurses and a five-
piece marching band. The cadets may not have been soldiers proper, but a
man could be forgiven for thinking as much: they were uniformed in
white pants and black shirts, they were well schooled in drill, and they
certainly presented a military face to the world. They promised, as do all
squads of drilled soldiers, might.

The Nationalists say, truthfully: they were unarmed.

The police say, truthfully: they were in military aspect, they got into
military formation, they obeyed military drill order, and they marched
out, to music, all forbidden. The parade itself was forbidden.

And it was. There is no doubt about this. Legally, the mayor had
rescinded the permit early in the afternoon. At an emergency conference
there at the intersection between Nationalist leaders and police officials,
the mayor again reiterated that the gathering was now technically illegal;
no permit to have a parade existed.

But what distinguishes the Ponce event from dozens of other routine
riot situations is what happened next. The police did not, in the preferred
fashion of the times, wade into the marchers and the families with trun-
cheons and clubs, whacking people left and right. You would expect that,
whether the place was Ponce or Dearborn; that's how unruly crowds were
treated in 1937. It happened at strikes and demonstrations all over America, and maybe even Toad Boring, atop his black horse in some strike-
busted Pennsylvania coal town, would know of such. But the police chose
not to do that.

Instead, they opened fire.

A remarkable sequence of photographs depicts these few moments. They do not quite rise to a threshold of proof of the Nationalists' allegation that the cops planned the massacre from the get-go and meant to teach the Nationalists a lesson they would never forget, if they even survived. But it does depict an appalling scenario, all chaos and blurry violence and death by gunshot in the gutter.

In the first photo, the cadets are lined up along the right side (as the photo is taken by José Luis Conde of the Puerto Rican newspaper *El Mundo,* looking south) of Marina Street; across from them is the crowd of spectators, gathered at the Nationalist headquarters possibly five deep, the crowd spilling around the corner down Aurora Street. Before and behind them are police formations, and the police have taken up a particularly menacing appearance. They are all in jodhpurs and riding boots, with Sam Browne belts on, as if dressed for cavalry battle. That may have been the fashion then, so to read into the wardrobe is perhaps going too far. Nevertheless, at the moment the shot is taken—it was appended to the ACLU's report on the incident, called "The Hays Commission Report on the Ponce Massacre"—they are clearly closing in, reaching for their revolvers.

This is almost exactly the moment it began. The leader of the cadets, defying the orders of the authorities, gave the signal to march. The band struck up "La Borinqueña," the Puerto Rican national anthem. A police officer raised his hand, ordering the marchers to stop.

A shot was fired.

No one knows who fired it, where it came from, whether it was even a shot. It could have been an auto in the next street backfiring. It could have been a firecracker. It could have been a nervous policeman whose front sight caught on the strap of his holster, so that as he jerked it free, he inadvertently pulled the trigger. But it almost certainly could not, would not, have been fired by anyone in the crowd. What would the point have been?

The second photo, by Carlos Torres Morales of the newspaper *El Imparcial* (who must have been standing two feet to the left or right of photographer Conde on the same second-story balcony overlooking the intersection), depicts the exact moment at which hell arrived at the corner of Aurora and Marina. A cloud of gun smoke arises in the center, and already the people in the crowd are falling back, beginning to run for cover. If you look carefully down Marina, you can see the submachine gunners setting up, adjusting their feet into the staggered firing position for better support as they raise their ten-pound tommy guns. The cadets haven't panicked yet, but their formation has come unglued as they cannot begin yet to figure out what is happening. Some of the nurses have left their formation, running across the street to party headquarters. And the band plays on.

The police, in a contagion of panic or savagery, drew and fired into the crowd. You can read their intent in their aggressive body postures, many leaning forward as they take up shooting positions or draw, many raising rifles or shotguns.

In the next seconds, all these men would fire. The submachine gun squad, most destructive of all, opened up. One can imagine the results of several Thompson guns spurting .45s at full cyclic rate from a range of about one hundred feet on a mass of people and, alas, some policemen as well (two died, almost certainly from the Thompson fire that sprayed wildly down Marina, through the crowd, to the police concentration).

The guns were loud. The crack of the reports was punishing, for each gun as it fires not only sends out a bullet but also a wave of muzzle gas propelling burnt particles of powder and lead shavings in a violent mist. Then there's the sound of the bullets hitting the pavement, the buildings alongside, the trees, the telephone poles: that's a secondary noise, yet it too is extremely powerful. And at each bullet strike, a splash of debris blossoms supersonically, filling the air with dust and grit. And finally there's the sound of the hits, and there were a lot of hits. Hunters know it well, that instantaneous signal of success when the bullet hits the game animal well and truly, a kind of dense, vibratory *WHAP*. No sound on earth is like it.

It was over in seconds.

Bodies lay everywhere. Many, fleeing the fusillades, fought their way into the only sanctuary available, which was the club. It soon became its own unique circle of hell: there were no linens to staunch the blood, and no room to lie down, so in a few seconds it became not only an abattoir but a crowded abattoir, and a very fearful one, for there was no guarantee at that time that the Thompson gunners, feeling their work undone, would not set up outside and proceed to riddle the place. Meanwhile, on the street, little scenes of atrocity were inscribed in the eyes of all who saw and would never forget them. One man, mortally wounded, wrote in his own blood, "¡Viva la Republica!" (Long live the Republic!) and "¡Abajo los Asesinos!" (Down with the assassins!) The cops clubbed a woman to death. They shot a man who was on his way home; he screamed "I am a National Guardsman" before the bullets took him down. A twelve-year-old girl was killed, as were many children. Another man writing in the medium of his own blood tried to inscribe the word "Valiente" on the wall, but died after the third letter.

The moaning, the crawling, the begging of the wounded were general. The air seethed with gun smoke, everything moved in a fog of disbelief and confusion, the police were in complete command, swaggering about, guns at the ready, looking for targets, the blood running in the gutters.

Nineteen people died, more than 150 were wounded, and, it's fair to say, the island was traumatized.

The ACLU, led by Arthur Garfield Hays, who was the organization's chairman, launched its immediate hearings and investigation, and issued a report in a month and a half. It concluded:

"1. The facts show that the affair of March 21st in Ponce was a MAS-SACRE. [Caps theirs.]

"2. Civil Liberties have been repeatedly denied during the last nine months by order of Governor Blanton Winship. He has failed to recognize the right of free speech and assemblage. Force has been threatened against those who would exercise these rights.

"3. The Ponce Massacre was due to the denial by the police of the civil rights of citizens to parade and assemble. This denial was ordered by the Governor of Puerto Rico."

And on and on and on.

Of course justice was vigorous and swift, in the Puerto Rican fashion. Here is the number of police officers convicted of crimes: 0. Here is the number of days they served in prison: 0. Here is the number of demotions and suspensions resulting from the event in police ranks: 0. And here is the number of apologies issued by Governor Winship: 0.

The various parties took their various lessons from these events. But perhaps the most salient lessons were the ones the Nationalists took, and who can blame them, looking at the bodies of the dead children and the pools of blood in the streets.

Their lesson—this is Don Pedro's conclusion, in prison, waiting for shipment to the federal pen; this is Oscar's conclusion, on a ship going to New York and hearing the news of the massacre from a radio room operator; this is twelve-year-old Griselio's conclusion, reading the pain and fury on the face of his big brother, Elio, on the face of his charismatic cousin, Blanca Canales; this is all of them in their towns and shops and bent over hoes, on steamships coming to America, in barrios in cold northern cities looking for work and hope, all of them—their lesson would have been something like: *Next time, we will have guns too.*

24. OSCAR ALONE

Oscar was being shot at from all sides. He stood out there, right at the foot of the steps, while four men from no distance farther than thirty feet (Birdzell), and more likely twenty feet, shot at him. He never flinched, he never panicked, he never really acknowledged the mortal peril he was in.

Oscar was shooting. The gun emptied itself in 13 percent increments each time he pulled the trigger. It leaped and barked in his hand, tossing spent casings to the side. He pirouetted this way and that, he twisted, he turned, he moved. He had astonishingly done exactly the correct thing from a tactical perspective. He moved slightly to the right, closer to the stairway to the Blair entrance, and between him and two of the men shooting at him (Boring and Davidson) was a wrought iron fence. They could *see* him. He was *there*. They could aim at him, as Floyd did, or they could point-shoot as Davidson did, with reasonable expectations, from that range at a target so close, of drawing copious amounts of blood. Yet they came up zero.

Is this because they were bad shots? No, indeed. In fact, they were superb shots. But what was happening is that as they fired at him, they were concentrated first of all, as they had been trained to do, on their sights. Thus the sights were crisp and clear to them, and that is exactly the path to accuracy with a handgun. In the background was the target, blurry but nevertheless distinct and immensely hittable. What they did not see was the wrought iron fence between them and the target, which had the attribute, though it was invisible to them, of a bulletproof barrier. Or at least it was bulletproof to those bullets.

They were firing the Treasury Department duty load, a round-nose .38 Special 158-grain bullet. When the bullet hit the wrought iron, it did not penetrate, though it must have made a hellacious reverberation. The lead, even moving at speed, was much softer than the wrought iron; instead, depending upon the angle at which the bullet struck the iron fencing, it either deflected, skewing off to left or right, its ballistic integrity and its lethal velocity hopelessly compromised, or it shattered, dissolving into a jet-propelled mist.

And that was what Oscar experienced. He did not feel the heavy whack of a bullet hitting him, but more the spray of fragments, extremely irritating but not lethal. One large one cut through his nostril. Another ticked an ear. There must have been a thump or a gouge of some sort when Toad's first bullet plowed through his hat and etched a groove in his skull, but he did not evince much discomfort and nothing interfered with his task at hand, which was to shoot back. He was so full of adrenaline and other chemicals that if he felt these minor wounds at all, he did not respond. The Secret Service agents had discovered that you cannot end a gunfight against a determined opponent by grazing him.

To end it, you must get a bullet deep into his body, rupture major blood-bearing vessels, arteries or veins, and cause him to rapidly exsanguinate; or you must break his load-bearing structures—his bones—and bring him to earth by shattering his struts so that he has nothing solid to keep him erect, and down he'll go, every time.

No shot did this to Oscar, not Floyd's, not Officer Davidson's. At the same time, from the street to which he'd rambled bloodily, Don Birdzell was bringing fire on Oscar but without much effect. Birdzell was moving, and nothing in his training had prepared him to shoot on the move. He was bleeding profusely from his leg, he was fighting shock, he was in great pain. He was shooting, as he has been trained to do, one-handed single-action, a position that requires a moment of stillness, a gathering of breath and strength and concentration, which has proved impossible in the chaos of the fight. So none of his shots struck home.

As for Oscar's own shooting, it was wild. "It bucked," he told his daughter much later. So he wasn't aiming, just laying out the rounds. They flew down the street, up in the sky. The few hundred-odd pedestrians in the immediate vicinity, now all of them gone to ground at the sounds of what has to be a gunfight, were extremely lucky that none of these shots struck them. Most bullets disappeared. One struck a window in a restaurant, and the papers the next day will be full of pictures of the puncture in the glass, the little jagged hole and the stress fracture shearing off at an angle. Another creased the tunic of a Metro police officer across the street.

It's doubtful that Oscar noticed when another figure emerged from the Blair House basement even as he was shooting and being shot at. It's doubtful that he noticed as his two primary antagonists moved toward that open door, moving down behind vegetation. It's doubtful that he noticed a shot coming his direction from the new antagonist.

It's doubtful, further, that he had any awareness of what was going on thirty-odd feet behind him, where Griselio, Les Coffelt, and Joe Downs are now engaged in their own mortal dance.

What he did notice is that his gun was suddenly empty. With a clack— the sound effects of guns are very dramatic—the slide locked back.

Oscar did the logical thing, the methodical thing, the Oscar thing.

In the middle of a mortal gunfight, he sat down on the steps to try to figure out how the hell to reload.

25. THE END'S RUN

Backfire.

That's what it had to be.

It's always just a backfire.

But there's another backfire . . . and another . . . and—

A maid screams.

Another maid screams.

At 2:20 P.M., Vince Mroz was sitting in the Secret Service office, which is right over the eastern entrance to Blair House, having just moved there in the push. Stout's in the room too, but the two aren't buddy-buddy.

Vince had heard gunfire before. He was a marine officer, even if he spent the war commanding marine contingents on aircraft carriers and never saw actual battle. He'd been involved in a gun incident just a few months earlier as well, so he knew the sound of gunfire. He was fast, he was big, he was athletic. Like all of them that day, it didn't take but a nanosecond for him to connect to the absolute reality of the moment. And like all of them, he didn't panic, he didn't freeze, he didn't think, he didn't hesitate or pause or wonder: he reacted.

He went to the window and he sees commotion: men bobbing and weaving, men running, and from the body language reads the urgency of the moment. He didn't even think: *It's happening.* He just went.

He was up, hitting the stairs, racing down the stairs, opening the big locked door under the office, which deposits him into the bright sunlight of the alley that runs along the eastern edge of Blair House, connecting Pennsylvania to H Street. He pivoted to the right, toward Pennsylvania, toward the action and the noise.

He saw Toad and Joe Davidson, guns drawn, coming at him down the alleyway from their initial firing point at the eastern guardhouse. They were running to the shelter of the corner of the building and as well toward the now opened door, through which they could not have gotten had he not opened it. Vince heard more fire, which, from his vantage point, he cannot identify. It has to be Oscar shooting wildly, Don Birdzell shooting through his injuries, and behind Oscar, way out of sight because of the angles but nevertheless auditorily clear, the exchange of shots initiated by Griselio on the western side of the front of the house.

Vince had his Colt .38 Detective Special in his hand, couldn't even remember drawing it.

The hammer came back, locked in place with a click, and he peered around the corner of Blair. A tree. Low vegetation. A blur of iron bars from the black wrought iron fence. A crowd of pedestrians across the street, hunched over. A trolley car stopped on Pennsylvania. The old War Office across the street.

And he saw Oscar Collazo.

Up came the gun. The sight went to Oscar.

He didn't instruct the finger to so behave; the finger knew. The finger was on its own. The finger decided.

The gun jolted in his hand as a 158-grain lead round-nose was launched toward Oscar.

And then Oscar seems to disappear.

Has he been hit?

Is he down?

At that moment another thought occurred to Vince. That is, it's rather ridiculous for all three of them, him, Toad, and Joe Davidson, to be hunkered down here right at the corner, with their limited visibility, their lack of connection to events, and, most importantly, their absence of shooting angles and targets.

Unlike other reactions, his next move is a conscious, deliberate decision. He knew you need angles to shoot from and at this moment there is no target.

Vince turned, and began his run. He raced through the basement corridor that ran parallel to Pennsylvania Avenue, through Blair, and on into Lee (there is no demarcation; inside, both houses are one house).

He ran, desperate to get through, to set up, to find another angle to shoot from, to win the fight.

26. GOOD HANDS

See that No. 14? That's a magnificent ballplayer. That's Otto Graham. Automatic Otto. Otto the Omnipotent. He came to Northwestern University on a basketball scholarship but freshman year he played intramural touch football and led Delta Upsilon to the Greek championship with an unbelievable passing arm. Pappy Waldorf, who coached NU's Wildcats, heard about Otto and went out to see him. The rest is sports history: he started for the Wildcats the next year and was soon enough setting Big Ten records.

So Otto was in the cathedral of Big Ten football called Dyche Stadium, and he was letting the ball fly. It was a crisp fall day, October 2, 1943, his senior year. Around him rose the stone towers of Dyche, solemn and vine-covered, a Parthenon of sports, a temple to the rigors of pure athleticism at the highest, most glamorous amateur level. And Otto is at the center of it. He's the American Golden Boy. There have been Golden Boys before—Red Grange, for one—and there'll be more Golden Boys, Frank Gifford, Paul Hornung to name two others, men upon whom fortune smiles so broadly it's actually a little awe-inspiring. But today, for now, at this instant, Automatic Otto is America's Golden Boy. Nothing could stop him.

Oops.

Hmmm, Otto's on his ass.

Hmmm. Otto's on his ass *again*.

Well, darn.

Otto's on his ass a third time. What the hell is this all about?

What it's about is a minor bump on Otto's inevitable march to glory. It's a bump in the form of a Michigan defensive end, big guy but fast and rangy too, who's juked his way through the line three times running and puts his shoulder at speed into Otto's fabulous midsection and knocks that million-dollar baby flat to the cold green earth of Dyche, with a turf sandwich to munch on.

There'll come a time, many years later, when Otto Graham, at the height of his glory as the championship-winning quarterback of the Cleveland Browns, is visiting the president of the United States, Dwight David Eisenhower, in the White House. He's standing there waiting, and suddenly a large man with blue eyes and a twinkly smile on his face is before him.

"Say, Mr. Graham, just wanted to say hello."

"Oh," said Otto, aware that the fellow in the suit somehow belongs here in these hallowed halls, is part of the staff or team or something. "Do I know you?"

"Well, you might say. I played end for Michigan and in '43 I smeared you three straight times."

"Oh," says Otto, laughing and remembering, and probably also remembering Northwestern lost, 21–7, "my head is still ringing. What's your name, what do you do here?"

"Vince Mroz. United States Secret Service."

That's Vince and he was a Golden Boy too. In fact, his was a different kind of gold but some would say a better gold: it didn't involve fame or glory or wealth, or anything coming easy to him out of sheer abundance of talent. But it was American gold in the form of the parable about the immigrant kid from some village in Poland who starts out with all the breaks against him—a father dead young, a lost farm (again!), a heavy-drinking stepfather, a rough town to grow up in—and overcomes it all, and goes on to a career of accomplishment and heroism. And meeting Otto Graham in the White House is nothing next to a better White House experience where he's able to introduce his mother—she stood by him all those years—to his boss, Dwight Eisenhower, the president of the United States, in the White House, and the president says to Mom, "You must be very proud of your son."

Vince and his three older sisters were the first of their family born in the United States. He was born in Stanley, Wisconsin (delivered by a midwife), where his father, a Polish immigrant, worked as a carpenter. He was one of seven children, the youngest (again! Griselio, Oscar, Floyd Boring!). But he remembers Wisconsin as a lost paradise (again!); his dad built the town dance hall. His whole family—dad on violin, older brother John (Jack), his brother Stanley, his sister, Mary—all played in the polka band. He was a popular kid, because the music hall was converted into a skating rink, and he'd been taught by his dad how to take the old skates and build them into scooters by mounting them on two-by-fours and then nailing the two-by-fours to apple crates. The whole vehicle would then be decorated with Nehi and Coke bottle caps, and all the kids wanted to have a scooter like that.

The family had to move to East Chicago, Indiana, a suburb of Gary, Indiana, the steel town at the toe of Lake Michigan, when Vince was two, after the small dairy farm in Wisconsin failed. Gary was one of the toughest, grittiest, ugliest cities in America, its lakeside location notwithstanding, with a constant gassy odor in the air, with the plants, like industrially franchised volcanoes, sprawling darkly across the landscape, belching smoke, steam, and gas into the air, emitting a hellish glow. It's safe to say that nobody wanted to live there except the steel furnaces, and because the steel furnaces were there, the people had to be. His dad worked in a cement factory; somehow they got by, returning in the summers to Wisconsin to help on an uncle's farm.

When he was seven, his father died. The pain is not commented upon in later interviews. It passes, unexpressed. Instead, the focus is upon his mother, how she scrounged for some while, presumably working in shops or whatever, and presumably the boys pitched in, but when Vince was twelve she married a man named Martin Gzik, another Polish immigrant who worked as a blacksmith for Inland Steel.

Martin was old-school. Martin saw no life ahead but work. For Martin, a man worked hard all day, he came home, he had dinner with his family that the wife prepared, then he had a pint of whiskey, and then he went to bed blurry and freed of memories, and the next day, it was exactly the same thing.

That is fine if you are Martin Gzik and, indeed, the essential ingredient to Martin Gzik and all the Martin Gziks of the world is the conviction that everyone is exactly like him, a furious laborer who wants a nice dinner, no worries about the rent, and his pint of whiskey every night.

But suppose you are not Martin Gzik? Suppose, moreover, you have a gift and it can take you and yours out of this place, and take them with you, liberate them from the life of working hard, eating in silence, drinking whiskey into blurry unconsciousness.

Vince had gifts. He could do many things well, and it turned out he was very bright. He was also big and graceful. He learned to dance in those days, when his older sister, Vernie (Veronica), taught him by the music of the radio. She was five years older than Vince, and her husband-to-be worked the night shift in the mills. So in the evenings, she'd turn on the old round-top wooden radio with the big yellow dial that the family had bought at Montgomery Ward and tune in to the big bands. "Come on, Vince," she'd say, "let's dance." She taught him the waltz, the two-step, the foxtrot, and he learned them well.

But the best thing he did was catch. He had great hands. If you threw him something—especially a ball, either round or oval, but leather, of course—it was as good as caught. He had good soft hands, and some kind of inner computer that calculated angles at warp speed and advised the body on how to adjust and position, whether to elongate or compact, the hands to open wide but stay relaxed, the fingers not brittle but rubbery, the torso relaxed, all of it adding up to the drama of the catch.

But Martin Gzik demanded a paycheck, not a wall of trophies.

That was the iron rule, and it is ironic in a way that a man who grew to be such an exemplar of law and order made his way in this world by violating the rule, in concert with his mom.

He doesn't know how she did it. But somehow she did. Martin, the boy has to stay late today. Martin, the boy has some school responsibilities, he can't come home early. Martin, Vince won't be here after school, he has to help some people with some things.

It was a beautiful lie, and it enabled him to break clear off a fake, go deep, and snare that long toss. And his senior season, he was offered a full scholarship to Michigan State.

He arrived at Michigan State in the early 1940s at a propitious time. It seemed that, on the whole, American law enforcement was in one of its periodic upgrading modes. It—"it" being somehow the collective will of the culture's senior executives, big-city chiefs, state police managers, federal supervisors, the whole upper stratum—has decided that the cop as high school grad who relied too much on muscle and not enough on brain had become too much the soul of law enforcement. This would take generations to change and in some places it never would. But in certain sectors the need to change was recognized; the new cop would be trained from the start as a professional; he'd be more than a high school grad; he'd have awareness of the law, of the latest in forensics, of a methodology of investigation; and, as important, he'd dominate by logic, coolness, and professionalism, not brute strength and the intimidation of a sap.

And it turns out one of the earliest cathedrals of the New Police Work was the School of Criminal Justice, and many of the guest instructors were members of the Michigan State Police. And that's where Vince was.

But it started earlier. As a child, he'd been a truant and a layabout at Catholic school because when you disappointed the nuns, you got the sharp edge of a ruler cracked across your hand. He hated that. He started ditching. Again: he's drawn to cops, but there's something in him that recoils at the administration of the roughest justice.

So his mother decides that education is more important than religion, and she pulls him out of Catholic school and enters him in the third grade at Franklin School, East Chicago, Indiana. He never misses a day. And he sees the patrol. Funny how it works: show the kid discipline enacted professionally and justly, power shared, responsibility granted, and he responds. He wanted to be a school patrol boy, and he ends up in a gunfight over the life of the president of the United States as a Secret Service agent.

He transfers to Riley School and he's on the Safety Patrol there. In high school he's the hall monitor. So there is something in him drawn, provoked, excited by the tasks of law enforcement.

Then there's the fluke of the roommate. He went to Michigan State on the football scholarship, got to campus early for preschool practice, and is roomed with a senior named Lou Smiley. Lou Smiley was what every senior should be for every freshman: he's handsome, a great athlete, a charmer, a decent man. And Lou Smiley was in the School of Criminal Justice, majoring in police administration, and after six weeks of rooming with Lou, that's what Vince signs up for. Gone are the thoughts of being an engineer (though he has an engineer's mind, a talent for math).

Vince eventually became one of the few men in the world to have won varsity letters at both Michigan State University and the University of Michigan and to be a member of the letter clubs and the alumni associations of both schools, which as everyone knows, hate each other quite routinely.

That's because after two years at Michigan State, he enlisted in the Marine Corps. The corps had a program called V-12 in those days, and more enlistments than it needed, so instead of shipping him to Guadalcanal, it shipped him to Ann Arbor. It must have seemed almost as evil a place to a Michigan State jock. But he was required to stay in school a year, waiting for his appointment to Officer Candidate School to take place, and so he played football, creamed Otto Graham three times running. Then it was off to the marines.

Near the end of January 1945, Marine Private Vince Mroz started palling around with another marine he met playing poker on the train from Camp Lejeune, North Carolina, to their new station at Quantico, Virginia. The marine's name was Tiny, of course, because he was six foot four. On weekends the two went to Washington to meet girls, particularly a girl named Dottie, who worked for the FBI's espionage division and whom Tiny would eventually marry.

When a special weekend arrived—the one Tiny had chosen to give The Ring to Dottie—military maneuver restricted all the men to base. Why don't you come here? Tiny asked Dottie.

"I'm not coming to Quantico with a bunch of hungover marines on a train going back to base," she told him. So why don't you bring Shirley, Tiny suggested, referring to Dottie's roommate, a petite woman who also worked at the FBI. Well, she has a date, came the reply, and doesn't think she can break it.

"Put Shirley on the phone," Tiny insisted, and when Dottie did, he told Shirley of his plans for the engagement ring and that he didn't want to leave it in the barracks because it might get stolen. Tiny passed the phone to Vince.

"You don't want to dwarf the romance, do you?" Vince told the woman he had never seen or talked to before. "Why don't you come on down? There's nothing we can do at the base except go to the NCO club and dance and have a few beers. The Andrews Sisters are performing at the base. Come on down."

"All right," said Shirley, a strong woman and nobody's fool, who graduated at sixteen from high school in her home town of Sheffield, Iowa, and had taught first and second grade before joining the FBI. "I'll break my date."

Vince and Tiny arrived at the station late and were on the opposite side of the train when the women got off.

"I want to see her legs before I see her face," Vince whispered, and the two lay flat on their bellies to see under the car. Dottie and Shirley, who could not see the prone figures on the other side of the tracks, were furious that the men were not there to greet them.

After the train pulled out, Vince and Tiny got up and walked over.

Vince towered over five-foot-three Shirley Gamm, who wore a gray suit and a hat with a broad brim that swept over her eyes and hid her face. Vince reached down and gently lifted the front of the brim.

"Hi Shirley," he said when he finally saw her eyes. "I'm Vince."

That night they danced and danced, and all the lessons Vernie had given her little brother proved their worth. "He was a beautiful dancer," Shirley remembered. "I guess that's the Polish in him." Three dates later, Shirley and Vince were engaged. Less than two months later, she pinned his second lieutenant's bars on him.

He spent what remained of the war in the Pacific commanding marine detachments on an aircraft carrier and a battleship and got out in the fall of 1946, a first lieutenant.

When he got out, it was back to Michigan State and football (the university president, "Uncle John" Hannah, interceded to get him housing on campus); he was married by this time to Shirley. He was one of the returning vets, that flood of men, a little older than they'd been, a lot smarter, and a whole lot tougher, who'd put their lives aside to win a war, and now had come back to reclaim those lives. They didn't have time to mess around, they'd already lost too much time. Vince was one of those, a senior in his mid-twenties with a wife, hardly a typical lost wet-behind-the-ears kid. And where he goes is straight into the United States Secret Service.

The service has decided, like the police all over America, to make that upgrade in polish and education. A kind of vein had been opened, being mined assiduously by the service from the raw materials at the Michigan State School of Criminal Justice. The Detroit office of the Secret Service handled the recruiting. There was a whole bunch of fellows who went directly to the service upon graduation, and they'd form a generation. Four other graduates from the year before, including Jerry Behn, had already joined the service. Of the graduation class of 1948, three went into the service directly: Vince, Ken Balge, and Bob Lapham. Rex Scouten, another graduate of that class, came in three months later. Stu Knight, later a director of the service, also graduated from that class but went first to the LAPD before later transferring to the Secret Service.

Vince's first day was July 12, 1948, at the Chicago office. The target of the field officers of the Secret Service, when they are not investigating those who've written nasty notes to the president, is counterfeiters (it's a department, after all, of the Treasury). And Vince had a run of chasing funny-money boys around the Windy City, especially that moment when a sting went wrong and an undercover agent who thought he'd been made drew and shot a suspect in the face. Vince and another agent—who had been staked out nearby—drove the superficially wounded man to the hospital, then to the hoosegow.

Nine months into his career, he pulled security at a speech the president, running for reelection, gave in Chicago. He and another agent, Charlie Peyton (an Indiana University graduate), were on the stage flanking the president. They stood there the whole time. But they had been discovered. Jim Rowley, head of the White House security detail as well as the forger of the alliance with Louie's, where all the agents bought their suits, liked what he saw. Vince and Charlie *looked* like Secret Service agents.

In January of 1949, Vince was sent on temporary duty to Washington for the inauguration; and in March, that was made a permanent posting. He had arrived.

He had arrived also at the end of his run. He was still thinking tactically. Just ahead, he heard the screams of a maid and could see by the light of the open door that there's an exit to the street at the far end of Lee House. But if he ducked out there, he's low, at street level, he'd have no angle to shoot from.

Instead he pivoted, raced up the steps, and reached the first floor of Lee, just behind the main door, which also allows him access to the street; but he'd be six feet up, he'd have a command of the situation, he'd have shots at Oscar, off to the left, if they are still needed, he'd have cover. It was the right move.

Vince flew to the door, threw it open, and stepped out, gun raised and cocked. He discovered to his amazement that while he and Toad and Joe Davidson have been shooting it out with one opponent at the east side of the house, a whole different gun battle has taken place here, in the west.

And what he saw filled him with horror.

27. THE COLOSSUS RHOADS

It is not known what the fifty-two-year-old Dr. Cornelius Packard Rhoads, director of the Sloan-Kettering Institute for Cancer Research in New York City, thought when he heard the news of the shootings at Blair House that day. From his credentials, you might presume he thought nothing, that a gunfight in the streets of Washington was as far removed from the refined venue in which he lived and worked as possible. He was a man of extraordinary talents and intelligence, and one of his nation's most gifted researchers. He supervised a staff of several hundred chemists, technicians, statisticians, librarians, and laboratory assistants, as well as scientists. So prodigious were his accomplishments that nine years later he wound up on the cover of *Time* magazine.

But in fact Dr. Rhoads had an intimate and unfortunate connection with what happened at Blair, dating back many years, to 1932 and a scandal of his own creation. His relationship to the gunfight was duly noted in Robert Donovan's *New Yorker* piece two years later, but appears to have excited little comment, and Dr. Rhoads went on with his industrious life, acquiring awards and accolades and a revered place in the medical pantheon.

But possibly at the moment when the news came, he had a moment of memory, a shudder, possibly even a spasm of deep regret. For as sure as Oscar's anguish over his father and Griselio's love of Don Pedro and Don Pedro's rage at the United States, Dr. Rhoads contributed his share to the mayhem and carnage that shattered that Indian summer day. Amazing that the actions of such a brilliant man could have such tragic repercussions and should forever stigmatize his memory, even if the *Time* cover story or the *New York Times* obituary didn't see fit to mention them. But they did and they do.

Cornelius Rhoads—nicknamed "Dusty"—was born in Springfield, Massachusetts, June 20, 1898, the son of an ophthalmologist, Dr.

George H. Rhoads. Clearly a gifted young man, he attended Bowdoin College, then went to Harvard Medical School, where he was class president and graduated cum laude in 1924. His years at Harvard make him a peer of Albizu Campos, who was there at the law school in those days. Perhaps the two passed each other in some Cambridge byway or jostled in a coffee shop or diner. But that is not the connection to the November 1 gunfight.

While Albizu Campos returned to Puerto Rico, Rhoads stayed in Boston; he did his internship in surgery at the Peter Bent Brigham Hospital in Boston. His next stop was the Trudeau Sanitarium in northern New York state's Adirondack Mountains, and two interpretations of this tour exist: the *Times* obit said he was a (research) fellow, but Susan E. Lederer, who studied Rhoads for a scholarly article, says he went there to recover from tuberculosis, which he had contracted as a surgical intern and, further, that it was this affliction that inspired Rhoads to go into research rather than practice.

He taught pathology at Harvard for a year, then in 1928, he joined the staff of the Rockefeller Institute for Medical Research. In 1931, he joined the Rockefeller Research Program upon the urging of Harvard hematologist William B. Castle, who asked Rhoads to go with him to Puerto Rico to do research for the newly formed Rockefeller Anemia Commission, which Castle headed. Their focus was to be anemia—believed to be caused by hookworm, and tropical sprue, an obscure and poorly understood disease.

He arrived in San Juan in June. He and Castle set up a laboratory at the Presbyterian Hospital and began systematically recruiting subjects for study. Although they called the subjects "patients," the recruited individuals were always the object of clinical study, even if many of them did receive treatment.

Initially, Rhoads enjoyed his work. He wrote a mentor in July, "The whole situation is nearly perfect. We have ample bed and laboratory space, excellent technical help and a most cooperative medical group to deal with. The climate is delightful and the country magnificent. I can imagine no more pleasant place to live."

But soon enough the novelty wore off; he was quarreling with Puerto Rican physicians, especially Garrido Morales, the epidemiologist for the insular government who had collaborated with Rhoads in collecting polio serum specimens in order to study a local outbreak of the disease. His letters also suggest that workplace conditions for the Rockefeller doctors were on the decline.

Luis Baldoni, a technical assistant in the lab, gave an unflattering description of Rhoads later, characterizing him as "a heavily built man, about 40 years old, six feet tall, he weighed about 180 pounds; his hair was black, skin pinky white, big greenish eyes of a penetrating look, big straight nose, medium sized mouth, a mustache like Chaplin." Baldoni said the doctor's face was "round and fat, with a thick beard, but he was always well shaved, his neck was short and fat; he was a man of rough manners and few words."

According to one published source, "On the night of 10 November 1931, Rhoads got drunk at a party, according to witnesses, and emerged to find his car [a Ford roadster] stripped and the tires flat." When he got back to his lab, apparently in a mood of agitation compounded by the liberating effects of the alcohol he had consumed, he sat down at a stenographer's desk and began to scrawl a note in longhand to a friend in Boston.

Dear Ferdie, he wrote to a man many believe was Boston researcher Fred Stewart,

> *I can get a damn fine job here and am tempted to take it. It would be ideal except for the Porto Ricans—they are beyond doubt the dirtiest, laziest, most degenerate and thievish race of men ever inhabiting this sphere. It makes you sick to inhabit the same island with them. They are even lower than the Italians. What the island needs is not public health work, but a tidal wave or something to totally exterminate the entire population. It might then be livable. I have done my best to further the process of extermination by killing off 8 and transplanting cancer into several more. The latter has not resulted in any fatalities so far. The matter of consideration for the patients' welfare plays no role here—in fact, all physicians take delight in the abuse and torture of the unfortunate subjects.*

Then he gave up, left it on his desk, and staggered to bed.

It was discovered two days later by technicians Aida Soegard and Luis Baldoni in the lab.

As Baldoni related, "On Thursday, November 12, 1931, I arrived to work at 7:30 A.M., at the foot of my microscope there was a paper folded in three parts and marked on the exterior 'F.W. Stewart' written in a corner in the handwriting of Dr. Rhoads; I put it on a little table next to me where Aida Soegard worked.

"Aida Soegard picked up the paper, opened it and read it, and very frightened . . . she told us its contents."

Soegard shared the letter with other women in the laboratory (but not Baldoni), and he says, "[E]veryone was terrified. Castle and Rhoads arrived and the girls made the letter immediately disappear; all knew that the letter had been written by Dr. Rhoads because all knew his writing.

"At 4 p.m. I got Miss Rafaela Carrasquillo . . . to give me the letter; after reading it, I kept it with me, as proof of the horrendous crime that Rhoads had committed; and from that date I have in my power that document."

Of course as the letter circulated, it created an uproar in the hospital, so intense that within another two days Rhoads called together all the commission employees and Puerto Rican doctors in the hospital to apologize profusely, trying to assure them of "the high regard and esteem in which I hold the Porto Ricans," according to the investigation conducted by Special Attorney José Ramón Quiñones later.

Baldoni recalled the speech, though not the precise words: "Here are several of his thoughts," he said, then assumed Dr. Rhoads's voice:

"I also know that this has caused a bad impression on all of you, but I want to tell you that I wrote that letter in a moment of [nerves]. It was for a friend of mine who has tuberculosis in the North and I want you to forgive me if I have offended you. After all, the letter never left. I have a high regard for Puerto Ricans. Of all the hospitals that I have seen in the world, I don't believe that any are as good as Presbyterian, and I have a very high regard for the honesty and diligence of the Puerto Ricans. After all, remember that the letter wasn't sent, and I ask you one more time to forgive me."

In the few days that he remained in Puerto Rico, Rhoads completely altered his brusque, imperious ways, and was much nicer to the women under his supervision. He sought out Baldoni and asked for forgiveness ("in an emotional tone"). A week later, when Baldoni had to go visit a sick aunt in Utuado, Rhoads gave him permission as well as a 10-peso loan.

When he sailed for the United States on December 10 with remaining commission members, he believed that all copies of the letter had been destroyed and the episode was over.

What he had not counted on—and perhaps could not imagine—was the fear he had generated among the staff, particularly the technician Luis Baldoni. Baldoni, suffering an attack of the flu, worried that he had been poisoned, and took some time off. When he returned, Rhoads had already left for America, but Baldoni continued to feel uneasy.

"The fear of losing my life because of poison or in another form, and the uneasiness that I had felt upon seeing that a horrible crime was committed without giving corresponding punishment to the doer of it, and fearing that a system existed to exterminate the Puerto Ricans in this form that no one could suspect, in the way that Rhoads described in his letter, and when I saw that no one in that hospital began the needed investigation before a situation of life and death for all, I gave my resignation to Dr. Castle."

In January 1932, Baldoni gave a copy of the letter to Albizu, who understood immediately that he had been given the gift of a propaganda gold mine, and set out immediately to publicize it. The arrival of the letter also coincided exactly with the Nationalists' political aspirations, for this was the year Albizu stood for the Senate as the head of a Nationalist slate. The Nationalists sent copies to organizations such as the League of Nations, the Pan-American Union, the Vatican, and the ACLU. In a cover note, José Lameiro, the Nationalist secretary, said the U.S. efforts to exterminate Puerto Ricans were like those mounted to wipe out the American Indians.

It became part of the vehicle the Nationalists rode that election cycle and created such a fuss that Rhoads, now back in the United States, felt impelled to answer. He called his letter "a fantastic and playful composition written entirely for my own diversion and intended as a parody."

That characterization did nothing to ameliorate Puerto Rican rage, much less to prevent the many investigations that took place. The affair was looked at by, among others, the then governor of Puerto Rico, James R. Beverley, who characterized Rhoads's letter as a "confession of murder" and a "libel against the people from Puerto Rico." Rhoads wired his apologies. Another investigator, Pedro Aponte Vázquez, discovered a 1932 letter from Beverley to the Rockefeller Foundation's associate director, saying that Rhoads had written another letter, "even worse than the first," that was "suppressed by the government" and presumably eventually destroyed.

The investigations came up with no criminal conduct. Eight patients had not died; no one was injected with cancer. But what seems to have infuriated the Puerto Ricans just as passionately was that Rhoads never suffered any professional consequences for his actions.

"Given the widely shared sense of the potential frustrations in dealing with locals and other challenges away from home, Rhoads' superiors accepted the explanation of his letter boasting of race extermination as a means to displace anger at the Puerto Ricans and the stress of a research program in the tropics," wrote researcher Susan E. Lederer.

Many Puerto Ricans, however, never forgot the Rhoads scandal and the way los americanos had simply sloughed it off, treated it as a joke, and thrown a mantle of collegial protection around the man.

One of them would recount the scandal bitterly much later.

"The Puerto Rican clinic assistant found a letter on the desk of this doctor, in which letter he confessed to a friend of his in the United States that he was bringing about a campaign for the extermination of the Puerto Rican people, because he considered the Puerto Rican people the most low down, lazy, dirty, and a lot more. I don't know. I can't recall all the names he gives the Puerto Ricans at the time, and in that campaign of extermination of the Puerto Rican people he had done his part by killing eight of his patients, and inoculating the virus of cancer in many more. . . . The American government not only failed to make investigation of that case, but also gave the man the means of escape from the island. You have him today working in cancer research in New York City."

His name was Oscar Collazo, who never forgot, and never forgave, and on November 1, 1950, went to war on those emotions.

28. OSCAR GOES DOWN

O scar sat on the steps of Blair in a strange universe: bullets whizzing and banging, men moving around to shoot or hide, the reports of the pistols, the spray of the near misses, where the bullets plunk stone or shear to supersonic mist when they hit the wrought iron fence. In all this chaos, Oscar sat down. Who would sit down in the middle of a gunfight?

Yet that too is part of the reality of a gunfight. People's minds operate in weird fashion, concentrating on this, ignoring that, the concentration and the obliviousness somewhat whimsical in their deployment. In the famous FBI gunfight between eight FBI agents and two heavily armed bank robbers behind the Suniland Shopping Center in Dade County, Florida, on April 11, 1986, it is reliably reported that one of the robbers, Michael Platt, already hit ten times (he was hit twelve times that day), climbed out of an automobile and walked toward a supine FBI agent who had been firing at him with a shotgun, and fired three times at close range. Then he walked back to the car, got into it, and tried to drive away. Meanwhile, batches of people were shooting at him. They all missed. But so did he. Standing near a downed man, he fired three times and missed each time. He didn't even know he missed. The man who was being shot at, an agent named Edmundo Mireles, Jr., didn't even know it happened either. He didn't notice the man near him, shooting point-blank at him. He was too busy doing exactly what Oscar was doing, reloading, a task made more difficult by the fact that his left arm had been shattered by a high-velocity .223 bullet fired by one of the robbers. Finally, he decided to give up on reloading—it was a shotgun he was fiddling with—and pulled his own .357 revolver, although it was loaded with .38 Special cartridges. In complete unawareness that someone had been shooting at him from close range, he got up and walked to the car in which Platt sat, trying to start it. Agent Mireles shot at Platt three times and at his partner, William Matix, three more. He hit on five of his six shots, ending the fight.

But consider the insanity of that transaction. From three feet, one man shoots at another and misses six times. The man he's shooting at doesn't even notice. That's a gunfight.

So when Oscar sat and after his methodical fashion reloaded, it may seem strange but it's not. It's not funny, it's not crazy, it's not wacky, it's not stupid, it's not absurd, it has nothing to do with any value anywhere in the civilized world. It's just a gunfight.

Oscar studied the problem. Certainly, he tried to remember what Griselio had told him in the room. Then, with his thumb, he pressed the release catch at the heel of the butt and the magazine popped from its secure hold in the butt, dropping a half inch or so. He seized it, pulled it out, and dropped it to the ground. He reached into his coat pocket and removed his second magazine, topped up with steel-jacketed 9mm cartridges. Now came the tricky part; he had to guide the magazine into the butt, yes, but not any which way. The cartridges must be facing the proper direction. Carefully, paying no attention to the shots coming at him or being fired in other areas of the fight, he placed the magazine correctly into the opening. He then guided the magazine smoothly up into the gun, felt it lock with a vibratory click (he would not be hearing with any discrimination at this point, because of the gunshots he fired and that were being fired at him, filling his ears with ringing). He hadn't any idea that the lever he hunted for was called the slide release, but when he tripped it, the compressed mainspring of the pistol spring decompressed, the slide flew forward with a jump, stripping a new cartridge from the magazine and placing it in the chamber, leaving the hammer cocked. The gun was ready to fire.

A speed reload under combat conditions is no small thing. Lots of people can't do it. When the gun quits the fight, they quit the fight. But Oscar, in his methodical way, has brought this improbability off.

He stood and made ready to—

And this seems to be where he noticed he has been hit. It's another oddness of a gunfight that it so concentrates your mind you recognize some small things and completely miss other large ones. He obsessed on loading the gun and he missed that he'd been shot. Possibly it's because in his highly adrenalized state, he was more or less inured to pain so he didn't feel even the most massive of traumas. Also, he wasn't hearing well, he wasn't seeing well. He was in a visual condition of extreme tunnel vision.

But at some point late in the reloading process or immediately upon its completion, Oscar's consciousness seems to have noted what his body had ignored: he had been hit in the chest.

Upon that recognition—he saw a smear of crimson stain spreading across his fine blue shirt, certainly felt a sudden burning sensation in that chest, running like a furrow across it, and finally noted a general achiness in his right arm, particularly inside the biceps—it occurred to him that he was about to die.

He went down. He landed on the sidewalk just next to the first step of Blair, face flat on the cold cement, the gun still in his right hand. His hat was on, but the collision with the ground somewhat dislodged it, so it was held atilt, canted slightly loose by the pressure of the step against his head. A trickle of blood from his head wound snaked its way down the side of his face. His left hand was outstretched above his head, fingers in repose, his right hand splayed to the right, perpendicular to the body, palm down, also relaxed, as if somehow he was glad it was, in some fashion, now over. He had as much dignity prone as he did upright; his trouser cuffs stayed tight to his ankle, exposing no untoward patch of silk sock; his shoes, highly buffed, stayed on and didn't fall off as happens so often when people hit the ground hard against their will. He looked very much like a fallen banker or senior law partner or investment counselor.

Oscar was hit, Oscar was down.

But who shot Oscar?

29. THE SECOND ASSAULT

The title of this book and many other accounts of November 1, 1950, notwithstanding, the event in question was not a single gunfight. It was actually two gunfights. They took place in almost, but not quite, the same time frame in almost but not quite the same space. They were next-door neighbors but they were very different in nature.

The first displayed surprise, reaction, courage, tactical intelligence, weird luck, the vagaries of ballistics and was a classic armed exchange over a relatively long period of time; it must have seemed like hours to its participants but it probably lasted 38.5 seconds. Some—none of the participants, mind you—even call it opera buffa, since it was set in motion by an unsure, untrained man fouling up with his firearm. But its primary characteristic was that it involved a lot of shooting but not much hitting.

The second gunfight was over very quickly; it was fast, so fast it almost defies belief; it was much shorter than the shootout at the Suniland Shopping Center in Dade County, Florida, and it may have been shorter even than the Gunfight at the O.K. Corral, which lasted about thirty seconds. It had no goofy twists. It just happened flat out. Running concurrently with and a little beyond the first fight, it probably lasted no more than twenty seconds. And yet during its course no less than the life of the president and fate of the United States were put in mortal danger. Moreover, its characteristics were the exact opposite of its neighbor: not much shooting, a lot of hitting. It was extremely deadly.

The first fight, between Oscar Collazo on one hand and on the other, Donald Birdzell, Floyd "Toad" Boring, Joseph Davidson, and Vince Mroz, took place essentially in front of Blair House, at the eastern end of the 135-foot frontage of the two-dwelling Blair-Lee complex along Pennsylvania Avenue diagonally across from the White House. The second gunfight transpired at the western end of that frontage, in front of the Lee House half of the complex, and it involved Griselio Torresola, Leslie Coffelt, Joseph Downs, and Harry S. Truman.

Why is it the "second" gunfight? What places it behind the first in chronology, if only by a few seconds? No audio or visual recordings of the event were made—it was, by thirty years, the pre-videotape world—and no overall eyewitness emerged to chronologize the materials beyond a doubt. True enough, but the testimony suggests almost beyond dispute that it took place—or rather, it began—after the first fight, and ran simultaneous to it and finished a few seconds later. That testimony comes from the survivors of the first fight, all of whom stated in their accounts and after-action reports and reiterated in later interviews that they had no idea the second fight even occurred. Again, this is the crazed world of the gunfight: it seems impossible, but a mortal struggle involving the firing of nearly a dozen gunshots at close range took place within a few feet of these men, and universally they did not notice it.

That's because they were busy trying to stay alive. What happened was dictated by the physiology of extreme circumstances. When Oscar's P.38 fired to begin the action, the sound of that report set off physical changes in the men at close hand. As they had been trained, they went into the fight half of the fight/flight response. The figure of Oscar filled reality for them and they continued to concentrate on the problem of Oscar at the exclusion of all other phenomena in the world.

If Griselio's gun had fired first, it is to that shot their attention would have been directed. Possibly then a nearer shot by Oscar would have redirected their attention back to him, but it was clearly the first shot that determined the course of the action and irrevocably oriented the eastern defenders to Oscar and the problem he posed. They were in what has been called the fog of war, or expressed in other iterations by the army combat guide quoted by A. J. Liebling, "In combat confusion is normal." That is all that happened. They looked at and committed to the immediate threat and they didn't come out of it for some minutes, even after the shooting was completed.

It is time to examine what happened to the immediate west.

Griselio Torresola, in his suit, his hat straight, his jacket buttoned, walked down the southern side of Pennsylvania Avenue, past the White House, past the old War Department now given to office space, and crossed Pennsylvania at the intersection of that avenue and 17th Street at a smart pace.

Then he turned right—east—at the corner of Pennsylvania and 17th and headed back down Pennsylvania, past the Court of Claims, headed back in the direction from which he was coming, until he reached the western boundary of Lee House. At this point he stopped momentarily. One hundred thirty-five feet ahead of him, he could see his partner, Oscar, just passing by the guardhouse at the eastern end of Blair House, then turning at the stairway to confront the back of an anonymous police officer who happened, by the whim of circumstance, to be facing not outward but inward. The timing was perfect. Each man had arrived at his destination simultaneously.

Griselio was also dressed up for his appointment with destiny and history. He had a gray chalkstriped suit on, highly shined shoes, a hat, a nice tie, a white shirt. He knew this would be the last day of his life, for he had no illusions about the results of guns. He had done enough shooting, seen enough rocks pulverized in the hills around Jayuya, to doubt the result of his enterprise.

Griselio reached the guardhouse at the western limit to Lee. According to one witness, he removed his pistol, gripped it with two hands, peeked in the westernmost window at the officer inside to mark his target, then stepped around the box into the doorway of the little structure to face the man.

Griselio thrust the shiny Luger forward with both hands, assuming what is now called the isosceles shooting position, and pointed it at the man in the booth. His finger flew to the trigger, yet so intent was he on completing the mission that he never really stopped. He kept moving, rotating left to right around the sitting man.

30. PIMIENTA

Think of him as a child of the river. Everyone who knew him did. He was the river boy, part fish, kissed by sun, untouched by cold or fear, who rode the currents and plunged the bottoms. Three people still alive who knew him intimately—his sister Angelina, his wife, Dilia, and his childhood chum and revolutionary compadre Heriberto Marín Torres—all think of the river when his name comes up and they place him in time and memory when he and they were children.

He was blond. He looked like a little German polliwog, shiny when wet, his hair plastered flat, and he was always wet. He loved the river, which is called the Río Grande de Jayuya. It was green and cool and it ran through the rocks. He loved to jump off a high one into a particular spot where the river almost formed a swimming hole, which the boys all called *La Suerte*, or "Luck" in English. He must have loved the feeling of gravity seizing him, the rush of the air as it roared by, then the impact as the river slapped him, then yielded, and down he swooped into green solitude, bubbles fizzing by left and right, the weeds twisting about him. Then with a shiver he would have kicked out of his descent and jetted to the surface amid a boiling whiteness as he broke out and felt the warmth and saw the brightness again. Above it tower the three green peaks—Los Tres Picachos—and in summer, when the sun blasted down even hotter here because this is in the mountains and the air is thin, he looked about and all is commotion and jubilation, because all the children go to the river.

Griselio was fearless. He could not stay out of the water. Once he jumped in before he could swim and Angelina fished him out and gave him hell. It didn't matter; he paid no attention. It was his nature to do the bold thing. Some imperative compelled him to risk. The dull life without challenge had no interest to him. His sister calls him *osado*, meaning daring, bold, audacious. She calls him *arriesgado*, meaning one who takes risks. She calls him *temerario*, rash, bold, temerarious, reckless. In fact, the woman he will marry—and in fact will still be married to November 1, 1950—first saw him in the river and maybe it was then that she fell in love, because he's such a pepper pot. Everybody knew him, because everybody in Coabey, five miles from the mountain town of Jayuya, knew the Torresolas.

As an assassin, Griselio had all the strikes against him: His childhood was happy. His father loved him and loved the family. He beat no one. He fed them all. Griselio was part of a family, a community, a culture. He was a good athlete, a loyal friend, popular with the girls, beloved by all. It sounds as if someone was assembling a presidential candidate rather than a presidential assassin.

Family is at the heart of it, nevertheless, and Griselio's shows that great families can turn boys in tragic directions just as surely as screwed-up ones. For Griselio, whatever you think of him, was forever obeying the mandates of family; he acted as he was raised, and in the end, by the rules of his family, he was a hero and a martyr, not a murderer.

The key is the remarkable woman named Blanca Canales. She was both Griselio's landlord and his cousin; she was his father's employer and his cousin. It's one of those complicated family things, with richer and poorer strains in the same genetic unit. The owner of the plantation was Don Rosario Canales, who was the father of Blanca; in his second marriage, Don Rosario married Consuelo Torresola, who was the sister of Griselio's father, that is, Angelina's and Griselio's aunt. Don Rosario died, Blanca inherited; Griselio's father moved with wife and four kids (Griselio, born July 2, 1925, was then two) to the Canales plantation in Coabey to work it with his sons in exchange for room and board. In other words, Blanca's family owned the land, Griselio's worked it. The crops were tobacco, beans, corn, and fruit, the whole unit self-sufficient. There was no poverty. Angelina remembers that "hens were raised, there was a cow, I remember there being two goats that were milked. We did not suffer from hunger."

But Blanca was a woman of progressive social beliefs; one might liken her, in American terms, to the well-born radical who inherits a position in society and then uses it as a leverage point by which to reform—or destroy, depending on your point of view—that same society. Some have

called her the "Puerto Rican Joan of Arc." Blanca was one of the few college-educated women of her generation, majoring in social work at the
University of Puerto Rico, and worked for a time for the Department of
Families. But eventually, she returned to Coabey, her eyes opened, her
indignation stoked, her senses of patriotism and reform entwined, and
took over the hacienda, a gray-balconied structure five miles east of
Jayuya. She was socially engaged; she was also, by accounts, engaging,
and soon founded something like a salon, where other socially engaged
sorts gathered, where children were welcomed. At the same time, in the
house on the same property, were the Torresola family, mother and father
and four kids, the children growing up absorbing her passion as naturally
as the air, the sunshine, the green mountains.

It is also said that Griselio's father, Clodomiro, was a remarkable man:
educated by tutors, he loved books and stories, and most nights in his
house, for the evening's entertainment, he engineered elaborate parlor
games such as Black Magic, a guessing game, and dramatic storytelling.
It's a romantic vision, typical of the nineteenth century, when such enter-
tainments were common: the father, who's worked hard all day in the
fields, nursing sustenance from his cousin's land, by night telling tales
from the *Arabian Nights* or Grimm's or Perrault, playing the parts, doing
the voices, aping the faces, and filling his children with love of self, of parents, of country, and a sense of the order of the world.

"My father was an exceptional human being," recalls Angelina. "He
taught me to read when I was about four years old. He would read all the
stories that are found in the *Tesoros de la Juventud* ["Treasures for Young
People"] and he would express them with a magical way, it seemed as if
we were seeing it happen." Clearly the man had a love of performing, a little snake of desire to be at the center of attention, but also to see his children laugh and provoke their minds, to make them see possibilities.

It turned out quickly enough that Griselio had gifts—the beauty was
one of them, the work ethic another, the love of family a third, the audac-
ity at the river another. But he was a fast learner in many ways, and the
fellow who always played shortstop, the toughest and most demanding
and most graceful position on the baseball field on *la vega*—the plain—
that the kids erected there on Blanca Canales's property that was the
focus of so much attention.

"He was very very light," remembers Heriberto Marín Torres, the old
friend from the valley, using an all but untranslatable Spanish expression

denoting quickness and agility. "He would steal bases. He was total *pimienta* [black pepper]."

They played baseball, they roamed the hills, they flirted with the girls, and on some nights they'd walk in from the mountains to the town and go to the movies. It could be anybody's boyhood. It could be Andy Hardy's boyhood.

Some have reported that the Torresolas were long a revolutionary family, and had taken part in the somewhat stunted history of the Puerto Rican independence movement from Spain, namely the abortive revolution at Lares in 1868. But Angelina herself denies it vehemently. There was no politics, she says, before the arrival of Don Pedro Albizu Campos to Jayuya in 1932. And then there was nothing but politics.

It seems that in 1928, Blanca had gone to Río Piedras, the university town near San Juan, and there she heard—as would, so much later, Oscar Collazo—a small speaker in a dark jacket and a bow tie, with fiery eyes, a little blurt of mustache, a man proud and unafraid who spoke of things as they could be. Blanca returned to Coabey and her little colony of Torresola cousins a true believer. Then, during the election of 1932, she invited the Great Man, the would-be Maximum Leader, to her house.

"That's the way it was," recalled Angelina, many years later, "because although we already had something of what Blanca related to us and with what she had interested us, well, prior to that, I don't remember politics being spoken about a great deal in my home. But after Blanca started to interest us in that matter, and after Don Pedro came, well, there's where it was that a [favorable] impression was made on all of us."

She goes on, "The [favorable] impression was mutual. Because, after him, our family, the Torresola family, he considered us his family. We were like *his* family."

This seems to be the germination point of the events of 1950, both in Puerto Rico and in front of Blair House, that long period of time during the election when Don Pedro was there, in the house; Oscar Collazo was there too, but from afar, as a campaign worker. But clearly the Torresolas are bonding in some powerful way, through the vessel of Blanca, with Don Pedro. Elio will end up leading the revolt in Jayuya (along with Blanca), Doris will end up the private secretary of Don Pedro and be wounded in the siege of his house, while Griselio . . .

Thus did Griselio's political leanings begin to manifest themselves as they apparently seized the entire family, which will in the end give up so much for Albizu Campos's idea of revolution. And if anyone is to fight for the revolution, it is the Torresolas.

For example, in 1946 when Griselio was twenty-one, he and his friend Heriberto went to Luquillo, a small town about twenty-three miles east of San Juan, to represent the Jayuya 4-H Club (of which Griselio is president) in a national contest, a kind of 4-H Jamboree. They took the train into town, they signed up, they were assigned to a tent. Every morning at the camp, the contestants began the day with the singing of the national anthem—the American national anthem. Griselio and his younger pal Heriberto do not sing; they are noticed and questioned.

"It's not *my* national anthem," says Griselio, and will not sing it.

A few nights later, he and Heriberto are introduced to others at a campfire meeting, and, Heriberto chuckles at the warm memory, "When we came in we were the most heavily applauded. I learned a lot from Griselio. He was, above all, a very serious young man. I learned his love for independence, his dedication to work. He was like a teacher to me. He was very smart, even brilliant, in spite of being so young and not having graduate degrees from a university."

Generally, the war years were pretty gentle ones in Puerto Rico. All the draft-age men are off to war; in the Nationalist camp, the fiery Don Pedro was in the Atlanta pen and though his minions do what they can to keep the flame burning, they lack his incandescence, his charisma, his ability to move the masses and to move the true believers even further. There's no record of anything particularly eventful occurring in the Torresola compound in Coabey, until 1944, when Griselio's father died suddenly in the night of a heart attack.

In 1947, Don Pedro was free at last, having served his ten years, the last of them in Oscar Collazo's own apartment building in the Bronx. The entire Nationalist Party showed up to welcome Don Pedro back, including Raimundo Díaz Pacheco's units of cadets in their black shirts and white trousers, squadded up in formation. The band blasted, the soldiers marched smartly, the crowds cheered the returning hero, the police agents took pictures. And soon Don Pedro was back in Jayuya, where he will rest from his ordeal and begin to plan the next step.

Security was a concern. Agents representing everyone from the Insular Police's Seguridad Interna (Internal Security) to the FBI and Naval Intelligence were tracking Don Pedro. In the mid-1940s they had also been watching a handful of people in Jayuya, including Elio and his father, Clodomiro. Following Don Pedro's return to the town, the number of Jayuya names on the list of people investigated by the Internal Security squad jumped dramatically; in 1948, the police added a few more Torresolas to the watch list, including one sloppily identified as "GLISEDIO."

With the intense surveillance of Don Pedro, the local Jayuya men, that is Griselio, Elio, and Carlos Irizarry, another prominent Nationalist who would with Elio lead the attack on the Jayuya post office in 1950 (along with Blanca Canales), organized an armed bodyguard, according to Heriberto Marín. After all, the night that Griselio and Heriberto arrived with Don Pedro, two carloads of Internal Security detectives showed up.

That was Griselio's introduction to firearms. He, his brother, and others of the inner circle in Jayuya began to pack pistols. The guns were Lugers donated to the cause by returning GIs, according to Heriberto, and it's a sure inference that among them must have been P.38s as well, for that was a sidearm GIs in Europe came across as often as Lugers.

René Torres Platet, a distant cousin of the Torresolas' (though of a later generation) and a Nationalist, came to know Elio, the older brother, well, and recalls that pistol practice began in 1948, after the return of Don Pedro and the imposition of Law 53, which made it illegal "to advocate violent actions against the Puerto Rican government in speech or writing." He recalls, "They [the bodyguards] follow[ed] him [Don Pedro] and they have to take [responsibility for] the security. . . . After that . . . they start practicing, shooting in the woods, in the . . . Coabey farm. . . . They just have pistols, no rifles. . . . They had the guns because they have to protect Don Pedro. Don Pedro was a target of many from the government, the U.S. government, the local government . . . so they have a security group for protecting him."

The bodyguards were therefore intimate with his planning, his intentions, his moods, his allegiances. But it was more than just a bodyguard group.

"It was . . . the group that was being organized for what was coming, which was the revolution," recalls Heriberto.

And it is during this time that Griselio has the sense of being special. He is the chosen son.

"Griselio was one of the persons that Don Pedro would always choose . . . whenever he had to travel outside of the neighborhood, to activities that would be carried out in Ponce, in Lares, in Cabo Rojo, and he was one of the persons that he [Don Pedro] trusted in a great deal. He had a lot of trust in Griselio."

Griselio even wrote to a newspaper to express his extraordinary devotion to Don Pedro Albizu Campos. It ran in the February 4, 1948, *El Universal*. "Each day," the young man proclaimed, "we have greater faith in the teachings of the master Albizu Campos."

In 1948, two things happened rapidly that to this day are somewhat mysterious. The first is that Griselio got married, and the second is that a month later he left for New York.

Dilia Rivera is a small brown woman, and the aging process has treated her worshipfully: like Angelina, she's stately and white-haired and elegant. But unlike Angelina, she is not serene. She seems still to radiate pain, as if she hasn't made peace yet, all these years later, with the end of her first marriage, the death of the father of her only child, and the slow passage of the years since those days more than a half century ago.

"He loved to swim," she says. "The first time I saw him was in the river. He was jumping from here to there all over, and I admired him." The boy in the river, blond and bold, jumping in and jumping out—that too is her first memory.

She was of—well, not wealthy in the American sense, but at least comfortable people. Her father owned a hacienda on a plantation. She'd been born in Guánica, then moved to Jayuya when she was eight or nine. That's when she first saw him; that may be when she fell in love with him too, though she won't say this.

"There was a hole where we would go swimming, and there were big rocks. We would all jump from there, and he had to jump from the highest one."

Then she left for a few years, and then returned and once again there was Griselio.

"He was the sort who people always knew. I always knew who he was."

The connection was immediate. It speaks to the passion of these two young people that they did not do things the usual way.

"He didn't seek permission from anyone [to see me]. I didn't either. That was very unusual for the time."

Both Angelina and Heriberto comment upon its suddenness. It just seemed to come from nowhere. Even Dilia seems a little stunned by it five decades later.

"We were talking at Blanca's house on the porch, and he just asked me to marry him and I said yes. I guess it was a surprise that he asked me. A judge married us. He came to Blanca's house and he married us there. After we got married, nobody knew we were getting married so there was no choice [except for the families to accept the union]."

Again, this is open to interpretation. The first interpretation is simple: he loved her, and in the culture of Puerto Rico, young people tend to marry at a very early age and begin a family. But a more conspiratorial imagination might conjure another reason: that in marrying Dilia, Griselio was protecting himself from selective service. As a married man, he would not be drafted, and therefore he was available, as one of the inner circle, to Don Pedro's directions in service to the revolution. She was moreover the daughter of a member of the Partido Popular Democrático. Her father was not a Nationalist, but was committed to the slower methodology of Governor Luis Muñoz Marín, concentrating on social and political development rather than quick independence. This in turn may explain Griselio's peculiar attitude toward her later in New York.

A month later, he was gone. He left for New York and Dilia moved from Blanca's house, where they had been living, to her father's house.

Why did Griselio go to New York? In one sense, this question needn't be answered. So many young Puerto Rican men went to New York in the late 1940s and early 1950s for the obvious economic reasons: there were job opportunities, there was a more vibrant economy, there was already a substantial colony with its support structures in place. You went to New York for the same reason that all immigrants go to New York or Cleveland or Chicago—for a better life. But Griselio's circumstances were far from typical: he had not been uprooted, there was no trauma of unemployment or family tragedy, no particular single event that made the trip necessary for survival. In fact, there seems to have been no pressing need. His family roots were deep in the soil of Coabey and Jayuya, and he had no children to support. His brother worked the farm, he could work with his brother, he could stay in a land he knew and loved.

One answer might be Law 53. This is the provision often called Puerto Rico's counterpart to the federal Alien Registration Act of 1940, better known as the Smith Act. Law 53 had been introduced late in the 1948 special legislative session—the last hours of the last day, in fact—and of it, University of Puerto Rico law professor David Helfeld said, "It can be assumed with confidence that . . . the basic cause [for introducing the legislation] was the return of Albizu Campos in December of 1947 and the consequent activation of his blackshirt followers who, it was commonly believed, were preparing for violence." Law 53 is why Heriberto himself left for New York in March of 1950; he felt that as a Nationalist he would never be able to get work in Puerto Rico and that he needed the new start. But again, his circumstances were different from Griselio's; he was much further down the economic order and much more vulnerable to economic predation. Griselio was connected to one of the oldest, most stable landowners in the area, the Canales family, and he had a secure life, maybe not a great life, but a life of honor and decency and plentitude there working with his brother on the farm.

Yet he goes, with much sadness, according to Heriberto. He went to New York in August of 1948. Blanca Canales herself supplied the answer: "Griselio went to New York for Don Pedro," she told Angelina. There seems to be no other compelling reason, and it becomes instantly clear that when he reaches New York, things change. This is something both Dilia and Heriberto agree on. Griselio was different.

The old Griselio—the pepper pot, the daring swimmer, the fast-handed shortstop, the joker, the most popular boy, the most handsome boy—that boy was gone. In his place is the New Griselio, who had become very much a loner. He drifted through jobs and he was in some sense disaffected. His employer at the bookstore El Siglo stated that "Griselio Torresola could hardly speak English, was very slow and had to be directed in everything he did." He fired him for being "careless, inefficient and lazy." He seemed to have no friends, at least to Dilia and Heriberto, or possibly he is shielding the two of them from what is the true purpose of his time in New York, which is the preparation for revolution in coordination with Don Pedro.

Yet if both Dilia and Heriberto saw him this way, there was another truth as well. It's clear from the FBI and Secret Service investigations that he was involved with Nationalists in New York, particularly Juan Bernardo Lebrón, a suspected gun-runner, and Juan Pietri Pérez, who had been elected president of the NPPR junta in June of 1949. With Lebrón, Griselio, under the name "Carlos González," purchased 9mm cartridges and Luger magazines from a sporting goods store in the Bronx called Morton's. The sales slip from this purchase turned up in the possession of another prominent New York Nationalist, Julio Pinto Gandía. The investigators noted that Griselio later registered at the Harris Hotel in Washington under the nom de guerre "Charles Gonzales."

Dilia's story is saddest. She arrived in New York December 27, 1948, after a wretched eight-hour flight from San Juan. Nobody was there to greet her at La Guardia. She was alone in the airport in a strange country. She took a cab to a friend's house in New York, and Griselio picked her up there.

But in New York, their relationship was different. Partly it was Dilia's intense rejection of New York. She hated it. She hated the filth, the noise, the vulgarity she saw everywhere, the drinking, the people sitting on the steps. This was, after all, an upper-class young lady of considerable grace and dignity suddenly thrust into the grimy melting pot in the coldest of months. But it's just as possible that New York seemed so horrible because there was such a change in Griselio and such a distance between them. He was seldom home, and he made no effort to introduce her to his circle of friends.

They lived in a single room in a boardinghouse, on Fifth Avenue at 110th Street; that can't have been pleasant. But it's also true that sometime in here Griselio had met a young woman named Carmen Dolores, who would become his common-law wife and the mother of his second daughter after Dilia left. In fact, Carmen Dolores came over and occasionally visited her and Griselio. But only Griselio and Carmen Dolores will know—and they aren't talking—the sequence of events in New York. Not even Dilia knows.

"He didn't take off with Carmen Dolores until after you left? Is that your sense?"

Dilia Rivera Torresola responds, "I guess. I don't know."

But in the Carmen Dolores–Dilia imbroglio, one can see certain principles at work. Griselio was indeed a new man, and the new woman was a signifier of that change. Dilia was the country girl, the girl from the valley of the Three Peaks in Coabey, and she fell in love with the boy and then the man he was, the bold, the daring, the gifted young fellow at home and in some sense the master of his world. But in his six months in New York essentially working underground for the revolution, he had to suppress that personality. In some sense, it ceased to exist for him out of sheer will. He needed a woman with whom he could share his political values, and it seems clear that he could not with Dilia.

She and Griselio fought over the man he had become. Now he was the new Griselio, the revolutionary Griselio, the underground man; how could he suppress that in her presence? It must have been miserable. Thus with Dilia he is awkward, silent, morose, unexpressive. He introduces her to no friends—"I never met anybody there [in New York]," she says—he does not take her into his social and professional life, which is based on Nationalist culture in Manhattan and the Bronx in the late 1940s and three quarters of 1950. He essentially drives her away.

"I left him," she would explain later. "I couldn't take any more. It's awful to say, but I couldn't. I could never get adjusted. Maybe if I had lived someplace else and had a place of my own."

With Carmen Dolores, another ardent Nationalist, he can be who he has become. Thus one premium that relationship immediately pays is in relaxation. He can be a secret agent with Carmen Dolores because she shares his beliefs and is part of Nationalist culture, knows the players and the players' wives and dreams herself of revolution. (She in fact will be arrested in 1954 in the aftermath of the assault on Congress by Lolita Lebrón, Rafael Cancel Miranda, Andrés Figueroa Cordero, and Irving Florés Rodríguez, and will serve time as part of that conspiracy.)

There are pictures in the Secret Service archives taken sometime in 1950 of Griselio, Carmen Dolores, and their new daughter. One could not look at them and say: Here is a presidential assassin. What one would say is: Here is a young father and his wife and his baby daughter and they are so in love with each other and so relaxed in each other's presence. Many of the photographs are taken in a New York snowfall, and you feel their pleasure at the strange beauty of this strange white fruit that's fallen from the sky.

Meanwhile, angrily, Dilia had returned to Puerto Rico. She will only see Griselio once more and she has not told him that she is pregnant.

Heriberto Marín had come to New York in March of 1950 to find work that he felt would be denied him in Puerto Rico because of a Law 53 · blacklist. One day he was walking up Fifth Avenue between 115th and 116th and went into a Puerto Rican bookstore called El Siglo because he's such an avid reader, and he was standing there, looking at books, and suddenly he felt a tap on his shoulder.

It was Griselio, to whom he had not spoken since Griselio left a year earlier and who has been mysteriously out of contact, with no news via Elio, no mail, no telephone calls. It seemed Griselio worked at El Siglo.

They chatted innocently enough—Heriberto asked if Griselio had any suggestions for employment and Griselio said no, it's hard to find a job.

But then, "Griselio invited me, that very evening—he asked me if I wanted to go eat at his house. I went, I met up with him there, and during the conversation I mentioned to him about the Nationalist Party and asked how nationalism was doing in New York. He told me he didn't want to know anything about that."

For whatever reason Griselio was suddenly denying all contact with nationalism.

"I asked him if he had any dealings with Don Pedro, and he said to me, 'I don't want to know about that.'"

Heriberto found this very strange because in the past, Griselio had talked endlessly about nationalism with him, had taken him to Blanca Canales's house to meet Don Pedro, had made him an ally in refusing to salute the American flag at the 4-H Club meeting in 1946.

"Griselio was friendly, the same, he was the same. But was he changed? Supposedly he was changed in political matters."

At no time did Griselio take his old friend to Nationalist activities. Two interpretations are possible: the first is that he genuinely was attempting to put the Nationalist Party behind him—but then why would he drive Dilia away for Carmen Dolores, why would he continue to talk to Don Pedro, why would he be active, as FBI documents prove, with other Nationalists? The other and more probable interpretation is that he was now the underground man: he wanted to keep his secret life in control and secure and he may not quite have trusted the way Heriberto just showed up accidentally in El Siglo, as the Nationalists were aware they were being monitored by federal agents to some degree (FBI documents report five different secret informants within the New York party cell).

A few weeks later in May or June of 1950, Heriberto, now employed (as a bill collector for a Puerto Rican travel agency), dropped in on Griselio unannounced in the evening.

"The second time that I went to Griselio's house, there was a young man there. And it was Oscar Collazo."

This confirms what Oscar's daughter, Zoraida, says, and it places Oscar and Griselio together before their meeting on the bridge the evening of October 29.

But possibly just as significantly, Griselio was extremely discreet about Oscar's role in the party.

"They didn't tell you that he had been the secretary [general] of the Nationalist Party?"

"Absolutely nothing."

Heriberto continues, "In the end of it all, we shared dinner, we ate that night. I did not become aware of anything else."

In other words, Oscar didn't say anything about being a Nationalist?

"No, no nothing. Nothing was spoken."

Nothing, he didn't say anything?

"Anything? Nothing, nothing, nothing, nothing. We continued visiting each other. I would visit him over there and converse with him, but we never again spoke of politics. Because with what Griselio told there at first when he said, 'Look, I don't want to know about any of that. If I've come here now to the United States it's because I don't want to know any more about nationalism or about Albizu Campos.' "

So perhaps not trusting him, perhaps not wishing to compromise him, given the private nature of their conversations, perhaps simply improvising as they went along, Oscar and Griselio play a charade for Heriberto, which is that theirs is a casual relationship, a friendship unconnected to politics, and Heriberto leaves that night suspecting nothing.

Griselio made a last trip to Puerto Rico on September 16, 1950—he departed Newark via a Continental Charters airliner to San Juan—and returned September 22, via Pan American, according to tickets found by Secret Service investigators. And it is beyond conjecture that during this strange journey of six days—why would an unemployed Puerto Rican man fly back to the island for six days, barring extraordinary circumstances, of which there were none—he went about putting his house in order and saying farewell to all that he knew and loved.

He saw Don Pedro. He had a conference with the Great Man September 21, and here he received the two letters that would be found later, those provocative missives that speak in generalities about "missions" and "duties," that may be conjured with to any end. It's certain that he made other visits as well: to his mother, Rosa, to his sister Doris, in San Juan, Don Pedro's private secretary.

Of the visits that can be documented, the first is to his sister Angelina

and her husband. Once she had been close to him; it is she who plucked
the young boy who could not swim yet from a raging, rain-swollen river
and beat him while trembling at the closeness of the call. But she had left
home at fifteen and gone off to marry and raise children (which is why
she avoided the political culture that consumed and, some would say,
destroyed the other three Torresola children). Since then they had not
been close. He visited her in San Juan sometime in that trip.

But Angelina noticed nothing different about him. "No! Nothing was
noticed about him. It [anything unusual about his sudden visit] never
occurred to us. He just showed up."

As for a feeling that this was some sort of farewell tour, she denies it
completely.

"No! No, no, there was none. We didn't become aware. [But] I don't
remember [the final conversation] anymore. I never knew he had those
qualities [the willingness to perform a mission with a pistol] in him."

One can argue that his very presence so suddenly was itself a revela-
tion indicating he knew what lay ahead; or one can argue, clearly, that he
was in San Juan, he hadn't seen his sister in years, and he had a free afternoon, so what the hell. He knocks on the door and has a nice little visit,
without significance.

Griselio then goes to Jayuya from San Juan. It's not an easy trip now,
but then it must have been even worse, six hours by slow bus over narrow
roads, up, up, and up. Yet nevertheless, Griselio makes the trip and sets
about his visiting. Certainly he saw Elio, but his wandering ways are such
that he went to say goodbye to his friend Heriberto's father. Sometime
between the 16th and the 21st, he knocks on the door and guess who
answers: it's Heriberto himself.

Unbeknown to Griselio, Heriberto had come home because he'd been
ordered to report to selective service for his physical. He wasn't sure he
was going to do it; he had to decide but he couldn't decide in New York.

"We were there for a while with the family, greeting one another—he
didn't know I had arrived—and he went to say hello to the older folks
[Heriberto's parents]. That [coincidence of Heriberto and Griselio showing up in Puerto Rico on the same day] was one of those things just by
chance that almost never happen, and the FBI thought that was so
strange, that both of us would have made a trip to Puerto Rico. Well, the
matter is that after being there for a while and he had said hello to my
parents and the family, he said, 'Let's go have a drink.' And we went and

we bought a bottle of Llave [rum] and we set down on the side of the roadway from the house to converse."

They sat there, their feet dangling off a bridge in the beautiful green valley, and had a drink, the two boyhood friends who'd become distant for whatever reason in New York where Griselio would not let his old pal be close to him. It is also odd that Griselio suggested a drink, for according to both Heriberto and Dilia he never drank.

"And then I asked him why he had come to Puerto Rico, and he said, 'Well, I wanted to see the older folks. It's been a while since I have been here, since I went to New York I haven't been here.' And he asked me, 'What about you?' And I said, 'Well I came because the army called me. I have to present myself a week later [for the physical].' And we were talking there for a while, talking about things. Yeah, yeah, remembering. And, when he said goodbye, he said, 'I have to go now, because tomorrow I shall leave early, I am leaving early.' He stayed only two days.

"So then, when we said goodbye to each other, he became somewhat sad. And he hugged me and he said, 'In case we don't see each other again.' There was something special about it. It still wells up emotion within me. It was, it was like the adios [final goodbye] of my brother, my friend, yes."

But Griselio had one final stop to make.

He had to see Dilia and the daughter he'd never seen before.

She was in her father's house about ten minutes' walk from Blanca Canales's place. It was a big house in the woods just above the valley floor, with a tin roof, far from the warehouse where they took the coffee to grind and store before shipment. Open a window and she could hear the Río Grande roll by. It had been her home since she left New York and where she lived when she gave birth to the baby she had once hoped to raise with Griselio in the traditions of the valley of the Three Peaks, traditions that would be continued by future generations of her family.

Dilia had dreamed. As their baby grew into childhood, Griselio would teach her how to swim in La Suerte. Maybe the girl would be as bold as her father and need a strong hand to pull her back when she strayed into rapids. Maybe she would jump from the high rocks around which the Río Grande swirled after mountain rains had swelled its flow, spilling mineral-rich water into the greenery flanking the river.

But Griselio was not there when the baby was born or in the weeks and months afterward. She named the baby Áurea, her mother's name, meaning golden, which fit the little blond girl perfectly. By mid-September 1950, Áurea was eight months old. Griselio had yet to see his daughter.

The valley was a good home for a child to grow up in and learn about nature and the world and people. There was support from family and the small, intimate community, and the weather was usually kind. On occasion Griselio's brother, Elio, would drop by the farm to make sure Dilia and the baby were all right. His visits were always welcome. Faithful Elio.

On a late September day in 1950, Dilia was upstairs with baby Áurea and Lola, a family maid, when a knock came to the door.

"Guess who's here," said Lola.

Dilia looked out the window and froze.

There he was, the man who had let her go. She had not seen him since those lonely, grim days in New York. Elio was by his side.

Dilia walked slowly down the stairs, holding the baby tightly in her arms, her baby, his baby. Áurea was wearing a little white dress.

Griselio stood at the doorway with his brother. He gave no apology for the long absence, no explanation. He didn't even look ill at ease.

On his shirt was a small gold crucifix with the dying Christ at its center, a crucifix that had been hers for years until she gave it to him on their wedding day. Griselio was not a religious man, and to this moment Dilia does not know why she gave him such a symbol of faith.

In front of the door where Dilia stood, Griselio gazed at his daughter for the first time and reached forward.

He took Áurea in his arms and embraced and kissed her. And while he held her, Griselio carefully unhooked the crucifix Dilia had given him on the day that was supposed to join them forever and pinned it on their daughter's dress.

Standing at the front door for perhaps a half hour, they talked. They spoke of Áurea, whether she was a good baby or not. The months between this moment and the hopeful time when Dilia and Griselio had exchanged vows before the judge—months that included those distant days in New York—vanished. If Griselio felt any pain deep inside, his face did not betray it.

Then Griselio handed the baby back to Dilia, said goodbye, and walked with his brother down the valley slope.

As she cradled the baby in her arms and started up the steps, Dilia quietly began to cry. Back in Áurea's room she handed the baby to Lola and broke down in sobs. She wept for Áurea, who would grow up without her father nearby. And she cried for her own loss, the loss of the wild, bold river boy she now realized she still loved.

31. POINT-BLANK

The range couldn't have been more than eighteen inches. He didn't have to aim. He sensed the muzzle of the gun on its direct line into his target. He shot with two hands for control and because if he stuck the gun out too far, possibly his target could react fast enough to grab the muzzle.

He didn't wait, he didn't think, he didn't talk or look or internalize. He pulled the trigger four times fast, the Luger's flash filling the dark space of the interior of the booth, possibly lighting the open eyes of the man he was shooting. Yet he was on the move, as the position of the wounds would later indicate; the penetrations followed a left-to-right pattern and the internal trajectories indicate that Griselio didn't pivot the gun, he kept the gun relatively straight as he rotated on his own left-to-right path around the booth. He was in a hurry.

The gun sent each steel-jacketed bullet out at approximately a thousand feet per second, stripping the empty shell out of the chamber and tossing it away, picking up and inserting a new one. Griselio easily could have fired his four shots in one second.

"That was the body of Leslie Coffelt whom I knew in life, lying on a slab at the D.C. morgue, unclothed," the deputy coroner, Dr. Christopher J. Murphy, would testify some weeks later. "I proceeded with my performance of the autopsy on the decedent. . . . My examination revealed this decedent had a gunshot wound of entrance in his left side ten inches below the junction of the two collar bones, [in the] breast bone, near the anterior auxiliary line, which would be at about the point where I am now pointing. This bullet took a course from left to right downward and backward, passing through the left kidney, the peritneous [sic] and intestines and mesentery in many places and lodged in the lumbar muscles and removed from the right flank two inches to the right of the spine, one inch above the great ileghm [sic] which would be about the point I am

223

pointing to, that is the point where I removed the bullet and marked that bullet on the base with the letter 'C' and turned it over to Sergeant Clark of the Homicide Squad at 10:30 P.M. on the night of November 1, 1950.

"I continued my autopsy and found that this decedent also had a gunshot wound of entrance four inches below the umbilicus or navel and two inches to the left of the midline, which would be about where I am pointing. That bullet took a course from before backwards and was not found by me. It passed through the intestines. I was not able to find it.

"There was also a gunshot wound of entrance in the mid axillary line two inches below. The mid axillary line is the line dropping from the angle under the arm, three inches below the one I have just described, which was four inches below the umbilicus, making this one six inches below the umbilicus. This bullet took a course from left to right and passed through the intestine in many places. I removed this bullet from the right flank past axillary fold two inches above the ileum, just about here [indicating]."

And so Leslie Coffelt was hit three times. The fourth bullet grazed the sleeve of his tunic. The results were expectable, even banal, in the world of forensic pathology, and tragic for all who knew, knew of, or loved him. Les must have jacked upright with the first shot almost to his feet, which is why the second and the third shots go so low, into the gut, and the fourth just missed him.

Griselio kept on moving, his progress taking him clear of the booth.

Leslie Coffelt began to slide down to his chair.

His pulse dropped. The blood loss was immediate. The pain, the shock, the surprise, the anger: what went through his mind in the split second after he was shot? Was he dying? He must have known that he was. Was he in shock? He had to be. Was he paralyzed? He must be. Down, down, down he slid, inside the booth, settling on the chair. He was bleeding to death.

Griselio came around the guardhouse and immediately encountered another target. This was Joseph Downs, the classic wrong place–wrong time guy. He was a White House policeman in civilian clothes; his job was to drive the panel truck known as the Grocery Wagon and purchase food for that day's Blair House dinner.

Downs, basically a tough Irish cop who was one of the best tennis players in Washington, had seen guns before and been in gun battles; he'd fought with the marines in Nicaragua in the 1920s, going into the service at seventeen to escape a rough upbringing in Cincinnati. He was wounded in the right side but kept on fighting, eventually killing the man who shot him.

Downs was a straitlaced religious man with a fondness for cigars and physical conditioning, a great basketball player with a shooter's touch. In fact, it may have been the extreme hardiness of his sports-hardened respiratory system and muscle tone that got him through the next few minutes.

He never had a chance either. He'd just paused to chat with the always friendly Les Coffelt, then proceeded down the walkway to the basement door at the west end of Blair. He heard a shot just behind him—though four were fired, he heard only one, according to his report—and turned to see a thin young man in a suit with a Luger in his right hand.

"I reached for my gun and as I did a shot struck in the right hip, stunning me and making it impossible for me to draw my gun. In my stunned condition it looked as if the man was moving toward me, as if intending to enter through [the] basement door.

"I turned toward the house and as I did two more shots were fired striking me in the back of the body and neck. One shot entered my right shoulder and traveled into my lungs, and the other struck a bone on the left side of my neck, glanced off, and then went through my left ear." The first bullet went into his abdomen and out again, punching a hole in his leather belt.

But even three 9mm bullets fired at close range didn't knock Joe Downs off his feet. He staggered onward, reached the door, and looked back. He couldn't see anything, though. "I couldn't determine much." His vision was blurred.

But he did have two quick thoughts: "They're after the president" and . . .

"I'm going to die."

Downs opened the door, slid in, and in another unrecorded moment of supreme heroism, slammed the door tightly behind him. Three bullets in him and he remembers to slam the door to keep the shooter out. In subsequent accounts of this event, no one, it seems, has focused on this act. It should have been focused upon. It was magnificent.

"Help, I'm shot," he cried. Then he staggered a few feet to the housekeeper's office and collapsed in a chair, to the horror of Miss Walker, the Blair House housekeeper. He asked her to call for a doctor—and a priest.

Meanwhile, on Pennsylvania, Griselio turned anew, giving up his pursuit of Joe Downs. What clearly attracted him was the sound of shots, though nobody was yet shooting at him.

Griselio turned to that sound, that is, to the south. There he saw the wounded Donald Birdzell clumsily aiming his third or fourth shot at Oscar. Griselio didn't hesitate. Again, his superb hand-eye coordination served him well, but something else did too. He took the longest shot of the engagement, lifted the Luger, aimed carefully, and pressed the trigger. Why was he so effective, when all the other shooters on the field missed so many shots? The answer is clear: he shot two-handed. He started the fight two-handed, according to witnesses across the street who saw the first shots, and then was so involved in the mechanics and the drama of his mission, he never diverged from it. In a gunfight, as many have observed, people tend to finish the way they start. Griselio wouldn't have thought to change his grip—his mind was on other matters.

The gun fired, and the toggle locked back, signifying an empty gun. That lack of a follow-up shot may have saved his target's life.

"I think I fired two or three rounds before I was struck again," Birdzell recounted, "this time in the left knee which knocked me down and I think I momentarily blacked out."

Consider that anomaly: Donald Birdzell goes through two years in a combat theater in World War II unscathed. Then in about twenty seconds he is shot twice on November 1, 1950, and both times in the knee.

But consider also Griselio's technique. He was shooting to kill. When he found a target, he hit it three times. Only because he is out of ammunition and must reload does he not pump two more into Donald. The missed fourth shot on Les almost certainly saved Donald Birdzell's life.

Griselio had fired at three men and downed them all. Two of them are out of the fight for good—Downs hit three times, Birdzell hit twice—and Leslie Coffelt, hit three times, has slumped down in his chair, bleeding profoundly, slipping into unconsciousness. And no one who is still standing has seen Griselio.

Griselio now stood to the immediate left of the Blair House steps, next to the hedge, beyond the guard booth. He was reloading, he was looking for new targets. He had evidently decided not to sprint forward and try to breach the defenses of the building. But he had a window here of possibly as many as ten seconds. It would be ended shortly, when Vince Mroz reached the end of his long run through the basement corridor and came out onto the top of the stairs at the entrance of Lee with Officer Charles Dodge, a White House policeman who had been in the housekeeper's office.

But for now, reloading, Griselio stood clear and unseen by any standing men. The only men who'd seen him were down.

Leslie Coffelt lay in his chair, dying.

32. THE MAN WHO LOVED GUNS

Not much had happened in Oranda, Virginia, since October 19, 1864. On that day, Jubal Early sent a few thousand of his best men through the fog and across Cedar Creek toward Union lines. Achieving surprise and inflicting heavy casualties, they drove the Federals back, almost out of the valley. Gray won the morning. But by the afternoon, Phil Sheridan had ridden hard from Winchester, found his troops in disarray, raised hell, and got them in order. They went back into the valley and by the end of the day had broken the Confederacy's grip on the Shenandoah for all time. It cost eight thousand lives. Blue won the afternoon, the valley, and the war.

But it was so quiet ever since, nobody thought much about that day. The battlefield lay three miles to the west of the town, and on any given day it was hard to remember that something so historic took place, so bloody, so tragic. War—or any kind of violence—was a long way from Oranda. The town was just a few houses and the church and the school and Mr. Horner's general store nestled in the folds of the green, green valley. The mountains lay all around, not towering but lining the horizon, the Blue Ridge one way, the Alleghenies the other, though the closest big hill is Signal Knob to the other side of Strasburg.

It was farm and stone country. People pulled a living from the land one way or the other, farming or in the quarries—and prayed hard. For fun they hunted or fished. You can't see a city anywhere you look, just the rolling green meadows, the tufts of vegetation or trees here or there, the grazing cattle, and the long shadows of the far mountains. If the sky is blue and the sky is bright, it could be paradise. It's a nice place to live and it's the sort of place that gets inside you and never, ever leaves. You may leave it, it never leaves you. That's the way it was in the 1920s for the Coffelt clan. Times were tough, but they had one another, they had their community, they had their God, they had their land. With those things, the Coffelt clan felt rich.

The kids dressed like ragamuffins, barefoot in their overalls and full of mischief. The one they call Etts is the jokester. They say Etts gets it from his daddy, Will, a carpenter. If he gets half a chance, Etts's daddy will nail someone's overalls to the bench and laugh when he tries to stand up and walk away. Etts has the same mentality. If you sit down around him, better reach back and make certain the chair's still there, because he'd be likely to pull it out on you. Nothing that really hurt anybody. Just something to have somebody laughing to start the day off. It got him beat up once in a while by older boys, but he never changed.

Etts was one of five Coffelts. They call him that, they say, because his young sister, Midge, could never pronounce his rightful name, which is Leslie. So in the valley, he's Etts. The others are Harry, Hollis, Norman, then Etts, and then Mildred, who was called Midge. Will Coffelt was the father and Effie Keller the mother—another old northwest Virginia family—and Will and Effie grew up a stone's throw from each other. They married in 1899, they built a house with their own hands, they brought five children into the world, and when Effie died, it was in the same house.

The church was a center of their life. As Irene Orndorff, an eighty-two-year-old Orandan who knew Les from the time he was ten, recalls, "They were real religious. Mr. Will Coffelt could say as pretty a prayer as anybody could stand in church and say it. They were real good. Miss Effie with her little basket, bless her heart, would take a basket of goodies to someone who was shut in. There was an old lady who lived across the creek, and Miss Effie helped make dresses and petticoats and then walked across Cedar Creek here over in Woodstock and took them over to that old lady to wear so she'd be warm in winter. That's dedication."

Etts was born in 1910, laughing from the start. Some of his brothers were different. Hollis was Mr. Perfect, that's what folks called him. He got that from his mother, Effie, a prissy woman, who liked to dress up and always wore a hat to church. Norman was just plain old Norm. He was a good guy, that's all. He didn't say much and if you saw him smile, something had to be really exciting. He was always there. And Harry, he was there and there and there.

If Etts wasn't playing ball or pulling pranks, he was hunting. He used to love to hunt. He'd hunt rabbits with a shotgun day in and day out, sometimes with his mother's dog, Buster, but Buster had a way of ruining the shot because he wouldn't wait for Les, he'd just go running crazily after the animal and send it scampering away. "Darn," Etts would say, "I had a nice shot at a rabbit and then Buster comes in." In the fall, he went deer hunting. When he was a boy, he saved up to buy a shotgun for rabbit hunting, and he kept that gun clean and shiny and owned it until the day he died.

He graduated from high school over at Strasburg and in those days you had to walk that far and back every day. There were no buses or cars. Seven miles as the crow flies. It didn't seem like much then, and nobody thought a single thing about it.

It may be that things were different then. Etts rose early in a room with his brothers and they all did chores right away, and so, being part of a mob, he never got the idea he was special. He was just part of something. They went downstairs, and Mama was already cooking breakfast. There wasn't much, but again, nobody got more. Folks understood you had to share.

Then he went to school. Now possibly if you go to school every morning in a mountain valley, barefoot, poor but proud and not a bit unhappy or ashamed of it, because it's like everybody, and you pass Mr. Horner's general store, a white clapboard building, then you turn right and head into "downtown" Oranda, which consists of one three-room schoolhouse, again white clapboard, with a steeple for the school bell and a flag, and you head in for your lessons but at the same time you see the Walnut Grove Church, which your daddy helped rebuild and which has Coffelts and Kellers and Hossenflips in the cemetery and they are all connected somehow and they're all linked by love, blood, and loyalty and the sky is blue, the valley green, and the mountains dark, well, what sort of a man do you turn out to be? The answer may be that you turn out to be like Leslie William Coffelt.

Etts grew up country, which means with hard work and also with dogs and guns. He never had a girlfriend because he was related to most of the women in the small town and besides, there were other pursuits. He graduated high school, second in his family (Mr. Perfect, Hollis, beat him to it), and he played sports. He took his religion seriously and never missed church. Etts never had a rebel bone in his body. He honored his mother and father and brothers and sister, he never missed a day of school, he never missed a Sunday in church. Why was Etts so good? It's a mystery. Some folks are just born that way.

"He was a wonderful person. To know him you loved him, that was all," recalled Irene Orndorff. "I knew him from the day I knew anybody in Oranda."

And the guns. His stepdaughter, Janie, remembers, "And he just had this thing for guns. He was a sharpshooter. Somewhere I have a plaque. It was his sharpshooter's award, and the Secret Service gives it every year to somebody, as I recall. In the service, I think on his service record you'll see that he was very good with guns."

In fact there are pictures taken in the 1930s when he was a teenage schoolboy. They show him laughing and joshing and posing for the camera with his pal Bob Lee, and they're playing cowboys after the fashion of the B pictures they must have seen in Strasburg on Saturday afternoons. They have that cowboy dream, of freedom, independence, beauty, honor, and decency, just like the movies taught then. But Etts is holding a real Colt's Peacemaker, like the iron used in the great American gunfights at the O.K. Corral or Dodge City or the Johnson County Wars. Probably nobody thought this sporting with a real Colt revolver was anything odd: then guns were a part of life. All the houses had them, all the men shot their deer in the fall—they needed the meat, so no one would be squeamish about such—and everyone knew how to skin a rabbit and make a stew or how to lead a duck so that the shot stream meets him where he'll be. And Etts had other guns too. He had a small, single-shot .22 rifle to cull the hogs every November. That was a part of the community celebration, pig-culling day; all the Orandans got together and culled the herd.

After high school graduation, Etts, like everybody, had to figure out a way to earn a living. It was 1928 and he took off for the nearest big city, Washington, D.C., two hours to the east. In a sense his daddy, Will, pioneered the way, because Will used to head into D.C. and find work carpentering, and the pay was much higher and he could sleep in his car during the week and come home on weekends. So to Etts, that was "The City."

There are of course stories about country folk who have to go to the city, and it changes them, somehow, into its own image. And they become slick and fast and talky and shady. It may have happened but it never happened to Etts. Mrs. Orndorff said it most eloquently. She'd been asked if he was a handsome boy, and she looked her questioner flat in the eyes and said, "He was pretty outside because he was pretty inside."

So into D.C. he went, looking for work, just with his strong back, sound common sense, and good heart. He became a policeman.

Why? Well, his stepdaughter, Janie, recalls simply, "From what I understand, he always wanted to be a policeman." So it can't be tracked to a certain thing, a certain experience, a turning point. One can assume the best, however, because with Etts you can usually assume the best. It seems sure he didn't become a policeman over issues like strength or power or blue uniforms or the big gun they all carried, but because it was a good way to help people.

He joined the department in 1929 and was assigned to Precinct 3, which ran down K Street, and he settled into the police life. He did it well, he advanced as steadily as anybody, he took notes on lectures, he wore the blue, he carried the Colt, he wrote the tickets.

Then in 1936 he quit for some reason. Maybe the pay wasn't high enough and he had to send more home to Mom and Dad in Oranda. It would have to be something like that. He worked as what was called an "engineer" then, and it seems to be some sort of building technician, probably taking care of mechanical problems and maintaining heating and cooling systems. For the longest time he was at the Lee-Sheraton Hotel, and then for some reason he switched to the G. C. Murphy Company. Then, for a time, he was a meat-cutter at the Safeway store on 17th Street.

Then there's Cressie. Again, it would be nice to tell how it was the Washington policeman came to meet a small-town Pennsylvania girl in the nation's capital training to be a nurse, but as Janie says, "The only family members that would know [how they met] are dead. His sister, Mildred, is dead; all of them are, I'm sure, dead."

But Janie also says that Cressie's family "adored him."

Cressie Elinor Morgan was from Uniontown, Pennsylvania. She was actually from Hopwood, a tiny town four miles outside of Uniontown, but since no one had ever heard of Hopwood, the family always said they came from Uniontown. Her father was not well-to-do, and she had siblings including a brother, Stanley, a sister Bunny and a sister Marie. The family used an outside privy and lit their home with kerosene lamps. Her mother worked at night and cared for her children during the day. Much of the family's food came from their garden.

And at some time in her life, Cressie did the unimaginable. For the late 1920s what she did was staggering. Whisper whisper, gossip gossip, that Cressie, she's exactly the type that such things happen to, a little too highfalutin for anybody else.

Cressie had a baby. The baby was named Cora Jane after her grand-mother and great-aunt. Unfortunately Cressie hadn't married the father.

There may have been a scandal but no one speaks of it anymore. In her fantasy life—evidently strong—Cressie insisted that the father was a doc-tor, but Janie looked and looked for her biological dad under the name she gave him, and never found him.

So Cressie went away and came back and the baby couldn't be acknowledged as Cressie's, and so it—maybe that's how Cressie always thought of Janie, as "it"—was given to an older married sister to raise.

Thus, when the engineer from Washington fell in love with Cressie and took her away to his city, it was probably the best thing that could happen to the family. Its embarrassing black-sheep daughter moved far enough away to quell rumors and Janie could grow up with her aunt, while visiting her mother and stepfather every summer.

They married October 5, 1937, in Prince George's County, Maryland, at the Forestville Methodist Episcopal Church, and moved into an apart-ment on Q Street.

In 1941, possibly because he now had two incomes (Cressie worked for a dentist, then as a saleslady at Hecht's), Les felt free enough to return to his preferred life: he rejoined the Metropolitan Police. His stepdaughter has to this day memorabilia that evoke this long-vanished American hero. There's a ticket book, containing a parking violation he issued on August 7, 1941, to someone who violated the 4:00 P.M.–to–6:00 P.M. parking ban in D.C. It's a strange, charged object, like something dark and mysterious from a medieval reliquary, this ancient government form laboriously laid out in Les's clear but clumsy handwriting, this being a carbon of the origi-nal, which denotes a miscreant's folly that must be rationalized to the state by paying a $3 fine. Somehow, in a way that photos don't and sec-ondary reading can't and interviews never will, it evokes his living pres-ence. It was in his belt that long, hot D.C. August sixty-four years ago as he haunted the streets in his blue serge, looking for parking violators.

In 1942, he requested and was awarded a transfer to the White House Police, a force that had been begun independently in 1922, comprising Metropolitan policemen and some military personnel, but was absorbed administratively (although perhaps not culturally) by the Secret Service in 1930 under the aegis of Herbert Hoover.

The war was on in 1942, and like everyone else, Leslie is drafted. He serves less than two years and never gets overseas, much less into combat. The story that Janie tells is that he started having fainting spells, and the army gave him a medical release. Could a man with a history of fainting spells become a member of the uniformed division of the Secret Service today and end up on the Protection Detail at the White House? Probably, indeed certainly, not. But it goes without saying it was different in those days. Everybody knew everybody, and if you were liked, as the friendly, loyal, earnest Les was, a place would be found for you without much fuss. So by 1945, Les was back on the White House Police Force.

Let's look at Les and Cressie in the late 1940s. There wasn't much money, even by the standards of the late 1940s. In 1949, for example, he made $3,917.67. By now they'd moved to the Arlington address, renting the one-bedroom apartment on Wayne Street off Lee Highway, and Janie, a high school graduate who's gotten a job through Les at the Veterans Administration, was living with them.

Church was important, and so was family. And so were the Masons. And so was work. He never missed a day or a service or a meeting. He loved his wife. Cressie was difficult—this is not a tale out of school; literally *everybody* agrees—but he loved her desperately and called her Baby. He was forever trying to settle the secret anger that flashed between Cressie and Janie, while Janie was secretly seeing the boy she would marry.

They visited a niece and nephew in Glen Burnie, Maryland, a suburb of Baltimore that lies a little to that city's south along Maryland Route 2. The nephew—Calvin was the son of his older brother Norman and had married and started a family—found Les full of life. He always brought presents for the small kids, Annette and Cynthia. Cynthia still remembers Les bringing her a dress. But with Cressie, predictably, there were problems. The nieces still remember Aunt Cressie as "lovely, but not friendly. Reserved." On one occasion, when the couple visited, and the family fixed up an upstairs room and fed Uncle Les and Aunt Cressie a fine meal, it came back through family sources that "someone" complained that they'd had to stay in the attic and that they hadn't been fed well enough.

And once the family visited Uncle Les in Arlington. Les proudly laid out his uniform with its shiny buttons and his cap and all his gear. When he brought out his Colt revolver his six-year-old niece Annette asked, "Have you ever shot anybody, Uncle Les?"

Les became serious and quiet.

"No," he told her—she remembers it to this day—"and I hope I never have to."

In the summer, Les and Cressie would visit Maryland. He loved to swim in the Chesapeake Bay, especially Alpine Beach, near Pasadena. He would go in the water even when it was too cold for everyone else.

In Hopwood, Pennsylvania, in the mountains just off Route 40, where Cressie's family lived, Les tried to teach his wife how to shoot, but she wasn't much interested in firing a gun. But her father and brother were, and Les enjoyed hunting with them when he got the chance.

And he'd go home to Oranda every October to hunt, usually by himself. In fact he went home in October of 1950 to hunt, and who should he run into but his old friend Irene Orndorff.

"He just loved to hunt rabbits. He loved to hear those beagles run. He would just hunt by himself. He said it the last time I talked to him—it couldn't have been over a month before [the Blair House incident]—he was out here hunting, and I went to put a letter in the box and he said, How's it going, Irene? I said, Just fine. And of course I always had a couple kids hanging on me, I had seven of them, and I said, We're doing okay. I said, How's Etts doing? He said, I'm doing good. He said, You know what? When I come up here and hear them beagles running, I'm in heaven. And I said, Well, bless your heart. He said, It's me, my beagles, the rabbits, and above all my God. He's always up there, isn't he, Irene?"

And now Les was shot, three times at close range with German steel-cased ammunition. He was slumping in his chair. He was dying.

33. THE DARK VISITORS

Who were these men? Not in the obvious sense of who were Oscar and Griselio as people, as husbands, as citizens, as believers, but who were they as types? Where do they fit in? The answer is, almost nowhere. They were different, certainly, from most other presidential assassins and would-be assassins.

There have been, in the history of the republic, fifteen such dark visitors who have reached out to strike either a president or a presidential candidate—the others were John Wilkes Booth (Abraham Lincoln), Leon Czolgosz (William McKinley), Sirhan Sirhan (Robert Kennedy), Giuseppe Zangara (Franklin Roosevelt; he killed Mayor Anton Cermak of Chicago instead), Arthur Bremer (George Wallace), Lee Harvey Oswald (John F. Kennedy), Samuel Byck (he aspired to kill Richard Nixon but instead murdered a policeman and a pilot), Lynette Alice "Squeaky" Fromme (Gerald Ford), Sara Jane Moore (Gerald Ford), Richard Lawrence (Andrew Jackson), Charles Guiteau (James Garfield), John Schrank (Theodore Roosevelt), and John Hinckley (Ronald Reagan). To understand, therefore, who Griselio and Oscar were, it's helpful to understand who they weren't.

Many had wretched childhoods in dysfunctional families (Oswald, Zangara), were beaten (Sirhan), made to feel as if they were nothing, held in contempt by father or mother (Czolgosz, Sirhan, Oswald, Byck, Fromme), if they are around, and one or the other or sometimes both are frequently absent (Oswald, Czolgosz, Moore, Zangara), in which case a stepparent of some sort, or the state itself, steps in and messes with the child's mind as savagely as possible. Still, usually, it's his father who beats him (Sirhan), doubts him, diminishes him, destroys him, tears him so apart that when he reassembles himself it's in some twisted format or other, laden with anguish and grievance, unburdened by morality, driven by narcissism, shorn of empathy and love.

In school the other kids torment him (Oswald, Byck, Sirhan). He's ugly, slow, a stammerer, he has acne, he's tragically shy, he's bereft of confidence. He has some form of attention deficit disorder or dyslexia, or maybe he's just plain stupid (Bremer, Zangara); this means that he's the butt of all classroom jokes, his teachers treat him like a burden if they notice him at all, and generally his condition could be described as abject misery. Naturally, he lacks coordination; if he's tossed a ball, he drops it, and soon no one will pick him for any games. Lacking physical vitality, he is picked on by other, stronger boys. He has no defenses; he has no one's shoulder upon which to cry. Thus, he curdles in solitude, festering, suffering, grieving for his own lost beauty, producing a species of pus in the brain, turning blacker, angrier, more hostile, more desperate with each tick of the clock, each new page of the calendar (Hinckley, Oswald).

Poverty is also a great help in the development of these strangers (Sirhan, Oswald, Czolgosz, Zangara). For many, their childhood is made intense by want, so that survival itself is an issue. That way they learn mistrust, fear, petty thievery, contempt for the system, contempt for the state, contempt for the family, the church, the school, the military service. Wherever they are, they are on the outside, looking in desperately, pretending all the while they don't need "in," and finally concluding that they must destroy "in."

They scuffle about in adult life. Poorly educated, depressed, friendless (Oswald, Byck, Sirhan, Czolgosz, Fromme, Moore, Zangara), they soon retreat into a world of their own manufacture, and it's a cruel place, where their will is absolute, their capacity to inflict pain endless (Hinckley, Zangara, Oswald). They will pay back all those who've hurt them over the years, and their fantasies are full of retribution, righteous vengeance, the triumph of their will. Their universe loses all contact with reality (Lawrence, Guiteau, Schrank), and it's not only a different drummer they hear but a different definition of music. Meanwhile, as failure coalesces with failure, their sense of aggrieved isolation accelerates. The world has never noticed them, never acknowledged them, never taken their pain into account (Hinckley, Byck). Therefore it too must be punished, and the vessel of punishment is always the same: the man who seems to head it all, who is smooth and confident and is held in respect and esteem, who radiates and attracts love, who is the father who beat them, the state that ignored them, all the girls who wouldn't love them, the club that expelled them, the coach who shouted at them when they dropped the ball, all of it, all of it rolled into one figure. From there the reach to the rifle or pistol isn't a long one, and in that one giddy second, when a tug on a trigger inflicts their will upon the world, for that time, and the time in flight as the bullet lasers to the target, that's the only moment in their miserable lives where they achieve happiness.

Yet none of these pathologies, these tendencies toward exile, bitterness, and violence, stalked Griselio or Oscar. Oscar and Griselio had almost no relationship whatsoever to that litany of oddballs, delusional fools, and narcissists. They were men connected to society, men with families they loved, children they treasured, futures they yearned for, full of hope and dreams. They were both in love. They honored the memory of their dead fathers. In every way they were estimable, but they were also soldiers, and they had a mission they believed would advance a cause they believed in ardently. So they go and do the thing, knowing that both death and calumny await them, and that they will be reviled for generations. They do it anyway, with melancholy and doubt, like all soldiers.

From afar, and even from close up, they were "normal"; no one would notice them in a crowd, where a surly Oswald, with his slouch and attitude, would stand out, or a completely crazy Guiteau, as loopy a man as ever lived, would and did draw continuous attention. Even a low-grade marginal like Sara Jane Moore, haunted by her father's rigid fundamentalist Baptism, seeking, then leaving respectable bourgeois life (she was a CPA), ended up so wiggy in her pursuit of a radical lifestyle that she attracted the notice of the FBI, who recruited her as a snitch, thus setting in motion the events that led her to open fire on Gerald Ford in search of redemption for her treason.

Thus James Clarke, a political scientist who has studied these people, classes Griselio and Oscar as classic "Type One" assassins, meaning purely political creatures, who never heard voices or received instructions from God or yearned for some form of human acknowledgment. They are, or so it seems, even more of the Type Ones than the other two examples Clarke cites, John Wilkes Booth (handsome and beloved, his hatred for Lincoln clearly marked him as far more pathological than Griselio and Oscar) and Sirhan (who was raised in a climate of violence in the Jerusalem of the late 1940s, saw his own brother die savagely, and was subsequently beaten harshly, then abandoned, by his own father).

If it can be explained, and possibly it can't, it can be said that these were men who were not afraid to die, not because they were sure of entry into an afterlife but because it was at the center of their definition of political manhood. Their lives were nothing next to the immensity and nobility of the cause. That's what made them so intense, so passionate, so seemingly out of reach of normal psychology. And that's what made them so dangerous.

34. MORTAL DANGER

Harry Truman had reached the window. He looked out. Before him he saw nothing. He almost certainly could not have reached the window in the first half of the fight. He was awakened, dazzled, confused, until finally, probably thirty seconds into it, he got out of bed and moved to the window. He could see Donald Birdzell, passed out on Pennsylvania Avenue, and possibly one other man—Griselio Torresola. But that of course meant Griselio could see him.

Like no man before or since in history, Harry Truman should have stayed in bed. Or, better, he should have rolled out of bed, crawled to a closet, climbed inside, closed the door, and huddled. What the nation needed at that precise moment was the one thing Harry Truman could not provide: cowardice.

He went to the window and even raised it, as he himself stated later and as several different accounts testify, most notably his secretary of the treasury, John Snyder. "There was a most unusual situation that could have been tragic, when during some of the firing, Mr. Truman came to the second-story window and looked out—raised it and looked out. The Secret Service immediately called to him to get back inside." On the front pages of newspapers across America the next day, a wire service photo of Blair House ran with a legend embossed by an AP graphic artist: although it misidentified the window from which the president looked out, it labeled it "Where President Viewed Gun Battle."

It can be said that was Harry Truman's nature. Other presidents might not have done so, but Truman had an active mind, a practical mind, a curious mind, and he did what his instincts told him to do. Thus, upon being roused from sleep by gunfire, his instincts demanded that he determine the source of the gunfire. Thus, he walked to the window. Thus, he potentially walked into the range of Griselio Torresola.

All previous accounts of this event have failed to recognize this. They have instead concentrated on the "folly" of Oscar and Griselio, how foolish and poorly planned their action was, how hopeless, because they couldn't have possibly gotten into Blair House and gotten up the steps past Stout and his tommy gun, past Toad and Joe Davidson and Vince Mroz and their Colts, up the stairs and through the door and there administered the coup de grâce.

But Griselio didn't have to.

Stewart Stout was out of the fight; he was back in the office getting the tommy gun out of the locked cabinet in the Blair House Secret Service office. Vince was out of the fight; he had ducked back inside and was running through the basement hallway and was probably a good fifteen seconds from arriving at the head of the Lee stairway. Toad and Joe Davidson were crouched at the corner of Blair, concentrating on Oscar, whom they had focused on exclusively. To them, Oscar was the nearest threat, which meant to them he was the only threat. Joe Downs had flopped into the housekeeper's office, yelling that he was shot because he was shot, three times. Donald Birdzell was unconscious in the street, a bullet through each knee. And Leslie Coffelt was in his booth, bleeding to death, sliding into a coma, three bullets in his body, his eyes glassy.

Griselio stood alone, undetected, unseen, at the foot of the Lee stairs. Nobody in the world knew he was there except the men he'd shot and an observer across the street in a second-floor window.

He reached into his coat pocket for another magazine. All he had to do was insert it, give a little tweak to the locked toggle of the Luger, which will fly forward, depositing a new steel-jacketed 9mm into the chamber.

And Harry Truman was at the window.

From where he stood, Griselio was thirty-one feet away from that window, which is not above the Blair House door as widely reported (that would put it over forty feet away), but one window bank closer to Lee House. Griselio was standing about seventeen feet from Lee House and had a substantial angle into that particular window so that he could have seen anyone standing in it. It is not known if the president leaned out, therefore making himself a better target, or if he simply stood still, and presented a thinner, smaller target. It is not known if Truman was there and Griselio saw Truman or Truman got there a few seconds later. It is not known if Griselio meant to stay there, having given up on his idea of penetrating the house; it is not known if he would have looked up at the right moment.

What is known, indisputably, is that a trained, determined assassin with extraordinary combat shooting skills and a known predilection for the highly accurate two-handed shooting stance stood with a gun he was loading, looking in the proper direction at the proper moment and unimpeded by any law enforcement agents. He had a clear shot at the window, and the president was either there or was within seconds of getting there.

What about the canopy? There was a canopy over the Lee stairway, a green canvas structure supported on metal framework. Wouldn't that have blocked Griselio's view of the window? The answer is no, and the reason is that Griselio, medium-sized by Puerto Rican standards, was by American standards tiny. He was five foot five. He could see under the canopy to the window easily.

The moment had arrived or was about to arrive. Griselio was ready, hungry, anxious to shoot. Vince Mroz was still ten seconds from his arrival and he was the only law enforcement agent with any chance of preventing Griselio from doing what Griselio had come to do.

Griselio was young, tense, loose, hot, dangerous, full of hormones, riding on a wave of victory, feeling powerful and triumphant. Griselio was a soldier on a mission. It would have taken but a flick of the eyes, a recognition of the possibility, a few more seconds, and the Alben Barkley administration would have begun.

The president of the United States was in mortal danger.

Nationalist Party Cadets ready to march in Ponce, March 21, 1937.
Police in foreground.

The Ponce Massacre begins.

3

Police—one dead, one with a shotgun, and one with a Thompson submachine gun—at Ponce during the massacre.

4

Pedro Albizu Campos giving a speech.

5

6

Rosa and Oscar Collazo in a picture taken about the time they were married in August 1940.

Griselio Torresola dancing with Carmen Dolores.

7

The bodies of two Puerto Rican Nationalists lie in the courtyard of La Fortaleza after an attack on the palace, where Governor Luis Muñoz Marín has his office. The governor was there at the time of the assault.

Blair House showing the paths of Griselio Torresola and Oscar Collazo.
The picture incorrectly identifies the window where Truman looked out.
The president actually appeared at the window to the left of the one
pointed out in the photograph.

White House Policeman
Leslie Coffelt at his post. The
picture adorns the front of a
Masonic tribute to him.

Elroy Sites tends to the grievously wounded White House
Policeman Leslie Coffelt.

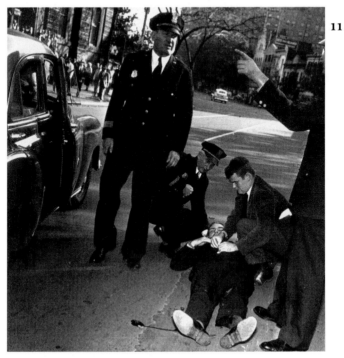

White House Policeman Donald Birdzell lies wounded
on Pennsylvania Avenue after the gun battle.

Secret Service Special Agent Vincent Mroz *(left)* in front of Blair House immediately after the attack. The body of Griselio Torresola, in fetal position, lies beneath the hedge in the middle of the picture.

Secret Service Special Agent Floyd Boring stands near the wounded
Oscar Collazo.

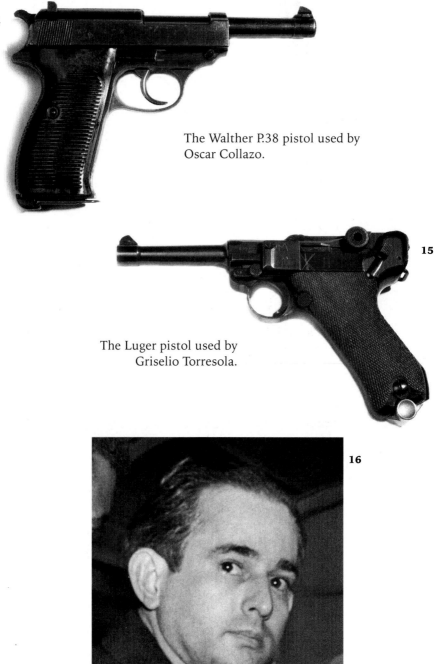

14 The Walther P.38 pistol used by Oscar Collazo.

15 The Luger pistol used by Griselio Torresola.

16 Oscar Collazo on the day of his verdict after being tried for the murder of Leslie Coffelt.

35. THE NEIGHBOR

The baby Kate was at her nap, and Judy would be home from St. Theresa's soon. When both were there, Ruth Boring had laundry to pick up, groceries to buy, and she always gave Judy some time in the park to play because the apartment was so small and an eight-year-old needs room to roam. Then there was dinner to be prepared because Toad will be—

There was a knock on the door.

Ruth answered, and standing before her was a neighbor. The neighbor was what was called in the tender euphemisms of the 1950s a "character," denoting some marginality of behavior that polite people hesitate to specify. Apparently she was an alcoholic.

Mrs. Jones, to use a pseudonym, looking more disheveled than ever, was rocking ever so slightly. Her face was strangely agitated.

"What is—"

"Ruth," blurted the woman, "have you seen the television or heard the radio? There's been a shooting at Blair House. Your husband is dead."

Ruth Boring was a cop's wife. She wasn't one for caterwauling, for scenes, for falling down, apart or sideways. She simply nodded and understood immediately what must be done.

She would go get Katie up. Then, her face controlled, her emotions kept in check, she would take Katie up the street to St. Theresa's and take Judy out of class and return home.

She didn't want her daughter to hear of her father's death from another child or a teacher.

36. AMERICAN GUNFIGHT

I n a gunfight there is no time, there is no clarity, there is no logical sequence of events. Things happen as they happen, and under massive stress men do what they will do. Physiological changes are incredible: IQs drop, fingers seem to balloon inefficiently, hearing shuts down, vision tunnels, peripheral perception vanishes. You can go around afterward and ask questions; you can draw up timelines and charts, and little stick figures illustrating movement by dashes or arrows, all of those techniques can in some sense reproduce and make comprehensible what happened, who moved where, who shot whom, why X did Y and not Z or A, and so forth and so on. Yet somehow when that is done, what results is a nice academic exercise that has some but not much real bearing on what was actually experienced.

So a true account of the 38.5 seconds of November 1, 1950, would consist of one very long sentence uninterrupted by punctuation because for each participant the world was contained between the first capital letter and the final period. It's unlikely that a rational thought occurred in the form of a sentence in anybody's mind. They just did what they had to by instinct or training in a world moving too fast for words, too dynamic for thought, too dangerous for deeper meaning. They survived, or they died. They just did the necessary, fast and hard, until it was over.

It is time, pray to God, Oscar pulls the gun points it at the officer and *Jesucristo* the gun does not go what is wrong and his breath goes away and he feels the scald of frustration and pulls the wretched thing to him what now he cannot remember what Griselio said this morning and he begins to hammer at the cursed thing with his hand while pushing levers and pulling things and *Jesucristo* now it fires hot jumping crazed, it bucks so hard, tossing something away leaping alive in his hand and the officer goes AH! and grips his knee which now spouts blood goes to one leg and begins to scuttle away drawing his own gun to shoot but Oscar who shoots at him—the gun bucks so!—he sees over the fence two other officers staring at him and he swings his gun toward them and his finger presses a trigger and AH! it hops again, spitting and tossing and he sees them bug-eyed but now they are moving too and

Grrrrrr Donald the bear feels the heat as he's on the worst damn job on the shift standing there by the stairway in his hot uniform in this hot weather all by himself for an hour his legs hurt his feet hurt he's not young anymore and maybe CLICK the noise comes and he turns because he knows exactly that sound he heard it in the Pacific so many times the sound of a gun snapping in some fashion and there before him he is astonished to see a little man in a suit beating comically at a pistol against his chest is this a movie what the hell is he shouldn't have a gun this is not BANG the gun fires he knows that sound so well but he feels a hot smack at his knee and goes down not believing for a second but he catches himself and understands at some deep clear sublime serene level that to stay there is to die and so he begins to scuttle, his leg leaking hot blood, he's not sure how he does it, he somehow gets beyond the man and lurches toward the street at the same time pulling his own revolver and spinning because he is not going by God to go down without returning fire he's shaking so much and in so much pain and the whole world is chaos and dazzle and he feels the hammer come back and BANG he's firing as he moves and

Floyd half in and half out of the doghouse catches some weird movement in his eye and turns and goddamn if some little guy isn't standing there with a German gun just behind Birdzell must be an army buddy it's a German gun even if he knows BIRDZELL WAS IN THE PACIFIC so why would it be a GERMAN GUN BANG the gun fires, the little guy Jesus Christ just shot Birdzell, Birdzell is down, it's happening can this be happening Floyd has his own Dick Special coming up in his hand and somebody seems to have already cocked it for him and there it is just like on the range front sight on the little guy's head or really his hat because he's wearing a hat and *let's finish this baby right here* BANG Floyd fires and is disappointed because he HAD HIM but the guy won't go down and BANGBANGBANGBANG in his ear riiiiiiiiiinnnnnnnnnnnnnnnnnnnggg- ggggg in his ear can't hear a goddamn thing, the little guy is down where is he where's my shot it's happening, where's my shot?

BANG a noise pulls the president from his sleep what the hell he sits up blinks the fog and spiderwebs out of his mind what the hell could that have been it sounded like a gunshot just what the hell is going on he slides out of bed and his feeling isn't fear at all or panic not even a little bit of it it's goddamn fury who the hell do these guys think they are shooting off guns here in the city don't they know guns are dangerous he knows he saw what guns could do in the first war and now he heads to the window to see just BANGBANG what the hell is going on

Joe Davidson is fast on the gun because he's a kind of a jumpy guy for some reason and he sees this little fellow twenty feet away just shoot Don Birdzell and he has no thought at all but to get the goddamn gun out and point no time to aim and whatever training he may have had it's out the window because he just wants to finish this little goddamn bastard before it's too late and the Official Police comes up and his trigger finger rocks BANGBANGBANGBANGBANG five just that fast he doesn't know if he hit anything Christ who could tell the little guy ducked down behind the iron fence he thought he saw the fence posts shiver as if hit and a black mist fly from them now he's got to find cover move to the house he's out here this guy could nail him find cover reload get more slugs in put this little bastard down

Oscar spins and shoots and spins and shoots BANGBANGBANG it's all a mess a blur he can't get up the steps now because bang bang bang shots come at it the whole world it is shooting at him and he shoots back crazily just putting the gun between him and them bang bang when will it stop it is so loud he cannot get up the stairs they are all shooting at him he sees them there he shoots again BANGBANG the gun jumps hot in his hand like it's alive then it's dead, it's broken the thing on top is stuck no it's empty reload RELOAD

Stout hears the sound and wonders, what the? and has to check so off he
goes, down the hall, turns left and looks out the door and sees nothing,
but hears BANGBANGBANG and realizes somebody's trying to shoot
their way in, TOMMYGUN and heads back to the office to the gunbox, ah
Christ, the seconds drag by, he still hears shooting which key, how to get
it in that tiny little slot FINALLY pulls the cabinet open out comes the
Thompson heavy dense and everything is there before him in absolute
clarity but his mouth so dry he locks in a stick magazine feels it click in
place puts two more clips in his pocket pulls back the bolt till it locks real
quick checks to see if the safety's OFF it is the gun is set to FULL AUTO
and finally FINALLY heads back to the

Vince hears the noise too thinks it's got to be a backfire but two more
come Jesus Christ so fresh in his ears he heard somebody shoot to kill
just a few months ago he looks out the window and sees a Chinese fire
drill everybody running this way that way BANGBANG shooting and he's
off in a flash he's fast down the damned stairwell to the big steel door he
unlocks it just in time to see Toad and Joe Davidson near the guardhouse
hunched aiming this is the real thing and he pivots a little sees the little
shooter ducking and weaving bang firing and Vince has his own Dick Special up hammer back he's a good shot too puts the sight there and bang
fires then now all three of us on this side Toad is looking for another shot
Davidson is too we need another angle on the guy so Vince spins back
inside takes off running like hell down the corridor hears screams HE'S
SHOT OH GOD HE'S SHOT to Lee and up the stairwell to get an angle
on the little guy

Griselio holds the Luger so many times he's fired it, and peeks in the window of the booth and sees the darkened silhouette of a guard sitting stoically in the chair and takes a breath and steps around it sees his darkness
fall across the face of the man in the booth and the Luger is there in two
hands close to his chest and the man begins to react but with his fast
ballplayer's reflexes Griselio is faster BANGBANGBANGBANG the Luger
just like in the hills with Elio and Carlos those were wonderful days they
were part of something important they were serving they would give up

their lives in a second for Don Pedro let the Internal Security try, just let them try we will fight to the last man and before him the man is stricken his eyes fill with pain and anger as the bullets strike him terribly pushing him back and down and if Griselio feels a thing for the shooting of a man he does not let it interfere with what must happen and he steps from the booth looking for targets

"Yes sir can I help you?" Les imagines himself saying to the fellow just before him now filling the entrance to the booth but maybe his mind isn't on what appears to be just another transaction it's happened a million times which way to the White House? is this the Smithsonian? that sort of thing so he's wondering what kind of mood Cressie will be in and hoping he can drive Janie home and that for once everything will just be fine his two girls will get along it would be so nice if say isn't that a gun he reacts faster than time jacking upright, going for his Colt BANG he only hears the first one and not the next ones but he feels each of them this can't be happening the gun the flash so bright in the darkness of the booth and the darkness of the man his legs go and he spills back into his chair and the man is gone oh Jesus I am going to die I am hit so bad but at the same time he grabs for something he knows so well that is his gun his Colt and he thinks somehow not in words but more like recovered knowledge from a far distant place I have to do something I have to move I have to shoot

Joe Downs walking into the basement of Lee not thinking of much with his bag of groceries he's just passed Les BANG he hears then BANG-BANGBANGBANGBANG what the hell could that be he turns and twenty feet away somebody's aiming at him what the hell is this he turns with no other options but he goes for his gun even if he already knows he's nailed and he doesn't hear the first one but he sure feels it WHACK right hip knocking him almost flat and he turns involuntarily WHACK WHACK hit again punches pain numbness staggers forward to the door turns shit the guy is gone shoves through the door screaming HELP ME I'M SHOT I'M SHOT but remembers somehow to slam the door, staggers then a few steps to somebody's office and spills in CALL THE DOCTOR I'M SHOT people are screaming HE'S SHOT HE'S SHOT HELP HIM and knows that it's him who's shot and then the lights go way dim on him he's shot he's shot he's shot

Oscar sits on the steps not hearing the whizz and bark of the bullets as they come screaming at him so concentrating on the reloading and with a snap and a clack the strange thing in his hand snaps alive he's ready he's reloaded he stands up and means to point at them but as he stands he notices he's been shot and when he sees the dark blot of blood on his beautiful blue shirt next to his tie and realizes now what a certain pain that hadn't fully registered at some earlier point signifies and suddenly he goes all woozy the world is black the sidewalk is coming up WHACK it hits him he lies there his nose squashed his hat on and off at once and he feels three separate tracks of blood running down his face and his whole left side feels numb I'm shot I'm dying I'm shot it's over

Griselio steps from the booth and spies a man in a suit ten feet away in the doorway opening it up and the Luger comes up and before you can know it he's fired three times bangbangbang the gun hops the shells eject, flying away, the man he shoots reacts, spins, is shot again, crashes through the door hard and he hears gunfire now and he turns past Oscar on the steps and sees who is shooting at Oscar an officer in the street who is hunched, holding a wounded knee, and Griselio with two hands his aim is true draws a bead

Donald is shaking bad as he fires he's fired five times now knows he has a sixth carefully thumbs back the hammer goddamn his knee hurts the little guy is down but you have to OH JESUS he's hit, the other goddamned knee he's been shot twice in two knees in twenty-five or so seconds oh baby this one hurts and down down he goes on the trolley tracks on the cobblestones and stays there oh it hurts so much there's so much blood oh God it hurts he's down it all goes away

The president arrives at his window and looks down upon the carnage sees an officer down in the street he sees a little man down on the steps and it's suddenly quiet is it over is it done he just stands there this can't be happening but it must be over it's like he's transfixed and a certain part of him is saying GET THE HELL AWAY FROM THE WINDOW but he can't move he's so damned astonished

The president is in the window he is thirty feet from Griselio who stands unnoticed at the stairway to Lee House the men on the other side haven't noticed him yet he's shot at three men and downed them all the president is thirty feet away and he has a straight line-of-sight picture to that window and there stands the president of the United States so he is very much in the kill zone . . . but Griselio is out of ammo he'd shot at his first two victims too many times, four and three apiece then one at the man in the street so now he must reload, the Luger toggle is locked back this moment can't be happening but it is there he's just got to get the new mag in and with his fast sure fingers it's not a problem the moment is here the president is here nobody has seen Griselio and possibly he thinks of Don Pedro Albizu Campos "each day we have greater faith in the teaching of the master Albizu Campos" I am death I am death the moment is here

Three bullets in him Les is dying and his heart is barely pumping his intestines are blown up his eyes aren't working he has nothing left his life's blood is running out of him like a broken faucet what is it in him that gets him moving but somehow shot to hell though he is he staggers out of the booth leaning against it and raises the Colt the hammer comes back and somehow though his arms would be trembling and his vision shutting down and the numbness spreading or perhaps it's pain that is spreading he knows how bad he's hit but he has this last little thing to do he has to do it please God let me have the strength to do it the gun comes up in his dim fuzzy vision his blood pressure is dropping his vital signs are fading tremors run through his body somehow he gets the hammer rotated backward and feels the click as it locks in the gun comes up shakily the whole thing has to be wobbly there has to be pain befuddlement regret awareness but through it all he finds the front sight he sees the little man a blur twenty feet away he can't know that nobody still in the fight except him has even seen the little man and his finger on the trigger like at practice so many thousands of times press press P-R-E-S-S

Griselio has the magazine almost into the gun when—

The bullet strikes him two inches above the ear on a slight upward angle and rockets through the outer portions of brain breaks skull into spray on the other side and spins free he is dead instantly he is so dead no thoughts but because it's not his deep brain that's destroyed a little twitch plays through his body like a dance a jig or something he falls but struggles to stay upright and the odd dynamic of motion propels him sideways over the low hedge to the grass and like a little mouse who wouldn't hurt anything his body orders his legs to compress and his arms to come in so that he's in the fetal position the side of his head blown out blood everywhere and that is how they find him

Les looks for another target still even now duty duty duty and he puts it together that there's been shooting and he forces the gun to the right and he hears someone screaming DON'T SHOOT, COFFELT, HE'S DOWN and so Les knows it's over, "he's down," that means it's over, by whatever mercy he has to know that no matter what happens he has won the fight he has done his duty he is so very tired, he settles back into the booth, down into his chair and he just sits holding the gun he hears nothing his eyes are blank his breathing is ragged blood everywhere he hears people running people yelling someone is there he puts the gun up but can find no strength and gently the gun is taken from him and he is led out but in his legs there is no strength and he slides down he's so tired he wants to rest to rest at last to rest there's nothing left to do at all for now the darkness comes the darkness comes the darkness comes the dark—

finally, it is over period stop the end.

37. THE GOOD SAMARITAN

Vince came out of the door to Lee fast and hard, looking for his shot. Close by his side was the White House police officer Charles Dodge, who'd joined him on his rush up the stairs after seeing Joe Downs stagger in the basement door, shot three times. Both men had their guns out.

There was nobody to shoot.

Everybody was down.

He beheld the horror of the gunfight. To his left, Vince saw Toad and Joe Davidson examining a fallen assailant. Across the street, citizens began to pick themselves up off the pavement now that the shooting was over. In the street a car had stopped and someone was helping a uniformed officer who had to be Donald Birdzell. Then, to his immediate forward and right, Vince saw someone struggling with a man he instantly identified as a seriously injured Les Coffelt.

Vince raced down.

He saw somebody pulling Coffelt out of the booth.

"I was right there. I assisted a total stranger. He looked like a worker, some kind or other, sort of a blue uniform on or something, shirt and trousers."

Someone had helped Les lie down on the pavement. Someone was there holding him, easing him to the ground, knotting up a jacket to form a pillow. His name was Elroy Sites, and he was nineteen, working as an apprentice electrician a half block away. When Sites heard the shots, he ran toward the sound.

It was the sign. There was something wrong with the sign. So the folks at Baylor Furniture Company, at 724 17th Street NW, halfway down the block from Pennsylvania, called R. Archie Burgess Electric on Georgia

Avenue and Burgess sent two men, Elroy Sites and Phil McLearer. They had just arrived and to get to the sign they had to get to the roof. At 2:20 P.M., Elroy and Phil were struggling with the ladder, setting it up so they could get up and figure out what was wrong with—

"It was like bang, bang, bang," Elroy Sites recalled.

He knew in a flash. He was a hunter, a rural Pennsylvania boy of nineteen who grew up around guns. He hunted with his uncle and was president of his high school rifle club. So he recognized the sound of shooting and he took off.

"I didn't say a word to him [McLearer]. I just went flying. I could run pretty fast in those days."

Elroy Sites never much even thought about why. He just knew somebody was getting shot and that meant somebody needed help and he never asked one way or the other. He went to help.

Figuring it took him ten seconds of reaction time, he says it then took him two minutes to get there, or, upon reflection, "probably not that long. I had to hold my tools down as I ran [he was wearing an electrician's belt]." But that was memory, not physics.

The distance, diagonally across the intersection, from Baylor Furniture to 1651 Pennsylvania, is 480 feet. He passed the Place Vendome Restaurant at 722 17th, the Crystal Valet Apartments at 720, Loretta Burdette's shoe repair store at 718, Eric Zuckerman's jewelry shop at 716, and the Keystone Hotel, at 714.

Astonishingly, Elroy Sites got to the fight before the last shot was fired.

"As I came around the corner I started to focus and I saw, I guess it was Birdzell out in the street. I don't remember anybody being with him and I just kept on going because I knew they were remodeling the White House and Truman was using the Blair House. I guess the next thing I saw was somebody laying at the foot of the stairs and his back toward the building [Oscar]. Beyond him at the next entrance there were two people, civilians, kicking something down [Floyd Boring and Joe Davidson]. As I got closer I saw this guy [Griselio] go over the hedge and I started heading, that's on the sidewalk."

He kept running "because there was still noise going on, I guess."

He heard shooting all the time that he ran.

"I think so. . . . I saw one jump over the hedge and I guess I sort of slowed down. I was just about at the guard box then. Then I heard the noise, it was like everything had stopped. There was nobody else around except the two down there [Floyd Boring and Joe Davidson at the other end of the property]."

Thus, inadvertently, Elroy Sites established the only timeline for the gunfight at Blair House. In re-creating his run from the location of 724 17th Street to the location of the Blair House westernmost guard post, researchers discovered that it took—ten seconds was allowed for his initial hearing of the shots and his reaction—a lot less than the two minutes Mr. Sites had estimated half a century later. It took 38.5 seconds. Therefore, the gunfight was 38.5 seconds long. Of course it may have been 38.4 or 38.9 or 36.1 or 39.2. But it was definitely between 36 and 40 seconds long.

When he arrived at the end of his run, Elroy Sites was alone on Pennsylvania Avenue in the immediate aftermath of the gunfight. He had seen Griselio go down, "trip, like he tripped or something," over the hedge and into the front yard of Lee, a bullet in his head. Les's was the last shot fired in the fight. Floyd and Joe hadn't seen Griselio and had inadvertently, in their focus on the downed Oscar, walked into Griselio's kill zone as he reloaded his Luger. It's not hard to guess what would have happened in the next few seconds: Griselio finishes loading, draws the pistol up, and with his two-handed marksmanship he kills or wounds them both. Then he begins to walk to that entrance and something catches his eye: it's the president of the United States looking out the window, now only twenty feet above him. Quickly he—

It never happened, of course. Elroy turned and noticed the wounded man in the booth. Leslie Coffelt, who had just taken what has to be considered the most important shot ever taken by an American police officer in history, an act made more heroic and more tragic and more remarkable by the nature of the wounds he had suffered, his rapidly collapsing physical state, the fear and pain that must have seized his mind, the weakness that suddenly afflicted his limbs.

This shot was one of the legends of the 1950s. Most boys heard of the ambushed White House policeman who fired one last shot that saved the president of the United States as he stood dying, after climbing to his feet. It was featured prominently as "The Battle of Blair House" in the Landmark Book, *The Story of the Secret Service,* part of a popular young adult series from Random House, where one of the current authors read it; he never forgot it and there's little doubt why: it was one of those comforting folk narratives, like the benign wisdom and mental acuity of J. Edgar Hoover's FBI, or the superiority of the F-86 Sabre Jet, or the righteousness of Our Boys in the Service that formed the foundation of a child's view of America in the 1950s.

Yet somehow it vanished from the collective imagination, possibly because it was too savage a moment, an explicit act of killing. Particularly after the 1960s and the anatomical specificity of the cranial evacuation that ended John F. Kennedy's life, as captured in slow motion on the Zapruder film, and the revulsions of Vietnam, the endless footage of burning monks and hooches and children, Leslie Coffelt's moment of will and commitment at the point of death seemed almost to be willfully forgotten, rejected by a culture that now celebrated gentleness, sensitivity, self-expression, and playing well with others.

Now Les had slipped back into the booth, still holding his gun, sitting on his chair, staring blankly out.

Elroy Sites recalls, "I heard Coffelt moaning and I went over and he looked up at me and raised his pistol. I just took my foot and pushed the pistol over and reached down and took the pistol out and put it in my belt. He never said a word to me. He was moaning very softly. I reached around and picked him up—he wasn't a big man but he wasn't light either, and at nineteen I was a lot stronger. I picked him up and got him through the door and walked a couple of steps because his legs were starting to crumble. I got him laid out there."

That was right in front of the booth.

"Yes, I had just lifted him out this way and I was trying not to hurt him anymore. I just picked him up at the shoulders. I sort of lifted him up through the doorway and then walked him a couple of steps and laid him down. He never said a word. He just seemed to be having trouble breathing, and I was trying to loosen his tie and I couldn't get it off. I guess I was getting nervous or something. I have a knife that I used for skinning wire and I took it and I cut [the tie] off. I unbuttoned his collar and happened to look up and there was somebody up there at the canopy holding a Thompson at me [this had to be Stout]. I just looked up at him and waited until everything was okay.

"There was somebody there in civilian clothes and I told him to give me his coat so he took his jacket off, and I rolled it up and made a pillow for [Les]. Then people started coming from all over. You could hear sirens and everything else. Then the basement door opened, and I hadn't even noticed it before, and [someone] said you'd better get inside there's another one in here, we need help. So I told him, you go and I'll look after [Les]. Like I say, he never closed his eyes but he never said a word. He was just moaning very quietly."

The memories collide, jangle together, meld, reemerge almost in stream of consciousness as Sites remembers this moment so long ago, images of Les and Griselio and Oscar and Floyd and Joe, all crushed into one stream of remembered imagery.

"Like I say, he never closed his eyes but he never said a word. He was just moaning very softly. At the time it was almost like you blink your eye and suddenly there was a lot of people there. . . . This guy came up and I told him to roll up his coat. I made a pillow, somebody came out the door, and I think it was a woman. I said we need help in there. . . . An ambulance came up, and they brought a stretcher back. I helped put him on the stretcher, and I gave the police captain his gun. They put him in the ambulance. Then I went around and worked on the sign."

That was it for Elroy Sites. Act of mercy accomplished, he did what men of his generation are known to do: he went back to work.

Meanwhile Vince turned from the melancholy task of getting Les onto the stretcher, and noticed what he had not seen before. There, lying on his side in the grass, was a little man. He was inside the hedge. His hands and legs were drawn up and he appeared to be tiny. His hat was askew on his head. An ugly smear of blood ran down his temple but otherwise he was unmarked in his gray suit. His pants legs were slightly hiked, revealing his well-shined shoes, his trim ankles. In his hand was a German Luger.

Vince was the first to reach him. He knew immediately that the man was dead but reached for a pulse anyway. There was none. He reached out and pried the blue-steel pistol from the tight grip. It was locked open, its toggle trapped back forming a triangle of pivoting steel, which breaks the sleekness of its lines. It looked broken, but Vince knew that was its standard unloaded condition. He knew too what to do next. The gun is evidence and evidence must be marked to establish a chain of custody so that no one may doubt its provenance. And thus he took out his car key and crudely inscribed his initials VPM on the left side of the firearm. It will be handed to a homicide cop and begin its long transit through the judicial system; and, many years later, it will end up in the Truman Library in Independence, Missouri, its beauty marred by his initials, on display next to Oscar's less elegant P.38.

Vince went through Griselio's pockets and found two magazines, loaded with the German surplus steel-cased 9mm ammunition. If he paused to think about it, he may have issued a shudder at the possibility of what might have ensued had the little man sleeping in the grass gotten his reload finished. But then he realized he didn't have to waste a thought, for such a possibility had vanished from the earth.

38. THE POLICEMEN'S WIVES

This is the policeman's wife's worst moment. This possibility is always there, always. It was not talked about, as if in not talking about it, it could be driven away. But they all know it couldn't. And they all know it can happen, has happened, will happen again. They've been to police funerals, they've been to wakes, they've made casseroles for the weeping widow and stood around in living rooms while family members agonized in grief just a few feet away. But preceding that horror was the waiting.

Ruth Boring sat in front of the blurry television set in her small apartment on a bright afternoon. The circular screen was her window on the world, and though the art of television news has not evolved into the sleek product it will ultimately become and still betrays its roots in radio, what she saw terrified her. The news was a jumble. No film, no graphics, no music, just broadcasters speaking urgently into a microphone, conveying messages of the shooting at Blair House, men killed, men wounded, the president is all right, with speculation on what is behind it, what happened, what is the news, what is the next thing, will there be an official statement?

Even as she endured this ordeal, so did the others. Shirley Mroz was at the grocery store with her baby daughter, Barbara, when "two city detectives came in and said President Truman had been shot. . . . I hurriedly tried to leave the market, pushing the stroller and carrying the groceries."

When she got home—the walk usually took fifteen minutes and she swears she made it in eight—she saw friends and neighbors sitting in the courtyard with their children. Nobody had any news. She left Barbara with one of them and hurried upstairs to use the phone, but it was ringing as she got in. It was a White House staffer who couldn't confirm whether Vince had been hit or not. Later, the news said that he had been shot in the hand—evidently, reporters had seen him pick up Griselio's Luger with a handkerchief and assumed he'd been wounded. "Five long hours passed before Vince came home and I could see he was safe." Janie Miller, Les's stepdaughter, was sitting two blocks away at the Veterans Administration at Vermont and K. In the same building was Helen Birdzell, older, tougher, more experienced. The two did not know each other and could not know that both are in the same dilemma and that in minutes news will arrive. For one it will be disturbing, for the other it will be devastating.

At Hecht's in downtown D.C. at 11th and F Streets, Cressie was standing on the floor in her department. She had no access to television or radio, but in Washington, irrespective of media, news travels fast. Somehow it reached her. She was shortly picked up by her friend Helen Gaines and driven to Emergency Hospital.

And possibly the worst of all was Barbara E. Allen, who was working at the Pentagon for the Joint Chiefs of Staff, when the word came that her husband, Bradley, the White House policeman, had been shot and killed. She was utterly distraught. She hadn't even realized by the time they called again to straighten it all out that Brad had taken the day off. Les Coffelt had taken his shift.

Meanwhile, in her apartment in Anacostia, far from the eyes of the public, in the privacy she demanded, Ruth Boring sat in silence, with one daughter next to her on the sofa, one daughter in her arms, watching, waiting for news, not knowing, haunted by her neighbor's news that Floyd was dead.

It comes. The phone. It can't have come soon enough even if the wait was only ten minutes. Decades later, Ruth Boring was reluctant to discuss this event. "It was such a sad day. I don't want to go back there."

She answered the phone.

It was U. E. Baughman's office. The chief of the Secret Service had news. Toad was all right.

She must have hugged the baby extra tight.

39. THE SCENE

T he young man didn't know why the trolley stopped.

He was just twenty-five, a Harvard graduate as yet truly untested in the world and unsure of himself. After service in the navy and a stab at journalism in upper New England, he'd come to a major city looking for work, some work, any kind of work, just to get in the business. One of the papers that seemed interested in him was the *Baltimore Sun*, stretching its mighty arms in the city on the bay. The *Sun* had a national reputation, what with the great H. L. Mencken still a beloved figure (though by 1948, he'd suffered his cruel stroke and no longer could read or write, while he remained ambulatory) and its network of foreign bureaus. If you were young and smart and believed there was a glamour to the Fourth Estate, you headed toward Baltimore. But it was raining when the train pulled into Penn Station in that city, and so he decided to stay aboard, and traveled forty more miles down the way to Washington.

He doubted that he had the skills, the talent, the ambition. He thought he'd try a newspaper called the *Washington Post*, sustained primarily by Shirley Povich's great sports column. It sadly trailed the *Daily News* and the *Star* in circulation. It was several notches down from the *Sun*, and a reject from the less than best wouldn't hurt as much as a rejection from the very best. So he walked in unannounced, and fate or luck or whatever smiled; it just so happened that someone had resigned, so there was an opening. In walked this handsome Ivy League kid with a Boston accent and a seeming ability to spell, write grammatically, and display occasional good sense. So he was hired on the "shit shift," as it was lovelessly called, starting work at three and going till eleven in metro. His job was basically rewriting handouts from civic groups.

A year or so later, he was riding to work on the trolley, 2:20 P.M. on an unseasonably hot fall day, down Pennsylvania Avenue, and suddenly the trolley stopped, middle of the street. Now what the hell?

Curiosity may have killed a thousand cats but it never harmed a reporter. So the young man got up and climbed down from the trolley and discovered himself standing on the street in front of Blair House. It was deadly quiet.

In front of him, a police officer lay in the street, blood pouring from both knees.

He looked to the left and he saw somebody lying just on the sidewalk in front of the Blair House steps, facedown in a suit.

Now wha—

Gunshot.

Even if you've never heard it, you know what it is. It can only be one thing and your reflexes are much faster than your conscious mind.

That was when the young man discovered himself lying on the ground. He doesn't remember much else, except that his nose was just above the trolley rail and the cobblestones were gritty.

He lay there for a bit.

There was no more shooting; he couldn't have known he had heard Les's shot into Griselio's head that ended the fight.

Finally he stood in that utter silence, as life began to return to the scene and people started to appear.

He realized that there had been an attempt on President Truman's life.

He got to work.

He was enterprising enough. Quickly he grabbed at another young man, this one in the blue tunic of the Washington Metropolitan Police. It was an on-the-fly interview at the dominant news event of the day.

The young officer's name was Private Marion R. Preston, twenty-four, a navy veteran who had been assigned to the White House precinct. He had been a policeman for less than thirteen months.

Breathlessly Preston recounted his story; breathlessly the young reporter wrote it down.

"I was at 17th and the avenue. That's when it started. First thing I heard was the shooting, maybe sixteen or twenty shots, like a machine gun, almost.

"I pulled out my gun and started running over. God knows what had happened, I thought to myself. On the way over, I knew I was getting shot at. I felt one bullet hit my tunic but I didn't know whether I had been hit. [Presumably this was one of Oscar's wild, unaimed shots.]

"There was much confusion in those few seconds, everybody shooting at everybody else. I decided I better stop and look the situation over. I couldn't see the president but the guns were still going.

"A policeman [Birdzell] was shooting from the middle of Pennsylvania Avenue. One of the civilians was shooting from behind the hedge, near the Lafayette Park side of Blair House [Oscar]. Another civilian was running into the Court of Claims building next door to Blair House. He looked kind of suspicious to me but I figured he might have been just an innocent bystander. [He was.]

"Anyway I didn't fire at him. I didn't fire a shot all day.

"The policeman that was firing from the middle of the avenue, I saw him go down, still firing.

"By the time I got in front of Blair House, the shooting was over. Everyone was lying there. I saw what had happened and turned in the [sentry] box and called the ambulance.

"I saw three people in civilian clothes that looked as if they were involved. They shot two of them and the third one was this guy that ran into the Court of Claims. I didn't shoot him because at that time, I didn't know who ought to be hit."

The young reporter got it all down; then he covered the event from the scene and called in information that would go in the main story, under the bylines of two distinguished *Post* reporters early in their careers, Chalmers M. Roberts, later a diplomatic correspondent and author, and police reporter Alfred E. Lewis, who broke the initial story about the Watergate break-in twenty-five years later.

For the young man, however, it was a swell day's work.

He still beams with pride when he tells the tale. Under the headline "Slug Creases Tunic of Police Pvt. in Gunplay," it ran, and, he recalled with pride, "It was my first goddamn front-page story."

The young reporter's name was Benjamin C. Bradlee, and he would make a name for himself as the *Washington Post*'s executive editor during both the scandals of the Pentagon Papers and Watergate.

Another young man who was early on the scene was the Secret Service agent Rex Scouten. He was in the agency office in the West Wing of the

White House and he'd heard his boss, Jim Rowley, cry, "Where's my tommy gun?" But Rex didn't wait for a tommy gun. He just got up and ran over there, joining a crowd of officers from the White House Police Force, led by Inspector Hobart Francis, a commanding figure with his hand on his gun on his hip.

Scouten got there and first of all he saw Floyd Boring standing next to Oscar Collazo, who lay flat on his belly on the sidewalk.

The smell of gun smoke still hung in the air, and all around there was that post-combat stillness as the world tries to reassemble itself from the mayhem that has been spilled into it. *Time* magazine even reported that "For a few seconds it was so quiet that the ding-ding of distant streetcars was clearly heard." The sun was bright, the buildings beautiful and stately, and nothing is as it should be because bodies lie everywhere, a crowd is beginning to arrive as people pick themselves up from the sidewalks all along Pennsylvania, and the sirens are rising in the distance.

At this moment, Floyd recognized Rex and said with a broad, hearty smile, "I think I plinked him right in the beanie."

Indeed, Oscar did appear to be plinked in the beanie, with blood running down his face; it would be a few seconds before they realized the little man was still alive.

"It wasn't too bad right then," Rex Scouten recalled many years later, "but then it turned into a hell of a lot of confusion after that. Floyd and the officers with him were still there where they should be on the east entrance to Blair House. Collazo was on the steps lying back on the steps. Birdzell was out in the street, still conscious."

But in just a few seconds, it all changed.

"The firemen, police, and ambulances came and people came. People on the street. There was a lot of confusion, milling around, and police trying to get the people back and getting Birdzell and Downs and Torresola and Collazo to the hospital."

Exhaustive photos were taken at the scene. The idea of "crime scene" had evidently not entered into police science as yet; no tape sealed the locality off, no barricades were erected, no sentries posted. The officers were so intent on getting the fallen to the hospital that, in the first few minutes at least, they never established elementary crowd control.

Almost immediately photographers appeared. This was the era of the Speed Graphic, the huge box camera that needed a flash to record images, and so one can imagine the Fellini-like atmosphere they provided to every great public event. In fact, many of the pictures that survive from those minutes—2:25 P.M. to 2:45 P.M., November 1, 1950—show photographers snapping pix of crowds of other photographers.

The pictures suggest pure surrealism: the popping of bulbs—that flash of unnatural, incandescent white light, dozens per second as more and more photogs arrive, the arrival of more and more cars, fire engines, motorcycles, and ambulances, and the tidal arrival of civilians from the street, drawn by hubbub and curiosity and the eerie glamour of violent death. It is not like the seedy alley where the FBI gunned down John Dillinger, and there are no film-noir stylizations, like brick alleyways, gutters, puddles of water or blood, garbage pails. Instead this strange public drama took place amid stately Georgian buildings well landscaped for the theater of government. Someone snaps a shot of Floyd and Oscar and it almost looks like a deer hunting picture, with Floyd standing proudly by his fallen prey, in his sunglasses and bow tie.

It was reported in *Time* magazine that at that second Harry Truman came to the window.

As *Time* dramatically puts it, "A hefty Secret Service man named Floyd Boring looked up, saw the President who had been aroused from a nap, peering out an upstairs window in his underwear. Boring bawled, 'Get back! Get back!' until the President stepped out of sight."

It didn't happen. Or at least it didn't happen to Floyd, who has no recollection of it.

Indeed, the account of a Secret Service man screaming "Get back" is something of an urban legend affiliated with the event. Neither of the living survivors of the fight, Floyd or Vince Mroz, can recall it happening. Neither Elroy Sites, the electrician who arrived to help Les Coffelt, nor reporter Bradlee recalled it either. And no surviving family members of Secret Service agents or White House police recall their illustrious relatives recounting such an event in private moments.

Then there's the reality of emotional drainage. At that point, as all combat narratives agree, survivors are in a kind of fog. Everything is moving slowly, their ears are ringing from the loud reports of the gunshots, they're sucking in oxygen, their brains are slowly withdrawing from animal unconsciousness of action. Why would anyone look up, why would anyone see the president, why would anyone say anything? All the reports of Truman at the window come from within Blair House, from Truman himself, from his wife, Bess, from stories told to Margaret by her parents, and so forth.

Clearly Truman came to the window much earlier, toward the end of the gunfight. He was but eight feet to the window from his bed on the second floor of Blair and the fight lasted 38.5 seconds. He could have covered the distance in five seconds; but assuming it took him some time to react, he probably didn't get there until the last five or six seconds. And that is why he was so shaken, more profoundly shaken than anyone ever knew. He saw dead and dying men. He was almost one himself.

"What happened, Floyd?" he asked a few minutes later.

"Well, Mr. President, it appears that some people aren't too friendly to you," is the official response, the one that made it into the history books. That's certainly not the brusque, truth-speaking Toad Boring of this account. More likely, Toad said something like, "Some sons of bitches tried to kill you, sir. But we took care of the bastards." He was never one for pulling punches.

In any event, the obligations of duty soon imposed themselves upon the chaos. Truman's press secretary, Charles Ross, arrived from the White House, and he had to know if the president still intended to go to Arlington National Cemetery for the dedication of the statue to Sir John Dill.

Harry Truman was not a man for shirking duty. And so, shaken or not, he agreed, overruling the Secret Service chief, U. E. Baughman, who'd arrived on the scene from the barber's chair a few blocks away. Baughman, fearing that the attempt was part of a larger, more coordinated attack, therefore ordered that the guard be quadrupled. And in a few minutes the cemetery team left for the site. It wasn't the usual two-car caravan but a whole retinue of vehicles, with armed Secret Service men standing up in the back seats of the convertible that followed the president's limousine to the cemetery, and a full complement of motorcycle policemen as well. Sirens blaring, squad cars in line, the whole convoy took off. It looked more like a trip by Joe Stalin than Harry Truman with his down-home style, at least for this one day.

The president gave his speech as planned, and it's fair to say he did what he had to do, did it well, got through the day. And in the days that followed, a number of gruff statements were issued by his press office on the subject of the shooting.

"Hell," he's reputed to have said, "if they'd made it up the steps, I'd have made them eat those guns," and much of America cheered at the toughness of the little guy.

Time magazine quoted him saying stoically, "A president has to expect those things." And it also quoted him as bragging to his chief-of-staff, Admiral William Leahy, "The only thing you have to worry about is bad luck. I never have bad luck."

But a picture taken just after Truman's speech at Arlington belies that official bravado. What we see is a man profoundly shaken: his eyes have that haunted, thousand-yard stare of the Iwo Jima survivor, his body is tense, there's not a relaxed line in his face, or a happy one.

He was deeply upset by the death of Leslie Coffelt. Some even believe that he chose not to run in 1952 because of his pain over the incident. Some say he was never the same again. Drew Pearson reported in his April 13, 1952, column in the *Post* that "An unreported factor behind President Truman's decision to retire was the anguish and strain that the Truman family still feels over the attempted assassination of the President on November 1, 1950, when Secret Service Agent [sic] Leslie Coffelt was killed."

Pearson reported that the president told Democratic congressman Morgan Moulder of Missouri, "Did you ever stop to think how you would feel if another man laid down his life for you? Well, that's the way I feel about Leslie Coffelt. It's men like him or some other good man who are really in danger in situations like that—not the President, but the men entrusted with his protection."

40. INSIDE THE SOCCER SHOE

During the events at Blair House, the man who could be said to be their author was under siege. Don Pedro Albizu Campos was trapped in his apartment, which doubled as Nationalist Party headquarters, at the corner of Calles Sol and Cruz, not more than six blocks from that other site of carnage, La Fortaleza, in Old San Juan.

The picturesque little intersection, so charmingly old-colonial, now looked like a scene out of the Second World War. Military and police vehicles were everywhere, as were barricades; soldiers, policemen, detectives crouched behind them, guns drawn. Searchlights had been brought in, and so had heavy weaponry. The building these forces surrounded had been shattered by machine gun fire, the louvers blown off the hinges, the stucco facade pockmarked by bullet impacts, the wooden balcony pierced and splintered in a hundred places.

The siege had lasted over three days. Immediately after the assault of La Fortaleza, agents of the Internal Security squad of the Insular Police were dispatched to the Club Nacionalista. When their car, Insular Police Car No. 1G-707, arrived at the intersection of Sol and Cruz (the time was about 12:15 P.M.), Albizu threw three homemade incendiary bombs at it. None of them exploded; but one broke the windshield of the police car. Doris Torresola, Albizu's secretary and the sister of both Elio and Griselio, also threw bombs from the balcony and fired shots at the policemen; additionally, Juan José Muñoz Matos, another young Nationalist, shot at the police. But in the ensuing exchange, Doris was wounded in the throat; eventually Doris and Muñoz Matos and another woman, Carmen María Pérez, surrendered and were led off to interrogation at police headquarters. But upstairs, there was no surrender.

Upstairs, the shots rang out in revolutionary defiance and it seemed that the old man was putting up a valiant struggle. He would not relent;

his mighty will would not buckle; no matter the odds, and with but a few firearms, he fought onward.

But like so many of the curiosities surrounding Don Pedro Albizu Campos, Harvard graduate, lawyer, politician, guru, father, and maximum revolutionary leader, this one is more complex than it seemed.

Don Pedro was indisputably there, in his apartment and party headquarters.

Shots indisputably came from that apartment, holding the police and National Guard soldiers at bay.

But Don Pedro didn't fire any of them.

"I do not know the reason," said the man who did the shooting, "but the truth is that he did not use the revolver. He did not use this revolver while I was there. Yes, I shot with the pistol, because I used all the bullets that I had. All the bullets I used and only two or three were left in the revolver."

And why didn't the Maximum Leader shoot?

It was a question people would ask for days.

"Albizu sends these boys to fight while he stays hidden in his house!" seems to be the gist of the complaint, something the press picked up in subsequent days.

And the answer was: "Well . . . because . . ." said Álvaro Rivera Walker to his interlocutor, the historian Miñi Seijo Bruno, and then lapsed into silence.

Rivera Walker, a Nationalist militant, had bravely crossed police lines sometime after 3:00 P.M. and joined Don Pedro in his apartment. It was no small thing; another sympathizer, Efraín López Corchado, a Nationalist from Mayagüez, tried the same trick at around 8:00 P.M.; in an exchange of fire, he was shot seven times by the police and died sometime later, without ever revealing what message he brought to Don Pedro from his city.

But somehow Rivera Walker made it into the apartment.

"I entered when the police had already been shooting inside the place and they responded to the fire. Two of the Nationalists that were there just took away the hurt Doris Torresola Roura. Then, it was I who entered."

He was unarmed. But he quickly found a revolver and joined the old man in the resistance. Or, more precisely, he became the resistance.

"He knew me. I visited him regularly. At times I slept at his house. My voice was known; because of this he welcomed me. I entered and there was a gun, another revolver, and another one. For the gun there were about seventy-five bullets and for the revolver there were about twenty-five or something."

He found himself in a blasted zone.

"Almost all the doors and windows had fallen from the bullets. This house was like a soccer shoe on the inside. You saw in all places as if there were little holes, and it was the bullets that did it.

"I remember that the police said to surrender ourselves and, when they placed themselves so that we could answer them, we answered their fire to keep them at a distance. It seems to me that after two days of this tension the police called us to talk. I don't remember if it was ten or fifteen minutes. Don Pedro went out on the balcony and I went out next to him. They asked us what we needed and we told them that we didn't need anything. We only wanted to know how the wounded Doris was. And that was it. It seems to me that we were there for three days and two nights."

He didn't know, but the plan to arrest Don Pedro had been worked out in some detail by the governor's office. It was a three-part orchestration of force, based on the idea that a dead Don Pedro would be more troublesome as a martyr than a live Don Pedro as a prisoner.

The plan is so detailed it provides a script for police officers to read from:

"Seeing that you have not complied with what by law we are asking of you," one such advisement states, "we shall proceed to carry out your arrest and in doing so we will utilize the means afforded to us by law."

As an overall operational guide, it states: "All men shall be instructed not to use any other level of violence beyond that which is necessary to carry out the arrest."

During the siege, Don Pedro and Rivera Walker talked about very little except their immediate survival.

"He told me that if we could find someone who made negotiations, perhaps in conversations we could find something in the future, but I told him that we didn't have to think about this, that we were sentenced to death or to jail, that there was no way to talk with anybody. . . . We no longer had any hope in winning revolutions, because we had heard on the radio the happenings on the island, but Don Pedro wanted foreigners to find out about what was going on in Puerto Rico."

Finally, by the third day, the police lost patience. So they resorted to phase 3 in the plan: "The gases shall be first thrust through the windows (then another discharge of gases)."

Again, Rivera Walker, the only man in the apartment with Don Pedro, narrated events to Miñi Seijo Bruno:

"The last night they attacked with gases. That night Don Pedro told me to lie down while he guarded and late in the night the attack came with tear gas. I do not know at what time this happened but it must have been 12 A.M. or 1 A.M., or around then."

The tear gas was delivered in heavy 40mm shells fired by large guns based on single-barrel shotgun action. They arrive with a howl and a thud, at considerable velocity, and that which they strike they destroy, being heavy and traveling at speed. They're also very hot to the touch and will start fires if they strike something volatile. They smash, they rip, they tear, they roll across the floor, and as they bounce and twist this way and that, they spew noxious gas, which assaults nose, eyes, ears, and throat. If you've ever been gassed or been through army basic training where one day part of the drill is exposure to intense tear gas, you know: nobody stands against tear gas.

"Gas is a thing that makes you lose your vision and breath," recalled Rivera Walker. "A person who receives gas cannot defend himself and I couldn't fight. So Don Pedro said to me, 'We have to get out of here.' And I said to him, 'Guard me while I put on my shirt and shoes,' but I didn't find my shoes. When I left the room, Don Pedro was at the start of the stairs waiting for me. . . .

"Then it occurred to me that because it was late at night, the town isn't observing, isn't watching, so it was an appropriate moment to assassinate Don Pedro without the town noticing, and then to say that [he] came down from there shooting with the intention of killing."

Rivera Walker was thinking clearly despite the tear gas. The fear of an assassination of Don Pedro was very real to the Nationalists, who understood the charisma of their leader and the fear and rage he inspired in the political structure. It may well be that the revolution of 1950 occurred when it did because the men around Don Pedro feared for his life and when he was put under siege decided to strike first. That's clearly what motivated Rivera Walker, gassed and exhausted though he might have been.

"It occurred to me," he said, "that he could avoid this by surrendering." What he meant is that by surrendering publicly, that is announcing to all observers on the street, presumably many among them reporters, that he and Don Pedro were giving up, he would be vouchsafing Don Pedro's life.

"I took a napkin that was on a table and I put it out on the balcony, indicating to them that we were surrendering, and they answered, 'Yes, come down, we know that you surrender.'

"But Don Pedro knew nothing about this. It was only my decision. Don Pedro was on the stairs trying to recover and waiting for me to come down. Then I dropped the napkin or tablecloth that we had, I left it on a broom that was there and we went down."

This is the source of a characterization from non-Nationalist Puerto Ricans that would haunt the old man for the rest of his life. It was that he was a tremendous coward who sent out the others to get arrested or killed, and then meekly waved a white handkerchief and surrendered.

Later, Governor Luis Muñoz Marín would make sport of the surrender flag by comparing it with the fighting spirit of other revolutionaries.

"For the humble barber of Santurce all that shrapnel [this is a reference to Vidal Santiago Díaz, Albizu's barber, who resisted arrest for several hours in a gun battle]; for he who put this into the barber's heart, for he who pushed him to that sacrifice, the towel at the end of the broom. . . ."

Rivera Walker finishes his tale in a tone of melancholy:

"Then we went down and came out of the house and they took us walking from the east like a square and they searched us."

A photographer snapped the moment of surrender and three days later that shot appeared in page size in *Life* magazine. It was offered in a kind of spirit of melodrama, at the conclusion to the spread on the assault on Blair House, a sort of denouement, saying to its millions of readers that he who put his heart into this, he who pushed them to their sacrifice, this was his squalid fate.

The man was old and in bedroom slippers, balloonish black slacks, striped pajama top. But it's not the seedy aspect of the clothes that so impressed; it was the look of hurt and confusion on Albizu's face. No other photograph ever recorded such ruin. In all his others, his eyes burn with ferocity and intelligence, his body language is taut and coiled, he is every inch a modern maximum leader. Not so here. Clearly he was exhausted, confused, possibly even, for the moment, broken.

In the apartment, according to the FBI report based on the police report, authorities found "9 incendiary bombs, a nickel-plated .45 Colt registered to Pedro Ulises Pabón; 26 cartridges for a .32 caliber revolver; one Czechoslovakian made Colt .25 auto with loaded clip and cartridge in the chamber; one Smith & Wesson .32 caliber revolver, loaded; 1 P-38 Luger [sic] with loaded clip and a cartridge in the chamber; and 33 .45 caliber cartridges. Also found in the street in front of the club were 12 homemade bombs and the remains of two other bombs allegedly thrown by PAC."

Temporarily, at least, in Puerto Rico as well as Blair House, it was over.

41. WHO SHOT OSCAR?

T here was no doubt about who shot Birdzell.

The wounded White House police officer Donald Birdzell lay in the emergency room of Emergency Hospital a few blocks from Blair House, to which all the wounded and the dying had been brought. There, as elsewhere, chaos reigned as people rushed and checked and triaged and did this or that.

"Who shot you?" a nurse asked Pappy.

"That joker right there," he said, pointing to the man next to him.

Oscar Collazo lay on another gurney, handcuffed to the thing, less than five feet from the man he'd shot and who'd tried to shoot him.

Meanwhile, surgeons worked frantically on Leslie Coffelt in one theater, and another team attended to the less severely wounded Joe Downs in another. Griselio's body was there too, for a later coroner's examination.

Oscar had been given a rough going-over. He wasn't beaten, but when it became clear his wounds were not serious and that he was in no immediate jeopardy, the priorities changed and information became more valuable and he was questioned relentlessly, without much kindness. Even wounded, in the fog of post-combat stress, roughly addressed and roughly handled by his interrogators, he kept to his narrative. What he admitted was carefully calculated, and one must admire, at least a little, his soldier's adherence to the duty of sticking to name, rank, serial number, and lie. He kept then—as forever—to the idea that it was just a crazy thing hatched between him and Griselio two nights earlier on the Willis Avenue Bridge. He denied any connection to the larger Puerto Rican Nationalist Party unit in New York, any influence of Don Pedro Albizu Campos. And the gringos bought it. As *Time* put it, "the wounded Collazo willingly told the tale of his crazy pilgrimage. He and his fellow plotter had known each other only two weeks. But they had agreed that the President should die, and that it was their sacred duty to kill him. Why? With flowery Latin eloquence, Oscar Collazo cried that his countrymen had been 'enslaved' and that Puerto Rico's politicians were 'tools' of the United States."

Oscar understood exactly how to limit the damage his failure had created for Don Pedro and he also understood how eager the Americans would be to have their stereotypes of Latin revolutionaries validated. He never flinched, he never shirked, and even with a bullet in him and a bunch of supremely annoyed Secret Service agents badgering him, he stuck to the line.

But why was he even alive to mislead?

One answer is the vagaries of the gunfight. He was shot at from distances of no more than twenty-five feet by four superb marksmen, Joe Davidson, Floyd Boring, Vince Mroz, and Don Birdzell, the latter three Secret Service Distinguished Shooters and competition shooters as well. Three of the four had been in firearms engagements before, and the fourth, Davidson, was an experienced police officer with lots of street time behind him. They were not green rookies, given to panic, and all of them performed with steely professionalism. They fired a total of fourteen shots, two by Floyd, one by Vince, six by Joe Davidson, and five by Donald Birdzell. And in fact they brought Oscar down. They won the fight by any standard.

But who shot Oscar?

One response might be, does it matter? It happened, someone shot him, and the rest is history. But it matters, if only to the record.

Nobody shot Oscar.

In all the shooting at Oscar, everybody missed. Everybody.

Over time, as memory has eroded and sense of centrality to the event has increased, both Floyd and Vince have claimed to have made the chest shot that brought Oscar down. Vince's claim is probably the more convincing. His single shot was taken from the eastern edge of Blair House at Oscar, who was most likely facing Floyd and Joe near the Blair House stairway nearly twenty-seven feet away. That would explain the radical angle of the shot that took Oscar down. It hit Oscar in the chest, but at an extremely shallow angle. Despite the photograph of him lying on the ground on his back, his shirt a bloody mess, the loss of blood was not serious. The bullet itself did not penetrate to blood-bearing organs, it did not shatter bone or vein or artery, it did not immediately traumatize him.

It scooted under the skin, left to right, across his chest, emerging from his right breast and then striking and shallowly penetrating his arm.

Thus it seems to make sense that it was Vince's shot. The angle adds up, as he was by far the farthest to the right for a left-to-right glancing shot, presuming, of course, that Oscar was standing still and arranged more or less directly east, an assumption impossible to confirm in the bobbing-and-weaving, ducking-and-shucking dynamic of a gunfight.

The case for Floyd is somewhat weaker, again based on the angles, though it is by no means dismissible. That case turns on the possibility that in the second that Floyd fired his second shot (he'd already taken the head shot, drilled the hat), Oscar had pivoted radically to his right. Since he was moving erratically, it's entirely possible, but of a slightly lesser degree of probability than Vince's case. No one says he twisted like that, but no one says he didn't, either. It can't be discounted, it can't be proved. Most accounts credit the shot as being Floyd's, including McCullough's biography of Truman. But this also represents a case of command courtesy; as the truth was either unknown or unknowable, the shot is ascribed to the commanding officer on the scene, that is, Floyd. And over the years, so described in print so many times, it has become something like conventional wisdom.

But it appears that neither Floyd nor Vince was in court March 2, 1951, when an FBI forensics examiner testified. According to that testimony, the bullet that was recovered from Oscar's arm bore the ballistic imprint of the rifling of the barrel of White House police officer Joe Davidson's .38 Colt Official Police. For some reason, that fact never made it into the legend of the affair, which credited the shot to the more glorious and exalted of the two services engaged that day, the Secret Service rather than the humble White House Police.

Joe Davidson shot Oscar.

Yes, but also no.

Davidson fired immediately in the beginning of the fight. He drew, and unlike everyone else there, he fired double-action, as is clear from Floyd's memory of the speed of the shots in his ear. That is, he didn't bother to cock, as he had been trained to do, but instead simply pulled the trigger on his revolver as fast as he could while pointing it in the general direction of the man who'd just shot Donald Birdzell. Floyd's testimony of the speed of the shooting supports that contention.

Yet Davidson's orientation to Oscar, which was almost 0 degrees, would seem to preclude the angle the bullet took through Oscar. More-over, the initial lack of blood, the lack of penetration, the lack of observ-able impact upon Oscar, his continuation in the fight even to the point of reloading, and finally the fact that none of the shooters actually saw Oscar go down as the direct result of a hit suggest that it was not one of David-son's shots.

The only theory that reconciles these disparate factors and links them to Davidson's early, hasty shots is that one of the bullets struck the wrought iron fence (which prevented so many of the other shots from hit-ting Oscar), and ricocheted hard left, hitting Oscar at a raking angle.

That explains so much: the bullet, striking the wrought iron, veers radically to the left (that is, from Davidson's orientation; from Oscar's it veers right). Also, having expended its energy against the iron, it loses considerable velocity. Thus when it strikes Oscar it does not bring with it the impact of a straight-on shot, which for a 158-grain lead slug traveling at 800 feet per second from the muzzle is about 300 foot-pounds. It is probably down to 400 feet per second because of the impact against the fence, and its energy is down as well—and as it courses across Oscar's chest, Oscar doesn't even notice it. This may seem impossible to readers who've seen hundreds of movies where bullets explode in geysers of fake blood, but in the literature of war and gunfights, the unnoticed wound is quite common. The reason is physiological: at that moment of high stress, the nervous system has all but shut down, and isn't receiving mes-sages from outlying posts. Thus the information "I've just been shot" doesn't reach a brain that is obsessed with identifying and destroying other targets or maneuvering the body it administers to avoid incoming fire.

Oscar, his hit as yet unnoticed (and since the angle has been so shal-low, the wound isn't bleeding much), continues to shoot and to fight, bobbing, weaving, not aiming, firing madly, his bullets speeding down the street to punch a hole in a policeman's tunic across the street or to frac-ture a window some blocks away. He even gets through a fast combat reload. He doesn't notice or respond to smaller wounds: his nostril is ticked, his earlobe, then there's Floyd's shot through his hat that engraves the top of the skull.

He moves, they move, the whole thing is crazy, and there comes a moment when he has finished his reloading and, since his vision has been directed down, to the lowered pistol he's been fiddling with, he suddenly notices blood burbling from his chest. At that moment the blocked message is suddenly permitted to continue its journey: I have been shot in the chest!

Oscar faints.

He swoons. Not from blood loss, not from pain, not from cowardice or anything like that: instead, from shock. He hasn't been brought to earth by a bullet at all; he's fainted, like a groom at a wedding or a soldier in a parade or even a super-brilliant child in the finals of a National Spelling Bee.

Again, this illuminates much. In his memoirs, never published in English, he recounts that he was really only out a few seconds, another indicator of a psychosomatic faint as opposed to a traumatic faint. During most of the time he lay on the ground in front of Blair House, he was conscious. He heard the agents talking, he felt them roughly frisking him for documents. That famous shot of him supine in front of Blair, in which the world assumes he's dead or seriously wounded: he's fully conscious and secretly taking it all in. Maybe in that moment of privacy, he gathered his strength for the duplicity he knew lay ahead. Or maybe he had the analytical capacity to appreciate the fact that his loss of consciousness almost certainly saved his life and maybe he thanked God he was fighting Secret Service and White House police personnel who had the discipline to stop shooting when he went down (Davidson: "Don't shoot, Coffelt, he's down!").

Whatever, he lay there, waiting to be hauled away, listening to it all. He was playing possum.

42. THE ROUNDUP

A tough, gruff ex–state policeman, like so many other Secret Service agents of the 1930s and 1940s, Carmine J. Motto was the star of the New York office, where his specialty was busting counterfeiters. But on the afternoon of November 1, 1950, he was called to headquarters on White Street and told to take as many agents as needed and make an investigation of Oscar Collazo's residence.

At that time, just a few hours after the shooting, the situation might charitably be described as pandemonium infected with panic. Nobody knew anything. Few if any Americans had even heard of the Nationalist Party of Puerto Rico or Don Pedro Albizu Campos. In Washington, the investigations were beginning with sudden urgency. Over at the FBI, J. Edgar Hoover ordered the preparation and release of several reports— printed on blue paper—on the history of Puerto Rican nationalism and his bureau's long history of shadowing the organization. With his characteristic brilliance at bureaucratic maneuver, he tried to establish instantly that no blame should be attached to himself or to his agency. Meanwhile, at the practical end of the operation, the grunts of law enforcement were called out to investigate and arrest fast.

The first part of this rough process was represented by Motto and his squad. When Motto arrived at Oscar's tenement on Brook Avenue in the Bronx, he found a circus. Chaos reigned in the streets outside. El Tango Restaurant and E. Salas Food Market formed a background to what looked like onlookers assembled for a parade.

"There were people thick as flies on the fire-escapes," noted the *New York Times* the next day. "Every window was crowded with men, women and children and the sidewalks were thronged. The air filled with excited chatter in liquid Spanish, and with soft murmuring." Meanwhile, press cameramen snapped off their Speed Graphics bulbs with that crisp pop, that odor, that brief, artificial crest of illumination. Cops everywhere were interviewing neighbors or trying to hold the crowd back.

So Motto's first issue was simple: he had to get through the door. This was not easy, as between his men and the apartment on the third floor stood half, or at least a third, of what seemed to be all humanity. As he retold the story in his book, *In Crime's Way: A Generation of U.S. Secret Service Adventures*, the solution was an outlawed football ploy called the flying wedge. The Secret Service team locked elbows, formed an arrowhead formation, and galloped forward. What worked at Harvard Yard during Teddy Roosevelt's day worked on Brook Avenue in the Bronx; the formation of Secret Service agents battered their way into the building and into the apartment.

There, they discovered even more chaos. As in Washington, the New York police had not cordoned the area off from the press, so much of the preliminary "investigating" was done by reporters, who were wildly tearing through everything. They had cornered Oscar's wife and his daughter; his two stepdaughters were at work and would arrive shortly. A hapless New York police inspector was in charge.

The inspector noted Motto's arrival, and came over. "For Christ's sake, Motto, where in hell have you guys been? We came over to give you some assistance. Let's go!"

"We were delayed," said Motto, in what may have been the understatement of the day. But in other respects, Motto was ready. This was his first big field command and he wasn't about to let it pass.

"Okay, here's what I want," Motto said. "Clear the apartment of everyone who isn't family. Post a guard at the door to interview anyone who wants to enter. I'll team an agent with one of your men and they'll make a detailed search of the apartment. Send for the emergency squad to search the basement, yard, air shafts, any place where weapons could be hidden. You and I will question Mrs. Collazo and the children."

The inspector bellowed the orders, and in two minutes all the ornery reporters and photographers were rounded up and shooed out of the apartment. The grunts of the police force took up their tasks, while Motto and the inspector interrogated Mrs. Collazo.

"Mrs. Collazo was as militant as her husband. She professed to know nothing about his trip to Washington, but supported whatever he did," Motto recalled.

She was, in short, as would be all the other Nationalists rounded up in the next several days, tight-mouthed. Indeed, she proved intractable. She never budged from her initial story. Eventually, Mrs. Collazo and her two daughters and stepdaughter were taken to headquarters. In his book Motto publishes a press photo of himself leaving the apartment with Rosa Collazo. Though the focus is tight on the front stoop as the lawman leads the suspect's wife down the steps with a certain delicacy, one can see from the crowds—people peer from the windows or from the doorway, a reporter stands at the stoop in horn-rimmed glasses, looking very Clark Kent—that it was still a mob scene. The stalwart Secret Service fellow is dapper in his double-breasted suit and fedora—he looks every inch a movie cop—and Rosa is meanwhile a study in composure and dignity. This is not to romanticize her but a simple truth; she is well dressed, entirely in control of her faculties, and her face betrays no agitation. She clutches her handbag; nothing in her body posture suggests fear, doubt, panic, terror. Only the presence (implied by the relationship of the two bodies) of Motto's guiding hand on her arm suggests an apprehension or the application of some kind of guiding force.

Meanwhile, the first search turned up nothing. "That was too incredible to believe! We conducted another search," wrote Motto.

"What the hell are you guys looking for—machine guns?" shouted the voluble Motto. "Cannons? Dynamite? I could care less about that stuff! I want to find out everything you can about this party and its members."

He ordered them to take everything that wasn't nailed down: "letters, pictures, notebooks, old Christmas cards, anything that can give us a lead on why this attempt took place and who else is involved. Tomorrow might be too late. There'll be all kinds of legal sanctions but right now, search."

Thus admonished, the searchers had much better luck. They found "hundreds of leads" that aided the investigation. An agent found a mimeograph machine under a bed as well as papers containing names and addresses of party members.

Surely, had Oscar thought it out, he would have realized that one necessary consequence of their actions would be a raid on their domiciles. But it appears never to have crossed his mind. He just took off, perhaps so intent on the nature and urgency of his mission that he left around piles of incriminating evidence that led federal authorities to his colleagues.

On the other hand, it can be seen as awareness that on some level the organization had been penetrated. FBI documents have revealed at least five confidential informants within party ranks. Presumably these men could have supplied the same information—possibly they already had— in short order. So securing already compromised information was of very little value, other than confirming what the informants had said. At the same time, the documents' presence simply gave law enforcement personnel something to crow about, and Motto did.

"The fruits of the search were also taken for further scrutiny. The night was long and arduous. Teams were sent out to locate and interview party members. By ten o'clock the next morning, we had located, interviewed, photographed, and fingerprinted every Puerto Rican Nationalist Party member in the New York area."

If Motto represents his actions at the Collazo apartment as a triumph of professional law enforcement, one less convinced is Carmen Zoraida Collazo, Oscar's daughter, who was fifteen at the time.

She had learned from her stepmother the night before that her father "had gone to Puerto Rico."

She returned from school at three o'clock and her stepmother sent her to the store to buy some steaks. When she got back from the store she saw a lot of people talking to her stepmother.

"Most of them were people from the press and from the TV programs, news programs. When I entered the building, the man downstairs said, 'Is your name Zoraida Collazo?' " She said yes.

"He said, you have a phone call. I go in the house and answer the phone and they ask me my name and I tell them my name and it was from a Spanish [-language] newspaper, *El Diario* [*de Nueva York*]. He said, What's your father's name? I gave him my father's name, and when they started asking me questions, I said, Why are you asking me these questions? He said, Because some people tried to kill President Truman. And I said, What does this have to do with me? So he said, One of them is your father, and he's either dead or wounded."

Police agents weren't far behind. Zoraida recalls that the officers were from the FBI, not the Secret Service. Possibly FBI agents were first on the scene, then later yielded to Motto's Secret Service team, though Motto does not acknowledge this. Or, possibly, Zoraida simply saw some flashed IDs and assumed the men were from the FBI, when they were really Secret Service.

Whoever they were, the agents told her her father was dead.

"I ran to one of the rooms in the back. I remember it so vividly. My God, every time I think about it it's like reliving it again. I ran to the back. I had some very tiny pictures of my father and I figured that they were going to take them, so I put them—you remember the bobby socks? I put them inside my bobby socks to keep them there, and I sat on the bed, closed my eyes, and I said, No, my father has to be alive, because if he were dead I'm sure I would have felt something. Because when you love a person so much you can even tell when something is going wrong. And so he has to be alive."

The officers kept them sitting on the sofa while they searched. At around six, when the last stepsister arrived, they were bundled up and removed to the White Street offices.

"When I got there, I felt like I was going to be arrested or put in prison, I don't know. They separated us. Two agents took one of my stepsisters. Two agents took my other stepsister. My stepmother was handcuffed and taken away. . . . I saw Griselio's wife. I saw her pass right by where I was sitting. She was also handcuffed and taken away. What was I thinking? I was thinking, I must make my father proud of me.

"Two agents were asking me questions. Who goes to your house? Do you know this man? I don't know anybody. But they had my school record already. They said, you're an outstanding student. How can you not know who goes to your house?"

Her answer—that her father made her go to bed at eight every night— did not please them.

What follows is melancholy. The details are unpleasant. It's not a scandal, not even close; but it does seem a lot for the full adult power of the state to be marshaled against a scared fifteen-year-old girl, who, after all, simply came home from school one day and found herself in a new world her father had just invented.

"This is what really hit me very hard. Because I didn't know that in a country where someone spoke about democracy they can take a fifteen-year-old girl, give her a record, take mug shots, keep her all night, no food. I had come home from school at three o'clock, they didn't let us cook. We had to sit there while they were asking all sorts of questions, and I tried to go and get a drink of water from the refrigerator and they stopped me. No, you cannot go in there. I said I must have something. Nothing like that. They shoved us in the car, took us downtown."

Were you allowed a lawyer?

"No, nothing like that. They didn't even say that. They separated us immediately. They took me someplace because I was the youngest and I was my father's only daughter. The others were his stepdaughters. They kept me longer. They told [my stepsisters] about one in the morning that they could leave. And Iris, the older, said we will not leave without my little sister. I will always remember that, because that was such a nice thing of her to do. So they told her she'd have to sit in the hallway. They had some benches, some long wooden benches. That's where my stepsisters sat to wait for me.

"I said to them [the agents] that I have to go to the bathroom, and they sent me with a male agent to the bathroom so I couldn't go. I didn't go. I didn't go in.

"They would eat in front of me, sandwiches and chocolate bars and stuff like that. They kept showing me thousands of pictures, and I kept saying, I don't know them, I don't know them. Even the ones that I knew I'd say, I don't know them, because I was so angry at this time. I was beginning to get angry. They showed me a picture of my father. The picture of where he is on the ground. But they covered where it said that he was wounded. And they said, Did you see your father's dead? You couldn't talk [if he were alive]. Why don't you talk [now] if you know something. I said, I don't know what you're talking about, I don't know anything. My father is dead, still I don't know anything. They said, Did the Nationalists tell you not to speak? Did they say they were going to harm you? I answered them, You don't know the Nationalists if you think that. I hadn't seen anybody from the party that day. Or any other day.

"Did the Russians pay your father? They wanted to link one thing [to another]. And I said no. I started laughing, actually, because it was so funny. We never had anything to do—as a matter of fact, there were some people from the party [NPPR] that were ousted from the party because they would speak about socialism or communism.

"After having me all night under questioning, they let me go early in the morning. I know we got home about seven o'clock."

Did they drive you home?

"No, we took the train. We had to take the train. We got there, we went to bed because we were exhausted, and about an hour later they were banging on the door again. They had it like that for three days. After three days we collapsed. Emotionally we collapsed. All three of us [the three daughters] had to be taken to the hospital. . . . They wouldn't let us sleep, and at all hours of the night, at three in the morning, they would bang on the door, and we had to open it for them. It was systematic harassment. Like to break us. But from us in the first place my father was very secretive about everything. He never would have gotten us involved. He never would have told us anything that could harm us in any way, so we didn't know anything. They were hammering us for what? They wanted to destroy us or something?"

In all, federal agents arrested eight people in New York on that and subsequent days. The two spouses were first on the list, Carmen Dolores Otero, the common-law wife of Griselio, and Rosa Collazo, the wife of Oscar. Both of these women were jailed on November 2, 1950, in lieu of $50,000 bail. After the women were held for twenty-seven days in jail without a hearing, the bail was reduced to $2,000. Judge John W. Clancy ruled that "the government had no right to hold the two women without giving them a hearing." He later told the *New York Times*, "There is no evidence against these women."

After spending fifty-one days in jail, Carmen Dolores Otero—who was pregnant with Griselio's son—was freed on her own recognizance. During her time in jail, she was not given a hearing, and was held although federal authorities admitted they had no evidence against her.

Two high-ranking Nationalists from the New York junta were arrested. They were Julio Pinto Gandía and Juan Bernardo Lebrón. Both were eventually charged as co-conspirators in the attempted assassination of President Truman. Both were jailed November 22, in lieu of $50,000 bail. They remained in prison until December 29, when, after the bail was reduced to $1,000, they were released. They were never tried or convicted of any crimes concerning the Blair House event.

Juan Cortés Cordero, who was Mrs. Collazo's uncle, was also picked up and held a few days. Also arrested, never tried, and eventually released, was Nationalist Party member Juan Correa. Meanwhile, in Puerto Rico, a similar but more extensive crackdown was ensuing. Immediate steps ordered by Governor Muñoz Marín included the suspension of vehicular traffic out of San Juan and the closing of public offices. Only police cars, army, the National Guard, firemen, doctors, and ambulances were allowed on the street after 3:00 A.M., Thursday, November 2 (that is, immediately after the arrest of Don Pedro). Residents of San Juan were advised to remain in their homes until further notice.

Government authorities, having dealt with insurrection in four different cities besides San Juan, clamped down hard. Including the three hundred armed Nationalists who surrendered November 2, about a thousand persons were rounded up. Many of them were communists, under the belief, widely stated by Muñoz Marín and others, that the communists had to be behind the uprising. However, no proof could be found of a widespread communist conspiracy, and within days, most were released.

Eight years later, the Governor's Committee on Civil Liberties disclosed that at the time of the insurrection, the division of Internal Security of the Puerto Rican police had a list of more than four thousand alleged Nationalist Party supporters but that fewer than one hundred were directly related to the insurrection.

Quickly enough, life returned to normal. By Friday, November 3, San Juan had reopened to business; the restrictions enacted on the second curtailing freedom of movement within certain areas of the island were lifted. Later that day, Muñoz Marín declared the uprising over.

Among those in prison: Elio Torresola, Doris Torresola, Blanca Canales, Pedro Albizu Campos, and Oscar Collazo.

Among the dead: Raimundo Díaz Pacheco and Griselio Torresola.

And, of course, Les Coffelt.

43. TAPS

The weather hadn't broken but clouds, low and dark, had moved in. It wasn't another bright scorcher but the temperature remained unseasonably warm, topping out at 76 at 2:30 P.M. on November 4, 1950, the day they buried Les Coffelt in Arlington National Cemetery.

The cemetery is one of the hallowed spots of American service culture. It spills across a series of low hills across the Potomac from Washington, united architecturally to the city by the thrust of Arlington Memorial Bridge, a causeway that's not merely a conduit of traffic, but also of the idea that duty to country sometimes involves dying violently. And from the cemetery itself, or from one of its many hills rolling with the grave markers of the dead, the city presents itself as an ideal, as if to argue that the sacrifice is worth it. It looms like a movie Rome across the river, white and beautiful and ceremonial. It's a view that never fails to stir, and on certain occasions, with the addition of muffled drums, solemn processions, stern men in their spotless dark uniforms, military or police, their well-dressed wives in black, grief well managed and well hidden behind the rigors of ceremony, the sense of tragedy amid beauty and splendor is crushing. So it was with Les.

The service was conducted at the Fort Myer Memorial Chapel, a small, red-brick building immediately adjacent to the cemetery, by Dean John W. Suter of the Washington Cathedral, and Lieutenant Colonel Robert M. Homiston, Fort Myer chaplain, from the Episcopal Book of Common Prayer.

Les's coffin had been carried to its place in the chapel by six of his fellow White House policemen in full regalia while "Private Coffelt's widow . . . walked slowly and heavily up the aisle before the service on the arms of her brother, an Army sergeant, and a close friend, a White House secretary."

The president was there—"calm but solemn," said the *New York*

286

Times—as were key members of his staff. U. E. Baughman and Jim Rowley represented Secret Service brass. The chief of the White House Police and dozens of agents and officers and their wives were also there. They had all come to mourn Les but also to celebrate him.

But unaccounted for in all this was Leslie's stepdaughter, Janie. She was just ignored. No provisions were made for her; Cressie never embraced her, never soothed her, never performed the obligations a mourning widow had for her freshly wounded daughter. In fact, Cressie had immediately packed up and moved in with her friend Helen Gaines and Helen's husband, and from that headquarters coordinated the funeral. Janie was left on her own. But that was Cressie.

So on this day, Janie arrived, with her fiancé and her fiancé's mother. The chapel was full; no space or seat had been saved for her. She saw her mother down front on the left hand of the tiny, packed house of worship, sitting next to her friend Helen and somehow the center of attention already, courted and honored by the many important officials of the occasion and seeming, somehow, to love it a little too much. An uncharitable person might say that Cressie had highjacked Les's death already, had made it a drama starring Cressie, had made it about Cressie. A kinder person might say that's how a woman with a powerful personality like Cressie's would express her grief.

Whichever theory, the immediate problem for Janie was simpler and less ambiguous: where to sit. There was no place to sit. Her mother wouldn't acknowledge her or wasn't looking for her and had saved no space. She was alone in her grief and there was no room. But then she saw a pew down close to the altar on the right, and she headed down there to squeeze in.

What followed is a moment so Washington, so of the system, so full of the cultural realities of an imperial city in full tribute's glow, that it should be studied. She slid into the pew and someone leaned over and said—there isn't a term for this tone in Washington, but everyone recognizes it, a kind of highly charged, high-theater lilt in which the courtier takes on the appurtenances of his liege lord, and seems to enjoy the pleasure a little too deeply—"I'm sorry, you have to leave, you can't sit here. This is for the president."

So Janie got up to walk out, disconsolately. The rank-pulling provided more pain. The hideous, humiliating reality of it was that she's just been kicked out of her stepfather's funeral.

But the little drama has not gone unnoticed. An officer from the Secret Service came over, bent, dark, and furious, and he leaned into the interlocutor's face and said fiercely, "This is Officer Coffelt's daughter and she can sit anyplace she wants!"

Janie sat down and got to hear as Dr. Suter read the fifteenth chapter, thirteenth verse, of the Gospel according to St. John, "Greater love hath no man than this, that a man lay down his life for his friends," and the service, with its encomiums and regrets, its sadness, its dignity, and its sense, finally, of closure, ensued.

Then the casket, draped in the flag, was moved to the caisson by the six White House policemen, and the procession left for the grave site a quarter mile away. "The President and Mrs. Truman left the chapel service with sorrow on their faces and moisture in their eyes," noted the *Times* reporter, Walter H. Waggoner.

Photographs taken that day show that the leaves had not yet fallen; at least Les, who loved the countryside so, had a mantling of greenery as he was taken to his final resting place. Six white horses pulled his caisson, accompanied, according to the ritual of full military honors that would become painfully famous thirteen years later, by a seventh, riderless. Muffled drums beat a steady tattoo for the solemn procession. A troop of ceremonial soldiers accompanied the horse-drawn carriage, followed by limousines packed with the dignitaries—including the president and his wife—who attended the service.

The committal was swift and when it was over, the pallbearers folded the flag into a tricorn, stars out, and presented it to the widow, who clutched it, sobbing.

Three volleys of rifle shots rang out, echoing among the hills and the trees. Then at last on a hilltop an army bugler sounded "Taps," beautiful, elegiac, simple. Anyone who's ever heard those mournful notes coming amid the gun smoke from the volleys in a valley full of the too-young dead under their rows upon rows of white markers knows the full power and pain of the ceremony.

44. OSCAR ON TRIAL

The headline in the *Washington Post* three days after the shooting said it succinctly enough: "U.S. to Seek Quick Trial of Collazo for Murder." One wonders now at the haste: perhaps the point was to make the larger statement that no one could assault the president of the United States without facing immediate and total consequences. Or perhaps the strategy was to get the quick conviction and death sentence against Oscar, then leverage that against him in an attempt to turn him on the issue of a larger conspiracy. Nevertheless, the entire affair was so rushed that the investigation somehow never caught up with the prosecution, and the prosecution never seriously challenged Oscar on his story or cast a wider net. The trial was limited, calling mostly immediate personnel from the event itself, and no investigators whatsoever. Perhaps the temptation of an easy conviction was too powerful for prosecutors: after all, they had their man cold and the drama played out without much surprise.

But that was still in the future. By November 8, 1950, a twenty-two-citizen grand jury had been convened. On that day, the government produced twelve witnesses to give their versions of the shooting, including a "surprise witness," John Gavounas, fifty-three, who, in the newspaperese of the era, was the "Cabbie [Who] Says He Took Gunmen to Death Site." Ultimately, twenty-three witnesses testified in the three-day hearing.

Oscar was indicted November 10, on first-degree murder charges. "In a four-count indictment returned by a Federal grand jury before Judge Edward A. Tamm of District Court, Collazo was indicted on two death-penalty charges of murder and two of assault with intent to kill," the *Washington Post* reported.

The prosecutor, George M. Fay, United States attorney, said that the case could reach trial in thirty days, though in fact it did not begin until late February of the following year.

Oscar had known from the very beginning exactly what he would say. He had his story and he stuck to it. Six days after the shooting, FBI executive D. M. Ladd was reporting to J. Edgar Hoover results of an interview with Oscar November 2, that "Collazo claimed he [Collazo] suggested that they kill the President and Torresola willingly joined him and told him he had two guns they could use. Collazo denied he had received any instructions from the NPPR to carry out the assassination and insisted it was entirely his own idea." Almost by default, that has become the accepted version of the incident, though for years the government tried to prove it inaccurate. In fact, from the very beginning the government had believed in the possibility of the wider conspiracy—by early evening November 1, the attorney general had sent a memorandum to Hoover that read, "In connection with the attempted assassination of the President today by Collazo and his associates, it is requested that the Bureau conduct an investigation to ascertain whether this attempt on the President's life is an overt act of a conspiracy which has for its purpose acts of violence, the overthrow of the Government or the assassination of public officials." Underneath, in Hoover's own scrawl, is the order, "ADAC Fletcher advised and instructed to conduct investigation as requested, 7 p.m., 11-1-50."

FBI and Secret Service documents reveal a wide-ranging but ultimately frustrating investigation as suspect after suspect claims to have not known Oscar well enough, not known Griselio at all, and to have been utterly surprised by what the two men did, and themselves to no longer be interested in Nationalist politics. The investigation turned up no document to demonstrate a wider conspiracy, and one tantalizing nugget—a report in a November 8 Earl Wilson column in the *New York Post* that the party elders in New York had held a lottery to pick the shooters—appeared to be unfounded, at least undocumentable. (That rumor has persisted for years.)

Meanwhile, Oscar refined his story several times in early interrogations until he finally found the version he liked the best: he and Griselio, who barely knew each other, met on the night of October 30 at the Willis Avenue Bridge and went forward from there, with an idea of going to Washington to "create a demonstration," by which they meant to attract the world's attention to what was going on in Puerto Rico. He refused absolutely to acknowledge any deeper conspiracy. He refused to plead insanity. He did what he did because he believed in it and he would face the consequences.

The United States of America vs. Oscar Collazo began February 27, 1951, at the District Court House, in front of Judge T. Alan Goldsborough. Fay represented the government, along with John W. Fihelly and John D. Lane, both assistant United States attorneys. Oscar was represented by three court-appointed lawyers, Kenneth D. Wood, Sidney S. Sachs, and Leo A. Rover.

The government opened its case with a recitation of the evidence against Oscar. Fay stated, "The evidence will show that on the evening of October 30, 1950, Collazo met Torresola again on the street in the Bronx, and they decided and they planned and plotted that evening to secure guns and ammunition and come to Washington with the intent and murderous purpose to assassinate the President of the United States."

After summing up Oscar's and Griselio's plan for a simultaneous attack from different directions on Blair House, the government lawyers began to call witnesses to establish the circumstances of death for Leslie Coffelt. They called Edward J. Tehaan, another White House police officer, who had identified Les's body in the D.C. morgue, then Dr. Christopher J. Murphy, the D.C. deputy coroner, who had actually known Les in life; Dr. Murphy described his autopsy on Les, his finding of two bullets (the third had apparently vanished during an operation at Emergency Hospital and it would have been "highly possible and probable that in using sponges to mop out the abdominal cavity, that that bullet would have been removed and dropped into a receptacle without anyone knowing it").

The jury of ten women and two men were presented with Exhibits B and C, that is, the bullets recovered from Les. It must have been quite a moment for each of them to hold in their hands the little twisted kernels of steel-jacketed German lead that had pierced Les as he sat in his booth that day. And there, small and polite and completely in control of his faculties, in a nice neat suit, sat the man who had participated in the assault. If he hadn't pulled the trigger on Les, he was still legally liable because, under federal law, anyone who aids and abets in the commission of a crime is guilty as a principal in that crime.

As the citizens passed around the recovered bullets, Murphy stated that "the intestine and all the internal abdominal organs, particularly the intestine and the mesentery, were practically blown to pieces, like an explosive reaction within the abdominal cavity, and they were torn and ripped in many, many places." He called them a "blast injury."

The accumulation of detail continued throughout the early days of the trial. Dr. Jerome Blaine Harrell, a surgeon at Emergency Hospital, further described the wounds. Paul Lee Yost, the White House Police property clerk, testified about the guns and uniforms carried and worn that day.

Then the eyewitnesses began with their 38.5 seconds' worth of narrative. Donald Birdzell told his story, identifying Oscar, followed by James E. Wade, the doorman at Blair, who saw Oscar pull his pistol and begin shooting. Next up was Joe Davidson, who re-created his experiences. He described the shooting in some detail and at some length: "Then Boring, I think he made some remark like he hit him in the head and then this Collazo, he looked up, and Boring went for the door [of Blair House] and I looked over at Collazo . . . I looked at him and I saw that he was going down again."

Floyd Boring was the next witness. He too spoke at length about the incident, including the empty clip he found on the ground next to Oscar and the full clip he found in Oscar's pocket. He was cross-examined by defense counsel, then gave way to Vince Mroz. "I immediately jumped the hedge and went to the man who was lying on the Lee House lawn because there were two civilians who were helping Officer Coffelt at the booth," Vince said, describing his approach to the dead Griselio.

The next witnesses were more tertiary to the main action. They consisted of a couple of D.C. traffic cops, one who'd witnessed the fight and came running over (he took Birdzell's gun from him), and another who saw Oscar with Birdzell in the emergency room and stood alongside another officer who found a paper bag with twenty-four 9mm cartridges and a spare clip in Griselio's pocket. Then came White House clerk John William McVicker, who was one of the civilians who helped Les Coffelt; he was followed by Elroy Sites, who also helped with Coffelt. Then came Matthew J. Cullen, Jr., a Bureau of the Budget employee, who was in the Executive Office Building looking out the window of his second-floor office. He appears to be the only one besides Les Coffelt and Joe Downs who actually saw Griselio. "Suddenly my attention was attracted by a small man moving strangely about the left side, near the window [of Les's booth]. . . . I noted that he was carrying a gun in front of him, holding it in both hands. He peered into the window on the left side of the booth and then moved quickly to the front of the booth and, holding the gun at about chest-level in both hands, he fired at least three shots into that booth."

The next witness, William Ellison Smith, a navy technician who worked in the White House kitchen, that is, in the Blair House kitchen during the Trumans' temporary occupation, saw Griselio jump over a hedge and begin to reload his pistol. "I saw his head shake. I didn't hear a shot. I saw his head shake, and I saw him fall."

Next Joe Downs described being hit as he walked in with the groceries. Then two nurses and a doctor talked about Oscar's behavior in the emergency room of Emergency Hospital, including one who said Oscar told her he wanted to kill President Truman.

Secret Service Agent Joseph J. Ellis, Jr., who rode with Oscar in the ambulance to the emergency room, gave the most damning testimony. He testified that he asked a nurse to ask Oscar, "Oscar, did you come here to Washington to try to shoot our president?" Oscar responded, "Yes, I did." Why? "Political reasons, so my country will be free." According to Ellis, Oscar went on in the ambulance with the story of Griselio, whom he said he had only known two weeks. "We decided to start a revolution; we had discussed before the Puerto Rican situation and the two of us decided at that time if we could come down here and assassinate the President we might cause a revolution." He said he didn't even know Griselio's first name. He then said to Ellis, "You are a Secret Service Agent, Mr. Ellis. If you had been there, I would have shot you, but there would be nothing personal about it. . . . I have no feeling of ill-will against the President. . . . I did not come down here to shoot Mr. Truman. I came here to kill the President of the United States."

There was discussion as to whether Oscar's incriminating comments should be allowed; the judge decided to let them in. Eventually, a D.C. police sergeant described the bullet holes the gunfight had left in the Blair-Lee property, and finally an FBI ballistics expert, George A. Berley, testified about the guns used, and identified the source of the bullet that clipped Oscar.

Now it was the defense's turn.

Poor Rover. He had nothing to work with. His contention in his opening statement was that Oscar had no idea Griselio was going to kill Officer Coffelt. "It was no part of any plan of Collazo's that there should be contemplated the killing of Officer Coffelt, or any other officer; that he did not know that Torresola had killed Mr. Coffelt until sometime later that day."

Then he called his only witness, Oscar Collazo.

Oscar had every intention of using the witness chair as a bully pulpit.

He would lecture the United States on its many derelictions, immoralities, and atrocities in Puerto Rico. His lawyer allowed this digression. There followed, under considerable leeway from Judge Goldsborough, a lengthy summation of Oscar's general grievances against the United States, including his first vision of Don Pedro Albizu Campos that night in 1932, his revulsion over Dr. Cornelius Rhoads's genocidal letter, his indignation over the Ponce Massacre, his belief that American capital "owned" Puerto Rico and had devastated the economy, and that America used tuberculosis and other diseases to oppress the poor people of the island. Though the government objected to the materiality of the lectures and Judge Goldsborough's forbearance wore very thin, the judge let Oscar vent.

Then came a curious episode in the trial. One of Oscar's lawyers, Leo Rover, approached the bench to explain a dilemma: he had been contacted by someone and offered a $500 donation with a hint of more to come if a new lawyer were allowed to come into the case and argue on Oscar's behalf by means of a plea of temporary insanity. The judge allowed Rover to ask Oscar about it and Oscar angrily rejected it, believing that it was a secret initiative of the colonial government, desirous of impugning the cause of nationalism by tainting it with association with mental instability. The episode, publicized the next day, established Oscar's bona fides as a martyr and political hero for those who agreed with him: he would not sacrifice his beliefs for a possibility of escaping the death penalty. The cause meant more than his life, and his behavior validated that concept. He literally preferred death before dishonor, even if few North Americans would agree that what he clung to represented honor.

Finally, the trial proceeded, and Oscar told his story of the two meetings with Griselio on the bridge, with some slight rearrangements. Now, he had never spoken to Griselio "two weeks before" the first night on the bridge, as he had first confessed. He only knew Griselio by sight from having seen him at several public meetings. He was surprised when Griselio showed up and proved to be as agitated as he was at the arrests of Albizu Campos's guards on October 27. He bought a pistol from Griselio for their presumed trip to Puerto Rico for $50 and on the next night received the P.38 and $15 in change. That same night, he, Oscar, was the one who'd come up with the idea of the "demonstration" in Washington as opposed to the previously agreed upon feckless trip to the island. It was all Oscar Oscar Oscar. Griselio was simply the pawn in Oscar's larger game of commitment to nationalism.

Then, finally, Rover yielded to Fay, and the cross-examination of Oscar Collazo began.

From a dramatic point of view, how much more satisfying if it had been a brilliant cross, a battle of wits and ideologies, with a brilliant prosecutor and a brilliant defendant slicing each other up in the best John Grisham fashion. But Fay limited himself to small, exact questions, seeking to lead Oscar down the path to the most immediate destination, his own guilt, and never hunted for bigger prey. Oscar, for his part, played dumb like a fox. Consistently, he tried to rope-a-dope his persecutor with seeming passivity, only to suddenly lash out with a swift, accurate blow.

Indeed, the most remarkable thing about the exchange was the willed transformation of Oscar's personality. Where his own attorney allowed him to expound on his political grudges against the United States, he was eloquent, complex, ironic, and the political was clearly the focus of his personality.

For example, Rover set him up to discuss the plight of schoolchildren on the island and he said, "I know of hundreds of thousands of school children in Puerto Rico who have to go the whole day without food, and still they have to go to a school to learn whatever they learn in a foreign language, because the Government of the United States does not allow them to learn in their own language."

Note how deftly he uses his own second language, how adroitly he contrasts the starvation with propaganda and how neatly he lays the crime at the feet of the government of the United States—succinct, elegant, effective, a man with a gift for language who's educated himself superbly.

Yet under cross, he's almost a mute. His answers are monosyllabic and surly, he plays stupid, and you can feel him straining to keep his lies as simple as possible so as not to trip himself up, not that the obvious Fay is trying to trip him up. Then, now and again, he scores neatly against the prosecutor.

Q: Who fired the first shot?
A: I did.
Q: Your gun didn't go off with the first shot, did it?
A: No sir. Anyway, I tried to shoot the first shot.
Q: You aimed it at Officer Birdzell who was standing in the center stairway of the Blair House?

A: Yes sir, I did.

Q: You meant to hit him?

A: I meant to hit him.

Q: You did hit him?

A: I did.

Q: You have not used a gun very often, you said.

A: No, sir.

Q: You knew that the gun could kill him if it hit him in a certain vital spot?

A: I don't know—maybe.

Q: You know that?

A: Maybe.

Q: You shot a .22 rifle and you have killed animals, have you not?

A: Yes sir.

Q: So you knew that when you shoot and if a bullet hits in a certain vital part, it would kill him?

A: If you aimed at that part, sure.

This is very clever. Without really stating it, Oscar has maneuvered Fay into laying before the jury the idea that possibly he didn't mean to kill Birdzell, presumably the last place Fay wanted to go. And Fay steps right into it.

Q: You didn't have a perfect aim?

A: As a matter of fact, I didn't even have a right sight [good sight picture].

Q: But you hit him?

A: I think I did.

He's quietly fencing here, appearing reasonable but being difficult. He plays this trick throughout, at one point tripping Fay up on his history with Albizu Campos, after the prosecutor had tried to allege that they'd shared the same house and Oscar brings it around to make the point that it was a different *room* in that house. Oscar is very exacting in his responses, rarely giving more than asked and often being so precise that he does not give the prosecutor what he wants if the question is somewhat off the mark.

"The following morning, on November 1, you and Torresola took out your guns and oiled and cleaned them that morning, that is correct, sir?"

"It was not in the morning, no sir."

You can almost hear Fay thinking ARGHHHHH! as he grits his teeth and asks, "When was it?"

"About noon."

Or, "And there were seven bullets [in the clip] in that gun, after you fired the first there were still six bullets and you fired them all [at Birdzell], didn't you?"

"I didn't fire at Mr. Birdzell."

In the end, the best that Fay can get from him is the admission that yes, he fired all his bullets (though he persists in the claim he aimed at nobody) and after reloading meant to shoot some more.

The cross-examination doesn't so much end as trickle out, ending on an objection by Rover that Judge Goldsborough sustained.

The jury took less than two hours and the headline summed it up: "Collazo Guilty of Blair House Murder; Death Is Mandatory."

45. DEEP CONSPIRACY

There is no doubt that Griselio Torresola and Oscar Collazo were guilty of conspiracy to murder the president of the United States. They met to talk about it, they acquired weapons to effect it, they traveled to do it, they reconned it, they planned it. Oscar never denied it; in fact it was the bedrock of his position in court, and he accepted the consequences full-out, straight-on.

But that is all he admitted, ever. And from his version of events has descended almost by default the grudgingly accepted theory of the case: that these two Puerto Ricans, in a frenzy of irrational passion, upset over events in Puerto Rico, threw this crazy thing together on the fly, and went down to Washington where they acted like Mexican bandits, and started shooting. Tragedy and foolishness resulted and the price was paid.

It says something either noble or perverse about Oscar that he preferred to be known as a fanatic rather than as a soldier. That's how total his commitment to the cause was and how far beyond ego and narcissism he was, for the linchpin of this argument was his own fanaticism. He didn't care. He let the world believe he was a simple fanatic, and refused to name names or testify against anyone.

As has been noted before, for years the Secret Service believed and tried to prove the deeper conspiracy—that as an act of political policy the Nationalist Party of Puerto Rico ordered Griselio to assassinate the president and he recruited Oscar to help him. The government believed that Pedro Albizu Campos, as part of his revolutionary plan for 1950, ordered two assassinations, one targeting Governor Luis Muñoz Marín, and the other President Harry S. Truman. These two events, along with the proclamation of a Free Republic of Puerto Rico in Jayuya, and cities in flames across the island, would have been the first steps in a war of revolutionary liberation.

The evidence never rose to a threshold of legal action. It may have been convincing, but still it was a series of inferences of intent, of patterns, of possibilities, of probabilities.

Let us briefly examine that evidence.

One must begin at the conceptual level. It is clear that the popularity of the NPPR was on the decline in the late 1940s. Through a program called Operation Bootstrap, the island's industrialization and economic diversification brought about better paying jobs, and better sociopolitical alertness. These reforms, according to scholar Esteban Jiménez, "took away from the [Nationalist Party] the theme of 'Yankees' as colonial overlords . . . The reforms also denied the [party] a base of support among the country's destitute peasantry." The diversification also broke the power of the U.S. sugar corporations, giving the government the ability to formulate its own policies and be responsive to the citizenry. A cultural aspect came into play as well: Puerto Ricans, by the late 1940s, had become secure in their identity as Spanish-Americans, and did not view it as contradictory to their loyalty to the United States. So "by 1948, not only had the economic and political themes of the Nationalists been neutralized, but the Puertorican people had regained their cultural awareness of the same Spanish cultural background defended by Albizu, in the context of the political association with the United States."

Thus, says Jiménez, that left but one theme to the Nationalists, *patria* for its own sake. In his speeches, Albizu defined *patria* as courage and sacrifice, "implying the reduced importance of the individual, who had the duty to sacrifice himself or herself if necessary for the aggrandizement of the national state."

This becomes an increasingly strident theme, particularly as party membership slipped. Countless speeches echo with the fire-and-brimstone rhetoric of a man who yearns for revolution, and his imagination is taken with images of destruction and death. It is clear that assassination as a policy and violence as a tendency were a part of the Albizu Campos mind-set, particularly in the late 1940s as he built toward revolution after ten frustrating years out of circulation in prison and in New York.

"The time of armed revolution is now. This is the hour—this is the hour. The hour for the independence of Puerto Rico is here. . . . The Yankee flag interests us only as a war trophy," he said at a speech April 16, 1948, at Plaza Barcelo, Barrio Obrero, Santurce.

Just a few months later, in a speech in Río Piedras, he evoked a macho metaphor and cast the conflict between cultures in intimate personal terms: "You were born a male for some reason. The one who allows himself to be struck by a man and does not strike back with all his strength in his heart does not have the right to exist. The one who raises his hand against you, punish him with death. That is why God has placed dignity in your face so that you may kill the one who touches it."

He explicitly named his targets in a speech in Ponce in March of 1949.

"I advise Muñoz Marín and Truman and all the bandits who wish to impose tyranny on Puerto Ricans that the patience of this country is running out. . . . Yes, and I advise Muñoz Marín to be ready for that day, and also President Truman, who sends those [troops] here to carry on the tyranny of the United States. One day our patience will end and the situation is going to be a little delicate. Yes, you will see much shooting here."

He may have reached his rhetorical crescendo in Cabo Rojo a little later: "He who does not arise pistol in hand or dagger, or with just an empty fist should die, and is not worthy of having been born in this country."

Beyond the conceptual level is the level of action. He had done this before. The Nationalists had practiced political assassination of important personages at least twice. The most famous of these cases is the murder of Colonel E. Francis Riggs in 1936 by two Nationalist followers in San Juan. One cannot say Pedro Albizu Campos "ordered" the event (especially since the assassins weren't around to explain their actions; they died within an hour in police custody); nor can one say he "ordered" the attempt on Judge Robert A. Cooper (it failed), who had presided over the trial of Albizu Campos (twice!) and found the means to send him to the federal penitentiary in Atlanta for ten years. Nevertheless, those events, as well as the attempt on Muñoz Marín led by Raimundo Díaz Pacheco on October 30, 1950, show that political assassination of opposition leadership was part of the culture; it was seen as a viable method for achieving political or revolutionary ends. If nothing else, it was a tradition within the party, and one can say that such a policy would not have existed without Albizu Campos's explicit permission. What is important here, this argument would run, is a clear pattern.

Moving toward the more specific, there is the overwhelming agreement of many in the party or in the culture who believe that Griselio and Oscar would not have done what they did without the express involvement of Albizu Campos. It was how Albizu Campos operated. According to Rafael Cancel Miranda, one of the shooters at the 1954 assault on the Congress, Don Pedro would put out an idea among his followers and carefully note who responded, marking the one that seemed most excited. Then, later, privately, he would approach that person and begin to charm or convince him quietly to perform the task.

There is some disagreement as to how explicit Albizu Campos's instructions may have been. Some would say Albizu Campos himself would have ordered the action with a high degree of specificity. Others would dilute his culpability by saying that he only ordered some kind of attempt, a "demonstration," and left it to Griselio to determine the form of that demonstration and that even at the ultimate moment—say, 2:19:59 P.M., November 1—Griselio and least of all Oscar had no clear idea of what they meant to do. Others would dilute Albizu's responsibility even more, by saying that there was nothing explicit in his behavior, he never "ordered" in the technical sense any behavior, but instead implied subverbally or by means of hinting, suggesting, cajoling, and nudging a certain course of action to an impressionable young man.

Clearly, Griselio, not Oscar (despite Oscar's testimony), was the key figure in the conspiracy. Griselio's sister Angelina believed that Pedro Albizu Campos ordered Griselio to his mission and his fate. "He did so," she said, admitting, "it's a deduction." She bases this, among other things, on the fact that she knew that Griselio was not interested in emigrating to the United States, but she was told by Blanca Canales that Griselio moved to New York "on Don Pedro's orders." The Torresola cousin René Torres Platet, who knew Elio well later on, agrees.

Griselio's actions themselves suggest the larger conspiracy. One was obtaining the handgun that he provided to Oscar. Oscar testified that Griselio somehow bought the gun for him sometime early on the thirtieth, and, while that is theoretically possible (FBI reports prove that Griselio was very busy that day in his home at the Hotel Clendenning, which makes it unlikely), the fact that the P.38 was also a German service automatic identified by serial number as wartime production and therefore clearly a bring-back from World War II, as was Griselio's Luger, suggests that its source too was Puerto Rico, where it may have been taken as a donation or bought by the Nationalists. Or possibly, it came from other weapons-acquisition initiatives of the party. It seems reasonable to conclude that the P.38 had been brought to America by Griselio to advance his revolutionary responsibilities.

And Griselio had been buying ammunition far in advance of the attempt at Blair House. On June 2, Juan Bernardo Lebrón and Griselio purchased two hundred rounds of 9mm ammunition for a Luger or P.38 from the Manhattan sporting goods store Morton's. Griselio used the same nom de guerre (Charles Gonzales) he used five months later when he checked into the Harris Hotel in Washington. He paid for that ammunition with check No. 25, in the amount of $50, drawn by Juan Pietri Pérez, treasurer of the New York branch of the Nationalist Party of Puerto Rico. On September 11, he bought another box of 9mm ammunition at Morton's. This clearly was one of his responsibilities, as the Nationalist official in New York Julio Pinto Gandía wrote a letter to Gonzalo Lebrón on October 28, in which he stated, "Torresola made a trip to Puerto Rico. His report on the ascendancy and decision of the movement are encouraging. We are at a decisive stage and the main fact is to collect the material that you know [weapons and ammunition, presumably] as soon as possible. Of course, I must tell you that the said material must be of the latest type."

Then there is the issue of that last trip to Puerto Rico, September 16 through 22, and Griselio's very odd behavior during it. In the first place, who paid for it? Griselio was unemployed, living on welfare. He had no visible means of support, and yet he was able to spend the money to buy his round-trip ticket. If there was no time constraint, a ship passage would have made far more sense for someone in his economic circumstances. Yet he had to get there fast, see Don Pedro, and return, all within a week. Next, after meeting with Don Pedro in San Juan, he makes the difficult trip to Jayuya to see "the old people." Why did he visit his relatives and friends and say farewell to them, as Heriberto Marín has stated? Why would he take Heriberto, an old pal whom he'd ignored in New York and to whom he'd stated categorically that he was done with politics, down to the creek with a bottle of rum, when he was a notorious teetotaler? Why would he be so emotional, and hug Heriberto and say goodbye? Why did he track down his still legal wife, Dilia, and see his elder daughter for the first time? Why did he give her a crucifix as a remembrance of him? Why in San Juan did he track down Angelina and her family? What was compelling him to spend most of his visit seeing the people who had counted in his life and saying farewell to them? These visits strongly suggest a man who knows his time on earth is extremely limited.

Then there is, according to Heriberto Marín, Griselio's reputation as a special favorite of Don Pedro's, the one who was trusted to do the difficult jobs. Clearly, Griselio was one of Don Pedro's most trusted agents.

A letter, found November 2, 1950, by FBI agents in the possession of Juan Bernardo Lebrón, the former president of the Manhattan branch of the Nationalist Party of Puerto Rico, whom the Secret Service believes bought the German surplus ammunition with Griselio, may be the single document that suggests a wider conspiracy. Lebrón, one of the many Nationalist Party members rounded up by law enforcement agencies in the immediate aftermath of the gun battle at Blair, was also suspected by FBI agents of receiving machine gun parts and ammunition from Chicago for shipment to Puerto Rico.

It's a letter sent by Elio Torresola to Griselio, dated July 16, 1950. Lebrón insisted to the FBI that in early October—Griselio was just back from Puerto Rico—Griselio gave the letter to Lebrón and asked him to figure out what it meant. And why would Griselio need an outsider's help in understanding a letter from his brother, particularly when he had just seen his brother? Possibly Lebrón's story doesn't hold a lot of water; possibly Griselio gave him the letter for another reason, Lebrón forgot he had it, and when he was picked up by the FBI and asked about the letter, he came up with the first fiction that occurred to him under interrogation pressure.

Lebrón continued with a somewhat bizarre story: he said that he read the letter and had no idea what it meant. "According to LEBRÓN," an FBI agent noted in his report, "Torresola then insisted that LEBRÓN should keep the letter and told LEBRÓN that he would give him twenty-four hours to figure out what the letter meant. LEBRÓN then put the letter in his wallet, intending to give it to Torresola the next time they met. LEBRÓN added that he never saw Torresola again and still does not know the meaning of the letter."

The letter *is* odd, a combination of buck-up morale boosting, domestic chitchat, and clandestine hugger-mugger of no known meaning.

> *My dear brother:*
>
> *I received your letter. Don't persist in writing to me in the way you have been doing. Continue strictly the advice we have given you when you left here. Nothing or nobody is to change the indications for the good of all. We do not need you here for anything and you must not come here for anything.*

*They are calling for obligatory military service . . . and if you come here the
only thing that will be done is to spoil everything.*

*Yesterday we had a surprise visit from Roberto. We read with great
interest Julito's documentation. We received the two presents. We are very
grateful for your kindness.*

*The relative of the little fat man gave us a pleasant surprise. Tell Juan
that I am writing to them with the same fountain pen that he sent me
which is a good one. Soon you will be visited by a friend of the family
whom you are to receive with much affection. . . .*

Your brother hugs you,

(Signed) ELIO

There follows a P.S. that advises Griselio he is not legally divorced.

Possibly the three paragraphs are some kind of crude code, suggesting
that shipments or messages between New York and San Juan were pro-
ceeding as planned. Possibly the last paragraph suggests that an emissary
from Don Pedro—"a friend of the family"—would arrive soon, with
orders, possibly to return home (as Griselio would two months later),
that should be obeyed.

All that is speculation, of course. Maybe there really were two presents, maybe a relative of a fat man did give them a pleasant surprise,
maybe this, maybe that. Far more interesting and revelatory is the
uncoded portion: "Don't persist in writing to me in the way you have
been doing. Continue strictly [to obey] the advice we have given you
when you left here. Nothing or nobody is to change the indications [direc-
tion] for the good of all. We do not need you here for anything and you
must not come here for anything. . . . If you come the only thing that will
be done is to spoil everything."

It sounds as if Griselio, in New York and understanding what lay ahead
and what he had been selected to do in one form or another, had grown
depressed. He had been writing blue, self-pitying letters to his older
brother, but Elio tells him authoritatively, "Stop writing me this stuff. Do
what you are told. Our plans are laid and you cannot change them now.
Do not come here, because your mission is in America; if you come home
and get drafted, that will screw up all our plans." It may be meaningless.
Perhaps Griselio merely wanted to change the plan in some regard. But
what's particularly unsettling about these events is that Insular Police
security reports prove that one of the men in consistent contact with

Pedro Albizu Campos at this time was none other than Elio Torresola. That seems to suggest that Elio had committed totally to the revolution and was intimately involved in its planning. He would be the last person, not the first, who would give Griselio some comfort.

Then a fair question: why on earth did Griselio give this letter to Lebrón? What possibly could he have gained by this? To understand, one must bear in mind that he gave the letter to Lebrón *after* he had been to Puerto Rico September 16–22, by which time he would have known that a dramatic, extremely dangerous action was in his future. That certainly seems strange.

And yet it isn't. It is actually part of a pattern that reflects Griselio's mind-set. It meshes perfectly with a certain vision of him: he is the melancholy commando, knowing that in a very short time he will die on a mission, and sad that he leaves his family, his wives—both legal and com-mon-law—and his two daughters and unborn son behind. Yet he feels locked into events by his culture, his upbringing, the stern admonitions of all he loves and respects, his brother, Elio, his mentor, Blanca Canales, and his Maximum Leader, Don Pedro. He has no choice.

So he yearns, even at this late date, to leave something behind, almost a testament by which he expresses his most precious truth: that he did what he did out of duty, not craziness, and that he did it as a sane, ratio-nal man, with feelings and fears. Thus he does three extraordinary things in his last days that somehow link him to, rather than apart from, the human community.

He gives the letter from Elio, which he must have felt carried the implication of his ambivalence, his regret, and his complicity in the move-ment, to Lebrón, aware that Lebrón would be taken by the FBI and the letter found. He had to understand that its contents would be scrutinized for meaning and its crude code penetrated. The act has the odd vibration of a suicide note or a confession.

Then, he writes a note to each of his daughters, as clearly they are in his mind that last day in New York. He knows he's not coming back; he wishes to leave a record of his love for them and let them know that now, at the very end, they are in his thoughts.

And then he engineers one of the case's most bizarre and most unex-plainable occurrences. He had two letters signed and dated September 21, 1950, from Albizu Campos that essentially tasked him with an important but unspecified mission and gave him access to Nationalist Party funds in

New York. This was evidence that led straight to "the old man," yet Griselio chose to *take* the two letters from Albizu Campos *with* him, rather than destroy them. It has puzzled all students of this case for fifty-odd years. Why on earth would he not destroy the letters, especially since his direct preparations for the mission were ongoing for three days and he had plenty of time to consider the implications of what he was about to do and the necessary consequences? He knew his pockets would be searched and that everything found in them would be tracked to its ultimate place of origin and meaning.

It may have been that it never occurred to him that there was any point to disguising his connection to Don Pedro and that, indeed, his connection to Don Pedro was the point. He couldn't have known that Oscar would survive and decide as a matter of policy to disassociate himself and Griselio from Don Pedro. Griselio could never have anticipated that.

And both letters were found within moments after that event, and they instantly and irrevocably link his actions to Don Pedro. In fact U. E. Baughman read the letters into the record at his press conference less than two hours after Griselio's death.

"My Dear Griselio," Don Pedro wrote, "If by any circumstance it may be necessary that you assume the leadership of the Movement in the United States, you will do it without any qualms. We leave everything concerning this affair to your high patriotism and sound discretion. I embrace you."

The other document, unaddressed and considered a memorandum by the FBI, read, "Griselio will draw the funds which he deems necessary to attend to the supreme necessities of the cause. He will be responsible directly to the Treasurer General. The Delegate will lend him all the cooperation necessary that his mission will be a triumph."

Surely the first message means: no matter what happens to me, you are to do your mission in the United States without qualms. And surely the second means: give Griselio anything he wants.

The psychological meaning of the letters is this: by allowing them to be found and by making sure the letter from Elio also was found, Griselio was making certain that the world knew he was a soldier. In order to do that, he had, in his own symbolic way, to confess to the conspiracy.

But another thing was found in Griselio's pockets, almost equally unbelievable, almost equally provocative. This was the address of no less than the most violent, the most dangerous, the most aggressive, the most notorious of the revolutionaries, and the most dead of them: the same Raimundo Díaz Pacheco, shot to pieces while trying to assassinate Governor Muñoz Marín October 30. That certainly links Griselio to the larger conspiracy. Clearly, Griselio wanted to be seen as a part of that effort.

The final circumstantial proof is the timing of the first meeting. Griselio went, disturbed, to Oscar the night of October 29, clearly upset. But the revolution had not begun.

That is to say, the first shots at Jayuya had not been fired. The assault on La Fortaleza was still sixteen hours away. The *New York Times* had no stories on events in San Juan. There were no revolutionary events in San Juan, except those noted by a small number of Nationalist Party members. Don Pedro's bodyguards had been arrested, and it was feared then that plans for the upcoming actions either had been or were soon to be discovered, based on the inevitable interrogations of these men. Additionally, on October 28, there had been a large prison break in San Juan, and many suspected Nationalist involvement. Security forces in the city were agitated and becoming more agitated. The Nationalists knew the jig was up. They may have seen the prison break or the arrest as the "outbreak" and decided to act immediately.

Thus the idea that Griselio and Oscar were upset by the outbreak of the revolution is proven fraudulent. The revolution hadn't begun. Only members of the conspiracy would understand the secret meanings of the arrests and the prison break and know that the revolution was coming and would act in accordance.

That is the state of the case. It's all hearsay, assumption, deduction. It seems to hold together, and although it wouldn't stand up in court, it should stand up in the court of consensus. On the other hand, maybe it's just vapors, patterns that don't exist except in the imagination of those looking for them.

But the truth is that more than half a century later, no hard information has come out from the inner party, from those on the scene, establishing the truth of what happened November 1, 1950.

Until Oscar spoke.

46. CRESSIE DOES HER DUTY

In January, Cressie Coffelt went to the one place in the world you would not expect: she went to Puerto Rico.

The invitation came from the Association of Members of the Insular Police of Puerto Rico, to attend their annual meeting in San Juan, January 16 and 17, 1951.

The invitation, sent by Lieutenant Francisco A. Nieves, president of the association, said, "Amongst the acts included in the varied program for the occasion there will be an homage to you as a token of sympathy and remembrance for the irreparable loss of your never forgotten husband who died an honorable death while complying with his duty in defending the life of our President, the Honorable Harry S. Truman."

It is unclear whether this was a trip stage-managed by the State Department in order to soothe any ill feelings between the United States and the commonwealth, or if it was genuinely spontaneous. As it worked out, the trip meant that Cressie missed by a day Janie's January 12 wedding.

"Between that [the wedding] and the duty of being here in Puerto Rico, I chose the latter so as to not disappoint the Puerto Ricans who have treated me so well," she told *El Mundo* January 13.

In Puerto Rico, her visit was widely covered. She arrived at San Juan airport on January 12 via Eastern Flight 658, aboard a shiny DC-6 that was part of "The Great Silver Fleet," with a traveling companion, Mrs. Marta Smith. It was a scene of some hubbub; a woman detective climbed up the stairway to the plane to present the grieving widow with a large rose bouquet, somewhat to the consternation of the passengers stacked up behind her, waiting to alight. Flashbulbs popped.

In a black hat with some sort of white ribbon festooning it, and the "distinctive star badge of the Orient Star," a Masonic emblem, yet otherwise in the black of mourning, she descended into a police ceremony, as dozens of Insular police officers in full uniforms were there to greet her, as well as an impressive cohort of executives in their pinstriped double-breasted suits.

"The Pontiac Company put a new car at Mrs. Coffelt and her companion's disposal, in which they were taken to the Hotel Caribe Hilton," reported *El Mundo*. "Several policemen with motorcycles headed the march toward the hotel blowing their sirens, followed by Mrs. Coffelt's car, Captain Benigno Soto's, and several jeeps of the Police."

Later in the trip, the UPI reported, "Mrs. Leslie Coffelt . . . received a gold medal from the Puerto Rican police and $4816.59 collected by school children at ceremonies conducted in her honor today."

Governor Muñoz Marín, himself the survivor of an assassination attempt, presented the medal.

A photo of that event, held at the Tapia Theater in San Juan, shows the earnest governor reading his prepared remarks from behind a phalanx of microphones, while Cressie sat a few feet away, eyeing him apprehensively. Nobody's smiling; nobody's happy; it seems like an extension of the funeral.

She told him, "I deeply appreciate this. I am here at the invitation of the people of Puerto Rico. Like any other American, I cannot hate a country for an act committed by one of its citizens. I shall always remember the kindness shown me by you and your good people. I thank you from the bottom of my heart."

A scroll from the "boys and girls of Puerto Rico" was presented to her. It read, "We want you to know our deep sympathy for you. We want you to know our admiration for a brave man, your husband, who kept true faith with duty and who gave the fullest measure of his devotions. . . .

"Two Puerto Ricans were instrumental in bringing tragedy to your home. But such men in no way represent us. We believe the courage of our people and their loyalty to the ideals of free men everywhere are being demonstrated day by day on the battlefields of Korea. The banners of the Sixty-fifth Infantry are true symbols of the faith and honor of Puerto Rico. They will keep our honor clean.

"As a token of good will from the children of Puerto Rico, as a symbol of our repudiation of the outrage committed against liberty and democracy, as a tribute to a brave man, we ask you to accept this remembrance. Our hearts go with it and our prayers that God may keep and comfort you."

47. OSCAR SPEAKS

O scar held his tongue from the moment Joe Davidson's .38 slug grooved his chest until the day he died, clinging always to the same story: the assassination was something he and Griselio dreamed up the night of the thirtieth, standing in the heat and humidity of the Willis Avenue Bridge, the cars streaming by just a few feet away, the two of them suspended, as it were, between the America that was Manhattan and the Puerto Rico that was the South Bronx.

But he broke his silence at least once. He broke it to Rosa Meneses Albizu Campos, the granddaughter of Pedro Albizu Campos. He trusted her and he wanted what happened truly remembered by someone of sympathy (an attorney herself, she is president of the latter-day Nationalist Party of Puerto Rico, which has become more of a rallying organization than a political force).

Meneses says she even taped the interview and has never disclosed its contents. Her attitude is best summed up by a comment she made from another interview with Gregorio Hernández Rivera, the one survivor of the attack on La Fortaleza, as a part of a kind of oral history project on the insurrection of 1950. Hernández gave her what has served as her ethic, in a way that almost surely sums up Oscar's feelings as well: "He told me a series of things that he never told anyone else. He did so for that very reason: to take care of the image of our Puerto Rican men and women, those who, all things considered, will shape the history of our motherland. And from the time that we write our history, we will do so just as it must be; but not now, not now, the way the empire should like for us to do. You understand?"

It is understood. So this is the history of what happened November 1, 1950, written the way Oscar told it, not the way the empire wanted it, through the medium of Rosa Meneses Albizu Campos.

The order was given by Albizu Campos.

"If that had not been an order that Albizu gave," said Meneses, "it would not have happened. No. Nobody would have dared to do that."

Griselio had been sent to the United States by Albizu to carry out the order.

"First of all," Meneses says, "there would be another factor as well: Griselio never wanted to go to the United States. He did not want to leave this—he never even thought about living in the U.S. He suddenly left—to the surprise of everybody, even his family—to live in the U.S."

Griselio went undercover.

"He [her grandfather Albizu] also worked these actions, like, for example, Griselio's. That is a work that falls under clandestine operations. He [Griselio], silently, without saying anything, giving it the appearance of being something else, he moved to the U.S. and he starts to acquaint himself with and identify people there that could take part in an action at a given time. I am sure from the information that I have gathered here and there that when he went over there, he did not know that that action would be taken on November 1, since the exact dates for the revolution were not known. It was not going to be in October of 1950. It was to be in 1952. The Blair House action was not to be on November 1, 1950. And, I am sure, that date was decided when he came over here in September . . . for three days.

"We don't know what the specific instructions were that Griselio had . . . because Oscar does not know that. I do know from Oscar that they were not the only two that were to go; there were others, and they went to pick the others up to go. But at the last minute . . . [the others] didn't appear. Griselio was counting on other men for that action, and they didn't appear, so that's why he went to Oscar. . . . These were [Griselio's] words [to Oscar]: 'I need you. Puerto Rico needs you.' "

Readers, aware now of the security arrangements at Blair, should briefly conjure with the idea of five men armed with German service automatics and steel-cased ammunition closing in on Blair House; the result would have been mayhem—and assassination. But it didn't happen that way. The others refused, for this reason or that. The two of them—Griselio, the trained guerrilla and assassin, and Oscar, the metal polisher—head to Washington. They don't ask why; they only do what the Maximum Leader has decreed, Griselio, after having lived with the knowledge of his own sure death for two years; Oscar, who knew nothing until that night, after having considered but a second. "History picked the two men that had to do that. Their life—the country, the independence of their country, came before their lives," Meneses says.

"Oscar tells me, 'I was not a versed person in military operations. I had no military training. I did not know how to use a weapon.' The one who was the—oh, what was the expression that Oscar would use? He would say that the hero was Griselio. Oscar always, always said that, because Oscar was a great man, not because he thought he was somebody, you know, he was a big man, a hero, a humble person, you know, very humble.

"Griselio quickly shows him [how to use a weapon], because Griselio was militarily trained. He knew all of these things because he was from Coabey, from Jayuya, from the group of revolutionaries that were being prepared in Jayuya."

She summed up, validating the classical conspiracy theory of 1950: "It was one and the same action of the 1950 revolution. It was part of that action. If the 1950 revolution had taken place, instead of on October 30, let's suppose it had been on November 5, the Blair House attack would have been on November 6, because it had to be consecutive. You see? Because this constituted the denouncement; they were the pieces to the pieces: one piece here in Puerto Rico, the other one Casa Blair, that other one the international denouncement at the U.N. with Thelma Mielke [who would speak before the U.N. in favor of Puerto Rican independence]. So, those are the pieces."

Meneses even confirms suspicions about Griselio's curious choice to carry with him the two letters from her grandfather.

"That would give him a dimension in which to place that action . . . one that was much more than simply murdering somebody. . . . It more or less gives a context to the action, which makes it an approach that's something different than a simple attempted murder. What is more, everybody knows who Pedro Albizu Campos is. And at that time, Pedro Albizu Campos was known. And that also establishes the level for Griselio, that this is not an assassination attempt, rather an action . . . which is not an attempt to commit murder, you know. It is a political action. It's trying to give that . . . sense of the action."

For good or ill, at last, it seems, Griselio gets to make his point. He seems to be reaching out of the grave, speaking first to his daughters and then to his wives and finally to the rest of us: he is saying, it was a mission. I did my duty by the lights of my culture, my upbringing. I faced the consequences and then I died.

He was the most reluctant of the assassins, yet in battle the most ferocious. He died for that which he believed. That is the only story, no matter what else the empire would make of it.

There is some corroborating evidence. On October 4, 1951, José A. Benítez, the executive auxiliary for the government district attorney, interrogated a former general secretary of the Nationalist Party.

At that time, this man had been convicted and was serving a jail sentence for his activities during the uprising of October 30 at La Princesa jail. But he was also disillusioned with the party, and was trying to separate from it; his activities had gotten him nothing but prison. He was also deeply upset that rumors circulated that he was one of the planned Fortaleza commandos and had refused to go ("That is a base lie of the biggest fabrication!"), and for that reason was thought a coward in the party's prison culture at La Princesa, where he was currently incarcerated. Moreover, there is some evidence that he agreed to this chat with the district attorney's man in exchange for a visit from his wife and daughter, as the DA's first inquiry to the prisoner is to inquire after the health and well-being of those two, who clearly had quite recently visited.

The interview was recorded and transcribed in Spanish. Somehow it ended up in Section V of the Luis Muñoz Marín Foundation Archives, catalogued as Series 1, General Correspondence, Nationalist Activities (231), Document 6. It appears never to have been shared with American authorities, or, at least, it is not referenced in any Secret Service or FBI documents accessed by the Freedom of Information Act or shared by other researchers. It simply lay in the files for years until a researcher found it.

It gives a window on the previously unseen and untestified to: a gossipy insider's account of events and culture within the upper ranks of the party in the days leading up to the revolution. The man had risen quickly in the hierarchy—from hanger-on to general secretary in forty-eight months, as his interlocutor notes with astonishment—chiefly on account of his youth and enthusiasm and, the most important fact, that Don Pedro evidently liked him and was particularly interested in bringing young people into an organization that, Don Pedro had discovered upon his return in 1947, was moribund. So at the conceptual level alone, here is clear testimony of what is perhaps already obvious, that Don Pedro was the driving force in the party and that things happened as he decreed them. "Nothing is done without his consent because he is the maximum leader in everything, and that's it," the man says at one point.

The conversation, over fifty pages' worth, wanders over the party land-scape of the previous few years, containing many revelations on the per-sonalities of the major players, the feuds between them, and so forth. One suggests that Don Pedro was sleeping with Doris Torresola in the party headquarters-apartment.

The former general secretary also had a number of acerbic opinions of some of the higher party officials, such as Julio Pinto Gandía, the New York junta chief.

"Is Pinto Gandía dangerous?"

"I think that if he has three or four drinks he can be dangerous, other-wise he's not."

But the man is most useful as a reporter on the plot to kill Harry Truman.

"———," asks his interrogator Benítez, "what is known about Tor-resola and Collazo, the guys that went to Washington?"

"Uh, Torresola came here to Puerto Rico."

"Tell me all that you know about that, because that's interesting."

"I know that he came here to Puerto Rico and he was here for fifteen or twenty days [it was actually six days, September 16–22]. In those fif-teen or twenty days he had various confidential face-to-face meetings with Albizu—you understand—strictly confidential; excuse me, that according to the news, according to what I was able to get from Elio, Tor-resola's brother, you know."

"Was he with you in the cell?"

"Yes, he was there in the cell with me. Well, uh, he [Griselio] came from New York with a message for Albizu, you see. He got the message to Albizu and he was here during several days. So, on that day, Albizu totally infused him—you understand."

"Do you think that Albizu planned what happened in Washington?"
"Yes."

"Are you convinced of that?"
"Yes."

"How is it that you arrive at that decision?"

"Torresola was, let's say, a man who was easy to infuse. They took Tor-resola out of Puerto Rico because he wanted to kill and kill. That's why he was taken out of Puerto Rico, at the party's official request. So, I can't say that I know this because so-and-so or John Doe told me but rather I have arrived at this conclusion on the basis of what I have heard. Any occurring attempt against Albizu or any revolt in Puerto Rico—you understand—they would go kill Truman."

The former general secretary then states that he heard this in his cell at La Princesa jail.

"Who had planned it, Albizu?"

"Albizu was the leader of everything. He was the maximum leader of the movement in everything; there is no one else there other than Albizu Campos—you understand—what he says goes; he that does not do so has a death penalty."

A second or two later Benítez asked, "So, Torresola came to Puerto Rico. He received the instruction to kill Truman—when? Do you know if it was to be when he heard that there had been shots fired here or something?"

"[Yes,] according to what I heard from Elio and from different guys here and there—you see I can't say that so-and-so took part in that, you see."

"That doesn't matter."

"There was knowledge," the prisoner continued, "among some of those closest to Albizu—you understand—the closest—that at the moment anybody touched Pedro Albizu Campos or if there was ever in Puerto Rico any attempt [on his life], they would kill Truman."

"So it just happened like that without any further instructional coordination?"

"No, sir [meaning, "no, no instructional coordination was necessary"]."

"In other words, when they became aware that in Puerto Rico many Nationalists had been arrested and that the disorder had already erupted, they acted over there [in the United States]."

"They were coldly waiting on the movement."

How reliable is this witness? He gets some facts wrong, like the length of Griselio's stay in Puerto Rico (though he gets right that there was indeed a visit). He makes a claim encountered nowhere else that Griselio "wanted to kill and kill. That's why he was taken out of Puerto Rico, at the party's official request." He also suggests that Griselio was first ordered to assassinate Truman in the September 20 conference with Albizu, when other evidence suggests that Griselio at least knew before then that he was expected to do something of a violent and destructive nature and may have known it involved President Truman.

On the other hand, the man had already been sentenced and so was not, in standard jailhouse snitch fashion, offering lies to prosecutors in exchange for a deal. He really had nothing to gain and wanted only to see his wife and daughter, get out of prison, and go on with his life.

And then he gets something so exactly right it suggests that his sources within the party were credible.

"What kind of an individual is Collazo?"

"From what I'm aware of, Collazo is a great stature of a man—an excellent character. From what I've been told, he is very intelligent; he is a good father, a good husband, a good son—a model man for the community. He is a man of extraordinary valor. And then he throws away his life for the homeland. I have been told he is an extraordinary man."

The man, by the way, in his eighties, is still alive and living in Puerto Rico, and for that reason his name is not divulged here; he refused to discuss this matter.

48. - - R-I- -

ome of the lessons of November 1, 1950, were immediately apparent to the federal government and the Secret Service. "The era of top security for presidents had arrived," an Ohio newspaperman told the Truman Library many years later.

Changes were immediate. The presidential limo was armored and supplied with running boards where agents could ride; the president no longer walked from Blair House to the White House; public access was limited to Blair House. The president's walks were rearranged: now his armored limo drove him to random places in the city so that his movements could not be anticipated. The *Chicago Sun-Times* wrote November 3 that the "President's guard [was now] on a War Footing."

The paper noted that "police guards in the metropolitan areas of Washington for blocks around the White House were doubled." West Executive Avenue, which was close by the Executive Office Wing, which contained the president's offices, was closed off.

"Nobody gets within what might be called a stone's hefty throw from the President or his family until he has stood and delivered himself of credentials proving he is on well-defined official business."

If the larger security lessons were learned, however, the smaller lessons were not. Amazingly, no one studied the 38.5 seconds of November 1 for their tactical revelations. Now, a half a century plus later, most of what could have been learned has become standard teaching for American police officers, but they remained undocumented and untranslated into policy for at least another quarter of a century, and there were several even more dispiriting police gun battles where, had the Blair House lessons been mastered, lives might have been saved. The Newhall, California, "massacre," where four California highway patrolmen were gunned down primarily because their training had been so poor, is one such example. They had been trained to shoot stationary targets in a target range environment and were unprepared for the aggressive, heavily armed felons who came at them. One of them was even found with collected spent cartridge casings in his pockets, meaning that even though under heavy fire, he had reverted to target range conditions and cleaned up his brass!

It didn't have to be so. The tactical lessons were clear from November 1.

First of all, police officers should carry powerful semiautomatic pistols. At Blair House, seven men, armed with revolvers, were almost overwhelmed by two men armed with automatic pistols. The 9mm automatics were not merely more powerful than the police Colt revolvers, but easier to manipulate, much faster to reload, and much easier to shoot accurately under pressure. Today, the Secret Service carries SIG-Sauer semiautos in a flat shooting caliber called .357 SIG, a 40-caliber necked down to .357-bore width, which is one of the best calibers for ending a gunfight fast by applying extreme shock to the opponent, irrespective of lethality. A .357 SIG round grooving Oscar's skull may well have put him to the pavement in a nanosecond with a very bad headache.

The second lesson is: shoot two-handed. The one-handed shooting techniques of the agents and officers turned out to be woefully inadequate. By contrast, Griselio, shooting with both hands on the gun, was able to operate with frightening efficiency. He took three men out of the fight in a very few seconds, including the longest effective shot in the fight, the one that hit Don Birdzell in the second knee; only the incredible courage of one of those men, to get himself back in the fight though fatally wounded, and to make a great shot, prevented what could have been a catastrophe. It's even possible that Les made that great shot two-handed himself, but it can't be stated with certainty as no witnesses saw that part of the fight. Meanwhile the Secret Service agents, firing one-handed, fired three shots—and all were ineffective. Don Birdzell fired five shots one-handed; he missed with all five. Police officer Joe Davidson fired six shots one-handed and only one of them, believed to be a ricochet, was effective, and not immediately.

Third, firearms training should be realistic, not bull's-eye-target based. The agents and officers were used to standing bolt-upright, taking their time, finding their grip, their sight picture, their breath control, then carefully squeezing off a shot. They were all very good at it, but so what? That kind of shooting never happens in real-world combat. Instead, as Blair House reveals, gunfights are fluid, dynamic, chaotic improvisations at

speed in highly adrenalized states of being, with a whole litany of physiological changes going on within the body, such as tunnel vision, auditory
exclusion, and loss of fine motor skills. In spite of those occlusions, one
moves and shoots simultaneously at targets in turn that are moving and
shooting simultaneously. Officers should be prepared for this; they should
not have to learn it on the job, where it may be too late.

But there was a larger lesson as well. It has to do with a society's need
for a certain kind of man. These men weren't only necessary on November 1, 1950, but at other dates in American history: December 7, 1941,
would be one, as would September 11, 2001, another, June 6, 1944. In
fact, they have always been necessary, and the tendency of modern culture
to devalue them—to find them crude and boorish and insensitive and
politically incorrect—is unfortunate.

What's the word that best describes them? It has not been evoked yet
here, for to throw it around loosely is to trivialize it. So it remains like a
clue in a crossword puzzle, a few letters of which are visible yet whose
meaning is still obscure.

As an exercise in imagination, let's pretend that Donald Birdzell, that
gruff, tough bear of a man, is all tied up in one of the crosswords that so
intrigued him. Imagine him at the breakfast table with Helen and Joan on
that promising-to-be-warm morning on the first day of November a few
minutes before he climbs into his Buick and heads to work. He's already
dressed but he hasn't put his tunic or his gun belt on, though both are on
the table.

Donald, with his large physique and blade of nose and piercing eyes, is
sucking down coffee—Black Magic, he called it, from his navy days—and
he's smoking Luckies, one after another, as the surgeon general's report is
still years down the road, and he's crouched over the previous Sunday's
Washington Post crossword. It's almost completed. Donald likes complete.
He likes neat, tidy, ordered, known, precise. He likes systems and he's a
man who believes in the elegance and justice of the system he's sworn to
defend and already has twice, in the navy and in the army.

Before him, however, a last set of blank squares tumbles downward
amid all the crisp letters. Its whiteness haunts him.

8 Down: Guy in tiff.

What the hell?

Donald should know. He's been in a fight or two. But he stares, thinks,
comes up dry.

-- R - I --

Guy in tiff.

"Helen, what could this be?" he might have asked.

Helen, busying herself with her makeup after fixing breakfast before departing for her own job at the Veterans Bureau, might have responded, "Don, honey, you know I don't have a head for those things."

"Joan, you got any idea?"

Joan says nothing.

Donald shrugs. Oh, well. Time to go. It'll be another hot one today. Maybe he's feeling old now; he's beyond forty, after all, he's walked beats, fought wars, been on the go and on his feet his whole life.

"Okay, hon," he says. "'Bye now, toots."

"Love you, sweetie," calls Helen from the bedroom.

Donald takes a last slug of Black Magic, takes his Colt revolver out of the holster, opens the cylinder to see six gleaming circles inscribed with the legend REMINGTON-PETERS .38 SPECIAL, restores the gun, cinches up the belt, then buckles it. He feels the weight of the revolver heavy on his waist. Then he pulls on his heavy winter tunic, buttons it, and sets his cap at a jaunty angle.

"Seeya, kid," he says to Joan.

He steps out the door and down the stairway to his Buick garaged in an alley behind the house. He climbs in, feels the vault-like clunk of the door as it joins with the chassis of the car. The Buick. Now there's a car. Never better. Nothing like it.

He pulls into traffic on Farragut Street, feeling the soft suspension of the car, makes a left-hand turn onto the four broad lanes of New Hampshire, climbs a hill, passes a circle and sees, in the rising sunlight, the federal city before him, the Capitol to the left, the squareness of the Lincoln Memorial to the right, and between them the high spire of the Washington Monument. If it was crowded, he knew all the back streets and could find his way fast. But it's not, so he just roars along. He loves to drive this hot little car, running it up to a light, then jamming on the brakes and feeling the chassis rock on the suspension springs.

He turns on the radio.

"—Rico, fighting continues as government troops retook the town of Jayuya high in the mountains and arrested—"

Then something flashes before his mind.

Now what the—

Guy in tiff.

8 Down.

- - R - I - -

Thought he had it. Then it vanished. Damn.

And then suddenly, unbidden, it pops to his mind.

Guy in tiff.

8 Down, with an R and an I.

W-A-R-R-I-O-R

Warrior!

Finally: complete.

EPILOGUE: DESTINIES

Pedro Albizu Campos

Pedro Albizu Campos was jailed for his participation in the insurrection of 1950, but later pardoned by Governor Luis Muñoz Marín. After the attack on Congress in 1954, he was jailed again. In prison his health declined, and he was released as a sick and dying old man. (Many of his adherents believe he was irradiated while in prison and his disease was in fact radiation poisoning.) He died in 1965. He is today celebrated by many in Puerto Rico, and his legend continues to grow.

Oscar Collazo

Oscar Collazo's death sentence was commuted by Harry Truman a few weeks before it was to be carried out in 1952. Oscar served a total of twenty-nine years in prison, most at the federal penitentiary at Leavenworth, Kansas, where he was a model inmate, mastering languages, reading voluminously, corresponding with family members and friends, and helping other inmates. He never renounced his Nationalist beliefs. In 1979, he was pardoned by President Jimmy Carter and went home a hero. He died in bed in 1994.

Harry Truman

Harry Truman decided not to run again in 1952 and instead went into retirement in Independence, Missouri, his beloved hometown. After many years as the town's most prominent senior citizen, he died in 1972.

Cressie Coffelt

Cressie Coffelt received a presidential appointment to work in the Interior Department during the years after Les's death, often relying on the Secret Service for small tasks and considerations and incurring some resentment. She never remarried and died in 1982. Her daughter, Janie, has kept Les's flame burning all these years.

Joseph Downs

Joe Downs recovered from his wounds and returned to duty on January 15, 1951. But his son, Jim, says the shooting, coming after the Nicaragua battle in which he was wounded, got to his nerves. After the Blair House attack, Downs gave up playing tennis, but kept his love of sports through-out his life. Downs retired from the force in 1956. He went to Miami, where he worked for the U.S. Customs Service, transferring to the Balti-more office in 1970. Three years later he retired again. In his later years, Downs kept busy taking tickets at a local movie theater. In July 1978, he died after suffering a heart attack at the age of seventy-two.

Donald Birdzell

Don Birdzell returned to work on January 15 of 1951—the same day that Joe Downs resumed his duties—and on that very day slipped on wet leaves on the pavement and seriously damaged a knee. He had to take another year off for recuperation. He retired from the White House Police in 1959; the next year he moved to Clearwater, Florida, where he enter-tained his grandkids. He died of complications from a broken hip in November of 1991 at the age of eighty-two.

Joseph Davidson

Joe Davidson rose to the rank of sergeant in the White House Police Force and retired in 1960 after suffering a heart attack. A second heart attack in 1965 was fatal. He was fifty-two years old when he died.

Stewart Stout

Stewart Stout was promoted to assistant to the special agent in charge of the White House detail in 1954. He traveled with John F. Kennedy to the Berlin Wall and was with the president's detail in Dallas on November 22, 1963. He was eventually promoted to special agent in charge of the spe-cial services division. He retired from the service on December 31, 1965. He died of a heart attack on December 30, 1974, at the age of sixty. At the time of his death he was an administrative assistant at the White House.

Floyd Boring

Floyd Boring retired from the Secret Service on March 1, 1967, with the rank of inspector. In retirement he worked a number of private security jobs including advance security of U.N. personnel coming to Washington, D.C., but eventually spent his time in his apartment in Silver Spring, Maryland, building handmade clocks and watching and enjoying his grandchildren. His wife, Ruth, died early in 2005. Though his health is somewhat shaky, the old warrior battles on.

Vince Mroz

Vince Mroz became head of the Charleston, West Virginia, and Kansas City, Missouri, offices of the Secret Service. He also served in the Chicago, Illinois, and Springfield, Illinois, offices and as an inspector in headquarters. He retired as deputy assistant director in 1974; and then, with his engineer's mind, succeeded at a variety of different careers, including supervisor of transportation for the Montgomery County School System. He retired in 1986. He now plays golf as often as possible and lives in Naples, Florida, where, eventually, he went to work for the Collier County Sheriff's Department as a director of the background investigative unit. He retired, for the third time, in August of 2001.

SOURCE NOTES

For this book, we relied on books, doctoral dissertations, master's theses, interviews, oral histories, trial testimony, historical archives, government documents released under Freedom of Information Act requests, written histories, newspapers, and our own observations. Weather information in several chapters comes from records kept by the National Climatic Data Center, National Oceanic and Atmospheric Administration. The following source notes do not include every resource consulted for the individual chapters; rather, they refer to sources which we relied upon primarily or sources directly quoted in the chapters.

Introduction

For the reaction in the continental United States to the assassination attempt: A *Time* story called the incident a "weird assassination plot" involving "irrational, unpredictable behavior," "The Presidency," *Time*, November 13, 1950, p. 22. "The acts of violence made no sense—except to Communists who thrive on disruption in the Caribbean and elsewhere," "Puerto Rico Revolt Endangers Truman," *Life*, November 13, 1950, p. 25. "The Puerto Ricans who tried to kill President Truman were as stupid as they were fanatical," "The Assassination Attempt," *The New Republic*, November 13, 1950. *The Nation* referred to the two men as "fanatical" and called the shooting a "crazy assault," "The Roots of the Tragedy," *The Nation*, November 11, 1950, p. 423. In a *Washington Daily News* column on November 3, 1950, entitled "Warped Life," Peter Edson labeled the incident "the crazy attempted assassination."

1: A Drive Around Washington

For Truman, we relied primarily on several histories, including *Truman*, by David McCullough; *The Autobiography of Harry S. Truman*, Robert H. Ferrell (ed.); *Harry S. Truman: A Life*, by Robert H. Ferrell; *Man of the People: A Life of Harry S. Truman*, by Alonzo L. Hamby; *Working with Truman: A Personal Memoir of the White House Years*, by Ken Hechler; and *Aspects of the Presidency*, by John

Hersey. Secret Service logs and White House appointment calendars yielded Truman's schedule. Material on the politics of the McCarran Act came from Michael J. Ybarra's *Washington Gone Crazy: Senator Pat McCarran and the Great American Communist Hunt*. The letter to Ethel Noland, dated September 24, 1950, is in "Papers of Mary Ethel Noland," Box 2, "Harry S. Truman to the Noland Family, 1950," Harry S. Truman Library, Independence, Missouri. The excerpt from Albizu Campos's speech is from "Albizu Campos Speaks," Smithsonian Folkways Recordings, No. P-2501 (2001).

2: Griselio Agonistes

For Griselio Torresola, the authors relied upon information obtained through interviews with his widow, Dilia Rivera, his sister Angelina Torresola, his life-long friend Heriberto Marín, and Oscar Collazo's daughter, Zoraida Collazo, as well as trial testimony and documents and reports obtained from the Federal Bureau of Investigation and the United States Secret Service under the Freedom of Information Act. We obtained information about guns and ammunition from the FBI and the Secret Service. We also referred to *The True Believer: Thoughts on the Nature of Mass Movements*, by Eric Hoffer.

3: Revolution

The authors relied primarily upon records of the Puerto Rican Insular Police, as well as FBI documents, along with the following books: *La Insurrección Nacionalista en Puerto Rico 1950*, by Miñi Seijo Bruno; *Las Llamas de la Aurora, Acercamiento a una Biografía de Pedro Albizu Campos*, by Marisa Rosado; *Puerto Rico: A Political and Cultural History*, by Arturo Morales-Carrión; and *Pedro Albizu Campos y el Nacionalismo Puertorriqueño*, by Luis Angel Ferrao. We also consulted *Albizu Campos: Puerto Rican Revolutionary*, by Federico Ribes Tovar; *The Basque History of the World*, by Mark Kurlansky; and *Our Bones Are Scattered: The Cawnpore Massacres and the Indian Mutiny of 1857*, by Andrew Ward. Further information was obtained from a series of articles published in 1979 by the Puerto Rican newspaper *El Vocero* concerning the revolution of 1950. The quotation describing Albizu Campos is from *Historia de la Nación Puertorriqueña*, by Juan Angel Silén, p. 22. The Nationalist Party insider who is quoted in this chapter is not identified because he is still living in Puerto Rico and declined to be interviewed for this book.

4: The Odd Couple

Information for this chapter was obtained from FBI reports and trial testimony. Information about Oscar Collazo's experience with guns was obtained from an interview with Nelson Canals, a Puerto Rican independence advocate.

5: Mr. Gonzales and Mr. De Silva Go to Washington

Information was obtained primarily from FBI and Secret Service documents, as well as books, including *Oscar Collazo Prisionero 70495*, by Carmen Zoraida Collazo; *The Assassins*, by Robert J. Donovan; *The WPA Guide to New York City*; and *Memorias*, by Rosa Collazo. Information was also obtained from interviews with Carmen Zoraida Collazo. The authors also consulted *The True Believer: Thoughts on the Nature of Mass Movements*, by Eric Hoffer (the quotation is from p. 66); and two articles, "Puerto Rico Revolt Endangers Truman," *Life*, November 13, 1950; and "Annals of Crime: A Demonstration at Blair House," Robert J. Donovan, *The New Yorker*, July 19, 1952.

6: Early Morning

We consulted *Aspects of the Presidency*, by John Hersey (the quotations regarding Truman's walking speed are from p. 37; "wonder and delight at this awesome stranger" is from p. 9; Truman's breakfast is from p. 34); *Truman*, by David McCullough (the quotation from Truman's diary is from p. 939); *Tumultuous Years: The Presidency of Harry S. Truman, 1949–1953*, by Robert J. Donovan ("I like them more than all the top-notchers" and "He would treat us almost like sons" are from p. 808); as well as *The United States Secret Service*, by Walter S. Bowen and Harry Edward Neal. We also relied upon interviews with former Secret Service agents, as well as an oral history by John Snyder. Further, we relied upon *Secret Service Chief*, by U. E. Baughman with Leonard Wallace Robinson.

7: Baby Starches the Shirts

We spent many hours with Jane Miller, Cressie Coffelt's daughter, talking with her about the family and reviewing her collection of Leslie Coffelt's personal documents. Other information in the chapter comes from various police sources. For information on Les Coffelt's Masonic activities, men associated with his lodge were interviewed. We also interviewed Irene Orndorff, who grew up in Oranda, Virginia, and who knew Leslie and his family throughout her life. Les Coffelt's height and weight came from a coroner's report quoted in an FBI document released under the Freedom of Information Act. As is the case with the other men on duty that day, we drove their routes to the places they parked. The information about Leslie working on his day off came from an e-mail sent by Officer Bradley Allen's granddaughter to the Secret Service. She said that Officer Allen, a good friend of Les Coffelt's, had been scheduled for duty but wanted to spend the day painting his house; Leslie agreed to sub for him.

8: Toad

For this chapter as well as Chapter 19, "Resurrection Man," we spent several hours interviewing Floyd and Ruth Boring. We also interviewed their nephew, Ed Boring, and Ruth's two sisters, Josephine Richer and Frances Spencer. Other agents familiar with the layout back then contributed to the description of the Secret Service office in the East Wing of the White House. The quotation on the proper grip for holding a revolver is from *The Colt Double Action Revolvers: A Shop Manual,* Vol. 1, by Jerry Kuhnhausen, p. 203.

9: The New Guy

Information for this chapter was obtained from interviews with Vincent Mroz. We also consulted various books about the Secret Service, including *The United States Secret Service,* by Walter S. Bowen and Harry Edward Neal; *Secret Service Chief,* by U. E. Baughman with Leonard Wallace Robinson; and *The Secret Service: The Hidden History of an Enigmatic Agency,* by Phillip H. Melanson with Peter F. Stevens.

10: The Buick Guy

This chapter was based upon interviews with Joseph King, Roy Birdzell, Ruth Birdzell, and Wilma Erwin, all relatives of Donald Birdzell, as well as various family documents.

11: The Guns

For this chapter, the authors relied upon trial testimony, as well as various books. For information on Blair House, the authors relied on *The Blair-Lee House: Guest House of the President,* by Eleanor Lee Templeman, and *The President's House,* by William Seale. The authors also consulted Randy Bumgardner, assistant manager of the Blair House, and toured Blair House. For information on the guns themselves, the authors relied on *The Luger Story,* by John Walter; *The Luger Handbook,* by Aarron Davis; *The Walther Handgun Story,* by Gene Gangarosa, Jr.; and *German Handguns,* by Ian Victor Hogg. The authors also relied on their own experiences; they have owned and fired all of the types of pistols used in the Blair House shooting. The description of the clothing worn by Oscar Collazo and Griselio Torresola comes from an FBI Laboratory Work Sheet obtained under the Freedom of Information Act. Oscar Collazo's daughter, Carmen Zoraida Collazo, said that the report on her father's attire was probably incorrect, for he was a modest dresser who never would have donned such gaudy socks.

12: The Ceremony

For this chapter, the authors interviewed family members of Justice M. Chambers, and obtained information from the History and Museums Division of the United States Marine Corps, and the National Marine Museum of the Marine Corps and Heritage Center. Additional information came from "Annals of Crime: A Demonstration at Blair House," Robert J. Donovan, *The New Yorker*, July 19, 1952. The quotation "I would much rather have that medal . . ." is from the article "Truman Gives No. 1 Medal to 15 Army Heroes," *Washington Post*, October 13, 1945. Information about Truman's schedule on November 1, 1950, was obtained from the Harry S. Truman Library in Independence, Missouri.

13: Indian Summer

The authors relied upon "The Attempt to Assassinate President Harry S. Truman," investigative studies for United States Secret Service Personnel, prepared by Leonard P. Hutchinson, special agent in charge of the Protection Research Section, United States Secret Service. The authors also consulted the White House duty roster for November 1, 1950. Further information was obtained from interviews with Vincent Mroz and Floyd Boring.

14: The Big Walk

For this chapter, the authors consulted *Puerto Rico: Cinco Siglos de Historia*, by Francisco A. Scarano, as well as trial testimony. The authors also consulted "Annals of Crime: A Demonstration at Blair House," Robert J. Donovan, *The New Yorker*, July 19, 1952. Additional information about the Riggs family and the Riggs National Bank was obtained from articles in the *Washington Post*, including "E. Francis Riggs Was Grandson of Banker Here," February 24, 1936; "Pittsburgh Bank to Buy Riggs; PNC Financial to Pay $705.2 Million for Embattled Washington Institution," July 17, 2004; and "New Money; With the Demise of Riggs Bank, All That's Left Is Jangling Change," May 16, 2005; and from the public information office of PNC Bank, which acquired the Riggs National Bank.

15: Oscar

Our understanding of Oscar Collazo was derived from interviews with his daughter, Carmen Zoraida Collazo, and from our review of his personal correspondence in the Colección Oscar Collazo at the University of Puerto Rico, including the following: to Chita (Iris), April 23, 1955 (No. 316) (regarding his work for his relatives); to Rosa, April 21, 1956 (No. 387) (regarding his brother Salvador); to Seymour Stein, September 21, 1969 (No. 1271) (regarding his love of nature); and to Rosa, December 10, 1955 (No. 354) (referring to the sacred soil of Coabey). We also reviewed FBI documents, and consulted "A History of Puerto Rican Radical Nationalism, 1920–1965," a doctoral dissertation by Jaime Ramírez-Barbot. Additional information was obtained from *The Assassins,* by Robert J. Donovan; and "Annals of Crime: A Demonstration at Blair House," by Robert J. Donovan, *The New Yorker,* July 19, 1952. The authors also consulted *The Face of Battle,* a book by military historian John Keegan, and *Albizu Campos: Puerto Rican Revolutionary,* by Federico Ribes Tovar.

16: "It Did Not Go Off"

Information for this chapter came from Secret Service and FBI files, as well as statements of Secret Service and White House police officers involved in the incident. We also reviewed Treasury Department Memo J-Co.-2-2271, p. 8, January 24, 1951, examining why Oscar Collazo's gun did not fire the first time he tried to shoot.

17: Pappy

This chapter was based upon interviews with Joseph King, Roy Birdzell, Ruth Birdzell, and Wilma Erwin, family members of Donald Birdzell, as well as family documents, including newspaper articles, pictures, and obituaries.

18: The Next Ten Seconds

This chapter is based upon FBI documents and witness statements.

19: Resurrection Man

Information for this chapter was obtained from an oral history and interviews of Floyd Boring. Information was also obtained from the *DuBois Morning Courier,* November 1934, and from documents and maps provided by the DuBois Historical Society and the DuBois Public Library. The authors also interviewed Josephine Richer and Frances Spencer, sisters of Ruth Boring, and visited the neighborhood where Floyd Boring grew up.

20: So Loud, So Fast

Information for this chapter comes from witness statements and interviews of Floyd Boring. The discussion of gunfights came from personal conversation with Clint Smith, director of Thunder Ranch, a nationally recognized center for firearms training. William Vanderpool, former supervisory agent of the

FBI ballistics lab at Quantico, Virginia, discussed the points of impact of various .38 Special loads with us.

21: Upstairs at Blair

For this chapter, the authors consulted *Truman,* by David McCullough (quoted material is from pp. 734–35, 768, 775); *Tumultuous Years: The Presidency of Harry S. Truman, 1949–1953,* by Robert J. Donovan; *The Korean War,* by Max Hastings; and *Washington Gone Crazy,* by Michael J. Ybarra.

22: Downstairs at Blair

This chapter was based upon interviews with Vincent Mroz and with two sons of Secret Service agent Stewart Stout, as well as witness statements, and the oral history of newsman Robert G. Nixon. The authors also consulted *Secret Service Chief,* by U. E. Baughman with Leonard Wallace Robinson.

23: Borinquen

Information for this chapter was obtained from Secret Service documents and the "Hays Commission Report on the Ponce Massacre," published by the American Civil Liberties Union, as well as various publications including *La Masacre de Ponce,* by Manuel E. Moraza Ortiz; *Patterns of Living in Puerto Rican Families,* by Lydia J. Roberts and Rosa Luisa Stefani; *From Colonia to Community: The History of Puerto Ricans in New York City, 1917–1948,* by Virginia E. Sánchez Korrol; *Down These Mean Streets,* by Piri Thomas; and *Puerto Rico: A Political and Cultural History,* by Arturo Morales-Carrión. We also consulted "A History of Puerto Rican Radical Nationalism, 1920–1965," a doctoral dissertation by Jaime Ramírez-Barbot.

24: Oscar Alone

For this chapter, the authors relied upon witness interviews, FBI documents, and interviews with Carmen Zoraida Collazo, daughter of Oscar Collazo.

25: The End's Run

Information in this chapter was obtained from interviews with Vincent Mroz, as well as FBI documents and witness statements.

26: Good Hands

This chapter was based upon interviews with Vincent Mroz, Shirley Mroz, and Rex Scouten. Some information on Otto Graham was obtained from Northwestern University.

27: *The Colossus Rhoads*

The authors relied upon a number of sources, including a book, *Necator Americanus,* by Pedro I. Aponte Vázquez, and various articles, including "51-Year Mystery: Did Doctor Kill 8?" by Robert Friedman, *Sunday Daily News,* June 20, 1982; "Dr. Rhoads Dies; Led Cancer Unit," *New York Times,* August 14, 1959, p. 21 (obituary); "Crusader Against Cancer," *New York Times,* August 15, 1959, p. 16 (editorial on death of Rhoads); "Revisiting a 1930s Scandal, AACR to Rename a Prize," by Douglas Starr, *Science,* Vol. 300, April 25, 2003, pp. 573–74; and " 'Porto Ricochet': Joking About Germs, Cancer, and Race Extermination in the 1930s," by Susan E. Lederer, *American Literary History,* 2002, pp. 720–46. The quotation from Oscar Collazo was from trial testimony. The quotations from Luis Baldoni are from "Did Rhoads Kill Albizu," by Pedro I. Aponte Vásquez, *Claridad,* January 14–20, 1983.

28: *Oscar Goes Down*

This chapter was based in part upon witness statements. The analysis of the Dade County, Florida, shoot-out comes in part from the analysis of W. French Anderson, M.D., referenced in Tactical Brief #7, Firearms Tactical Institute, July 1998.

29: *The Second Assault*

For this chapter, the authors concluded that the gunfight lasted about 38.5 seconds because that is the time it took to re-create Elroy Sites's run from where he was working when the first shot went off to Leslie Coffelt's booth, where he arrived at the end of the gunfight (see Chapter 37). Information about the gunfight was also obtained from witness interviews. The authors also consulted *Mollie & Other War Pieces,* by A. J. Liebling, and *The Army Combat Guide.*

30: *Pimienta*

This chapter was based upon interviews with Angelina Torresola, Heriberto Marín Torres, René Torres Platet, and Dilia Rivera, as well as on FBI and Secret Service documents and records of the Puerto Rican insular police. For additional information about Law 53, the authors consulted "Discrimination for Political Beliefs and Associations," *Revista del Colegio de Abogados de Puerto Rico,* November 1964, p. 65.

31: *Point-Blank*

This chapter was based primarily upon witness reports, trial testimony, the examination of the coroner's report as quoted by FBI documents, and the examination of trial testimony by William S. Queale, M.D., who is board-certified in internal medicine and frequently reviews medical examiners' reports and provides opinions on the cause of death.

32: The Man Who Loved Guns

Information for this chapter was based upon interviews with Coffelt family friend Irene Orndorff and Jane Miller, Les Coffelt's stepdaughter, as well as interviews with other Coffelt family members and the authors' review of family documents and memorabilia.

33: The Dark Visitors

For this chapter, the authors consulted *American Assassins: The Darker Side of Politics,* by James W. Clarke; "Presidential Assassinations and Assaults: Characteristics and Impact on Protective Procedures," by Frederick M. Kaiser; and *Assassination and Political Violence: A Report to the National Commission on the Causes and Prevention of Violence,* by James F. Kirkham, Sheldon G. Levy, and William J. Crotty. Information about Griselio Torresola and Oscar Collazo was obtained from interviews with family members and friends, as well as FBI and Secret Service documents.

34: Mortal Danger

Information for this chapter was obtained from witness interviews, trial testimony, and an oral history by John Snyder. Additionally, the authors consulted various books about Harry Truman. The authors also examined and measured the exterior of Blair House and the angles from which shots were fired based on photographs taken at the time and participant interviews.

35: The Neighbor

This chapter was based upon interviews with Floyd Boring and Ruth Boring.

36: American Gunfight

This chapter is based upon participant statements and interviews.

37: The Good Samaritan

Information for this chapter was based upon interviews with Vincent Mroz, Floyd Boring, and Elroy Sites. Information on the businesses on 17th Street at the time of the shooting came from the 1954 D.C. City Guide and the 1954 edition of *Baist's Real Estate Atlas of Surveys of Washington, D.C.,* Vol. I; for the sake of the narrative, the authors took the liberty of assuming that these businesses were there at the time of the shooting, though they caution the readers that they can't be sure. The authors also examined the weapon used by Griselio Torresola in the Blair House shooting; it is on display at the Truman Museum in Independence, Missouri.

38: *The Policemen's Wives*

This chapter is based upon interviews with Shirley Mroz, Jane Miller, and Ruth Boring, and upon the e-mail sent by Officer Bradley Allen's granddaughter to the Secret Service, which was cited for chapter 7.

39: *The Scene*

This chapter is based upon interviews with Benjamin Bradlee, Floyd Boring, and Rex Scouten, as well as articles in *Time*, November 13, 1950; and *The Washington Post*, "Slug Creases Tunic of Police Pvt. in Gunplay," November 2, 1950. The authors also reviewed photographs published in various newspapers at the time. The Drew Pearson column referred to in this chapter was published in *The Washington Post*, April 13, 1952.

40: *Inside the Soccer Shoe*

This chapter is based upon FBI files and upon records obtained from the archives of the Fundación Luis Muñoz Marín. The authors also consulted *La Insurrección Nacionalista en Puerto Rico 1950*, by Miñi Seijo Bruno. The *Life* magazine article referred to in this chapter was published November 13, 1950. The quotation from Luis Muñoz Marín is from his autobiography, *Memorias*.

41: *Who Shot Oscar?*

This chapter contains the authors' deductions based upon witness interviews and statements, trial testimony, and an FBI report on the bullets obtained at the scene.

42: *The Roundup*

The authors obtained much of the information for this chapter from the book *In Crime's Way: A Generation of U.S. Secret Service Adventures*, by Carmine J. Motto. Additional information was obtained from interviews with Carmen Zoraida Collazo, from the files of the Fundación Luis Muñoz Marín in Puerto Rico, from FBI documents, and from newspaper accounts at the time, including articles published in the *New York Times*, November 2, 1950, November 28, 1950, and December 3, 1950. The authors also consulted "A History of Puerto Rican Radical Nationalism, 1920–1965," a doctoral dissertation by Jaime Ramírez-Barbot.

43: Taps

Information for this chapter was obtained from articles published at the time in various newspapers, including the *New York Times,* as well as interviews with Jane Miller.

44: Oscar on Trial

Information for this chapter came from the Oscar Collazo trial transcript, FBI and Secret Service documents, a November 2, 1950, article in the *Washington Post,* and various newspaper accounts at the time of the trial.

45: Deep Conspiracy

Information for this chapter was obtained from interviews with Angelina Torresola and Heriberto Marín Torres, as well as FBI and Secret Service documents. The authors also relied upon a master's thesis, "The 1950 Nationalist Revolt in Puerto Rico," by Esteban Jiménez, written in the fall of 1997 (the quotations are from pp. 68, 71–72).

46: Cressie Does Her Duty

This chapter was based upon newspaper articles of the time, including a January 13, 1950, article in *El Mundo,* and interviews with Jane Miller, daughter of Cressie Coffelt.

47: Oscar Speaks

This chapter is based upon an interview with Rosa Meneses Albizu Campos, as well as on records from the archives of the Fundación Luis Muñoz Marín in Puerto Rico.

48: - - R - I - -

The authors obtained information for this chapter from records of the Truman Library, newspaper accounts of the time, interviews with Joseph King, Roy Birdzell, Ruth Birdzell, and Wilma Erwin, relatives of Donald Birdzell, as well as various family documents. Additional information was obtained from Lewis C. Merletti, former director of the Secret Service. Ballistic information on the .357 Sig comes from *Stopping Power: A Practical Analysis of the Latest Handgun Ammunition,* by Evan Marshall and Edwin Sanow.

BIBLIOGRAPHY

Printed Sources

Acosta, Ivonne. *La Palabra Como Delito: Los Discursos por Los que Condenaron a Pedro Albizu Campos, 1948–1950.* Sections translated by Regina Jacqueline Galasso at the request of the authors. San Juan, PR: Editorial Cultural, 2000.

Aponte Vázquez, Pedro I. "Did Rhoads Kill Albizu," *Claridad,* January 14–20, 1983.

———. *Pedro Albizu Campos: Su Persecución por el F.B.I.* Sections translated by Regina Jacqueline Galasso at the request of the authors. San Juan, PR: Publicaciones René, 1991.

———. *The Unsolved Case of Dr. Cornelius P. Rhoads: An Indictment.* San Juan, PR: Publicaciones René, 2005.

Arce de Vázquez, Margot, et al. (eds.). *Pedro Albizu Campos, Reflexiones Sobre Su Vida y Su Obra.* Sections translated by Regina Jacqueline Galasso at the request of the authors. Río Piedras, PR: Editorial Marién, 1991.

Artwohl, Alexis, and Loren W. Christensen. *Deadly Force Encounters: What Cops Need to Know to Mentally and Physically Prepare for and Survive a Gunfight.* Boulder: Paladin Press, 1997.

Austin, Dolores Stockton Helffrich. "Albizu Campos and the Development of a Nationalist Ideology, 1922–1932." Master's thesis, University of Wisconsin, 1983.

Barkley, Alben W. *That Reminds Me—.* Garden City: Doubleday, 1954.

Baughman, U. E., with Leonard Wallace Robinson. *Secret Service Chief.* New York: Harper & Row, 1961.

Bender, Lynn-Darrell (ed.). *The American Presence in Puerto Rico.* Hato Rey, PR: Publicaciones Puertorriqueñas, 1998.

Berner, Brad K. *The Spanish-American War: A Historical Dictionary: Historical Dictionaries of War, Revolution, and Civil Unrest.* No. 8. Lanham, MD: Scarecrow Press, 1998.

Bernier-Grand, Carmen T. *Poet and Politician of Puerto Rico: Don Luis Muñoz Marín*. New York: Orchard Books, 1995.

Bhana, Surendra. "The Development of Puerto Rican Autonomy Under the Truman Administration, 1945–1952." Dissertation, Graduate School of the University of Kansas, nd.

———. *The United States and the Development of the Puerto Rican Status Question, 1936–1968*. Lawrence: University Press of Kansas, 1975.

Bowen, Walter S., and Harry Edward Neal. *The United States Secret Service*. Philadelphia: Chilton, 1960.

Burnett, Christina Duffy, and Burke Marshall (eds.). *Foreign in a Domestic Sense: Puerto Rico, American Expansion, and the Constitution*. Durham: Duke University Press, 2001.

Carrión, Juan Manuel, Teresa C. Gracia Ruiz, and Carlos Rodríguez Fraticelli. *La Nación Puertorriqueña: Ensayos en Torno a Pedro Albizu Campos*. Sections translated by Regina Jacqueline Galasso at the request of the authors. San Juan, PR: Editorial de la Universidad de Puerto Rico, 1993.

Clark, Victor S., et al. (eds.). *Porto Rico and Its Problems*. Washington: Brookings Institution, 1930. Reprint edition, New York: Arno Press, 1975.

Clarke, James W. *American Assassins: The Darker Side of Politics*. Princeton: Princeton University Press, 1982.

Claster, Daniel S. *Bad Guys and Good Guys: Moral Polarization and Crime. Contributions in Criminology and Penology*, No. 36. Westport, CT: Greenwood Press, 1992.

Collazo, Carmen Zoraida. *Oscar Collazo Prisionero 70495*. Sections translated by Regina Jacqueline Galasso at the request of the authors. Chicago: Editorial Coquí, 1976.

Collazo Cortez, Lydia. *Memorias de Rosa Collazo / recopilado por Lydia Collazo Cortez*. Sections translated by Regina Jacqueline Galasso at the request of the authors. [Puerto Rico: s.n.], 1993.

Dávila, Arlene M. *Sponsored Identities: Cultural Politics in Puerto Rico*. Philadelphia: Temple University Press, 1997.

Davis, Aarron. *The Luger Handbook*. Iola, WI: Krause Publications, 1997.

Dietz, James L. *Economic History of Puerto Rico: Institutional Change and Capitalist Development*. Princeton: Princeton University Press, 1986.

Donovan, Robert J. "Annals of Crime: A Demonstration at Blair House." *The New Yorker*, July 19, 1952.

———. *The Assassins*. New York: Harper & Brothers, 1955.

———. *Tumultuous Years: The Presidency of Harry S. Truman, 1949–1953*. New York: W. W. Norton, 1982.

Dorman, Michael. *The Secret Service Story.* New York: Dell, 1967.

Duany, Jorge. *The Puerto Rican Nation on the Move: Identities on the Island and in the United States.* Chapel Hill: University of North Carolina Press, 2002.

Federal Writers Project, with an introduction by William H. Whyte. *The WPA Guide to New York City.* New York: New Press, 1992.

Fernández, Ronald. *The Disenchanted Island: Puerto Rico and the United States in the Twentieth Century.* Westport, CT: Praeger, 1996.

———. *Prisoners of Colonialism: The Struggle for Justice in Puerto Rico.* Monroe, ME: Common Courage Press, 1994.

Ferrao, Luis Angel. *Pedro Albizu Campos y el Nacionalismo Puertorriqueño.* Sections translated by Regina Jacqueline Galasso at the request of the authors. Editorial Cultural, 1990.

Ferrell, Robert H. *Harry S. Truman: A Life.* Columbia: University of Missouri Press, 1994.

Ferrell, Robert H. (ed.). *The Autobiography of Harry S. Truman.* Columbia: University of Missouri Press, 2002.

Fields, Alonzo. *My 24 Years in the White House.* New York: Coward-McCann, 1961.

Fogle, Jeanne. *Proximity to Power: Neighbors to the Presidents Near Lafayette Square.* Washington, D.C.: Tour de Force Publications, 1999.

Gangarosa, Gene, Jr. *The Walther Handgun Story.* Wayne, NJ: Stoeger, 1999.

Goodsell, Charles T. *Administration of a Revolution.* Cambridge: Harvard University Press, 1965.

Hacket, William H. *The Nationalist Party.* (For the Committee on Interior and Insular Affairs) Washington, D.C.: U.S. Government Printing Office, 1951.

Hamby, Alonzo L. *Man of the People: A Life of Harry S. Truman.* New York: Oxford University Press, 1995.

Hastings, Max. *The Korean War.* New York: Simon & Schuster, 1987.

Hechler, Ken. *Working with Truman: A Personal Memoir of the White House Years.* Columbia: University of Missouri Press, 1982.

Helfeld, David M. *Discrimination for Political Beliefs and Associations.* Revista del Colegio de Abogados de Puerto Rico, November 1964.

Hersey, John, with introduction by Robert A. Dahl. *Aspects of the Presidency.* New Haven: Ticknor & Fields, 1980.

Hoffer, Eric. *The True Believer: Thoughts on the Nature of Mass Movements.* New York: Perennial Classics, 2002.

Hogg, Ian Victor. *German Handguns: The Complete Book of the Pistols and Revolvers of Germany, 1869 to the Present.* London: Greenhill, 2001.

Hornik, Michael Sam. "Nationalist Sentiment in Puerto Rico from the American Invasion Until the Foundation of the *Partido Nacionalista, 1898–1922.*" Dissertation, State University of New York at Buffalo, 1972.

Iglesias, César Andreu (ed.). *Memoirs of Bernardo Vega: A Contribution to the History of the Puerto Rican Community in New York.* Translated by Juan Flores. New York: Monthly Review Press, 1984.

Jayuya, Tierra de Altura. Puerto Rico: Fundación Puertorriqueña Humanidades.

Jiménez de Wagenheim, Olga. *Puerto Rico's Revolt for Independence: El Grito de Lares.* Boulder: Westview Press, 1985.

Kaiser, Frederick M. "Presidential Assassinations and Assaults: Characteristics and Impact on Protective Procedures." *Presidential Studies Quarterly.*

Keegan, John. *The Face of Battle.* New York: Vintage, 1977.

Kirkendall, Richard S. (ed.). *The Harry S. Truman Encyclopedia.* Boston: G. K. Hall, 1989.

Kirkham, James F., Sheldon G. Levy, and William J. Crotty. *Assassination and Political Violence: A Report to the National Commission on the Causes and Prevention of Violence.* Vol. 8. Washington, D.C.: U.S. Government Printing Office, 1969.

Klinger, David. *Into the Kill Zone: A Cop's Eye View of Deadly Force.* San Francisco: Jossey-Bass, 2004.

Kuhn, Ferdinand. *The Story of the Secret Service.* New York: Random House, 1957.

Kuhnhausen, Jerry. *The Colt Double Action Revolvers: A Shop Manual.* Vol. 1. Edited by Noel Kuhnhausen. McCall, ID: VSP Publishers, 1988.

Kurlansky, Mark. *The Basque History of the World.* New York: Penguin, 1999.

Lewis, Gordon K. *Puerto Rico: Freedom and Power in the Caribbean.* New York: Monthly Review Press, 1963.

Libbey, James K. *Dear Alben: Mr. Barkley of Kentucky.* Lexington: University Press of Kentucky, 1979.

Liebling, A. J. *Mollie & Other War Pieces.* New York: Schocken Books, 1964.

López, Alfredo. *The Puerto Rican Papers: Notes on the Re-Emergence of a Nation.* Indianapolis: Bobbs-Merrill, 1973.

Maldonado, A. W. *Teodoro Moscoso and Puerto Rico's Operation Bootstrap.* Gainesville: University Press of Florida, 1997.

Maldonado-Denis, Manuel. *La Conciencia Nacional Puertorriqueña por Pedro Albizu Campos.* Sections translated by Regina Jacqueline Galasso at the request of the authors. San Juan, PR: Ediciones Compromiso, 1984.

———. *Puerto Rico: A Socio-Historic Interpretation.* Translated by Elena Vialo. New York: Random House, 1972.

Marín Torres, Heriberto. *Eran Ellos*. Sections translated by Regina Jacqueline Galasso at the request of the authors. Río Piedras, PR: Ediciones Ciba, 3rd edition, 2000.

Marqués, René. *The Docile Puerto Rican*. Philadelphia: Temple University Press, 1976.

Marshall, Evan, and Edwin Sanow. *Stopping Power: A Practical Analysis of the Latest Handgun Ammunition*. Boulder, CO: Paladin, 2001.

Mathews, Thomas. *Puerto Rican Politics and the New Deal*. Gainesville: University of Florida Press, 1960.

McCarthy, Dennis V. N., with Philip W. Smith. *Protecting the President: The Inside Story of a Secret Service Agent*. New York: William Morrow, 1985.

McCullough, David. *Truman*. New York: Simon & Schuster, 1992.

Melanson, Philip H., with Peter F. Stevens. *The Secret Service: The Hidden History of an Enigmatic Agency*. New York: Carroll & Graf, 2002.

Meneses de Albizu Campos, Laura. *Albizu Campos y la Independencia de Puerto Rico*. Sections translated by Regina Jacqueline Galasso at the request of the authors. San Juan, PR: 1961.

Morales-Carrión, Arturo. *Puerto Rico: A Political and Cultural History*. New York: W. W. Norton, 1983.

———. *Puerto Rico and the Non Hispanic Caribbean: A Study in the Decline of Spanish Exclusivism*. Río Piedras, PR: University of Puerto Rico, 1971.

Moraza Ortiz, Manuel E. *La Masacre de Ponce*. Sections translated by Regina Jacqueline Galasso at the request of the authors. Hato Rey, PR: Publicaciones Puertorriqueñas, 2001.

Morris, Edmund. *The Rise of Theodore Roosevelt*. New York: Modern Library, 2001.

Morris, Nancy. *Puerto Rico: Culture, Politics, and Identity*. Westport, CT: Praeger, 1995.

Motto, Carmine J. *In Crime's Way: A Generation of U.S. Secret Service Adventures*. Boca Raton: CRC Press, 2000.

Muñoz Marín, Luis. *Memorias: Luis Muñoz Marín: Autobiografía Pública, 1940–1952*. Sections translated by Joaquín Sánchez and Johnnie Benningfield II at the request of the authors. San Juan, PR: Fundación Luis Muñoz Marín, 2nd edition, 2003.

Neal, Harry Edward. *The Secret Service in Action*. New York: Elsevier/Nelson Books, 1980.

Neelley, Ewing Edward, Jr. "Alben W. Barkley: The Image of the Southern Political Orator." Doctoral thesis, University of Illinois at Urbana-Champaign, 1987.

Negrón-Muntaner, Frances, and Ramón Grosfoguel (eds.). *Puerto Rican Jam: Rethinking Colonialism and Nationalism.* Minneapolis: University of Minnesota Press, 1997.

Nonte, Major George C. *The Walther P-38 Pistol.* El Dorado, AR: Desert Publications, 1975.

O'Toole, G. J. A. *The Spanish War: An American Epic—1898.* New York: W. W. Norton, 1984.

Pentz, William C. *The City of DuBois.* Press of Gray Printing Co., 1932.

Pérez, Louis A., Jr. *The War of 1898: The United States and Cuba in History and Historiography.* Chapel Hill: University of North Carolina Press, 1998.

Picó, Fernando. *Puerto Rico 1898: The War After the War.* Princeton: Markus Wiener, 2004.

"Puerto Rico Revolt Endangers Truman." *Life,* November 13, 1950.

Ramírez-Barbot, Jaime. "A History of Puerto Rican Radical Nationalism, 1920–1965." Doctoral dissertation, Ohio State University, 1973.

Ramírez Lavandero, Marcos (ed.). *Documents on the Constitutional Relationship of Puerto Rico and the United States.* Washington, D.C.: Puerto Rico Federal Affairs Administration, 3rd edition, 1988.

Report of the Commission of Inquiry on Civil Rights in Puerto Rico (Hays Commission Report). Princeton: Princeton University Library, 2002.

Ribes Tovar, Federico. *Albizu Campos: Puerto Rican Revolutionary.* New York: Plus Ultra Educational Publishers, 1971.

Rivera Ramos, Efrén. *The Legal Construction of Identity: The Judicial and Social Legacy of American Colonialism in Puerto Rico.* Washington, D.C.: American Psychological Association, 2001.

Roberts, Lydia J., and Rosa Luisa Stefani. *Patterns of Living in Puerto Rican Families.* Río Piedras, PR: University of Puerto Rico, 1949.

Rosado, Marisa. *Las Llamas de la Aurora, Acercamiento a una Biografía de Pedro Albizu Campos.* San Juan, Puerto Rico: [s.n.], 1992 (Santo Domingo, República Dominicana: Editora Corripio).

Roth, Mitchel P., "Oscar Collazo: Portrait of a Puerto Rican Nationalist and the Attempted Assassination of Harry S. Truman." Paper presented at a meeting of the American Society of Criminology in San Francisco, November 2000.

Sánchez Korrol, Virginia E. *From Colonia to Community: The History of Puerto Ricans in New York City, 1917–1948.* Westport: Greenwood Press, 1983.

Scarano, Francisco A. *Puerto Rico: Cinco Siglos de Historia.* Sections translated by Joaquín Sánchez and Johnnie Benningfield II at the request of the authors. Mexico: McGraw-Hill, 2000.

Seale, William. *The President's House: A History*. Vols. 1 and 2. Washington, D.C.: White House Historical Association with the cooperation of the National Geographic Society, 1986.

Seijo Bruno, Miñi. *La Insurrección Nacionalista en Puerto Rico 1950*. Sections translated by Regina Jacqueline Galasso at the request of the authors. Río Piedras, PR: Editorial Edil, 1989.

Silén, Juan Angel. *Historia de la Nación Puertorriqueña*. Sections translated by Regina Jacqueline Galasso at the request of the authors. Río Piedras, PR: Editorial Edil, 1973.

———. *Pedro Albizu Campos*. Sections translated by Regina Jacqueline Galasso at the request of the author. Río Piedras, PR: Editorial Antillana, 1976.

———. *We, the Puerto Rican People: A Story of Oppression and Resistance*. New York: Monthly Review Press, 1971.

Smith, Elbert B. *Francis Preston Blair*. New York: Free Press, 1980.

Smith, Kenneth R., Jr. "The Truman Assassination Attempt in the American Consciousness." Doctoral thesis, Central Connecticut State University, 2003.

Status of Puerto Rico: Selected Background Studies Prepared for the United States–Puerto Rico Commission on the Status of Puerto Rico. Washington, D.C., 1966. Reprint edition, New York: Arno Press, 1975.

Steinberg, Alfred. *The Man from Missouri: The Life and Times of Harry S. Truman*. New York: G. P. Putnam's Sons, 1962.

Stephens, Jean Marie. "The Attempt to Assassinate President Truman." Master's thesis, St. Louis University, 1969.

Stevens-Arroyo, Antonio M. "Catholicism As Civilization: Contemporary Reflections on the Political Philosophy of Pedro Albizu Campos." Seminar paper, Brooklyn College, City University of New York, 1992.

———. "The Political Philosophy of Pedro Albizu Campos." Master's thesis, New York University, 1975.

———. *The Political Philosophy of Pedro Albizu Campos: Its Theory and Practice*. Occasional Papers No. 13. New York University, 1974.

Stueck, William. *Rethinking the Korean War: A New Diplomatic and Strategic History*. Princeton: Princeton University Press, 2002.

Templeman, Eleanor Lee. *The Blair-Lee House: Guest House of the President*. McLean, VA: EPM Publications, 1980.

Thomas, Hugh. *Rivers of Gold: The Rise of the Spanish Empire, from Columbus to Magellan*. New York: Random House, 2003.

Thomas, Piri. *Down These Mean Streets*. New York: Knopf, 1967.

Torres, Benjamín. *Pedro Albizu Campos: Obras Escogidas, 1923–1936, Tomo IV.* Sections translated by Regina Jacqueline Galasso at the request of the authors. Mexico: Editorial Claves Latinoamericanas, 1987.

Trask, David F. *The War with Spain in 1898.* Lincoln: University of Nebraska Press, 1996.

Trías Monge, José. *Puerto Rico: The Trials of the Oldest Colony in the World.* New Haven: Yale University Press, 1997.

Truman, Harry S. *Mr. Citizen.* New York: Bernard Geis, 1960.

Truman, Margaret. *Bess W. Truman.* New York: Macmillan, 1986.

Vázquez Medina, Raúl. *Verdadera Historia de la Masacre de Ponce.* Sections translated by Regina Jacqueline Galasso at the request of the authors. Ponce, PR: Instituto de Cultura Puertorriqueña, 2001.

Wagenheim, Kal, and Olga Jiménez de Wagenheim (eds.). *The Puerto Ricans: A Documentary History.* Princeton: Markus Wiener, 2002.

Walter, John. *The Luger Story: The Standard History of the World's Most Famous Handgun.* London: Greenhill, 2001.

Ward, Andrew. *Our Bones Are Scattered: The Cawnpore Massacres and the Indian Mutiny of 1857.* New York: Henry Holt, 1996.

White, Trumbull. *Puerto Rico and Its People.* New York: Frederick A. Stokes, 1938.

Ybarra, Michael J. *Washington Gone Crazy: Senator Pat McCarran and the Great American Communist Hunt.* Hanover, NH: Steerforth Press, 2004.

Youngblood, Rufus W. *20 Years in the Secret Service: My Life with Five Presidents.* New York: Simon & Schuster, 1973.

Zavala, Iris M., and Rafael Rodríguez (eds.). *The Intellectual Roots of Independence: An Anthology of Puerto Rican Political Essays.* New York: Monthly Review Press, 1980.

Zimmermann, Warren. *First Great Triumph: How Five Americans Made Their Country a World Power.* New York: Farrar, Straus & Giroux, 2002.

Audio/Visual

Reclamando Patria: Entrevista con Oscar Collazo, Rafael Cancel Miranda e Irvin Flores. Center for Latin and Caribbean Studies, Video, 1980.

The Secret Service: 1865 to the Present, the Inside Story. Vols. 1 and 2. All-American Television and Quorum Communications and A&E Television Networks, Video, 1995.

The Truman Tapes: In His Own Voice. HarperCollins, Audiotapes, 1997.

Truman, The American Experience. Turner Home Entertainment, Video, 1987.

Truman, The Presidents Collection. Turner Home Entertainment, Video, 1997.

Interviews and Oral Histories

Rosa Meneses Albizu Campos, interview by the authors, September 2004.

Miguel Eduardo Bernier Siman, sworn statement taken by José C. Aponte (special government prosecutor) in Ponce, Puerto Rico, January 26, 1951. Fundación Luís Muñoz Marín. Translated by Johnnie Benningfield II at the request of the authors.

Roy Birdzell, interview by the authors, 2005.

Ruth Birdzell, interview by the authors, 2005.

Ed Boring, interview by the authors, April 1, 2004.

Floyd M. Boring (U.S. Secret Service agent assigned to the White House, 1944–67), oral history interview by Niel M. Johnson in Temple Hills, MO, September 21, 1988, and interviews by the authors, 2004 and 2005.

Manuel Bernardo Caballer Rodríguez, sworn statement taken by José C. Aponte (special government prosecutor) in Ponce, Puerto Rico, January 22, 1951. Fundación Luís Muñoz Marín. Translated by Johnnie Benningfield II at the request of the authors.

Mike Chambers, interview by the authors, 2004.

Carmen Zoraida Collazo, interviews by the authors, 2004 and 2005.

Matthew J. Connelly (appointments secretary to the president, 1945–53), oral history interview by Jerry N. Hess in New York, NY, August 21, 1968.

Rafael Demetrio Cournier Santiago, sworn statement taken by José C. Aponte (special government prosecutor) in Ponce, Puerto Rico, January 21, 1951. Fundación Luís Muñoz Marín. Translated by Johnnie Benningfield II at the request of the authors.

Jim Downs, interview by the authors, 2004.

Wilma Erwin, interview by the authors, 2005.

Antonio González Marín, interview by the authors, September 22, 2004. Translated by Johnnie Benningfield II at the request of the authors.

Wallace H. Graham (President Truman's personal White House physician, 1945–53; Truman family doctor, 1945–82), oral history interview by Niel M. Johnson in Independence, MO, March 30, 1989.

Charles W. Higginbotham, interviews by the authors, July 12, 2004, and 2005.

Joseph F. King, interviews by the authors, March 11, 2004, and 2005.

Pedro Enrique Gerardino Ludesse Lluveras, sworn statement taken by José C. Aponte (special government prosecutor) in Ponce, Puerto Rico, January 26, 1951. Fundación Luís Muñoz Marín. Translated by Johnnie Benningfield II at the request of the authors.

Heriberto Marín Torres, interviews by the author, 2004 and 2005. Interpreted and translated by Johnnie Benningfield II at the request of the authors.

Alejandro Medina Rodríguez, sworn statement taken by José C. Aponte (special government prosecutor) in Arecibo, Puerto Rico, January 22, 1951. Fundación Luís Muñoz Marín. Translated by Johnnie Benningfield II at the request of the authors.

Jane Miller, interviews by the authors, 2004–2005.

Greg Mroz, interviews by the authors, 2004.

Vincent Mroz, interviews by the authors, 2004 and 2005.

Josephine Richer and Frances Spencer, interview by the authors, April 1, 2004.

Dilia Rivera, interviews by the authors, April 12, 2004.

James J. Rowley (Secret Service agent in charge of White House detail during the Truman administration), oral history interview by Niel M. Johnson in Kensington, MD, September 20, 1988.

Pat Schaffer, interviews by the authors, 2004.

Rex Scouten, interviews by the authors, 2004 and 2005.

Elroy Sites, interview by the authors, June 1, 2004.

John W. Snyder (secretary of the treasury in the Truman administration, 1946–53), oral history interview by Jerry N. Hess in Washington, D.C., April 2, 1969.

William Vanderpool, interview by the authors, May 2005.

Annette Coffelt Wade, interview by the authors, 2004.

[Name withheld by the authors], interview by Mr. José A. Benítez (executive auxiliary for the government district attorney) at the Policía Insular police station, October 4, 1951. Fundación Luís Muñoz Marín. Translated by Johnnie Benningfield II at the request of the authors.

ACKNOWLEDGMENTS

This book could not have been possible without the assistance of many people who gave time, experience, passion, and in some cases painful memories to two bland interlocutors from different worlds. In recompense we only promised fairness and thoroughness; we hope we have lived up to those promises. We and we alone are responsible for the conclusions and interpretations, and they are blameless, and they should be thanked for their considerable efforts.

Of course the first two are the two living Secret Service veterans of that day at Blair. Floyd Boring welcomed us into his home from the start and sat patiently through what must have seemed an endless series of chats about the most mundane of matters. He was never the sort to make a big deal of any of this in the first place, and his wife, Ruth, made even less of a big deal over it, but they were warm and generous. Sadly, Ruth died early in 2005.

Vince Mroz was equally patient, equally friendly, equally open. On close to half a dozen occasions he stood still for our inquiries, as did his wife, Shirley. He was even available for late night phone checks on obscure facts or lost data.

Jane Miller, Les Coffelt's stepdaughter, had the most painful memories—hers are of loss and grief—but again she shared with us willingly her thoughts of what had to be one of the worst days of her life. She also helped us reconstruct the life that Les and Cressie had built for themselves in the little house on North Wayne Street in Arlington, and she let us dig through her sizable collection of mementos of her stepfather's life. Her daughter, Donna Tobin, in whose home the interviews took place, was engaged as well in our quest. Members of the Masonic Lodge to which Les was so devoted—especially the secretary, Dean Clatterbuck—generously shared information about the organization and Les's involvement.

Joseph King, one of Don Birdzell's nephews, recalled his uncle's presence so vividly that one felt that the fourth person in the room was old Don himself, rollicking with laughter. Again, he let us glimpse in intimate detail a figure who'd previously been just a name in a few books and articles, and we hope we have brought Don to life, with his Luckies, his Buicks, and his endless cups of Black Magic. Roy Birdzell, Ruth Birdzell, and Wilma Erwin, Don's living siblings, were also helpful in recollecting their brother.

Rex Scouten, a Secret Service agent who'd been on duty that day in the White House and who knew our heroes well, graciously helped us re-create the scene outside Blair in the immediate aftermath of the event and gave us insights into the personalities of the agents and officers involved. We reached Mr. Scouten through the influence of architectural historian William Seale, who wrote *The President's House,* and who also was instrumental in giving us a perspective not only on the buildings he knows so well but on the personnel who inhabit them during working hours.

White House policeman (and later chief of the White House Police) Charles Higginbotham also shared his memories of the time and place and the men he knew. He too got to the scene immediately; as important, he'd stood or sat on duty in the guard posts ringing Blair House and he knew and shared details of the culture of the White House Police in 1950. He was extremely generous with time and candid in his assessments.

A number of the children or relatives of the other agents or officers involved pitched in. Michael Stout and Stewart Stout III remembered their father for us, as did Jim Downs. Annette Coffelt Wade talked freely with us about her Uncle Les and Aunt Cressie. Pat Schaffer and Mike Chambers, two of Colonel Justice Marion Chambers's children, re-created for us the Rose Garden scene when their father received the Congressional Medal of Honor from President Truman. Ivo Facchine, of the DuBois Historical Society, helped us understand that Pennsylvania city. Sarah Mauck, president of the Strasburg Historical Society, generously shared her time introducing us to the world in which Les Coffelt grew up and to people who knew him.

Then, graciously, Elroy Sites recalled for us his adventures that day, when he went from apprentice electrician to volunteer emergency medical technician in 38.5 seconds; if nobody has ever thanked him for his courage then, please let us do it now.

Michael Sampson, the Secret Service archivist, worked hard at finding the documentation that the two bland strangers required. We seemed to hit it off with Mike from the start, and his attention to us was always full-bore and professional. He invited us to see what he had and he helped us see what we had to get. In the Secret Service we also had good relationships with a series of agents in charge of public information duties who understood instinctively that we had a great story to tell and should be helped to tell it.

Lewis Curtis, of the Web site Cartridgecollectors.com, sent us a long memo detailing the vagaries of 9mm steel-case ammunition, enabling us to make sense of the cartridges Griselio and Oscar fired that day; Vince Mroz's son Greg, a retired Secret Service agent himself, discussed his agency's duty rounds of the 1950s with us, for the other side of that part of the story.

A note should be made of the support we received from good friend Gary Goldberg. Gary, a hail-fellow-well-met of mysterious connections and networking skills, turned out to have more contacts in the service by far than Hunter, the nominal Washington journalist; it was in fact Gary who managed to put us together with Deputy Assistant Director James F. Tomsheck, Office of Government and Public Affairs, to get this whole damn ball rolling in the first place. Later, he stage-managed an introduction to Lewis C. Merletti, a former Secret Service chief, whose influence was helpful.

Randy Bumgardner, the assistant manager of Blair House, took us on a tour of that building and seeing it up close from the inside was so helpful in imagining what went on there that day; he also read the appropriate parts of the manuscript and caught a number of potentially embarrassing errors, as did Candace Shireman, associate curator at Blair House.

The same is true of Randy Sowell and Elizabeth Safly, archivists at the Truman Library in Independence, who indefatigably hunted out answers to our dozens of questions and provided interviews and fact sheets and archived materials. Thanks to Mark Beveridge of the Truman Museum, we were able to examine—carefully and not with our own hands—Griselio's, Oscar's, and Floyd's handguns, during which time we got the close-up gun photos in this book (from photographer Phil Licata). Just as important, however, was the vivid charge that such relics invariably carry with them, a provocation to the imagination and a fuel to the spirit: there they were, the things themselves, as nondescript as the thousands of other service weapons of the era and yet abuzz with the charisma of history.

In Puerto Rico (Bainbridge went five times, Hunter once) we were treated well and found people willing to speak openly of what were no doubt painful memories, about which they had ambivalent feelings.

Nelson Canals, our first translator and a well-known progressive gadfly who seems to know everybody, was our facilitator on early trips, setting up interviews, then translating them for us. We met Nelson through Babs and Miguel Vilar. Babs is Bainbridge's cousin, her husband a retired Episcopal minister with connections in the progressive community in Puerto Rico and a pure devotion to his island nation. Both proved extremely valuable to us as general counselors on matters of Puerto Rican culture and history.

Later Johnnie Benningfield II came aboard for his language skills. A professional court translator with superb real-time talents, he also gave not only his knowledge and ability, but something substantially more: his spirit, which infused the project, and ability to develop information as well as any reporter. Joaquín Sánchez of San Juan also used his considerable linguistic skills in translating with precision several publications in Spanish. Finally, the Johns Hopkins scholar Regina Jacqueline Galasso did a great deal of textual translation for us, all of it first-rate, as well as helped us cut through at least some of the mysteries of a culture not our own.

In the Nationalist community, we would like to think we made friends, or at least, as we struggled to be fair and to tell this story not only from the North American but also from the Puerto Rican point of view, didn't make enemies.

Oscar Collazo's daughter, Carmen Zoraida Collazo, wanted her father's story told, and sat still for far too many interviews, going back over her memories and trying to re-create what must have been an extraordinarily bad day for her. She never flinched; she believed in the project to such an extent that she became another facilitator, arranging for introductions within the community that otherwise we might not have gotten.

Chief among these was Rosa Meneses Albizu Campos, Don Pedro's granddaughter and head of the Nationalist Party in its later, nonviolent configuration. She shared with us her insights and memories as well as her recollection of the only interview with Oscar in which he acknowledged the deeper conspiracy.

Then there was Heriberto Marín Torres, a fighter at Jayuya with Elio Torresola (seven years' jail time) and childhood friend of Griselio's, as well as a friend in New York in the period leading up to the assassination attempt. He's a terrific—even noble—fellow and was generous with his time and memory. We hope that through his eyes and the eyes of our next acknowledgee that Griselio, the mystery man in the affair, has been brought to some kind of life.

That acknowledgee is Griselio's surviving sister, Angelina. Again, the generosity is heartwarming: she took us, norteamericanos, one tall and fair, one fat and bald, into her home and warmly recalled her brother's life, times, and personality. If the pall of tragedy overhung the conversation, we were not aware of it. She was a great and friendly interview. René Torres Platet, her cousin, was a facilitator of these interviews, as was Nelson Canals.

Rafael Cancel Miranda, poet, patriot, and one of the shooters at the U.S. Congress in 1954, recalled Don Pedro's operating procedures for us in an interview in his home in Mayagüez, Puerto Rico.

Another veteran of the 1950 revolution, Antonio González Marín, shared memories.

Back in America, Griselio's widow, Dilia Rivera, spoke to us twice in her home in a Northeast state and once in Puerto Rico, in a house she owns a short walk from the river where Griselio swam as a boy. Again, many of her memories are not happy, but heroically she confronted them for our edification.

In the academic world we benefited from the expertise and knowledge of many. First, at the University of Puerto Rico, Roberto De León González opened many doors and had many suggestions, all of them wise. The staff at the Fundación Luis Muñoz Marín were extremely helpful in pointing out useful documents in their archives. Then the scholars at Centro de Estudios Puertorriqueños at Hunter College in New York City, repository of a vast collection of resources on Puerto Rico, were generous in sharing a host of documents, including FBI files on Pedro Albizu Campos, which had been obtained through Freedom of Information Act requests. Ramón Bosque Pérez was particularly helpful, as were Félix V. Matos Rodríguez, Pedro Juan Hernández, Nélida Pérez, and Jorge Matos.

Then, Princeton scholar Christina Duffy Burnett made some acute and helpful comments on the manuscript. Dr. William S. Queale, Bainbridge's personal physician, who frequently reviews medical examiners' reports to provide opinions about causes of death, studied testimony and documents describing Leslie Coffelt's wounds and helped us understand how he died. Finally, Mitchel Roth of the College of Criminal Justice at Sam Houston State University in Huntsville, Texas, allowed us to use his paper "Oscar Collazo: Portrait of a Puerto Rican Nationalist and the Attempted Assassination of Harry S. Truman," as well as the FBI files he had obtained via FOIA requests.

For our own FOIA actions, we relied on the guidance of Emilio Cividanes, Esq., of Washington, D.C., and through his advice we coaxed many heretofore unseen documents out of the gears of the bureaucracy.

On the administrative side, we were helped by part-time researcher Grant Huang, who actually ran the distance from Elroy Sites's ladder to Blair House to come up with the 38.5-seconds figure. Sally Harkay served as John Bainbridge's assistant as our research materials grew too voluminous for one man to manage. Without her, the piles of documentation that grew in his study would have become unmanageable and unusable. Dawn Tesar typed many of the interview transcripts with speed, precision, and enthusiasm, sometimes under great pressure. John's friends Neil Grauer and Kerry Caputo dissected early versions of the manuscript and offered good advice that was taken.

Stephen Hunter has many of the usual suspects to thank, and one new one. Valued friends Bob Lopez—he tragically died this year—and Lenne Miller gave insightful commentary early on, as did *Washington Post* colleague and nonfiction ace David Von Drehle, who once hired him and now is stuck with him as pal and hanger-on for the rest of his life. Also at the *Post*, the great Ben Bradlee shared his memories of the event. And the equally great Bob Woodward gave Hunter a long and illuminating talking-to about the mysteries of the form he is master of, the nonfiction narrative.

Then there are the professionals. Both Esther Newberg, of ICM, and the great Michael Korda, of Simon & Schuster, got this book from the second it was pitched. They were willing to underwrite the experiment. Their wisdom and guidance have been important throughout. And David Rosenthal, Simon & Schuster's irrepressible publisher, pitched in with his usual acumen and enthusiasm. But at a certain point, the material had gotten too dense. It had acquired the shape of the Paramount mountain on Hunter's dining room table and to look upon it was to feel a soul-deep ache. Thus he called an old colleague at the *Baltimore Sun*, Alison Chaplin, and said what to him was the ugliest word in the English language: "index."

She said, "You know, I've always wanted to try my hand at that!"

And she did, fabulously, saving one author's efforts and making accessible again that which had disappeared under torrents of sloth and slop.

And of course Bainbridge and Hunter would both like to thank the women who got us through the past two years of frenzy. John's wife, Katherine, also an attorney, brought a meticulous mind and a first-rate editorial talent to bear on the project. Her steadiness and insight illuminated the project from start to finish. Her brilliance, endurance, and ability to see both the forest and all the trees—not to mention her devoted companionship—were indispensable to John.

Hunter's own wife-to-be, Jean Marbella, was her own usual Gibraltar, listening patiently to his rages of doubt and depression and more or less keeping him not only afloat but on course during the whole thing, even through a couple of late-book health crises.

Thanks to all of them!

INDEX

Acevedo, Roberto, 19, 32

Acheson, Dean, 60, 157, 158

Albizu Campos, Pedro:

  adoption of Catholicism by, 27–28

  army experience of, 26–27

  arrest vs. martyrdom of, 269–71, 284

  assassinations and, 16, 109, 122,
    125, 299–301, 310–11

  birth and family background of,
    23–25

  bodyguards of, 22, 23, 38–39, 93,
    211–12, 294, 307

  and conspiracy theory, 298–303,
    305–6

  death of, 323

  documents from, 13–14, 38, 39,
    218, 303, 305–7, 312

  early years of, 174, 175

  elections lost by, 29, 120–21

  Griselio as trusted apostle of, 15,
    34, 44, 110, 211–12, 214, 250,
    300–303, 311–12

  and Griselio in New York, 13–14,
    15, 214, 218, 301, 311

  and Griselio in Puerto Rico, 218,
    302, 305, 314

  and Griselio's commitment to the
    cause, 13–14, 15, 39, 110, 250,
    311–12

  at Harvard, 25–26, 27, 28

  influence of, 13, 14, 15, 21, 38, 110,
    115, 119–21, 125, 271, 273,
    294, 300–302, 312, 313–15

  as "Maximum Leader," El Maestro,
    or "The Old Man," 8, 315

  in New York, 14, 30, 123, 124–25,
    210, 296, 299

  as Oscar's inspiration and mentor,
    41, 118–19, 121, 125, 294,
    300–301

  outlaw period of, 29–31

  pardoned, 323

  physical appearance and personality
    of, 13, 23–25, 26, 28, 125, 209,
    271

  political development of, 28–29

  and Ponce massacre, 179–80

  in prison, 30, 120, 123–24, 125,
    174, 179, 210, 285, 299, 300, 323

  rage against U.S. by, 24, 26, 28, 29,
    91, 127, 171, 299

  revolution promoted by, 10, 13, 14,
    24, 29–31, 121, 125, 210, 214,
    298, 299–300

  and Rhoads letter, 198

  schooling of, 25, 175

  speeches of, 9–10, 118–19,
    299–300

Albizu Campos, Pedro (*continued*)
　surveillance of, 8–9, 210–11
　trapped in his home, 18, 21–23,
　　33–35, 36, 267–72
　wife of, 28, 121
　zealotry of, 24, 118–20, 179–80
Albizu Campos, Rosa Meneses,
　310–12
Albizu Romero, Alejandro "El Viz-
　caíno," 24
Alien and Sedition Acts (1798), 7
Alien Registration Act/Smith Act
　(1940), 213
Allen, Barbara E., 259
Allen, Bradley H., Jr., 56, 259
American Civil Liberties Union
　(ACLU), 175, 177, 179
anticommunism, 6–7, 157–58, 285
Aponte Vázquez, Pedro, 198
Arlington National Cemetery, 286
Army, U.S.:
　Albizu's experience in, 26–27
　in Puerto Rico, 171
　racism of, 26
Army Corps of Engineers, 89
assassins, 236–39
　Beauchamp and Rosado, 109, 123,
　　124
　Booth, 236, 238
　Bremer, 236, 237
　Byck, 236, 237
　Czolgosz, 75–76, 236, 237
　Fromme, 236, 237
　Guiteau, 236, 237, 238
　Hinckley, 236, 237
　Lawrence, 236, 237
　Moore, 236, 237, 238
　new suits bought by, 41, 45, 205
　Oswald, 41, 236, 237, 238
　rituals of, 41–42
　Schrank, 236, 237
　Sirhan, 236, 237, 238
　"Type One," 238–39

　Zangara, 236
　see also Collazo, Oscar; Torresola,
　　Griselio
atomic bomb, 157
Ayers, Eben, 53

Baldoni, Luis, 196–98
Balge, Ken, 192
Barkley, Alben, 7, 242
Basques, zealotry of, 23
Baughman, U. E.:
　book by, 164
　at Coffelt's funeral, 287
　and conspiracy possibility, 306
　and gunfight, 163–65, 259, 265,
　　306
　and recruitment, 77–78
　and rings of defense, 164–65
　on Stout's action, 163–65
　and Truman's morning walks, 52
Beauchamp, Elias, 109, 123, 124
Behn, Jerry, 192
Benítez, José A., 313–16
Berley, George A., 293
Beverley, James R., 198
Birdzell, Donald, 83–85, 319–21
　after the gunfight, 252, 253, 273,
　　292, 324
　in the army, 136
　birth and early years of, 133–37
　Colt Official Police weapon of, 84,
　　318, 320
　death of, 324
　on duty, 66, 83–84, 106, 245
　and gunfight, 108, 129, 132, 137,
　　138–39, 153, 155, 181, 182,
　　185, 203, 226, 240, 245, 246,
　　249, 262, 263, 273, 274, 275,
　　295–96, 318
　and Helen, 83, 84, 134–35
　knee wounds of, 132, 137, 138–39,
　　226, 249, 273, 318
　in Metropolitan Police, 135

and the navy, 133–35, 136
physical appearance and personality
  of, 83, 84, 135
as trial witness, 292
in White House Police Force, 136,
  137
Birdzell, Helen Murphy, 83, 84,
  134–35, 259
Birdzell, Ivan, 136–37
Birdzell, Kenneth, 137
Birdzell, William Isaac and Iva May,
  133
Blair, Francis Preston, Sr., 89
Blair-Lee House:
  design of, 88
  events after gunfight, 262–64
  gunfight at, *see* gunfight
  history of, 88–89
  security details of, 80, 89–90,
    104–8, 111, 154, 155, 161, 162,
    164, 311, 317, 318
  staff in, 66, 160, 165, 225
  Truman living in, 6, 53, 60, 66–67,
    73, 88, 253
Bogart, Humphrey, 64
Booth, John Wilkes, 236, 238
Boring, Earl Cleveland, 144, 146
Boring, Floyd M. "Toad," 62–73, 161
  after the gunfight, 252, 253, 254,
    263, 264
  on duty, 64, 90, 106, 108, 143, 151,
    275
  early years of, 144–47
  family of, 52, 63, 243
  and football, 65, 141–44
  and gunfight, 129, 139–40, 151,
    152–55, 181, 182, 184–85, 193,
    203, 241, 243, 245–46, 247,
    263, 274–75, 276
  gun of, 64, 68–70, 94, 140,
    152–53, 154
  physical appearance and personality
    of, 62, 64–65, 143, 146, 150

previous lethal confrontations of,
  71–73
retirement of, 325
and Ruth, *see* Boring, Ruth Lehner
and Secret Service, 63, 64, 65–66
as senior officer, 74, 78, 79, 81, 275
in state police, 71, 147–48
as suit guy, 63–64
in target practice, 153
as trial witness, 292
and Truman's safety, 151, 264, 265
whistle swallowed by, 145–46
Boring, Frances Mary Murray, 144
Boring, Ruth Lehner, 150
  death of, 325
  marriage of Toad and, 62, 63, 64,
    65, 148–49
  as policeman's wife, 72, 243, 258,
    259
Borinquen, 5, 22, 170; *see also* Puerto
  Rico
Bradlee, Benjamin C., 260–62, 264
Bremer, Arthur, 236, 237
British East India Company, 27
bronchoscope, invention of, 146
Bruno, Miñi Seijo, 268, 270
Byck, Samuel, 236, 237

Campos, Juliana, 24, 25
Canales, Blanca:
  and Albizu, 115, 121, 209, 214
  family of, 207
  influence of, 13, 34, 115, 127,
    207–8, 209, 305
  in Jayuya, 22, 47, 115, 121, 209,
    211
  and Ponce Massacre, 180
  in prison, 285
Canales, Rosario, 207
Canals, Nelson, 37
Cancel Miranda, Rafael, 216, 301
Carrasquillo, Rafaela, 197
Carter, Jimmy, Oscar pardoned by, 323

Castle, William B., 195, 197, 198
Cates, C. B., 102
Central Intelligence Agency (CIA), and
	Korean War, 100
Cermak, Anton, 80, 236
Chambers, Marion, 101–3
Chiang Kai-shek, 156
China:
	communism in, 156, 157
	and Korean War, 159
Clarke, James, 238
Coast Guard, U.S., shooting range, 67
Coffelt, Cressie "Baby," 56–59
	child of, 59, 232–33
	death of, 324
	and Eastern Star, 56, 308
	later years of, 323–24
	and Les's death, 259, 286, 287, 308
	marriage of Les and, 54, 57, 233
	personality of, 57, 234
	Puerto Rico trip of, 308–9
Coffelt, Janie, 54–60, 233
	and Les's death, 259, 287–88, 324
	memories of Les, 56, 57, 58, 59,
		231, 232, 234
	personality of, 57
	wedding of, 58, 308
Coffelt, Leslie, 54–61, 228–35
	burial of, 286–88
	childhood of, 229–31
	death of, 223–24, 227, 235,
		247–48, 251, 252, 255–56, 259,
		266, 273, 285, 291, 292, 293,
		308
	on duty, 66, 90, 104–5, 248, 251
	family background of, 228–29, 230
	Griselio shot by, 250–51, 254–55,
		261, 318
	and gunfight, 155, 183, 204,
		223–24, 226, 248, 250–51,
		254–56, 261, 277
	and guns, 55–56, 94, 230–31,
		234–35, 250, 291

	marriage of, 54, 57, 233; *see also*
		Coffelt, Cressie
	as Mason, 56
	physical appearance and
		personality of, 54–55, 56, 84,
		231, 234
	as police officer, 232, 233
	and Secret Service, 231, 233
	and White House Police Force, 56,
		233
	and World War II, 234
Coffelt, Will and Effie, 229, 231
Collazo, Carmen Zoraida (daughter),
	113, 123, 126
	and Don Pedro, 124–25
	and Griselio, 127, 217
	and investigation, 281–84
Collazo, Oscar:
	after the gunfight, 253, 263, 273,
		280, 285
	Albizu as inspiration and mentor
		of, 41, 118–19, 121, 294,
		300–301
	and Albizu in New York, 14, 30,
		124–25, 296
	apartment of, 40–41, 123, 126,
		278–81
	birth and early years of, 113–15
	and Carmen (first wife), 122
	commitment to the cause, 15, 16,
		31, 39, 94, 110, 118–21, 127,
		171, 179–80, 238–39, 280, 290,
		293–94, 298, 311–12
	and conspiracy theory, 298,
		300–301, 307, 312
	daughter of, *see* Collazo, Carmen
		Zoraida
	death of, 323
	emigration to U.S., 115–16, 122
	family background of, 113, 170
	and gunfight, 108, 112, 128–32,
		138–39, 152–55, 181–83, 185,
		200–202, 203, 204, 205, 241,

244–45, 246, 249, 262, 263,
  274–77, 295–96, 297
gun purchased by, 16, 37–38,
  93–97, 257, 294, 301
at Harris Hotel, 47–49, 95, 98–99,
  123
immigrants helped by, 126
inexperience with weapons, 93–96,
  98–99, 110, 129–32, 139, 154
jobs of, 15, 41, 122–23, 125–26
memoirs of, 277
and Nationalist Party, 31, 36, 39,
  94, 120–22, 124–25, 127, 209,
  218, 284, 290, 294, 323
in New York, 14, 30, 117, 122, 123,
  124–25, 210, 217–18, 296
nom de guerre of, 48
pardoned, 323
physical appearance and personality
  of, 14, 15, 16, 38, 42, 44, 95, 98,
  110–11, 123, 126, 236, 238,
  284, 295, 316
planning the attack, 14–17, 38–39,
  49, 90–91, 111, 291, 298
and Ponce Massacre, 179–80
preparations by, 41–42, 109–12,
  311–12
in prison, 285, 323
and Rhoads letter, 199, 294
and Rosa, 16, 41, 44, 48, 123, 126
sightseeing in Washington, 86–91,
  289
stories told by, 38, 129–30,
  273–74, 277, 290, 293–97, 306,
  310–16
travel to Washington, 42, 46–49
trial of, 289–97
Collazo, Rosa Cortés:
  daughters of, 123
  and investigation, 279–80, 282,
    284
  and Oscar, 16, 41, 44, 48, 123, 126
Collazo Gago, Eduardo, 113

Colón, Orlando, 174
Colón Delgado, Oscar, 9
Columbus, Christopher, 5, 23, 170
Conde, José Luis, 177
Congress, U.S., 1954 assault on, 216,
  301
Cooper, Robert A., 124, 300
Correa, Juan, 284
Corretjer, Juan Antonio, 27
Cortelyou, George B., 76
Cortés Cordero, Juan, 284
Cuba, and Spanish rule, 172
Cullen, Matthew J., Jr., 292
Czolgosz, Leon, 75–76, 236, 237

Davidson, Joe:
  after the gunfight, 252, 253, 254,
    324
  Colt Official Police weapon of, 275
  death of, 324
  on duty, 66, 106, 108
  and gunfight, 129, 139, 140, 155,
    181, 184–85, 193, 203, 241,
    246, 247, 274, 275–76, 277,
    318
  Oscar shot by, 275–76
  as trial witness, 292
Dávila, Carmelo, 32
De Silva, Anthony (nom de guerre),
  48
Dewey, Thomas E., 156
Díaz Pacheco, Raimundo, 30, 94, 125,
  210
  and La Fortaleza attack, 18–20,
    31–32, 300
  as martyr to the cause, 32, 39, 285,
    307
Diego, José de, 118
Dill, Sir John, 80, 103, 265
Dillinger, John, 264
Dodge, Charles, 227, 252
Donovan, Robert, 113, 122, 194
Douglas, Paul, 11

Downs, Joe:
  after the gunfight, 273, 324
  background of, 224–25
  death of, 324
  on duty, 66, 106–7
  on grocery detail, 107, 164, 224,
    248
  and gunfight, 155, 183, 204,
    225–26, 248–49, 252, 263
  as trial witness, 293
Drake, Sir Francis, 21
DuBois, Pennsylvania, 144–45

Early, Jubal, 228
Eastman, Max, 116
Eden, Sir Anthony, 103
Eisenhower, Dwight D., 162, 187
Ellis, Joseph J., Jr., 293
Eran Ellos (Marín Torres), 44–45

Fay, George M., 289, 291, 295–97
Federal Bureau of Investigation (FBI):
  academic requirements of, 78
  Collazo file of, 127, 290
  and executive protection, 77, 290
  forensics reports of, 275, 293
  legends of, 255
  Nationalist Party reports by, 29–31,
    36, 214, 217, 271–72, 278,
    280–81
  post-gunfight investigation by,
    278–84, 290, 303, 306
  in Suniland gunfight, 200–201, 203
  surveillance of radicals by, 173,
    210–11, 238, 278, 290, 301
fight/flight response, 204
Figueroa Cordero, Andrés, 216
Florés Rodríguez, Irving, 216
fog of war, 204, 256, 264
Ford, Gerald, 236, 238
Francis, Hobart, 263
Franks, Sir Oliver, 103
Frenchy (USCG), 68, 73

Friml, Rudolf, 100
Fromme, Lynette Alice "Squeaky,"
    236, 237
Fuchs, Klaus, 6, 157
Fuller, Sam, 94

Gage, Lyman, 76
Gainer Corporation, 41, 125
Gaines, Helen, 259, 287
Garfield, James, 236
Gavounas, John, 289
Géigel Polanco, Vicente, 31
Goldsborough, T. Alan, 291, 294
Gonzales, Charles/Carlos (nom de
    guerre), 48, 214–15, 302
Gonzáles Cortea, Antonio, 174
Graham, Otto, 186–87, 190
Great Indian Mutiny, 27
Griffith, Clark, 56
Guiteau, Charles, 236, 237, 238
gunfight:
  alternate scenarios of, 128–29, 132,
    165, 254, 264
  auditory exclusion in, 154, 183,
    204, 264, 276, 319
  Birdzell hit, returning fire in, 132,
    137, 138–39, 153, 155, 181,
    182, 185, 226, 245, 246, 249,
    262, 273, 274, 275, 295–96, 318
  Coffelt shot and killed in, 223–24,
    226, 235, 247–48, 250–51, 273
  Coffelt's legendary shot in, 250–51,
    254–55, 261, 318
  conspiracy theory of, 16, 298–307,
    312
  and crime scene, 263–64
  Davidson shooting in, 140, 155,
    181, 203, 246, 274, 275–76, 318
  Downs hit in, 225–26, 248–49, 252
  duration of, 164–65, 203, 244, 254,
    265, 317
  end of, 252, 261, 263
  first actions of, 108, 112, 131

first shot failure in, 128, 129–32
fog of war in, 204, 256, 264
Griselio shooting, hit in, 155, 205,
 223, 224, 226, 247–48, 249,
 250, 251, 254, 261, 292–93
ineffectual firing in, 181–83, 203,
 274, 318
lessons learned from, 317–19
media stories about, 258–59,
 261–62, 263–64, 271, 273–74
Oscar shooting, hit in, 128,
 131–32, 138–39, 152–55,
 181–83, 200–202, 204, 244–45,
 246, 249, 262, 263, 274–77
Oscar's stories about, 273–74, 277,
 290, 295–97, 310–16
planning of, 12–17, 90–91
primal consciousness in, 154,
 244–51, 276, 319
second assault in, 203–5
Toad shooting in, 139–40, 152–55,
 181, 182, 203, 245–46, 263,
 274–75, 276
Truman as target in, 240–42, 246,
 254, 258, 261, 264–65, 274
unpredictable and illogical events
 in, 153–55, 200–202, 203, 204,
 244, 274, 318–19
Vince shooting in, 184–85, 247,
 274–75
Gunfight at the O.K. Corral, 203
guns:
 actuator of, 163
 Birdzell and, 84, 318, 320
 blast injury from, 291
 Coffelt and, 55–56, 94, 230–31,
 234–35, 250, 291
 Colt Official Police revolver, 55, 84,
 275, 318, 320
 Devil's paintbrush, 32
 double-action, 93, 140, 155, 275
 dry-snapping, 70
 grease guns, 18–19, 31

Griselio and, 37, 39, 91, 91–94, 98,
 211, 250, 256–57, 292, 301
ineffectual firing of, 181–83, 274,
 318
isosceles shooting position for, 205
lessons learned about, 318–19
locked in rack, 107, 162–63, 165,
 241, 247
Luger, 37, 39, 92–93, 94, 98, 211,
 256, 301
machine gun, 32
metal polishing of, 123
Mroz and, 79, 94, 185, 247, 256
9mm cartridge of, 91, 97
oiling of, 97
Oscar and, 16, 37–38, 91, 93–99,
 110, 129–32, 139, 154, 181,
 182, 200–202, 244–45, 246,
 257, 294, 295–97, 301
P.38, 37, 91–92, 93–94, 95–98,
 130, 139, 181, 257
realistic training in use of, 318–19
recoil of, 153, 154
reloading, 97, 152–53, 183, 200,
 201, 226, 318
of revolutionaries, 22, 31, 94,
 107–8, 211, 214–15, 271–72,
 301–2
revolvers, 68–70, 94, 95, 130
safety mechanism of, 96, 131
semiautomatic, 93, 95, 139, 154,
 318
shooting to kill, 226
SIG-Sauer semiautos, 318
single-action, 130
superior firepower, 32, 318
target practice with, 67–70,
 152–53, 317–19
Thompson submachine (tommy
 gun), 107–8, 162–63, 178, 247
Toad Boring and, 64, 68–70, 94,
 140, 152–53, 154
two-handed shooting, 226, 318

guns (*continued*)
  unpredictable results from,
    152–53, 274–77
  wadcutters, 153
Gzik, Martin, 188–89

Harrell, Jerome Blaine, 292
Harris Hotel, Washington, 47–49, 95,
    98–99, 123, 215, 302
Hays, Arthur Garfield, 179
H-bomb, 157
Helfeld, David, 214
Hemingway, Ernest, 116
Hernández Rivera, Gregorio, 18, 30,
    32–33, 310
Hersey, John, 50, 51, 53
Hinckley, John, 236, 237
Hiraldo Resto, Domingo, 19, 32
Hiss, Alger, 6, 157
Hoffer, Eric, 15, 41, 47
Holden, William, 79
Homiston, Robert M., 286
Hoover, Herbert, 233
Hoover, J. Edgar, 77, 107, 162, 255,
    278, 290
Hume, Paul, 6

Ignatius Loyola, 23
In Crime's Way (Motto), 279
Irizarry, Carlos, 115, 211

Jackson, Andrew, 89, 236
Jayuya, Puerto Rico, 22, 34, 47,
    114–15, 211, 307
Jesuits, formation of, 23
Jiménez, Esteban, 299
Jones Act, 172–73

Keegan, John, 114
Kellerman, Roy, 79
Kennedy, John F., 79, 159, 161, 236,
    255, 324
Kennedy, Robert F., 236
King, Joe, 134, 136

Knight, Stu, 192
Korean War, 100, 158, 159
Krupa, Gene, 161

"La Borinqueña," 177
Ladd, D. M., 290
La Fortaleza:
  attack on, 31–33, 47, 94, 267, 300,
    307, 310
  deaths at, 32–33, 36
  lessons of, 47
  Muños Marín at, 20, 31
  preparations for attack on, 18–21
Lameiro, José, 198
Langer, Bill, 8, 10–11
Lapham, Bob, 192
Law 53 (*ley de la mordaza*), 173, 211,
    213–14
Lawrence, Richard, 236, 237
Leahy, William, 266
Lebrón, Gonzalo, 302
Lebrón, Juan Bernardo, 214, 284, 302,
    303, 305
Lebrón, Lolita, 216
Lederer, Susan E., 195, 199
Lee, Bob, 231
Lee, Samuel Phillips and Elizabeth
    Blair, 89
Lee House, *see* Blair-Lee House
Lewis, Alfred E., 262
Lewis, Sinclair, 145
Liebling, A. J., 204
Lincoln, Abraham, 236, 238
López, Irma, 43
López, Manuel, 36–37
López Corchado, Efraín, 268
López Dávila, Trinidad, 113
Louie's, suits from, 63–64, 81
Lovell, Joseph, 88–89

MacArthur, Douglas, 158, 159
Mahan, Alfred T., 172
Marine Corps, U.S., 76, 190
Marín Torres, Heriberto:

book by, 44–45
and Griselio in New York, 212, 214,
    216–18
on Griselio's childhood, 206,
    208–9, 210
and Griselio's return visit to Puerto
    Rico, 219–20, 302
and Nationalist Party, 211, 217,
    303
and revolution, 211
Marshall, George C., 102
Matix, William, 201
Matthews, Francis, 102
Maxim, Sir Hiram, 32
McCann, Jerry, 62, 66, 79
McCarran, Pat, 6–7, 158
McCarran Act, 6–8, 11, 158
McCarthy, Joseph, 6, 157
McCullough, David, 156, 275
McKinley, William, 75–76, 236
McLearer, Phil, 253
McVicker, John William, 292
Mencken, H. L., 260
Meneses, Laura, 28
Metropolitan Police, Washington,
    D.C., 77, 135, 261–62
Michigan State University, School of
    Criminal Justice, 77, 190, 192
Mielke, Thelma, 312
Milburn, John, 75
Miles, Nelson A., 5, 171, 172
Mireles, Edmundo, Jr., 200
Monroe Doctrine, 172
Moore, Sara Jane, 236, 237, 238
Morales, Garrido, 195
Motto, Carmine J., 278–81
Moulder, Morgan, 266
Mroz, Shirley Gamm, 81, 82, 191–92,
    258–59
Mroz, Vincent P., 78–82, 187–93
    after the gunfight, 252, 264
    birth and background of, 74, 79,
        187–88, 190
    on duty, 66, 90, 105–6, 107, 161,

162, 164, 184, 187
    family of, 79, 81, 258
    and football, 189, 190, 192
    and Griselio, 256–57, 258, 292
    and gunfight, 184–85, 193, 203,
        226–27, 241, 242, 247, 274–75
    gun of, 79, 94, 185, 247
    at Michigan State, 189–90, 192
    physical appearance and personality
        of, 74, 79–80, 188
    retirement of, 325
    and Secret Service, 78–79, 192
    and Shirley, 81, 82, 191–92
    as trial witness, 292
Muñoz Marín, Luis:
    Albizu pardoned by, 323
    attempted assassination of, 16, 21,
        47, 298, 300, 307
    as governor, 213, 271, 309
    at La Fortaleza, 20, 31
    and post-gunfight roundup, 284–85
Muñoz Matos, Juan José, 22, 34, 267
Murphy, Christopher J., 223–24, 291

Nationalist Party of Puerto Rico
    (NPPR):
    Cadet Corps of, 19, 29, 30, 94, 109,
        122, 125, 130, 176, 177, 210
    and communists, 285
    and conspiracy theory, 298–307, 312
    current role of, 310
    decline of, 299, 313
    and elections, 29, 120–21
    flag of, 118
    gun-running for, 214–15, 301, 303
    informants within, 281
    La Fortaleza assault by, 19–21,
        31–33, 36, 47, 94, 267, 300,
        307
    leader of, *see* Albizu Campos, Pedro
    New York junta of, 39, 43, 122,
        124–25, 214, 216, 217–18, 281,
        284, 302, 306
    and Ponce Massacre, 124, 174–80

Nationalist Party of Puerto Rico
(NPPR) (*continued*)
post-gunfight investigations of,
278–85, 290
prison interview and, 313–16
rejection of, 174
and revolution, 13, 14, 15, 16–17,
18–21, 22, 24, 30–31, 174, 211,
214, 270, 312
and Rhoads letter, 198
and siege at Albizu's home, 267–72
and Spanish rule, 172
surveillance of, 210–11, 214, 217
and Truman attack, 22, 294, 315
and U.S. colonialism, 21, 30, 127
violence espoused by, 8–10, 16, 22,
29–30, 91, 120, 123, 124, 174,
300
zealots in, 15, 21, 32–33, 39,
179–80, 209–10, 294
Naval Intelligence:
reports by, 24
surveillance of radicals by, 173,
210–11
Newhall, California, massacre, 317–18
Nieves, Francisco A., 308
Nixon, Richard M., 157, 236
Nixon, Robert G., 166
Noland, Ethel, 11

O'Brian, Hugh, 162
O'Hara, John, 145
Operation Bootstrap, 299
Orbeta, Enrique de, 175
Orndorff, Irene, 229, 231, 235
Oswald, Lee Harvey, 41, 236, 237, 238
Otero, Carmen Dolores, 42, 45–46,
215, 216, 217, 282, 284
Ovidio López, Manuel, 43

Pan-American Exposition (1901), 75
Parker, Dorothy, 116
Pearson, Drew, 266

Pennsylvania State Police, 76–77,
147–48, 149–50
Pérez, Carmen María, 22, 34, 267
Pérez, Juan Pietri, 43, 214, 302
Perkins, Max, 116
Peters, Theodore, 6
Peyton, Charlie, 193
Pinto Gandía, Julio, 43, 215, 284, 302,
314
Platt, Michael, 200
Ponce, Puerto Rico:
as city of rebellion, 24
massacre in, 108, 124, 174–80, 294
U.S. landing in, 171
Ponce de León, Juan, 170
Povich, Shirley, 260
Preston, Marion R., 261–62
Puerto Rico, 167–80
as *Borinquen*, 5, 22, 170
cigars from, 168–69
communists in, 285
economic problems in, 169–70,
173
emigration to U.S. from, 116, 122
flag of, 117–18
Free Republic of, 16, 22, 29, 43,
298
geography of, 167
judicial system in, 124
and Law 53 (*ley de la mordaza*), 173,
211, 213–14
national anthem of, 177
national identity in, 299
nationalists in, *see* Nationalist Party
of Puerto Rico
and New York community, 116–17,
167, 213
Operation Bootstrap in, 299
as paradise, 115, 167–68
plans to return to, 15, 16, 125, 167
Ponce Massacre in, 108, 124,
174–80, 294
population of, 169

post-gunfight roundup in, 284–85

Riggs murder in, 30, 109, 123, 124, 174, 300

shaping the history of, 310

tourist destinations in, 168, 169

U.S. presence in, 20, 30, 127, 170–74, 274, 294, 299–300

Quiñones, José Ramón, 197

Ramírez-Barbot, Jaime, 124

Reagan, Ronald, 236

Rector, Dudley, 54

Rentzel, Delos W., 100

Reveron, Ana, 117

Rhoads, Cornelius Packard "Dusty," 194–99, 294

Rhoads, George H., 195

Ribes Tovar, Federico, 24

Rice, Grantland, 142

Riggs, E. Francis, 30, 109, 123, 124, 174, 300

Riggs National Bank, 109

Rivera, Dilia (Torresola), 44, 206, 212–13, 215–16, 217, 220–22, 302

Rivera Walker, Álvaro, 268–71

Roberts, Chalmers M., 262

Robinson, Leonard Wallace, 164

Rockefeller Anemia Commission, 195, 198

Rockefeller, Nelson A., 100

Roosevelt, Franklin D., 67, 149
attempted assassination of, 80, 236
death of, 50, 150

Roosevelt, Franklin D., Jr., 161

Roosevelt, Theodore, 76, 236

Rosado, Hiram, 109, 123, 124

Rosado, Marisa, 24

Rosenberg, Julius and Ethel, 6

Ross, Charlie, 166, 265

Rover, Leo A., 291, 293, 294, 295

Rowley, Jim, 81, 165–66, 193, 263, 287

Sachs, Sidney S., 291

St. Valentine's Day Massacre, 107

Santiago Díaz, Vidal, 271

Schrank, John, 236, 237

Scouten, Rex, 52, 79, 192, 262–63

Secret Service, U.S.:
after the gunfight, 274, 317–18
at Blair House, 89–90, 104–8, 161
buddy network in, 66, 76–77, 234
conspiracy theory of, 16, 298
counterfeiting detail of, 192
culture of, 74–78
and daily routine, 80–81
detail to protect the president, 50–52, 53, 67, 75, 76, 77, 78, 81, 103, 138, 150–51, 154, 163–65, 193, 264, 265, 266, 274, 317
Distinguished Marksmanship Awards in, 68, 231, 274
flying wedge formation of, 279
formation of, 75
and gunfight, 128, 240, 262–63, 264, 274, 275, 318
hierarchy within, 77
Investigative Branch, 77
and McKinley assassination, 75–76
and Nationalist Party, 214, 216
no security system in, 50, 66, 75, 263, 317
pistol teams of, 71
post-gunfight investigation by, 278–81, 287, 290
Protection Detail, 77, 78, 80, 149–50
Qualification (target practice) in, 67–70, 152–53, 317–19
rings of defense in, 164–65
rotation "push" system of, 67, 80
state police recruitment for, 147, 149–50
sworn to sacrifice, 74–75, 76

Secret Service, U.S. (*continued*)
  university recruitment for, 77–78,
    192–93
  White House office of, 65–66, 76,
    149–50, 165–66
  and White House Police, 66, 76, 77,
    233
Secret Service Chief (Baughman), 164
Sepoy Rebellion, India, 27
Sheridan, Phil, 228
Sherman, F. P., 102
Shields, Bill, 79
Sirhan, Sirhan, 236, 237, 238
Sites, Elroy, 252–56, 264, 292
Smiley, Lou, 190
Smith, Marta, 308
Smith, William Ellison, 292–93
Smith Act/Alien Registration Act
    (1940), 213
Snyder, John W., 51, 240
Soegard, Aida, 196–97
Soto, Benigno, 309
Spanish-American War, 171, 172
Stewart, Fred, 196
Story of the Secret Service, The
    (Landmark), 254
Stout, Stu:
  after the gunfight, 324
  death of, 324
  on duty, 66, 105–6, 161, 162–65, 255
  and gunfight, 162–65, 241, 247
  physical appearance and personality
    of, 107, 161, 162
  protecting the president, 163–65,
    324
  and Secret Service, 78, 161–62,
    163–64
  as state trooper, 161
  and tommy gun, 108, 162–63, 241,
    247
Suárez Díaz, Rafael Manuel, 120
Sully, Thomas, 89
Sundry Civil Expenses Act (1906), 76

Suniland Shopping Center, Florida,
    gunfight in, 200–201, 203
Suter, Dean John W., 286, 288
Symington, W. Stuart, 103

Tagore, Rabindranath, 27
Tamm, Edward A., 289
"Taps," 288
Tehaan, Edward J., 291
Terry, Charles, 25
Thomas, Piri, 167
Thomas, R. M., 102
Tiny (marine), 191
Tormos Diego, José, 175
Torres Medina, Manuel, 19, 32
Torres Morales, Carlos, 177
Torresola, Angelina, 115, 206–7, 209,
    212, 218–19, 301, 302
Torresola, Carmen (Otero), 42, 45–46,
    215, 216, 217, 282, 284
Torresola, Clodomiro, 208, 210, 211
Torresola, Doris:
  and Albizu, 22, 34, 209, 314
  arrest of, 47, 267, 268, 285
  injury of, 34, 47, 209, 267, 268,
    269
Torresola, Elio:
  and Griselio, 221, 303–7, 314
  in Jayuya, 22, 34, 47, 115, 209, 211
  party connections of, 127, 211
  and Ponce massacre, 180
  in prison, 285
Torresola, Griselio:
  Albizu as inspiration and mentor
    of, 13–14, 15, 44, 110, 214, 250,
    300–303, 311–12, 314
  and Albizu in Puerto Rico, 218,
    302, 305, 314
  as Albizu's bodyguard, 38–39, 93,
    211–12
  birth and background of, 12–13,
    114, 120, 206–8
  commitment to the cause, 13–14,

15, 16, 31, 36–37, 39, 91, 110,
171, 180, 238–39, 247–48, 250,
290, 311–13
and conspiracy theory, 298,
300–307
death of, 251, 256–57, 261, 263,
273, 285, 292, 293
family of, 42, 44, 45–46, 115, 121,
206–9
and gunfight, 155, 183, 204–5, 223,
224, 226–27, 240–42, 247–48,
249, 250, 251, 253, 254, 292
at Harris Hotel, 47–49, 95, 215, 302
jobs of, 15, 217
letters and documents of, 13–14,
38, 39, 45, 218, 303–7, 312
Luger of, 37, 39, 92–93, 250,
256–57, 301
and Nationalist Party, 31, 36, 44, 45,
127, 210–11, 214, 216, 305–7
in New York, 12–15, 34, 35, 43,
212, 213–18, 301, 304, 306, 311
nom de guerre of, 48, 214–15, 302
and Oscar's gun, 16, 37–38, 94–98,
130, 244, 294, 301
and Oscar's story, 273–74, 290,
293, 294, 296, 306, 310
physical appearance and personality
of, 12, 15, 38, 44–45, 91,
110–11, 205, 206–7, 208, 216,
236, 238, 305, 314
planning the attack, 12–17, 36–37,
38–39, 49, 90–91, 111, 291,
298
political development of, 209–12
and Ponce Massacre, 180
preparations by, 42–46, 109–12,
127, 214–15, 311–12
residence of, 42–44
return to Puerto Rico, 218–20, 302,
305, 314–15
sightseeing in Washington, 86–91,
289

travel to Washington, 46–49
Truman and, 298, 301, 311–12,
315
and wives, 212–13, 215–16, 217,
220–22
Torres Platet, René, 211, 301
Treasury Cash Room, 67
Treasury Department, 75, 152, 181
Truman, Bess, 6, 53, 67, 88, 103, 265
Truman, Harry S.:
on Bill of Rights, 7
and Coffelt's death, 266, 286, 288
conspiracy against, 16, 39, 131,
166, 203, 266, 293, 298, 300,
301, 311–12, 314–15
daily schedule for, 80–81, 100–103,
156, 265–66
death of, 323
dental work on, 158–59
and domestic issues, 157–58
early morning walks of, 50–52, 67,
81, 317
and gunfight, 128, 160, 204,
240–42, 246, 249–50, 264–65
and his daughter, 5–6, 11
and international issues, 156,
157–59
and McCarran Act, 7–8, 11
Oscar's sentence commuted by,
323
physical appearance and personality
of, 53, 103, 156, 240, 266
retirement of, 266, 323
and Secret Service, 50–52, 67, 81,
103, 150–51
as swimmer, 81, 151
Truman, Margaret, 5–6, 11, 67, 88,
265
Truman Library and Museum, 92,
256–57

*The United States of America vs. Oscar
Collazo*, 291–97

Valera, Eamon de, 27
Vaughan, Harry, 157
VERMONT (Russian bomb), 157

Wade, James E., 160, 165, 292
Waggoner, Walter H., 288
Wake Island, 159
Walker, Miss (Blair housekeeper), 225
Wallace, Fred, 67
Wallace, George, 236
warriors, society's need for, 319–21
Wayne, John, 148
White House:
 remodeling of, 87–88, 253
 Rose Garden, 101
 Secret Service office of, 65–66, 76,
  149–50, 165–66
 tunnel under, 67
White House Police:
 after the gunfight, 287
 at Blair House, 89, 106, 108, 164

and gunfight, 275
rotation system of, 67, 80
and Secret Service, 66, 76, 77,
 233
Wilson, Earl, 290
Wilson, Jim, 148
Wilson, Woodrow, 27
Winship, Blanton, 175, 179
Wood, Kenneth D., 291
World War I, 26
World War II:
 and Birdzell family, 136–37
 Chambers in, 101–3
 and Coffelt, 234
 guns from, 94
 lessons of, 138
 and Puerto Rico, 124

Yost, Paul Lee, 292

Zangara, Giuseppe, 236, 237